BONUS SHORT STORIES

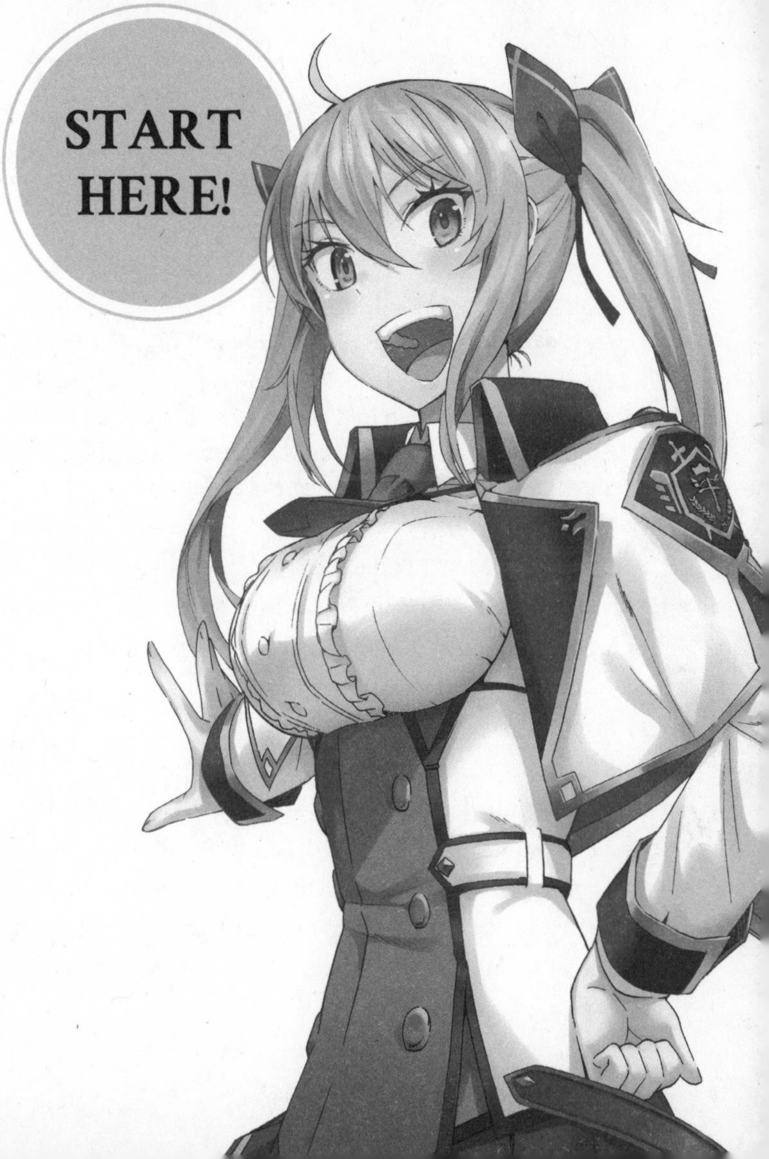
START
HERE!

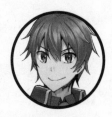

✦ Allen Rodol's Growth ✦

It was seven at night. Allen had just returned to the dorm after his duel with Dodriel Barton. He was currently getting in his daily practice swings in the forest next to the dorm.

"Hah! Yah! Ho!"

He started at three in the afternoon, which meant it had already been four hours, but he wasn't showing any signs of stopping. Given how his eyes were sparkling like a young child, he could have gone all night.

Th-this is a dream come true!

Allen's billion-plus years of training had improved his sword-craft dramatically. He hadn't had any time to process that before he entered the duel with Dodriel—and ended up winning with an overwhelming skill advantage he didn't know he had. He returned to the dorm in a confused trance, and now that he had finally found some downtime, he was savoring the joy he felt at his growth for all it was worth.

I understand the sword like I never have before!

➡

Techniques and concepts he had never been able to grasp—the ideal angles to swing his sword, when to shift his body weight, when to slow down and when to speed up—had been drilled to his core. The "essence of swordcraft" now dwelled within him. The weight of the sword in his hands, the sound of the blade cutting through air, and his awareness as he prepared each strike all felt perfectly natural.

Ha-ha, this is a total blast!

A single leaf fell before Allen as he absorbed himself in swinging his sword.

"Eighth Style—Eight-Span Crow!"

Eight sharp slashes caught the leaf in the air and tore it to shreds. Immediately afterward, loud clapping echoed throughout the clearing. Allen turned around to see an enormous bear—actually, it was Ms. Paula, standing at more than two meters tall and clapping her hands.

"Well done, Allen! When did you become such a pro? Did you find some kind of trick to help with your training?"

"U-Uh, well…I guess you could say that," Allen answered evasively before sheathing his sword. *There's no way I can tell her about the 100-Million-Year Button…*

She would think he had gone insane if he tried to explain the experience he went through. There was no reason to worry her like that.

"I guess this is how boys are—take your eyes off one for three days, and he'll become a man before you know it!" Ms. Paula exclaimed with a satisfied smile, giving a few proud nods. "All right, I think I'll start on dinner. Today's menu is a large helping of curry with lots of vegetables and meat! We need to

➡

put some meat on those bones so you can get as big as me one day!"

"A-ha-ha… I'll do my best…" *I don't think I'll ever be as big as Ms. Paula…*

Allen smiled awkwardly and followed Ms. Paula back to the dorm.

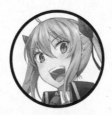

✦ Lia Vesteria's Misunderstanding ✦

In Arlond, the capital city of Vesteria Kingdom, Lia Vesteria was about to board her flight to the neighboring country of Liengard. It was the day of the Thousand Blade Academy entrance ceremony.

"All right, Father. It's time for me to go," she said.

Standing next to the royal family's private aircraft and waving to her was Lia's father—Gris Vesteria, the king of Vesteria. He was bawling without a care for the eyes around them.

"Oh, Lia, my adorable little girl… Are you really leaving me?" he asked.

"D-don't cry like that… There are people watching us," Lia said.

Lia and Gris were surrounded by a group of capable royal

➡

guards on high alert for any threats, and beyond them was a crowd of citizens hoping to get a glimpse of the princess as she departed.

"I'm not here as the king of Vesteria, I'm here as a father who loves his daughter very much! I couldn't care less about what people think! That all feels so trivial next to the worry that is tearing my heart asunder..."

"I appreciate the concern, but I'll be fine. I'll call you as soon as I arrive, and I'll make sure to contact you regularly. And don't forget, Liengard is a very safe country."

"That may be so, but..."

Gris was the very definition of a doting father, and he was doing all he could to convince his daughter to stay. Rather than rebuff him cruelly, Lia searched sincerely for the words to put him at ease.

"Nothing is going to happen to me. On the off chance I do run into any trouble, I have Dragon King Fafnir to protect me!"

Gris made a complicated expression at the mention of her Soul Attire, and nodded.

"...I see that your resolve is strong. I won't stop you. Just let me say one more thing."

"What is it?"

"I know I've told you this many times since you were a small child, but you mustn't forget: all men are wolves! No matter how kind a man may appear, he is always hiding vulgar thoughts in his heart! You can't let your guard down, no matter what happens. You especially cannot invite one into your room!"

➡

"Don't worry, I know. Okay, it's time for me to go now."

"Bye, Lia. I'll pray for your safety!"

Gris waved emphatically as she walked away, and feeling slightly embarrassed, Lia returned his waves until she boarded the plane.

"Whew…"

Lia sat down in her plane seat and looked through a schedule she had been given for her first year at Thousand Blade Academy.

"Hmm… The first big event is the Elite Five Holy Festival. That's what I thought," she said aloud. She flipped through the pages until a single piece of paper fell out. It was the letter that Reia Lasnote, the chairwoman of Thousand Blade Academy, sent to her a few days ago.

"Oh yeah… She said there's a 'bona fide superstar' among the new students this year. I wonder what kind of person they are. Reia values strength more than anyone, so they must be truly incredible to earn such praise from her… Are they the child of a distinguished noble family? The favorite pupil of a famous school of swordcraft? A naturally gifted swordfighter who can use Soul Attire? Ha-ha, I'm looking forward to meeting them."

In reality, the "bona fide superstar" was a self-taught nobody from the boonies who hadn't even developed his Soul Attire and was ridiculed by his peers as the Reject Swordsman… But Lia couldn't possibly have known that at the time.

➡

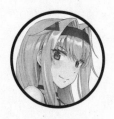

✦ Rose Valencia's Decision ✦

Rose Valencia opened her eyes. She was lying in the Sword Fighting Festival infirmary after her shocking defeat by the mysterious swordsman named Allen Rodol.

"Wh-where am I…?"

She awoke to fluorescent light, an unfamiliar ceiling, and the smell of disinfectant. Having no idea how she ended up in that bed, Rose sat up in a daze.

"Oh, you're awake."

"Are… Are you Reia Lasnote?! The Black Fist?!"

Rose went bolt upright, reaching for her trusty sword beside her pillow.

"Whoa, slow down, there. No need to be on guard. I swear I don't bite," Reia responded with a wry smile. She took a sip from a glass on the table. "Man, that was a great match. The crowd was going crazy."

"…Oh… I lost…"

Finally realizing what happened, Rose closed her mouth tight and clenched her fists. She was clearly upset about the loss.

"So, tell me about Allen Rodol. Was he strong?" Reia asked.

➡

Rose nodded gravely.

"…Yes. I don't know exactly how he defeated me, but he is unbelievably skilled. His sword carries generations of diligent experimentation and study. It was like I was fighting a true blademaster who had lived for an eternity…"

"Interesting. He must be good to earn such high praise from you…"

Reia crossed her arms, apparently deep in thought.

"So… What business do you have with me?" Rose asked after getting out of bed and swiftly tidying up her appearance.

"Hm? Oh, I came to do a little scouting."

"Scouting?"

"Rose Valencia, sole inheritor of the famous Cherry Blossom Blade School of Swordcraft… I want you to enroll at Thousand Blade Academy," Reia declared, handing her an entrance guide for Thousand Blade Academy.

Rose shook her head without hesitation.

"I appreciate the offer, but I have to decline. I must search for that mysterious swordsman named Allen Rodol."

"Hmm, I see. What would you do if I told you that Allen Rodol might be enrolling at Thousand Blade?"

"What?! Is that true?!"

After Rose demanded that Reia share everything she knew about Allen, she finalized her decision to enroll at Thousand Blade.

I KEPT PRESSING THE 100-MILLION-YEAR BUTTON AND CAME OUT ON TOP

~THE UNBEATABLE REJECT SWORDSMAN~

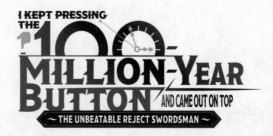

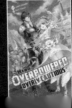
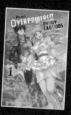

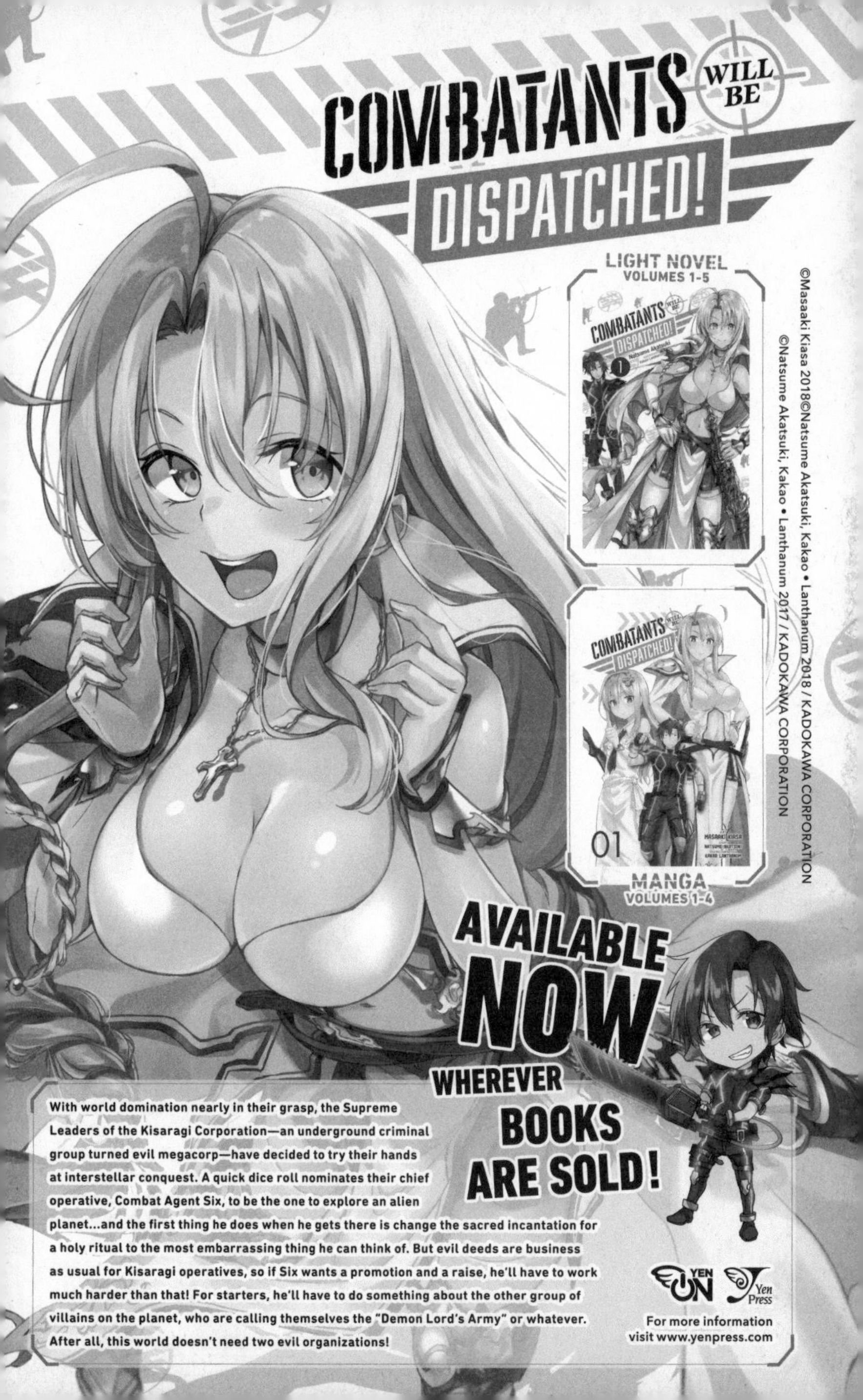
COMBATANTS WILL BE DISPATCHED!
LIGHT NOVEL
VOLUMES 1-5
MANGA
VOLUMES 1-4
AVAILABLE NOW
WHEREVER BOOKS ARE SOLD!
With world domination nearly in their grasp, the Supreme Leaders of the Kisaragi Corporation—an underground criminal group turned evil megacorp—have decided to try their hands at interstellar conquest. A quick dice roll nominates their chief operative, Combat Agent Six, to be the one to explore an alien planet...and the first thing he does when he gets there is change the sacred incantation for a holy ritual to the most embarrassing thing he can think of. But evil deeds are business as usual for Kisaragi operatives, so if Six wants a promotion and a raise, he'll have to work much harder than that! For starters, he'll have to do something about the other group of villains on the planet, who are calling themselves the "Demon Lord's Army" or whatever. After all, this world doesn't need two evil organizations!
For more information visit www.yenpress.com
©Masaaki Kiasa 2018©Natsume Akatsuki, Kakao • Lanthanum 2018 / KADOKAWA CORPORATION
©Natsume Akatsuki, Kakao • Lanthanum 2017 / KADOKAWA CORPORATION

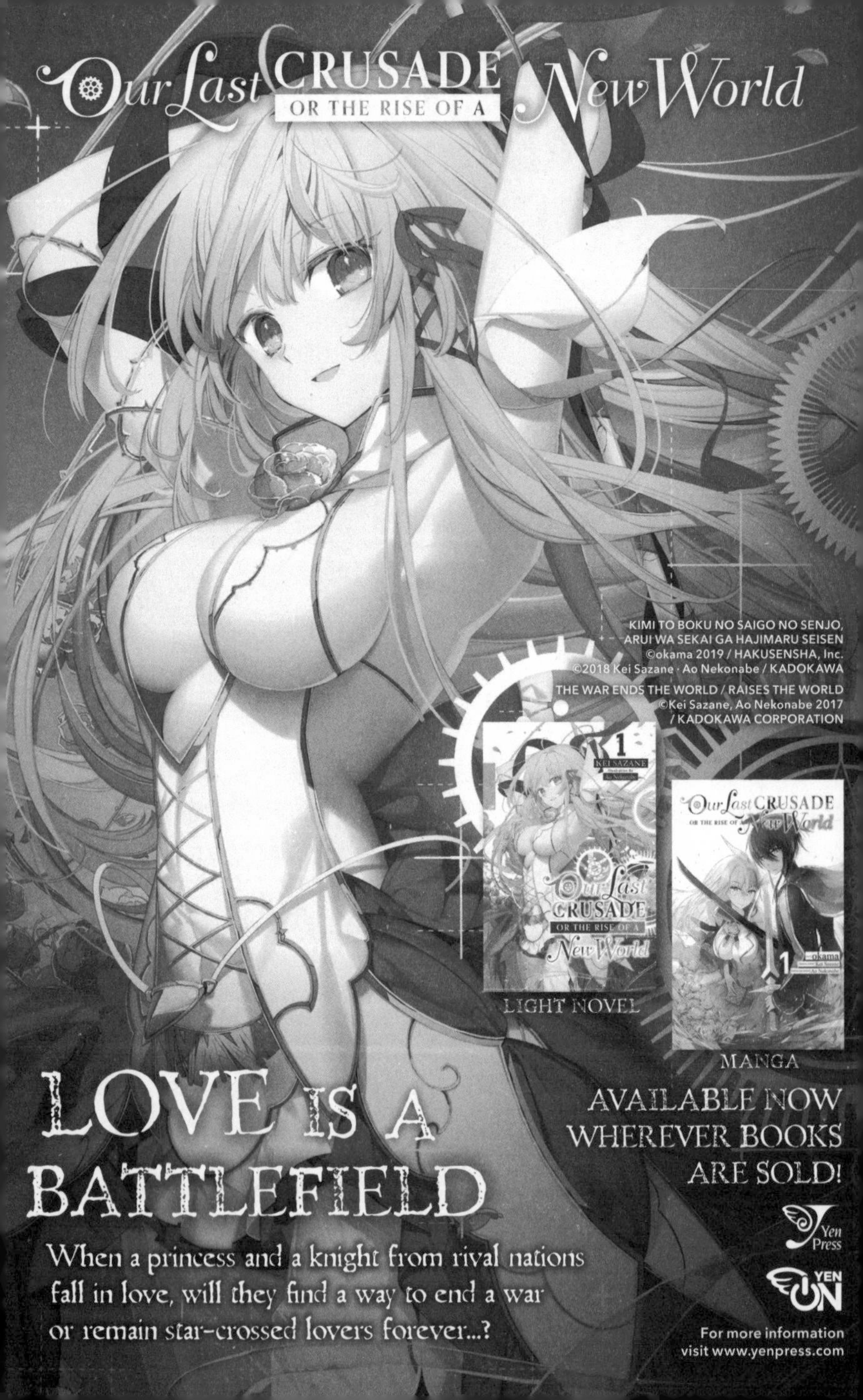

Our Last CRUSADE OR THE RISE OF A New World
KIMI TO BOKU NO SAIGO NO SENJO, ARUI WA SEKAI GA HAJIMARU SEISEN
©okama 2019 / HAKUSENSHA, Inc.
©2018 Kei Sazane · Ao Nekonabe / KADOKAWA
THE WAR ENDS THE WORLD / RAISES THE WORLD
©Kei Sazane, Ao Nekonabe 2017 / KADOKAWA CORPORATION
1
KEI SAZANE
Our Last CRUSADE OR THE RISE OF A New World
LIGHT NOVEL
Our Last CRUSADE OR THE RISE OF A New World
1
okama
MANGA
LOVE IS A BATTLEFIELD
When a princess and a knight from rival nations fall in love, will they find a way to end a war or remain star-crossed lovers forever...?
AVAILABLE NOW WHEREVER BOOKS ARE SOLD!
Yen Press
YEN ON
For more information visit www.yenpress.com

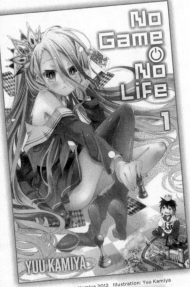
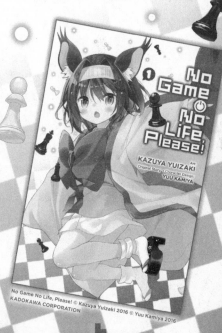

  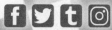

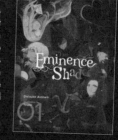

Read the light novel that inspired the hit anime series!

Re:ZeRo
-Starting Life in Another World-

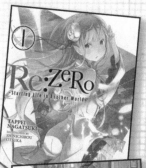

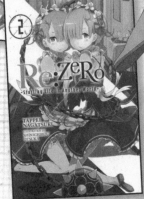

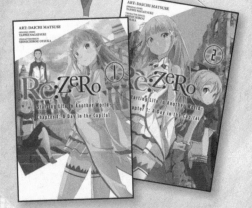

Also be sure to check out the manga series!

AVAILABLE NOW!

www.YenPress.com

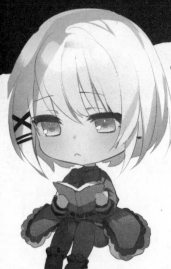

The Detective Is Already Dead

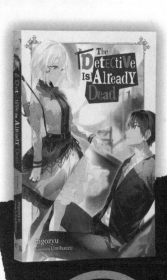

When the story begins without its hero

Kimihiko Kimizuka has always been a magnet for trouble and intrigue. For as long as he can remember, he's been stumbling across murder scenes or receiving mysterious attaché cases to transport. When he met Siesta, a brilliant detective fighting a secret war against an organization of pseudohumans, he couldn't resist the call to become her assistant and join her on an epic journey across the world.

...Until a year ago, that is. Now he's returned to a relatively normal and tepid life, knowing the adventure must be over. After all, the detective is already dead.

Volume 3 available wherever books are sold!

YEN ON
YenPress.com

TANTEI HA MO, SHINDEIRU. Vol. 1
©nigozyu 2019
Illustration: Umibouzu
KADOKAWA CORPORATION

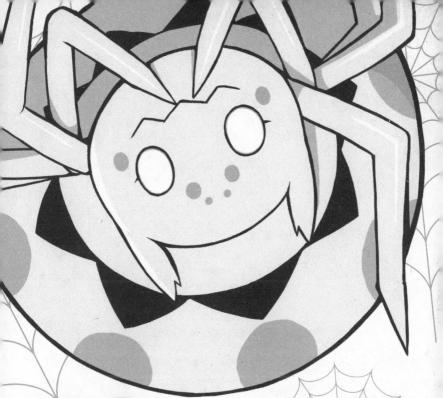

So I'm a Spider, So What?

Manga Vol. 1-11
Light Novel Vol. 1-14

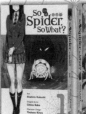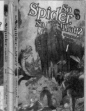

AVAILABLE NOW!

YOU CAN ALSO KEEP UP WITH THE MANGA SIMUL-PUB EVERY MONTH ONLINE!

I'm gonna survive—just watch me!

I was your average, everyday high school girl, but now I've been reborn in a magical world...as a spider?! How am I supposed to survive in this big, scary dungeon as one of the weakest monsters? I gotta figure out the rules to this QUICK, or I'll be kissing my short second life good-bye...

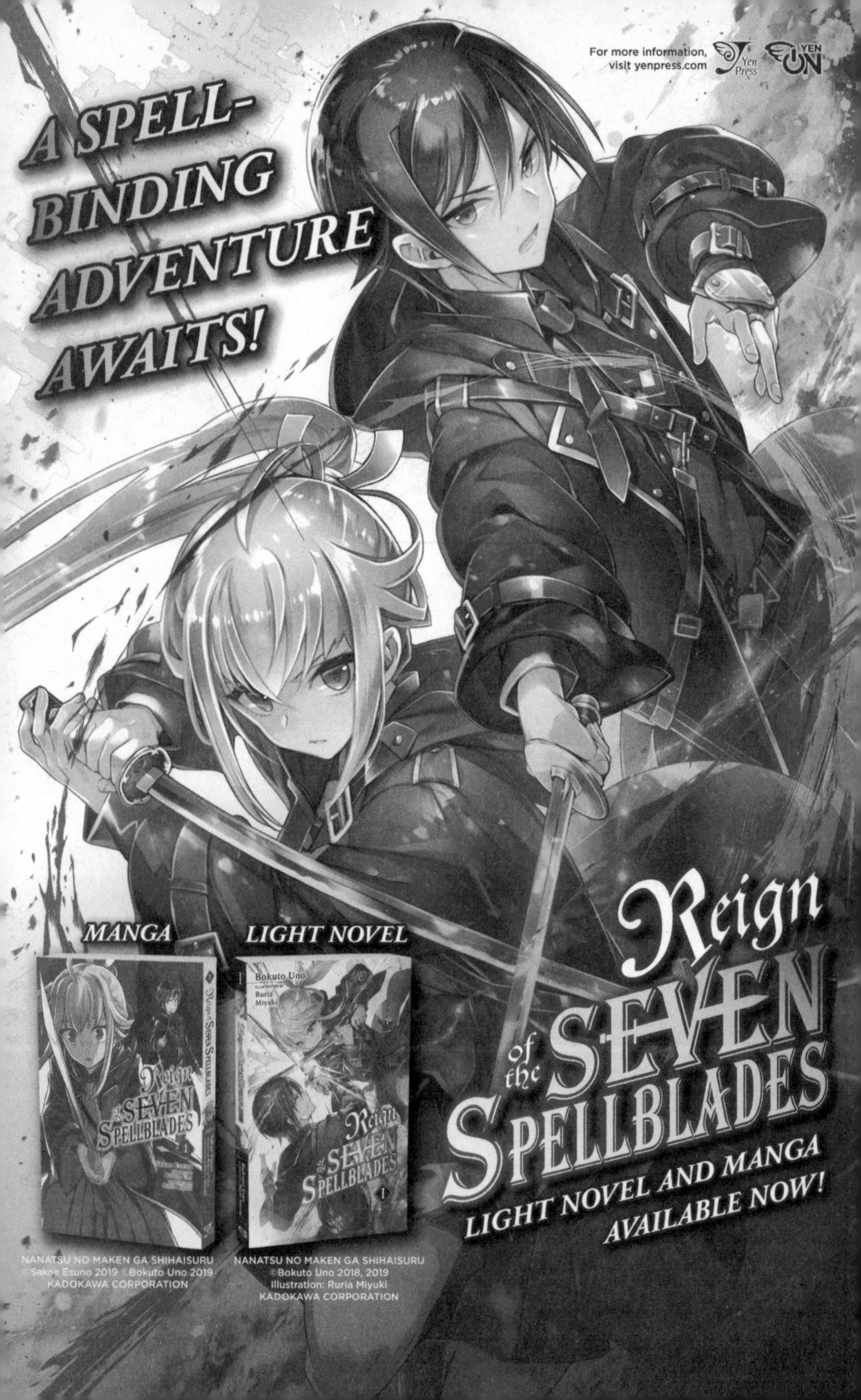
For more information, visit yenpress.com
Yen Press
YEN ON
A SPELL-BINDING ADVENTURE AWAITS!
MANGA
LIGHT NOVEL
Reign of the SEVEN SPELLBLADES
LIGHT NOVEL AND MANGA AVAILABLE NOW!
NANATSU NO MAKEN GA SHIHAISURU
©Sakae Esuno 2019 ©Bokuto Uno 2019
KADOKAWA CORPORATION
NANATSU NO MAKEN GA SHIHAISURU
©Bokuto Uno 2018, 2019
Illustration: Ruria Miyuki
KADOKAWA CORPORATION

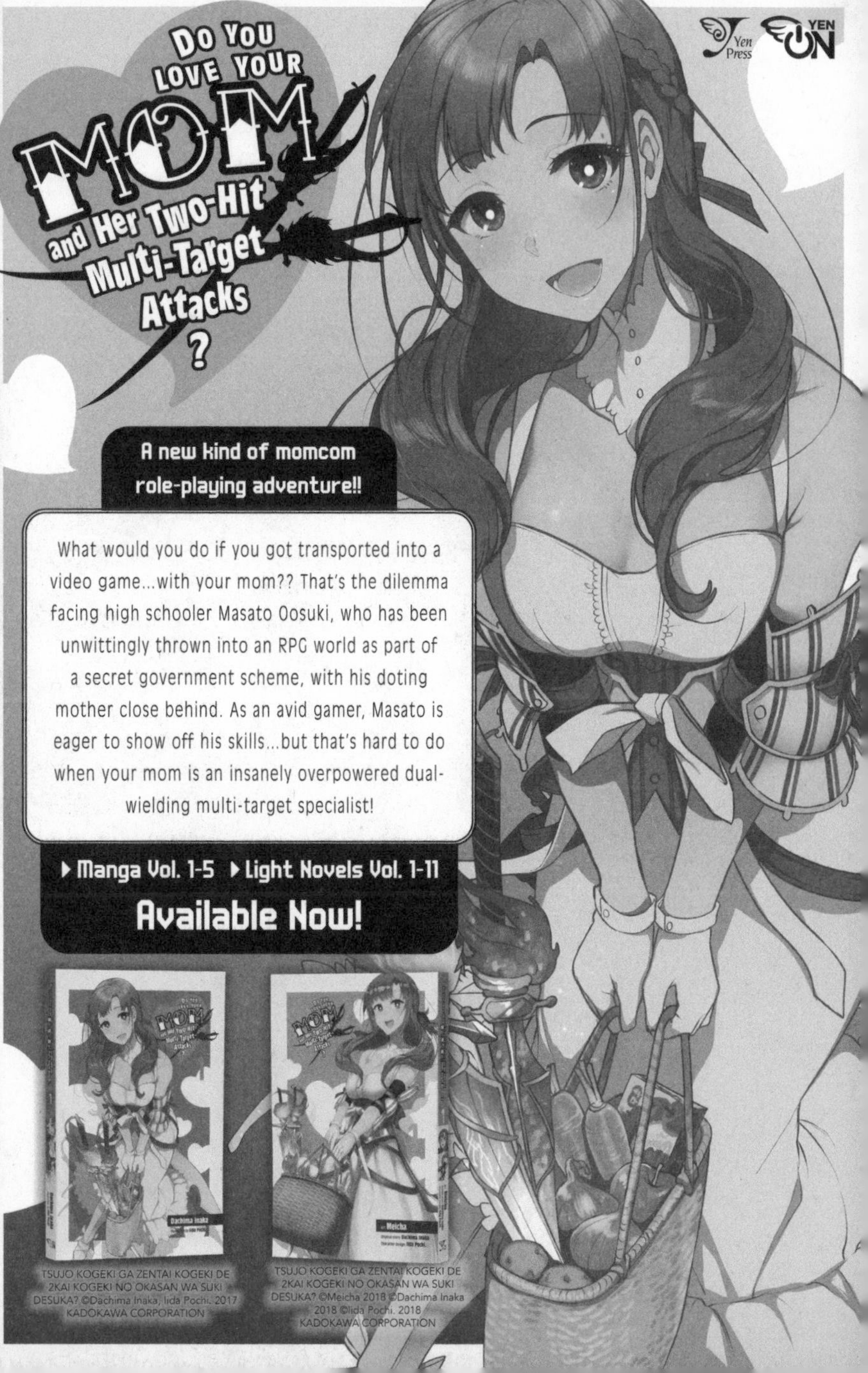
Yen Press
YEN ON
Do You Love Your Mom and Her Two-Hit Multi-Target Attacks?
A new kind of momcom role-playing adventure!!
What would you do if you got transported into a video game...with your mom?? That's the dilemma facing high schooler Masato Oosuki, who has been unwittingly thrown into an RPG world as part of a secret government scheme, with his doting mother close behind. As an avid gamer, Masato is eager to show off his skills...but that's hard to do when your mom is an insanely overpowered dual-wielding multi-target specialist!
▶ Manga Vol. 1-5 ▶ Light Novels Vol. 1-11
Available Now!
Dachima Inaka
Meicha
TSUJO KOGEKI GA ZENTAI KOGEKI DE 2KAI KOGEKI NO OKASAN WA SUKI DESUKA? ©Dachima Inaka, Iida Pochi. 2017 KADOKAWA CORPORATION
TSUJO KOGEKI GA ZENTAI KOGEKI DE 2KAI KOGEKI NO OKASAN WA SUKI DESUKA? ©Meicha 2018 ©Dachima Inaka 2018 ©Iida Pochi. 2018 KADOKAWA CORPORATION

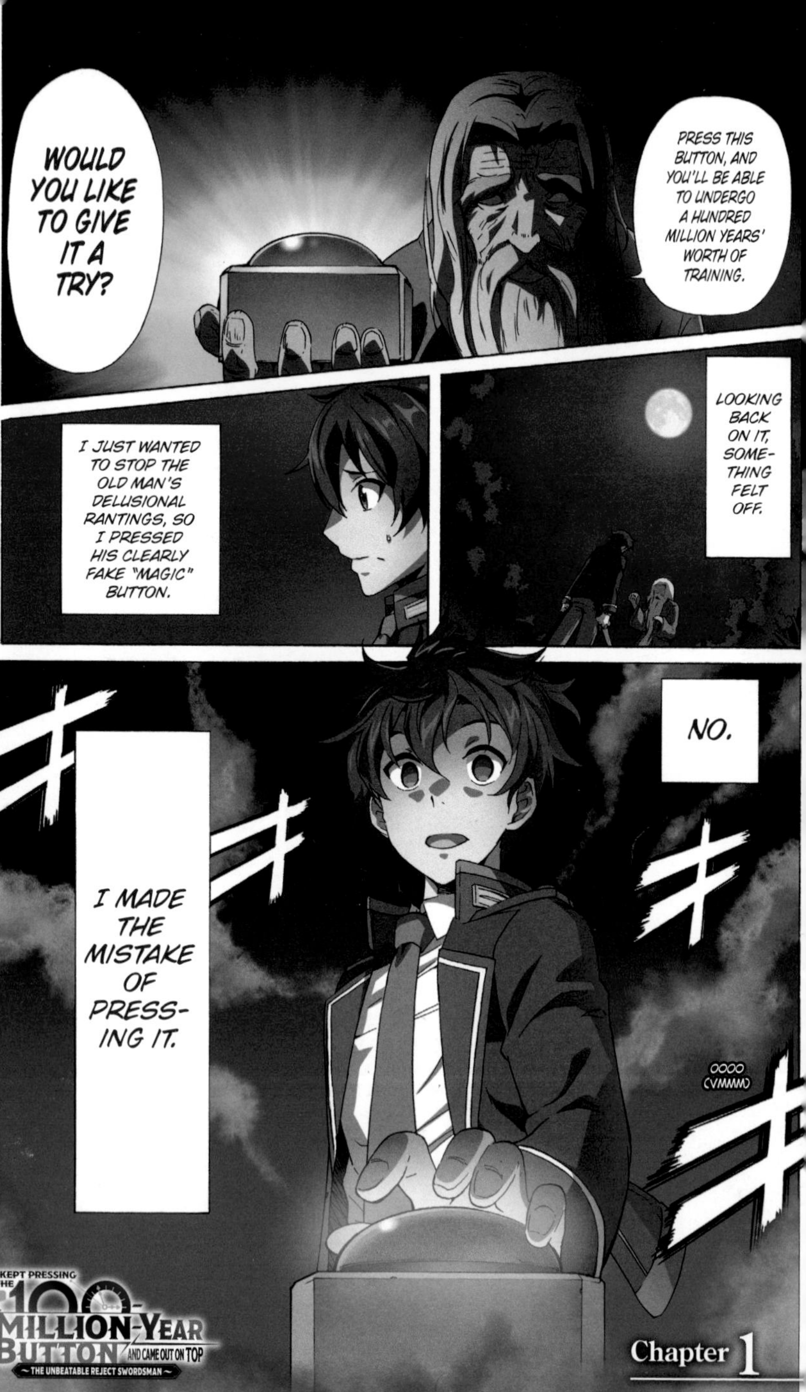
PRESS THIS BUTTON, AND YOU'LL BE ABLE TO UNDERGO A HUNDRED MILLION YEARS' WORTH OF TRAINING.
WOULD YOU LIKE TO GIVE IT A TRY?
LOOKING BACK ON IT, SOMETHING FELT OFF.
I JUST WANTED TO STOP THE OLD MAN'S DELUSIONAL RANTINGS, SO I PRESSED HIS CLEARLY FAKE "MAGIC" BUTTON.
NO.
I MADE THE MISTAKE OF PRESSING IT.
OOOO (VMMM)
I KEPT PRESSING THE 100-MILLION-YEAR BUTTON AND CAME OUT ON TOP
~THE UNBEATABLE REJECT SWORDSMAN~
Chapter 1

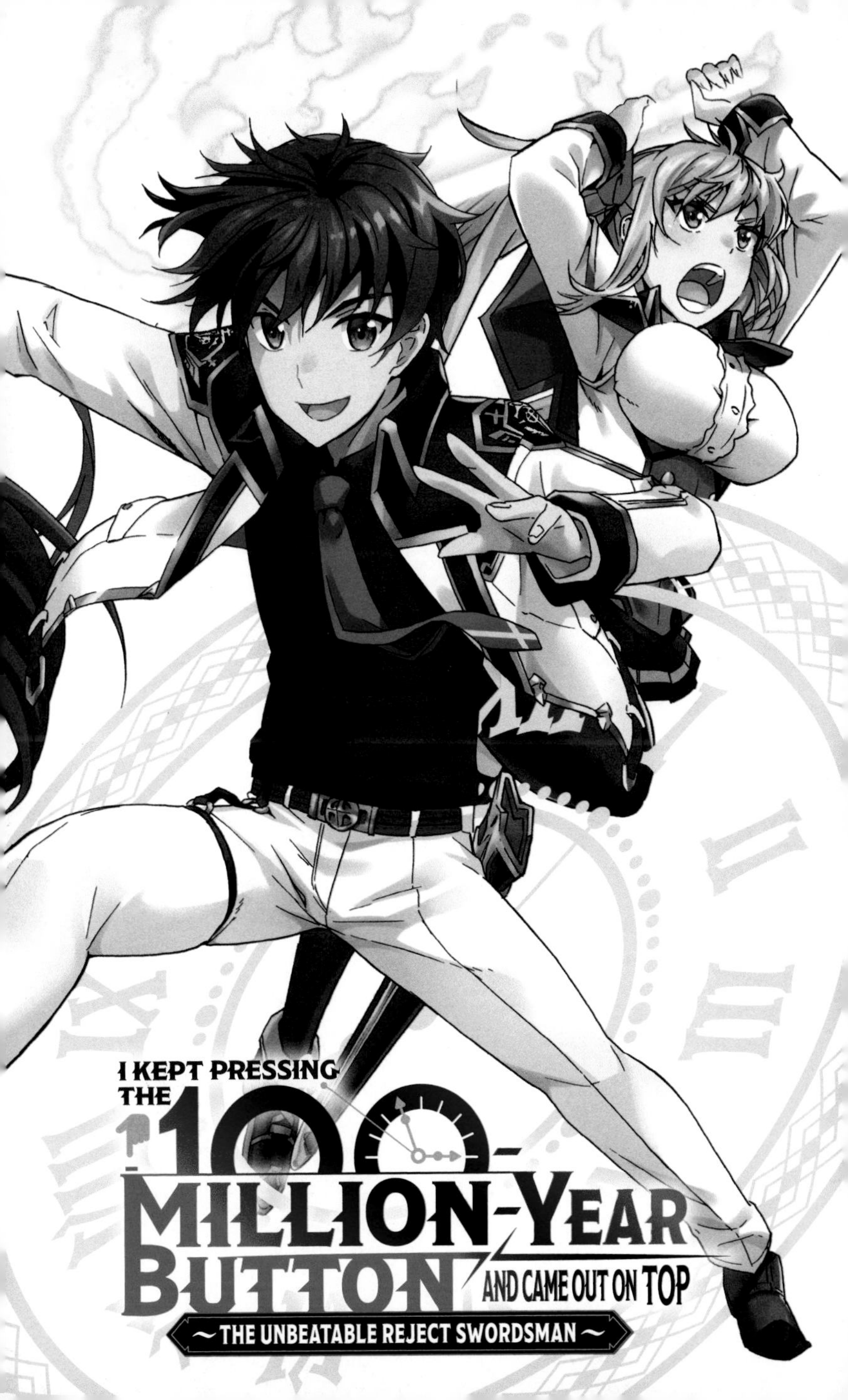
I KEPT PRESSING THE 100-MILLION-YEAR BUTTON AND CAME OUT ON TOP
~THE UNBEATABLE REJECT SWORDSMAN~

YUTARO SHIDO

Original Story
SYUICHI TSUKISHIMA

Character Design
MOKYU

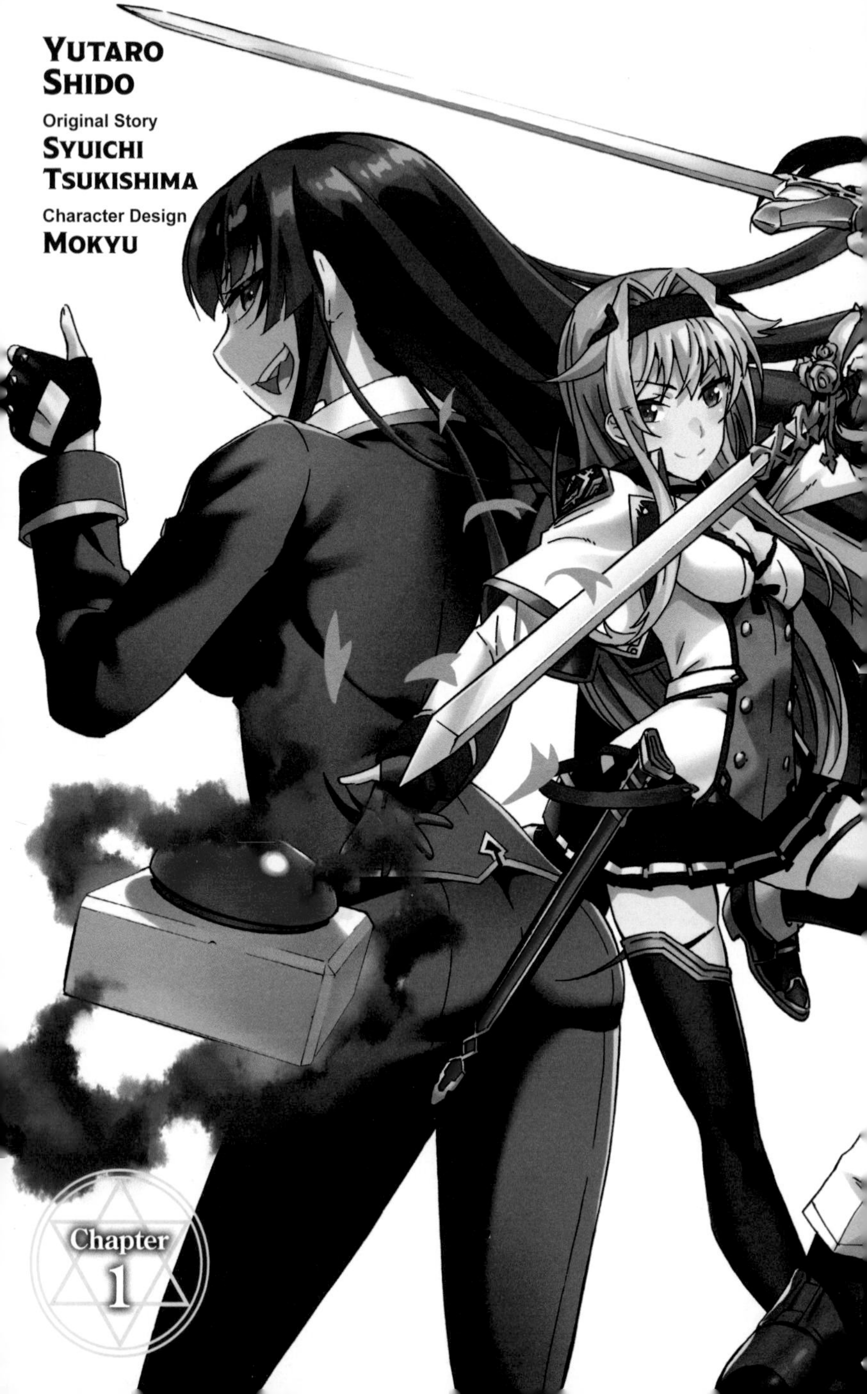

Chapter 1

CONTENTS

Chapter 1
001

Chapter 2
071

Chapter 3
107

Chapter 4
145

Chapter 5
183

Preview
222

Bonus Novel
244

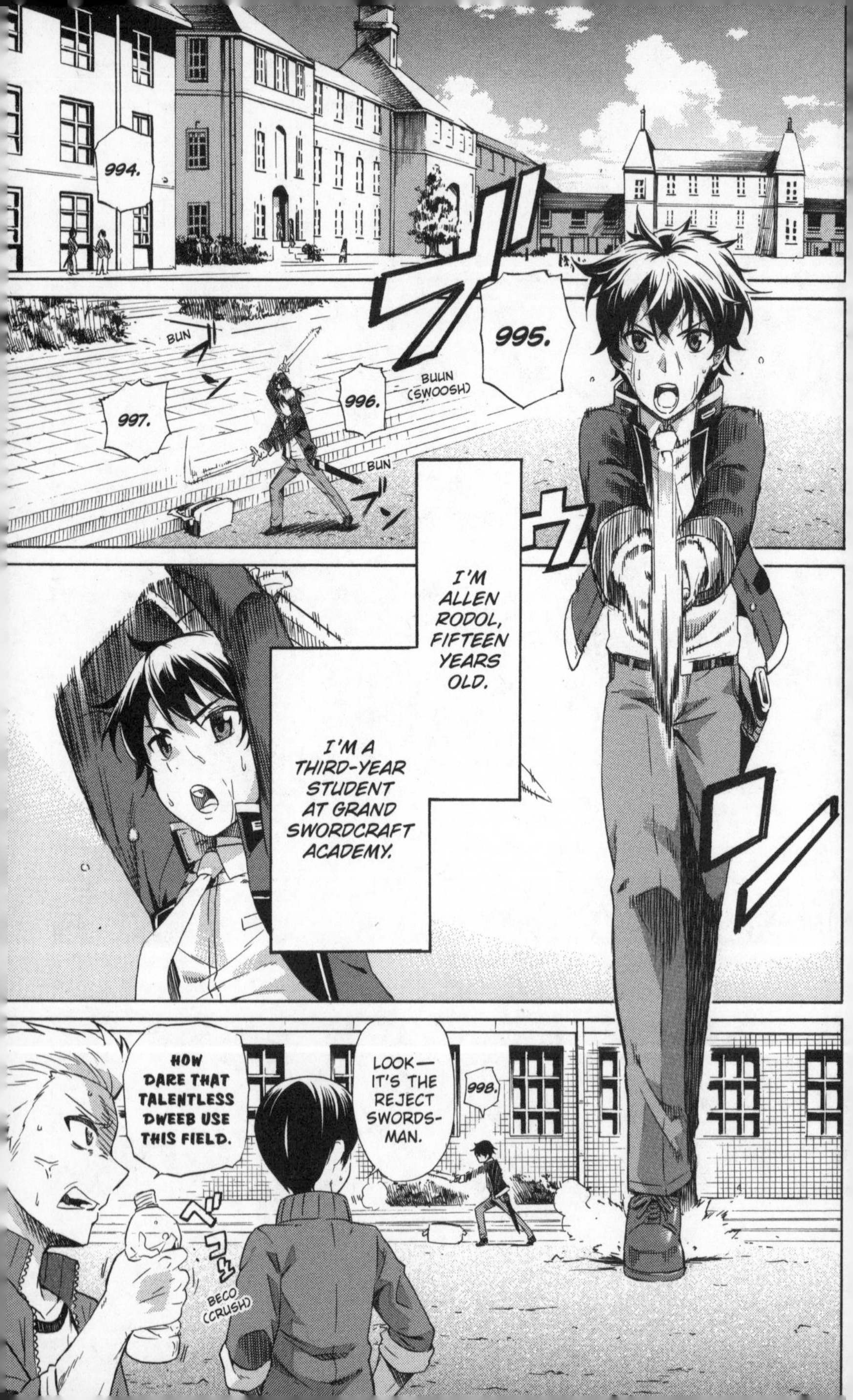
994.
995.
BUUN (SWOOSH)
996.
BUN
997.
BUN
I'M ALLEN RODOL, FIFTEEN YEARS OLD.
I'M A THIRD-YEAR STUDENT AT GRAND SWORDCRAFT ACADEMY.
998.
LOOK— IT'S THE REJECT SWORDS-MAN.
HOW DARE THAT TALENTLESS DWEEB USE THIS FIELD.
BECO (CRUSH)

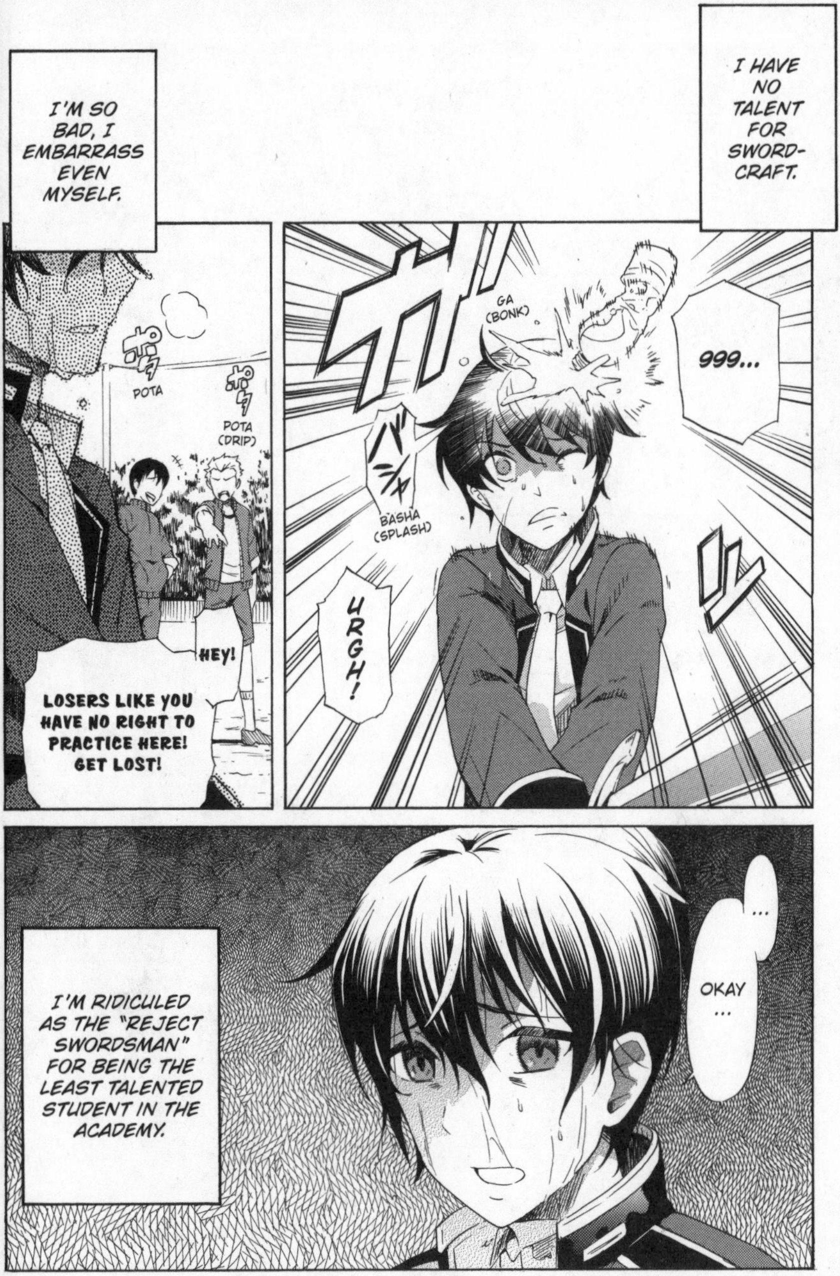

I HAVE NO TALENT FOR SWORD-CRAFT.
999...
GA (BONK)
BASHA (SPLASH)
URGH!
I'M SO BAD, I EMBARRASS EVEN MYSELF.
POTA
POTA (DRIP)
HEY!
LOSERS LIKE YOU HAVE NO RIGHT TO PRACTICE HERE! GET LOST!
... OKAY ...
I'M RIDICULED AS THE "REJECT SWORDSMAN" FOR BEING THE LEAST TALENTED STUDENT IN THE ACADEMY.

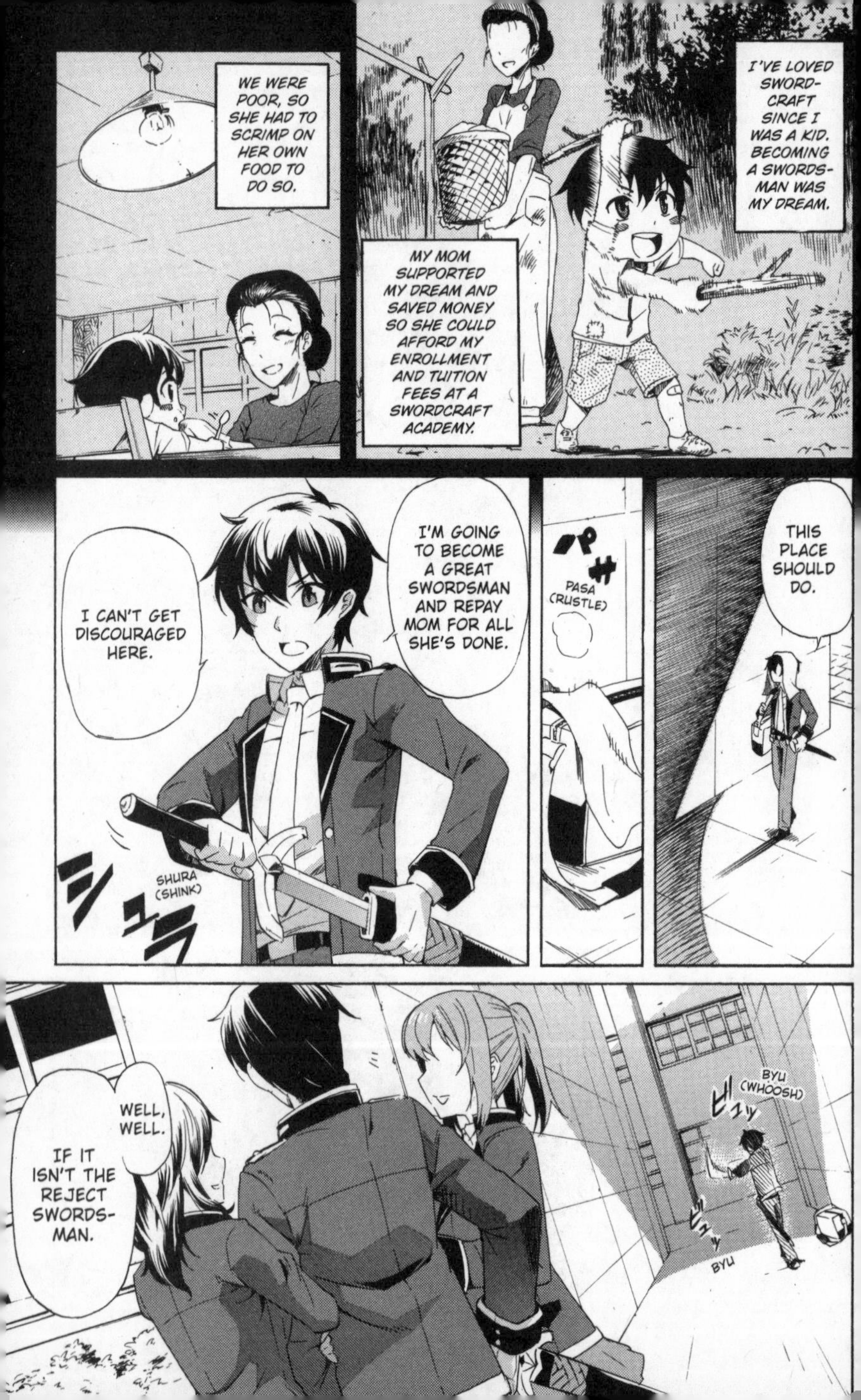
I'VE LOVED SWORDCRAFT SINCE I WAS A KID. BECOMING A SWORDSMAN WAS MY DREAM.
MY MOM SUPPORTED MY DREAM AND SAVED MONEY SO SHE COULD AFFORD MY ENROLLMENT AND TUITION FEES AT A SWORDCRAFT ACADEMY.
WE WERE POOR, SO SHE HAD TO SCRIMP ON HER OWN FOOD TO DO SO.
THIS PLACE SHOULD DO.
PASA (RUSTLE)
I'M GOING TO BECOME A GREAT SWORDSMAN AND REPAY MOM FOR ALL SHE'S DONE.
I CAN'T GET DISCOURAGED HERE.
SHURA (SHINK)
BYU (WHOOSH)
BYU
WELL, WELL.
IF IT ISN'T THE REJECT SWORDSMAN.

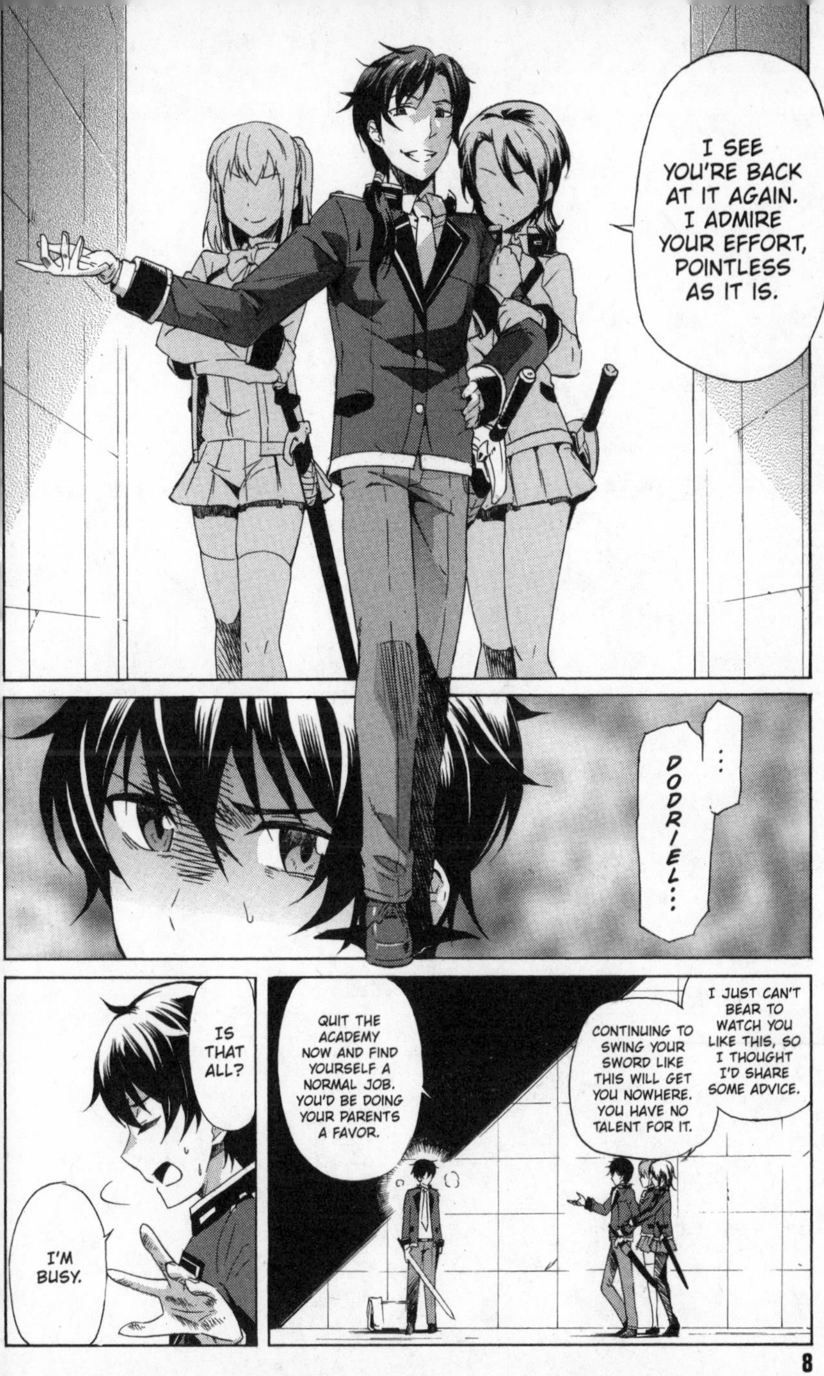
I SEE YOU'RE BACK AT IT AGAIN. I ADMIRE YOUR EFFORT, POINTLESS AS IT IS.
...
DODRIEL...
I JUST CAN'T BEAR TO WATCH YOU LIKE THIS, SO I THOUGHT I'D SHARE SOME ADVICE.
CONTINUING TO SWING YOUR SWORD LIKE THIS WILL GET YOU NOWHERE. YOU HAVE NO TALENT FOR IT.
QUIT THE ACADEMY NOW AND FIND YOURSELF A NORMAL JOB. YOU'D BE DOING YOUR PARENTS A FAVOR.
IS THAT ALL?
I'M BUSY.

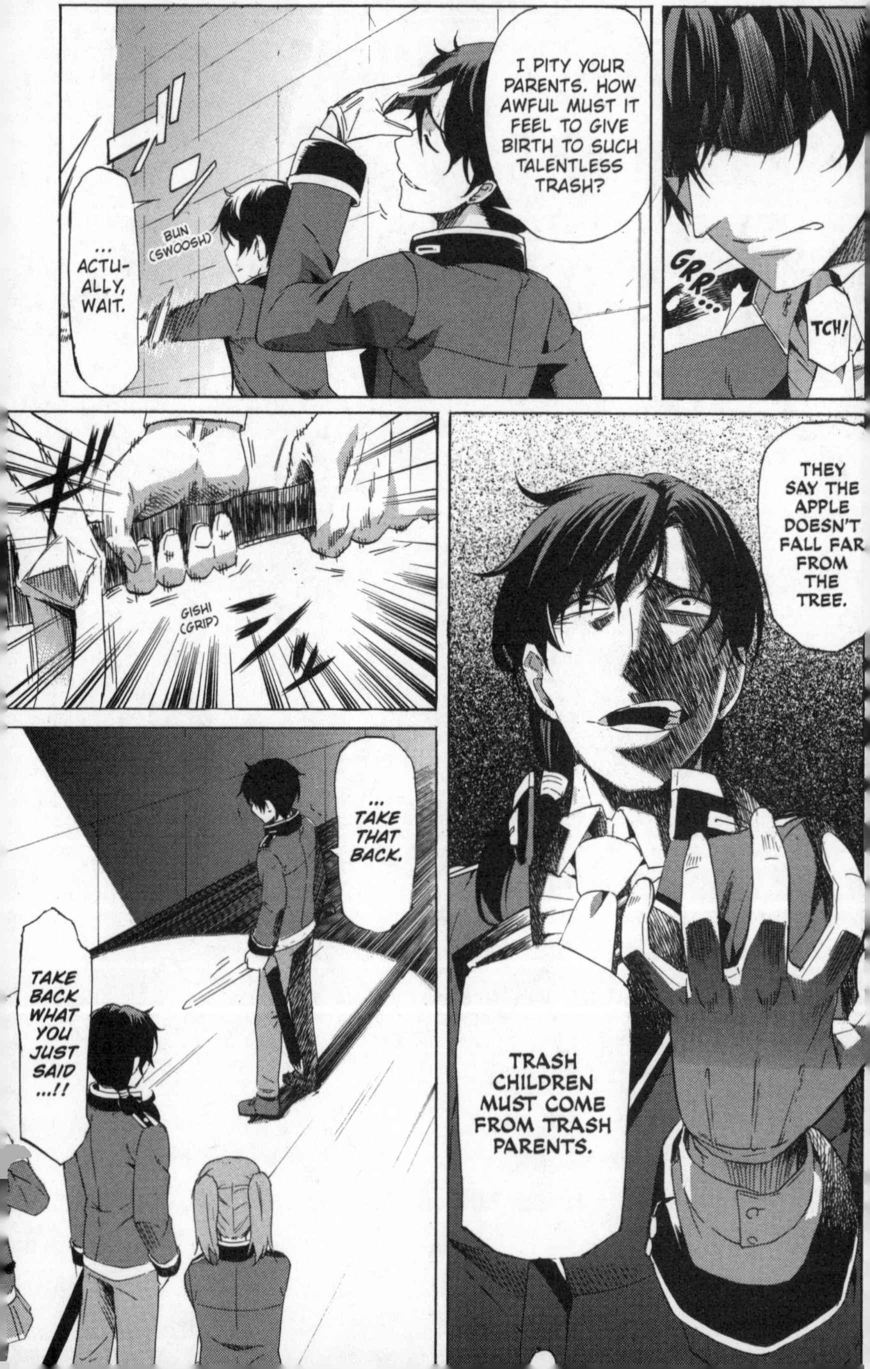
GRR...
TCH!
I PITY YOUR PARENTS. HOW AWFUL MUST IT FEEL TO GIVE BIRTH TO SUCH TALENTLESS TRASH?
BUN (SWOOSH)
... ACTUALLY, WAIT.
THEY SAY THE APPLE DOESN'T FALL FAR FROM THE TREE.
TRASH CHILDREN MUST COME FROM TRASH PARENTS.
GISHI (GRIP)
... TAKE THAT BACK.
TAKE BACK WHAT YOU JUST SAID ...!!

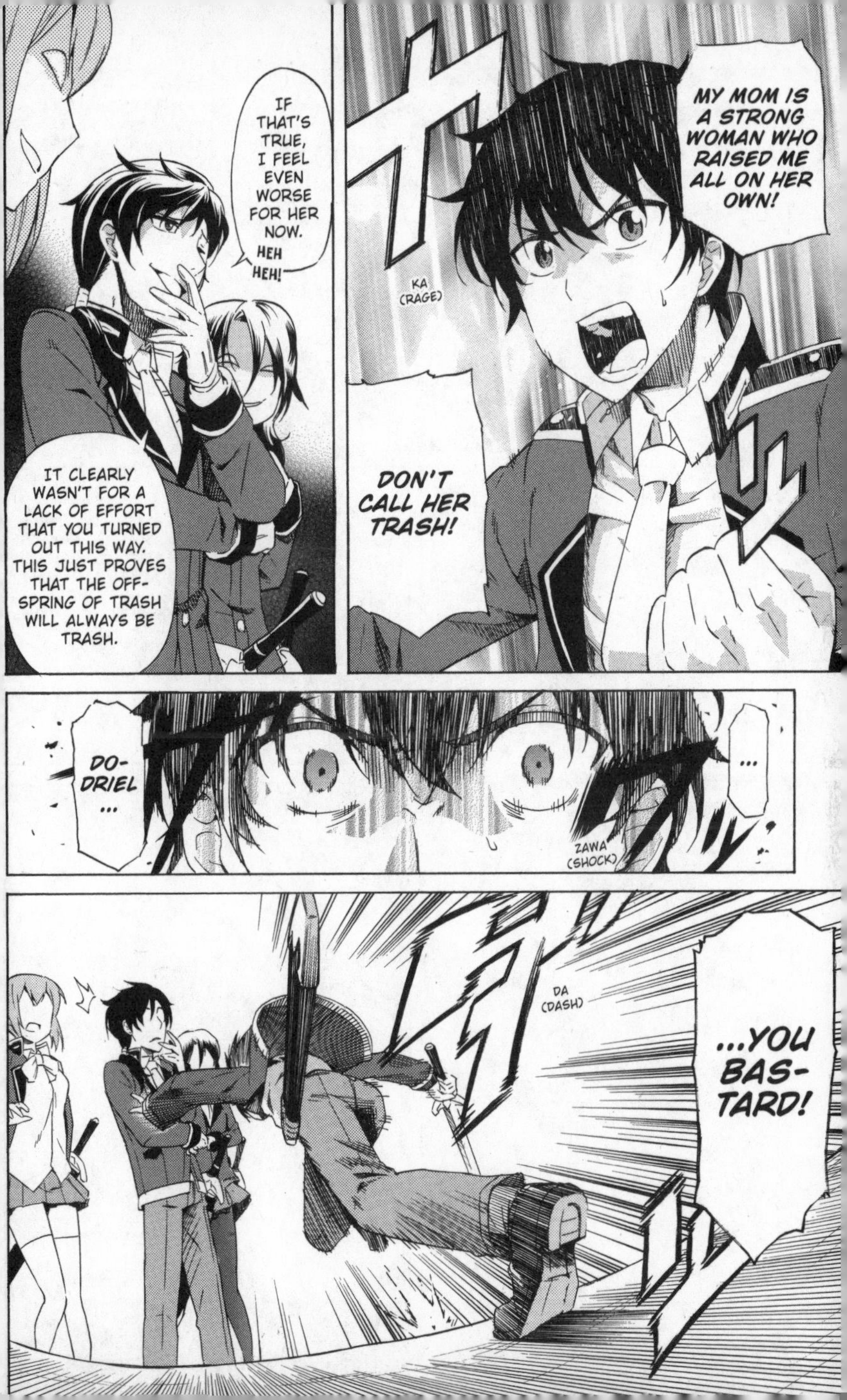
MY MOM IS A STRONG WOMAN WHO RAISED ME ALL ON HER OWN!
KA (RAGE)
DON'T CALL HER TRASH!
IF THAT'S TRUE, I FEEL EVEN WORSE FOR HER NOW. HEH HEH!
IT CLEARLY WASN'T FOR A LACK OF EFFORT THAT YOU TURNED OUT THIS WAY. THIS JUST PROVES THAT THE OFF-SPRING OF TRASH WILL ALWAYS BE TRASH.
...
ZAWA (SHOCK)
DO-DRIEL ...
...YOU BAS-TARD!
DA (DASH)

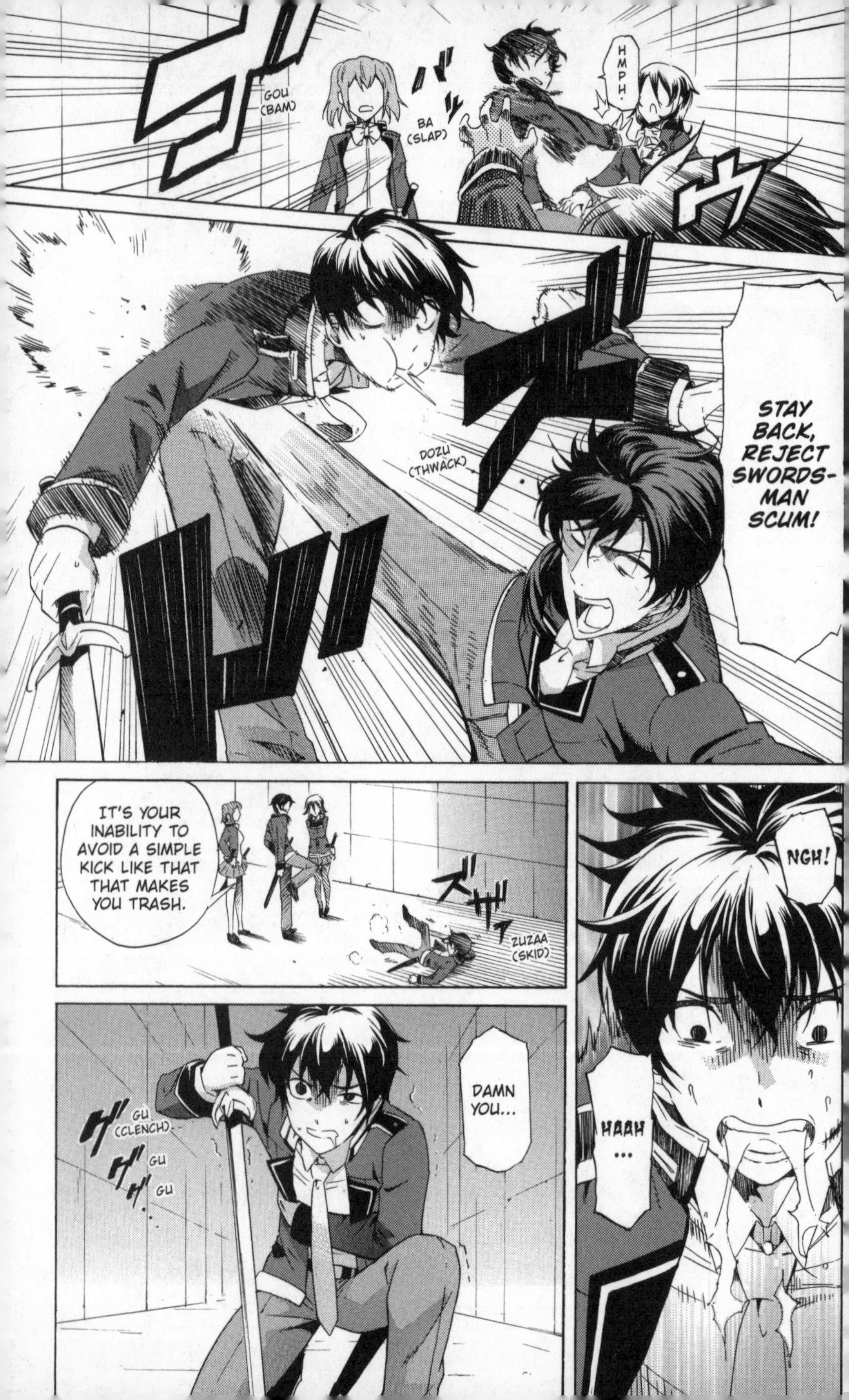
HMPH.
BA (SLAP)
GOU (BAM)
STAY BACK, REJECT SWORDSMAN SCUM!
DOZU (THWACK)
NGH!
HAAH ...
IT'S YOUR INABILITY TO AVOID A SIMPLE KICK LIKE THAT THAT MAKES YOU TRASH.
ZUZAA (SKID)
DAMN YOU...
GU (CLENCH)
GU
GU

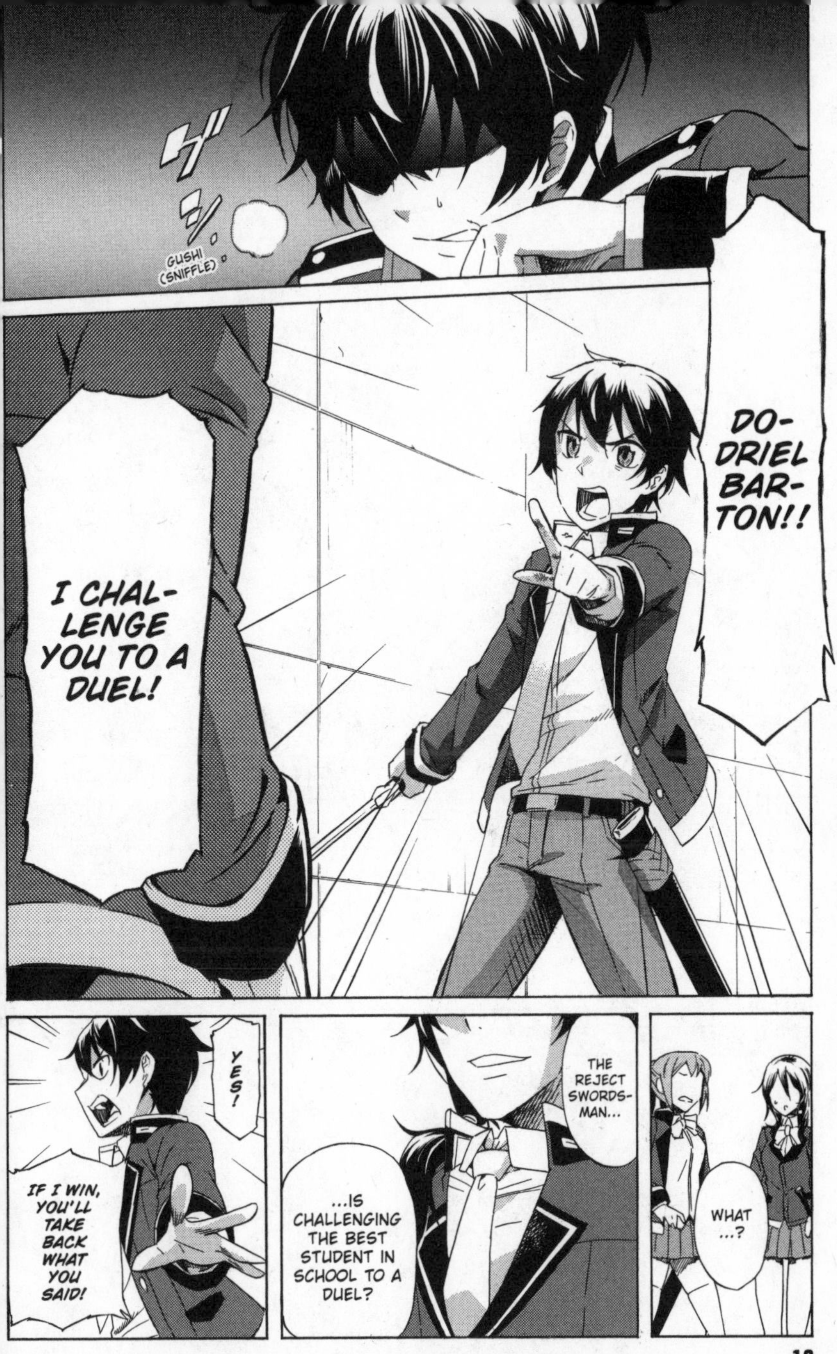
GUSHI (SNIFFLE)
DO-DRIEL BARTON!!
I CHALLENGE YOU TO A DUEL!
WHAT ...?
THE REJECT SWORDSMAN...
...IS CHALLENGING THE BEST STUDENT IN SCHOOL TO A DUEL?
YES!
IF I WIN, YOU'LL TAKE BACK WHAT YOU SAID!

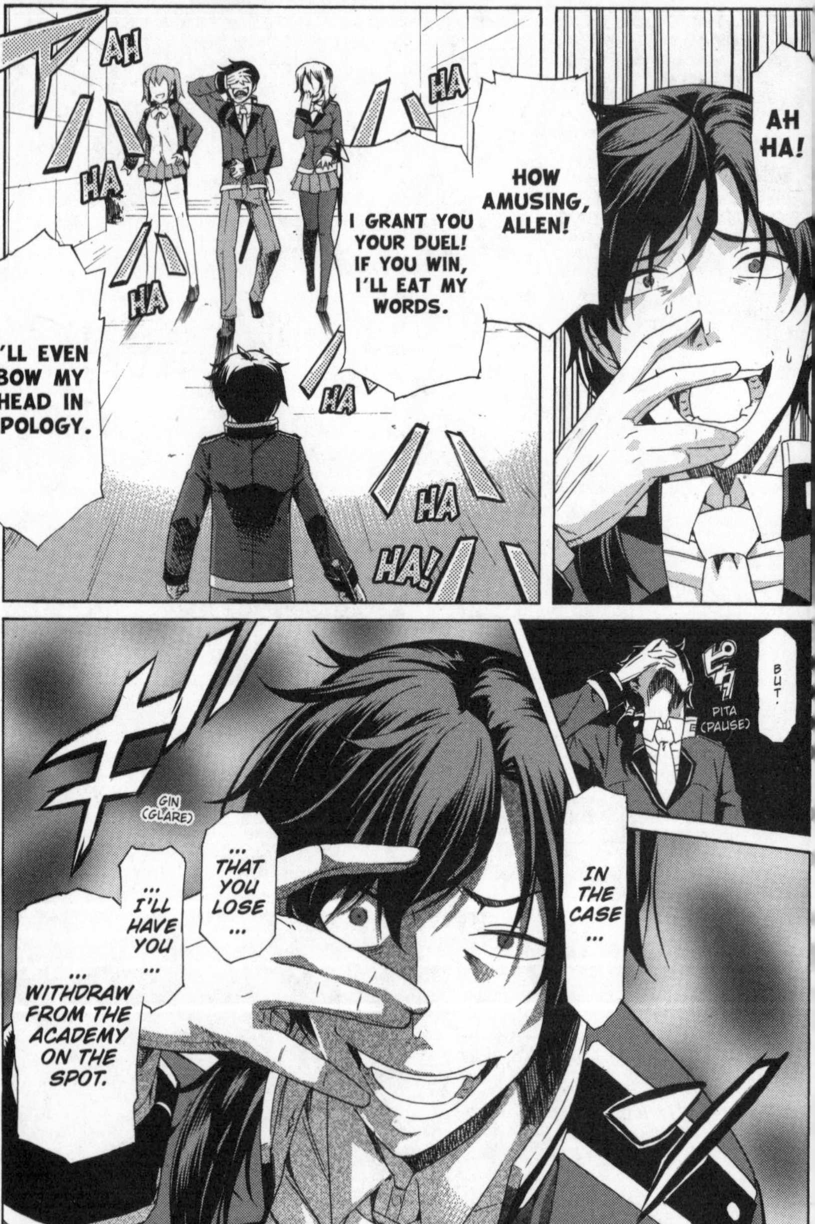
AH HA!
HOW AMUSING, ALLEN!
I GRANT YOU YOUR DUEL! IF YOU WIN, I'LL EAT MY WORDS.
AH
HA
HA
HA
I'LL EVEN BOW MY HEAD IN APOLOGY.
HA
HA
HA!
BUT.
PITA (PAUSE)
IN THE CASE ...
... THAT YOU LOSE ...
... I'LL HAVE YOU ...
... WITHDRAW FROM THE ACADEMY ON THE SPOT.
GIN (GLARE)

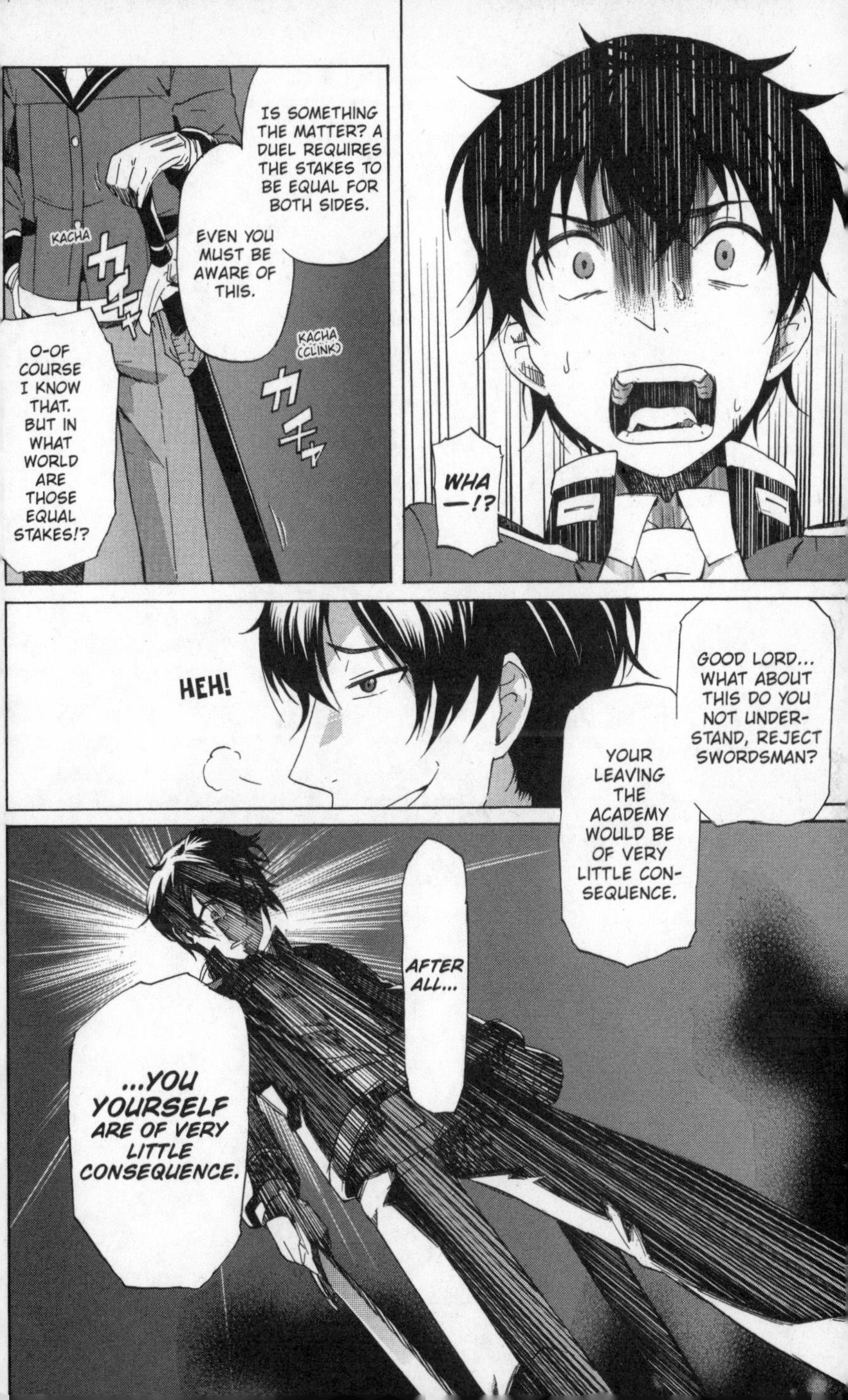
WHA—!?
IS SOMETHING THE MATTER? A DUEL REQUIRES THE STAKES TO BE EQUAL FOR BOTH SIDES.
EVEN YOU MUST BE AWARE OF THIS.
KACHA (CLINK)
KACHA
O-OF COURSE I KNOW THAT. BUT IN WHAT WORLD ARE THOSE EQUAL STAKES!?
GOOD LORD... WHAT ABOUT THIS DO YOU NOT UNDERSTAND, REJECT SWORDSMAN?
HEH!
YOUR LEAVING THE ACADEMY WOULD BE OF VERY LITTLE CONSEQUENCE.
AFTER ALL...
...YOU YOURSELF ARE OF VERY LITTLE CONSEQUENCE.

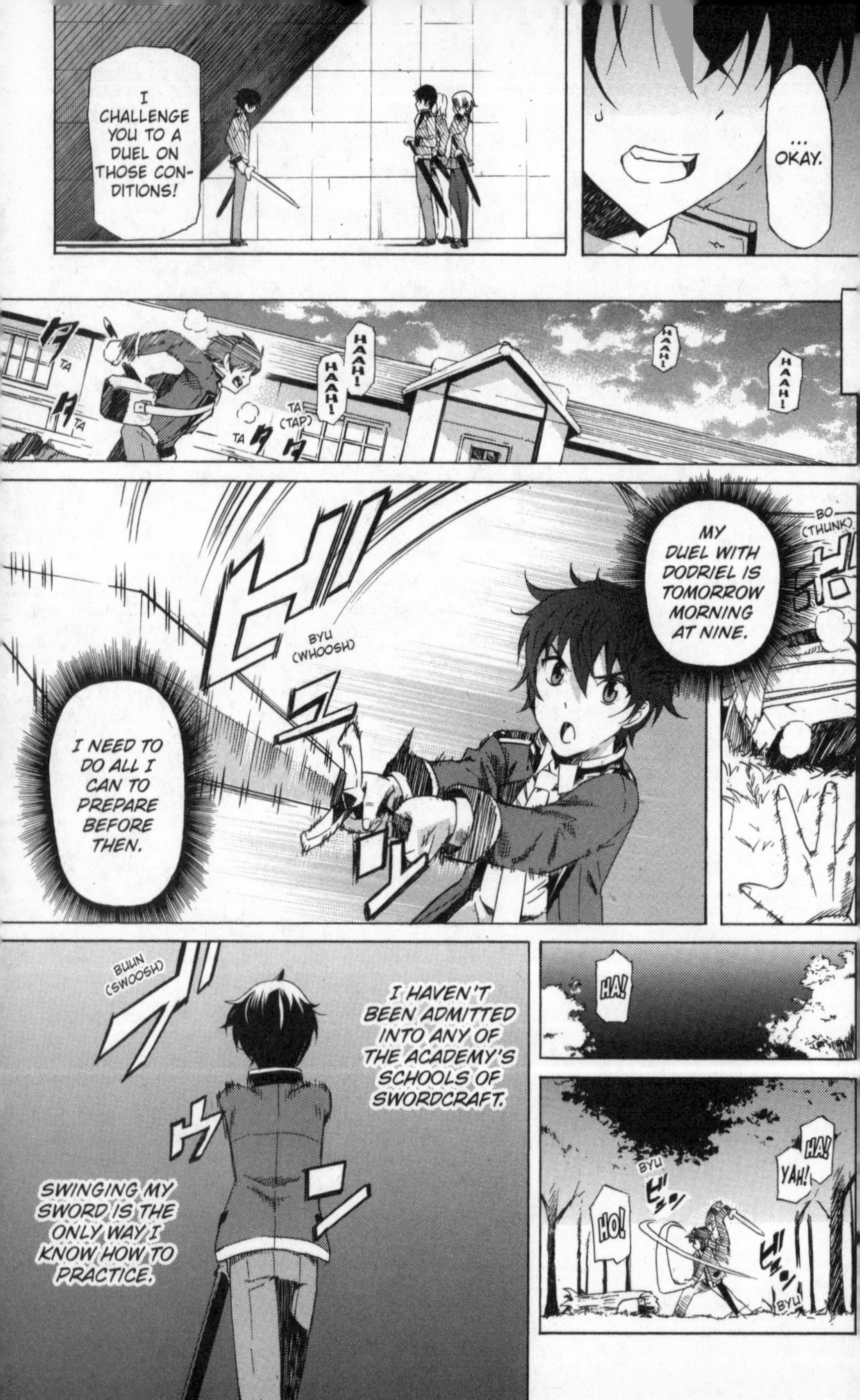
... OKAY.
I CHALLENGE YOU TO A DUEL ON THOSE CONDITIONS!
HAAH!
HAAH!
HAAH!
HAAH!
TA (TAP)
TA
TA
TA
BO (THUNK)
MY DUEL WITH DODRIEL IS TOMORROW MORNING AT NINE.
BYU (WHOOSH)
I NEED TO DO ALL I CAN TO PREPARE BEFORE THEN.
HA!
HA!
YAH!
BYU
HO!
BYU
BUUN (SWOOSH)
I HAVEN'T BEEN ADMITTED INTO ANY OF THE ACADEMY'S SCHOOLS OF SWORDCRAFT.
SWINGING MY SWORD IS THE ONLY WAY I KNOW HOW TO PRACTICE.

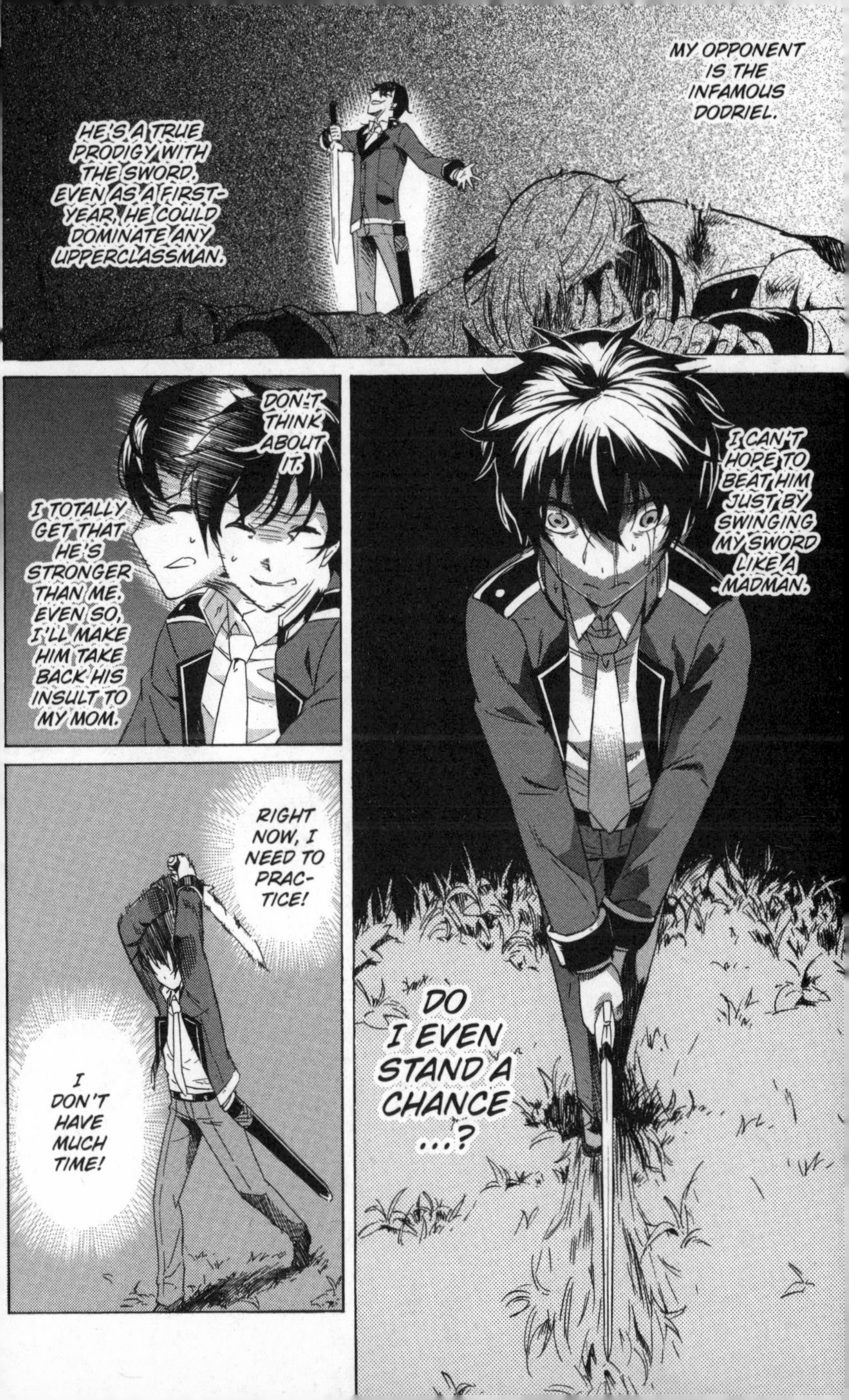
MY OPPONENT IS THE INFAMOUS DODRIEL.
HE'S A TRUE PRODIGY WITH THE SWORD. EVEN AS A FIRST-YEAR, HE COULD DOMINATE ANY UPPERCLASSMAN.
I CAN'T HOPE TO BEAT HIM JUST BY SWINGING MY SWORD LIKE A MADMAN.
DO I EVEN STAND A CHANCE ...?
DON'T THINK ABOUT IT.
I TOTALLY GET THAT HE'S STRONGER THAN ME. EVEN SO, I'LL MAKE HIM TAKE BACK HIS INSULT TO MY MOM.
RIGHT NOW, I NEED TO PRAC-TICE!
I DON'T HAVE MUCH TIME!

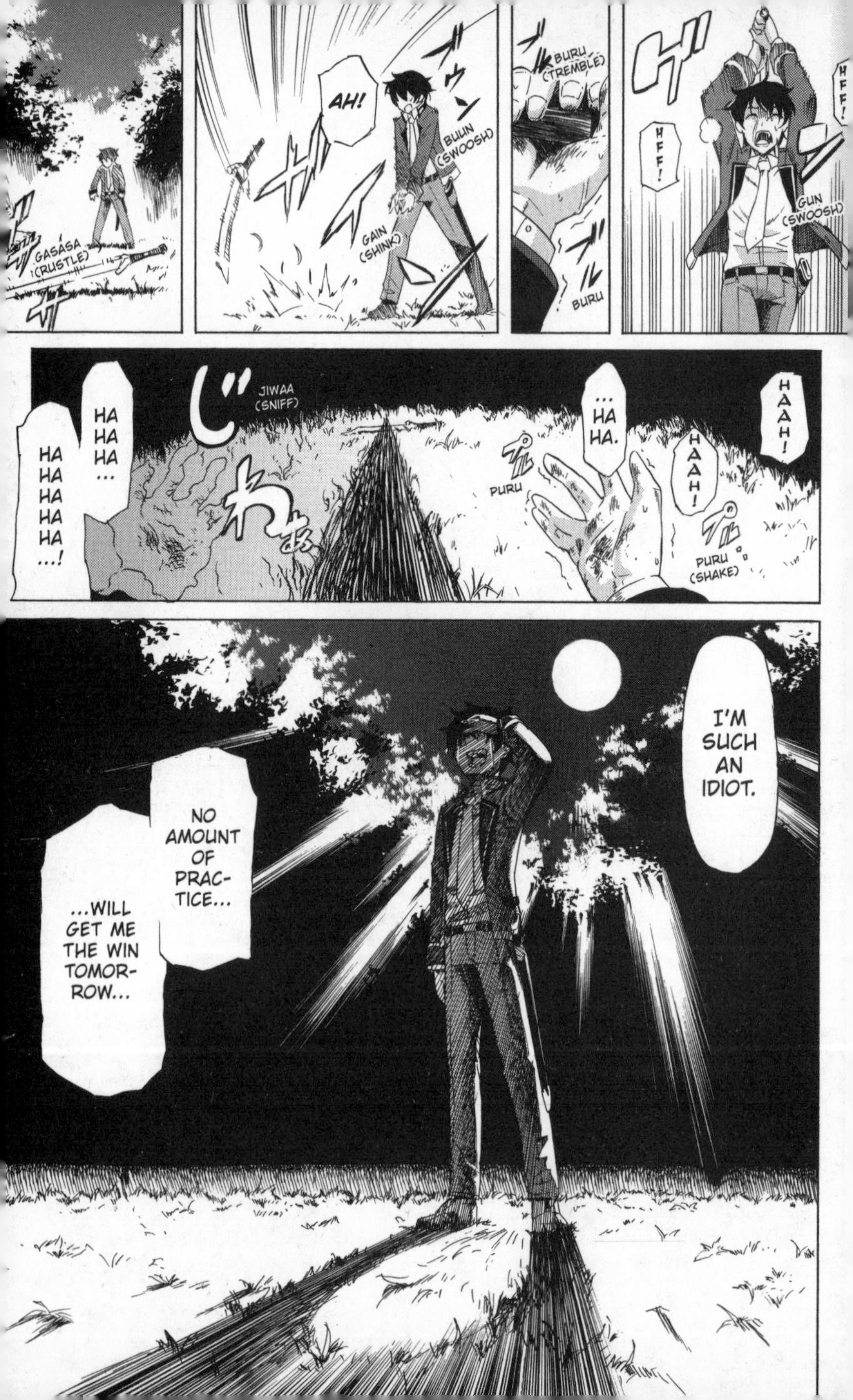
HFF!
HFF!
GUN (SWOOSH)
BURU (TREMBLE)
BURU
AH!
BUUN (SWOOSH)
GAIN (SHINK)
GASASA (RUSTLE)
HAAAH!
HAAAH!
PURU (SHAKE)
...HA HA HA.
PURU
JIWAA (SNIFF)
HA HA HA...
HA HA HA HA HA...!
I'M SUCH AN IDIOT.
NO AMOUNT OF PRAC-TICE...
...WILL GET ME THE WIN TOMOR-ROW...

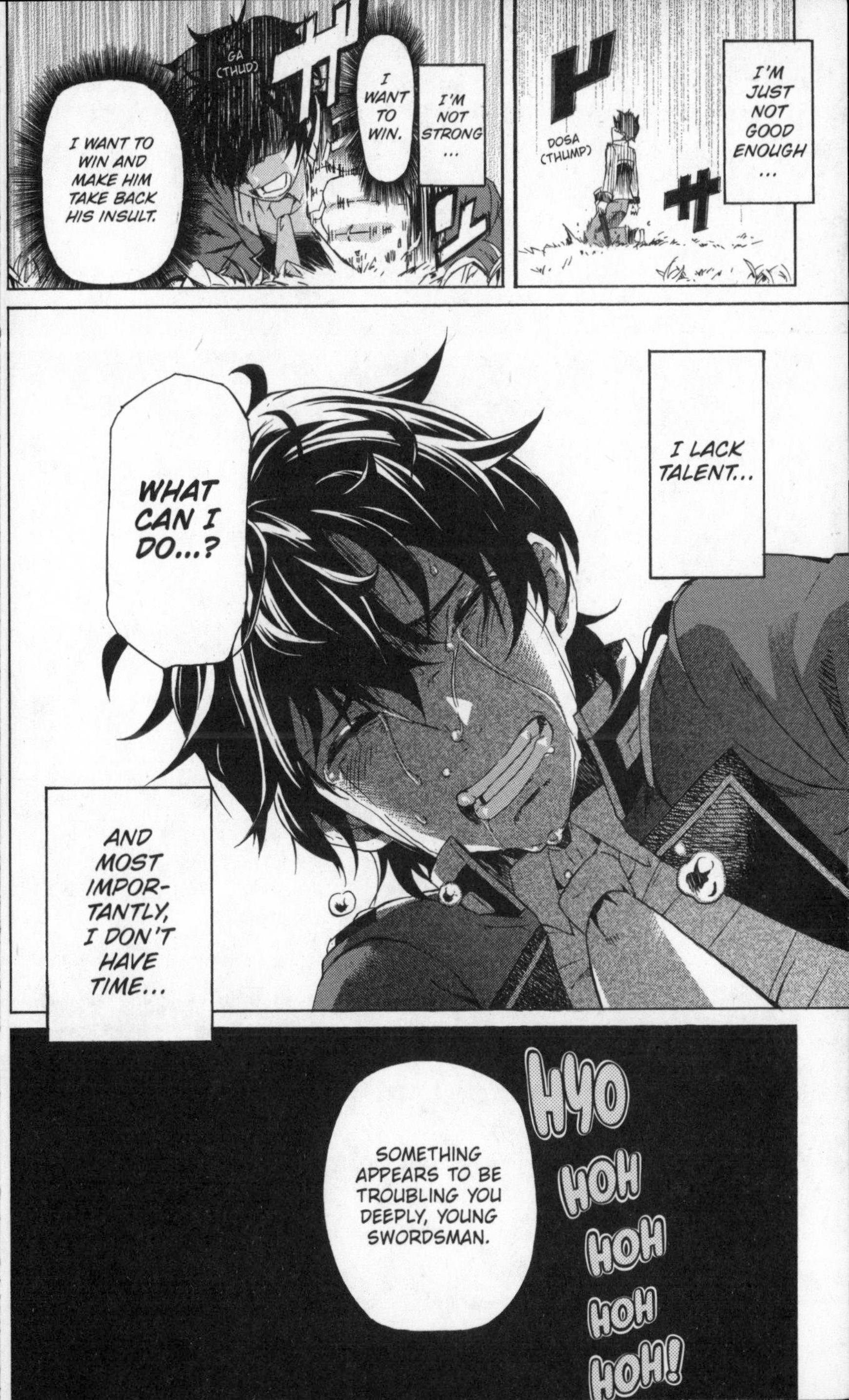
I'M JUST NOT GOOD ENOUGH...
DOSA (THUMP)
I'M NOT STRONG...
I WANT TO WIN.
GA (THUD)
I WANT TO WIN AND MAKE HIM TAKE BACK HIS INSULT.
I LACK TALENT...
WHAT CAN I DO...?
AND MOST IMPOR-TANTLY, I DON'T HAVE TIME...
HYO HOH HOH HOH HOH!
SOMETHING APPEARS TO BE TROUBLING YOU DEEPLY, YOUNG SWORDSMAN.

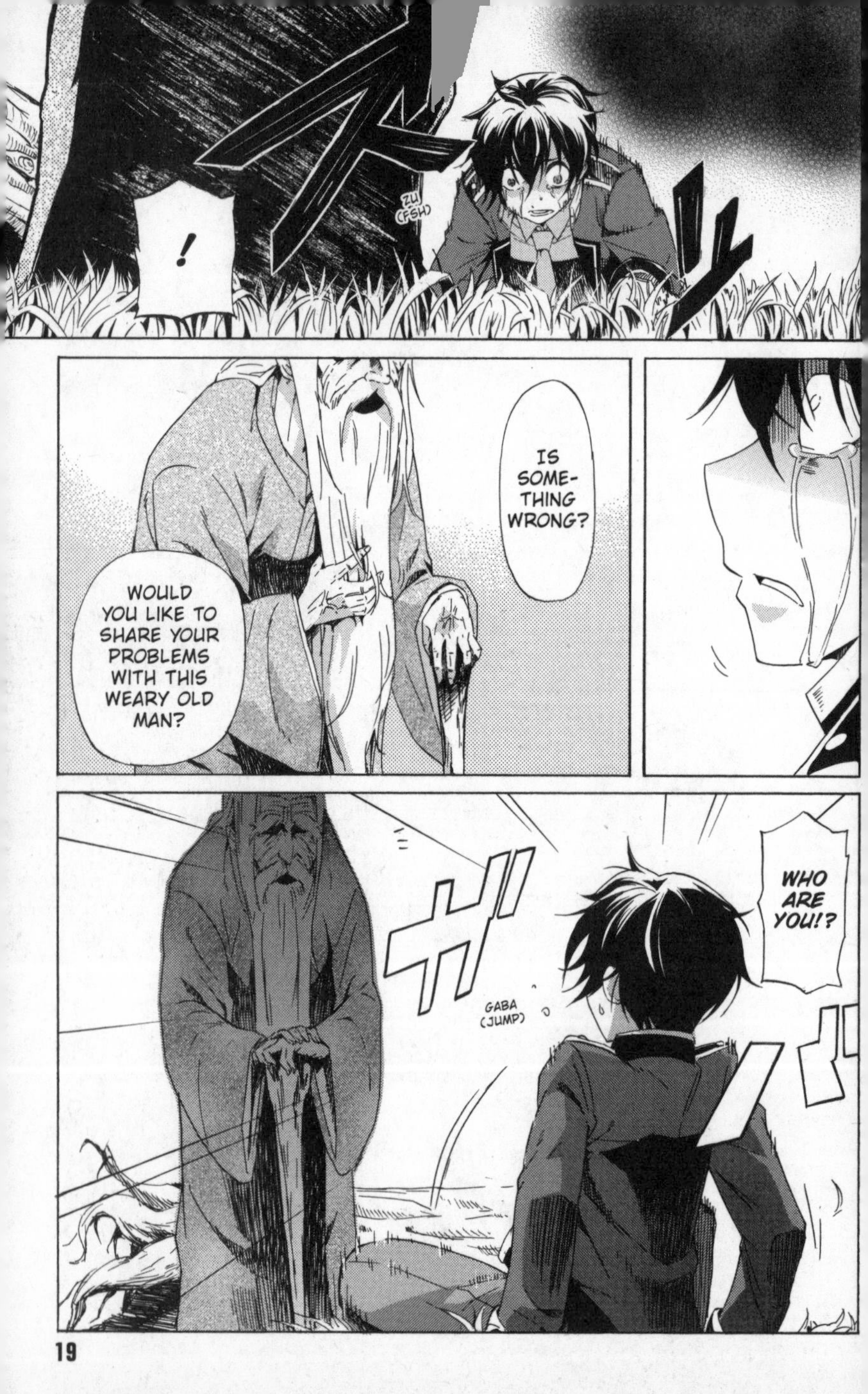
ZU (FSH)
!
IS SOME-THING WRONG?
WOULD YOU LIKE TO SHARE YOUR PROBLEMS WITH THIS WEARY OLD MAN?
WHO ARE YOU!?
GABA (JUMP)

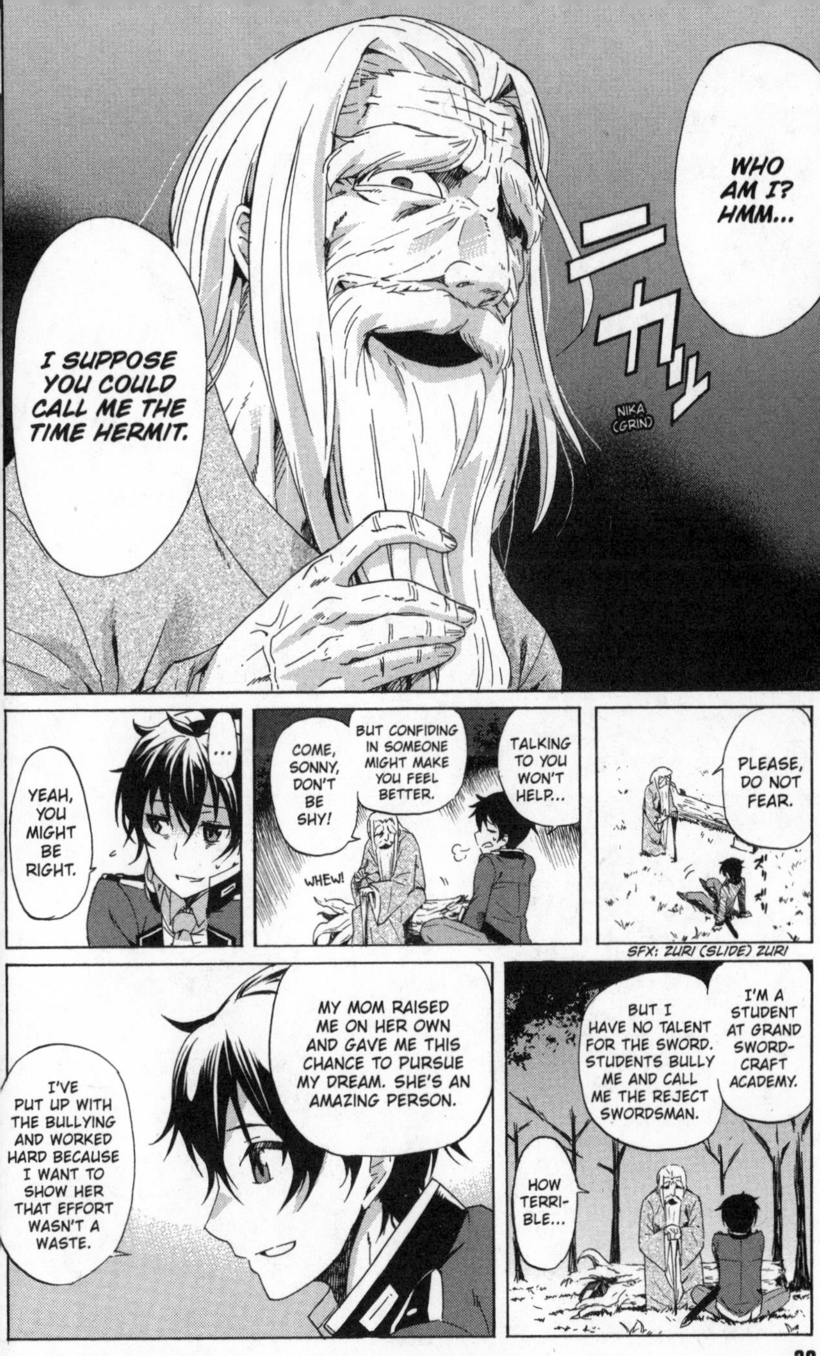
WHO AM I? HMM...
NIKA (GRIN)
I SUPPOSE YOU COULD CALL ME THE TIME HERMIT.
PLEASE, DO NOT FEAR.
SFX: ZURI (SLIDE) ZURI
TALKING TO YOU WON'T HELP...
WHEW!
BUT CONFIDING IN SOMEONE MIGHT MAKE YOU FEEL BETTER.
COME, SONNY, DON'T BE SHY!
...
YEAH, YOU MIGHT BE RIGHT.
I'M A STUDENT AT GRAND SWORD-CRAFT ACADEMY.
BUT I HAVE NO TALENT FOR THE SWORD. STUDENTS BULLY ME AND CALL ME THE REJECT SWORDSMAN.
HOW TERRIBLE...
MY MOM RAISED ME ON HER OWN AND GAVE ME THIS CHANCE TO PURSUE MY DREAM. SHE'S AN AMAZING PERSON.
I'VE PUT UP WITH THE BULLYING AND WORKED HARD BECAUSE I WANT TO SHOW HER THAT EFFORT WASN'T A WASTE.

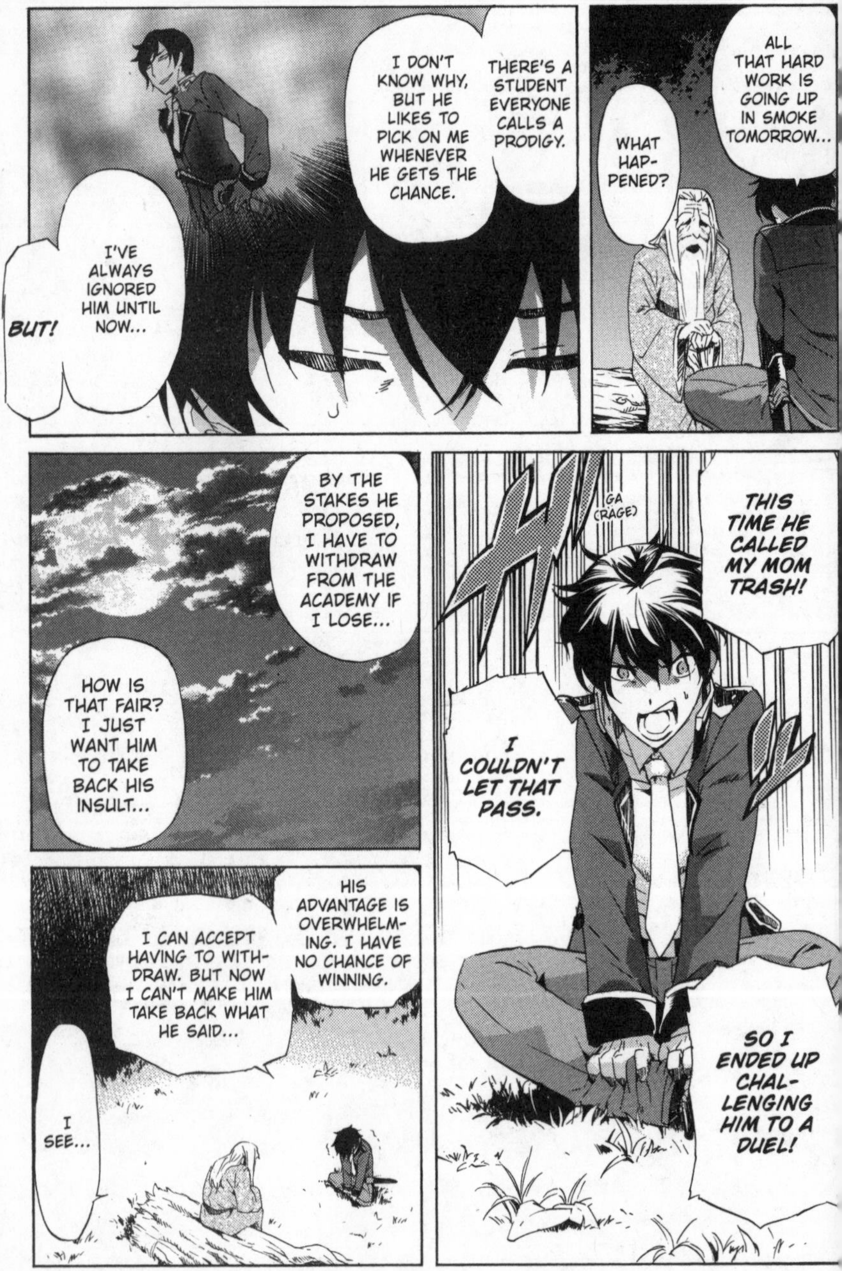
ALL THAT HARD WORK IS GOING UP IN SMOKE TOMORROW...
WHAT HAPPENED?
THERE'S A STUDENT EVERYONE CALLS A PRODIGY.
I DON'T KNOW WHY, BUT HE LIKES TO PICK ON ME WHENEVER HE GETS THE CHANCE.
I'VE ALWAYS IGNORED HIM UNTIL NOW...
BUT!
THIS TIME HE CALLED MY MOM TRASH!
GA (RAGE)
I COULDN'T LET THAT PASS.
SO I ENDED UP CHAL-LENGING HIM TO A DUEL!
BY THE STAKES HE PROPOSED, I HAVE TO WITHDRAW FROM THE ACADEMY IF I LOSE...
HOW IS THAT FAIR? I JUST WANT HIM TO TAKE BACK HIS INSULT...
HIS ADVANTAGE IS OVERWHELM-ING. I HAVE NO CHANCE OF WINNING.
I CAN ACCEPT HAVING TO WITH-DRAW. BUT NOW I CAN'T MAKE HIM TAKE BACK WHAT HE SAID...
I SEE...

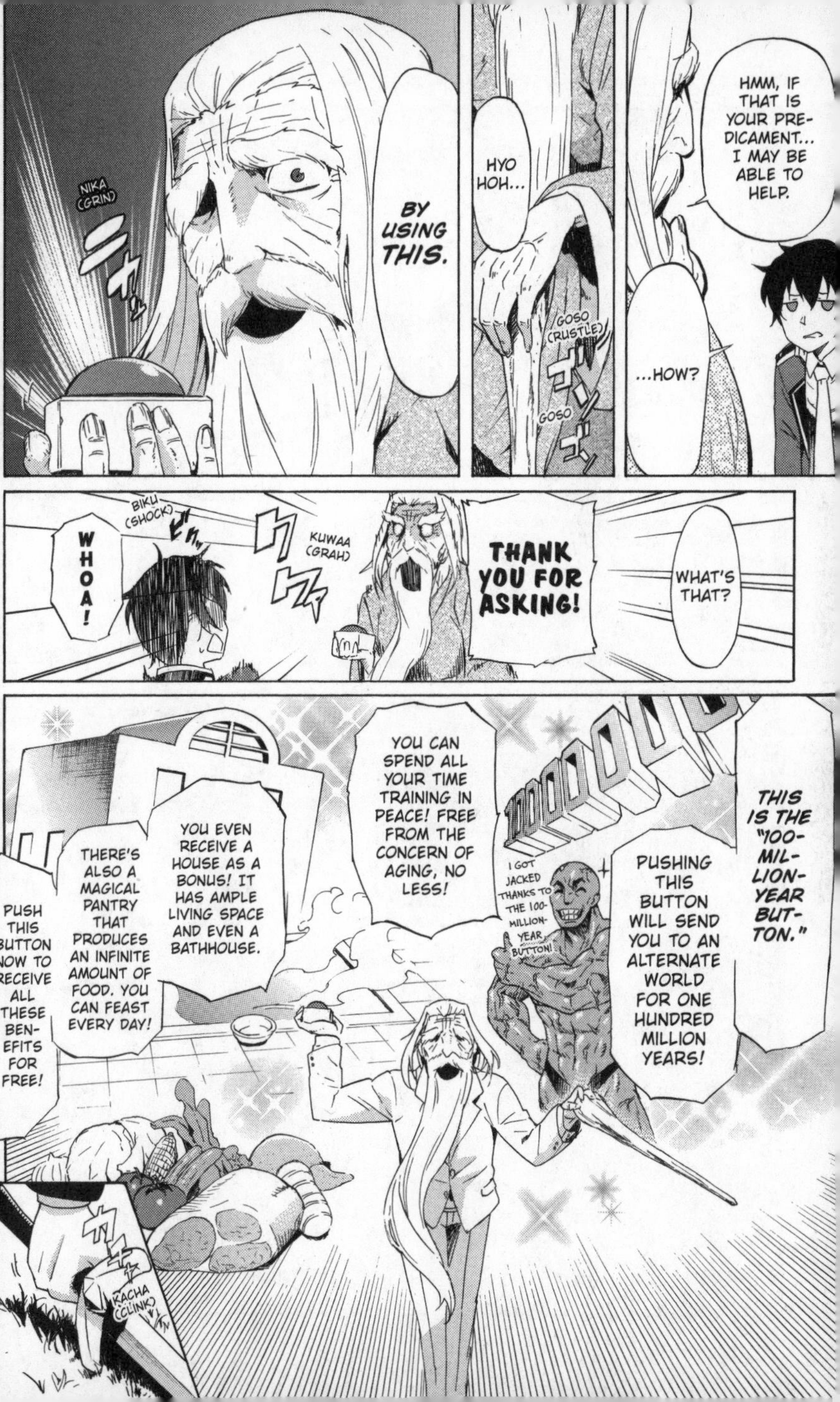
HMM, IF THAT IS YOUR PREDICAMENT... I MAY BE ABLE TO HELP.
...HOW?
HYO HOH...
GOSO (RUSTLE)
GOSO
BY USING THIS.
NIKA (GRIN)
WHAT'S THAT?
THANK YOU FOR ASKING!
KUWAA (GRAH)
BIKU (SHOCK)
WHOA!
THIS IS THE "100-MILLION-YEAR BUTTON."
PUSHING THIS BUTTON WILL SEND YOU TO AN ALTERNATE WORLD FOR ONE HUNDRED MILLION YEARS!
I GOT JACKED THANKS TO THE 100-MILLION-YEAR BUTTON!
YOU CAN SPEND ALL YOUR TIME TRAINING IN PEACE! FREE FROM THE CONCERN OF AGING, NO LESS!
YOU EVEN RECEIVE A HOUSE AS A BONUS! IT HAS AMPLE LIVING SPACE AND EVEN A BATHHOUSE.
THERE'S ALSO A MAGICAL PANTRY THAT PRODUCES AN INFINITE AMOUNT OF FOOD. YOU CAN FEAST EVERY DAY!
PUSH THIS BUTTON NOW TO RECEIVE ALL THESE BENEFITS FOR FREE!
KACHA (CLINK)

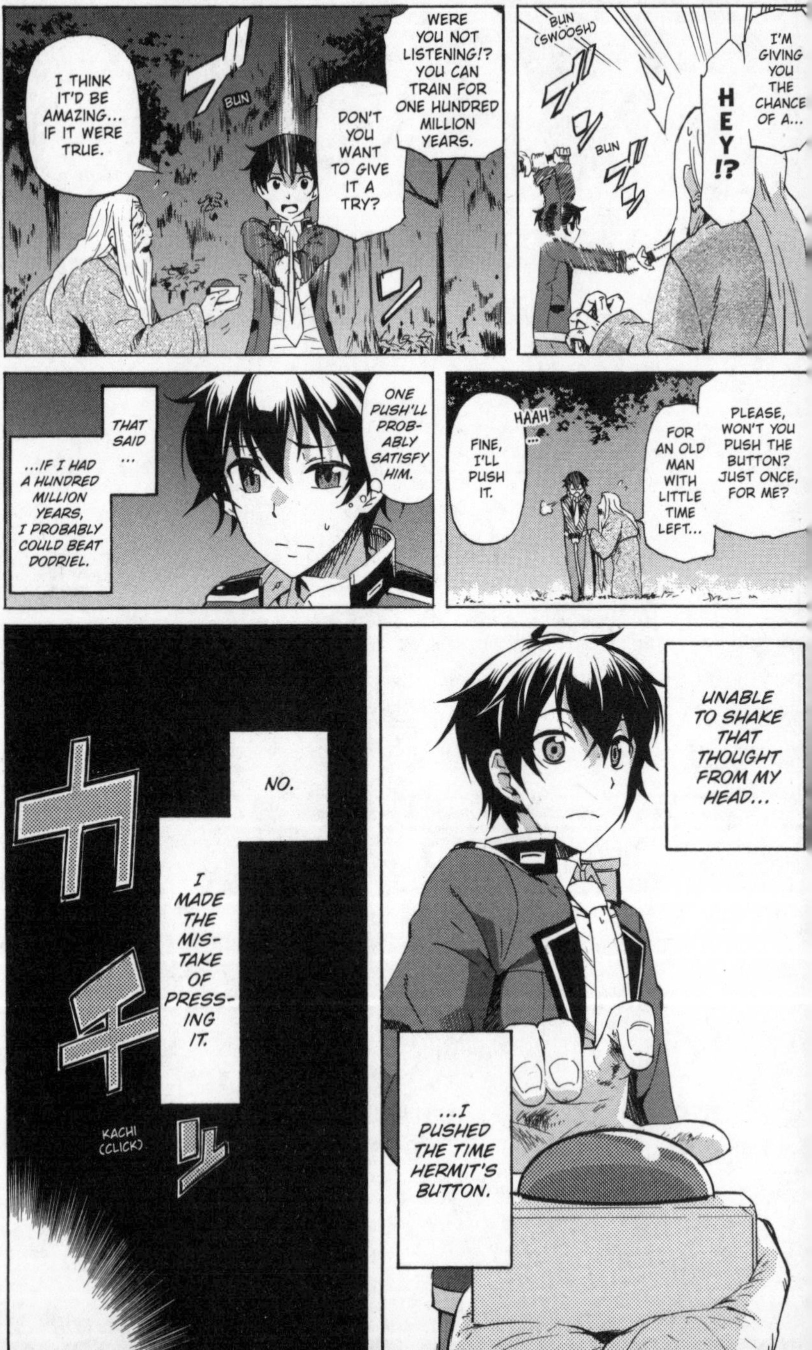
I'M GIVING YOU THE CHANCE OF A...
HEY!?
BUN (SWOOSH)
BUN
WERE YOU NOT LISTENING!? YOU CAN TRAIN FOR ONE HUNDRED MILLION YEARS.
DON'T YOU WANT TO GIVE IT A TRY?
BUN
I THINK IT'D BE AMAZING... IF IT WERE TRUE.
PLEASE, WON'T YOU PUSH THE BUTTON? JUST ONCE, FOR ME?
FOR AN OLD MAN WITH LITTLE TIME LEFT...
HAAH...
FINE, I'LL PUSH IT.
ONE PUSH'LL PROBABLY SATISFY HIM.
THAT SAID...
...IF I HAD A HUNDRED MILLION YEARS, I PROBABLY COULD BEAT DODRIEL.
UNABLE TO SHAKE THAT THOUGHT FROM MY HEAD...
...I PUSHED THE TIME HERMIT'S BUTTON.
NO.
I MADE THE MISTAKE OF PRESSING IT.
KACHI (CLICK)

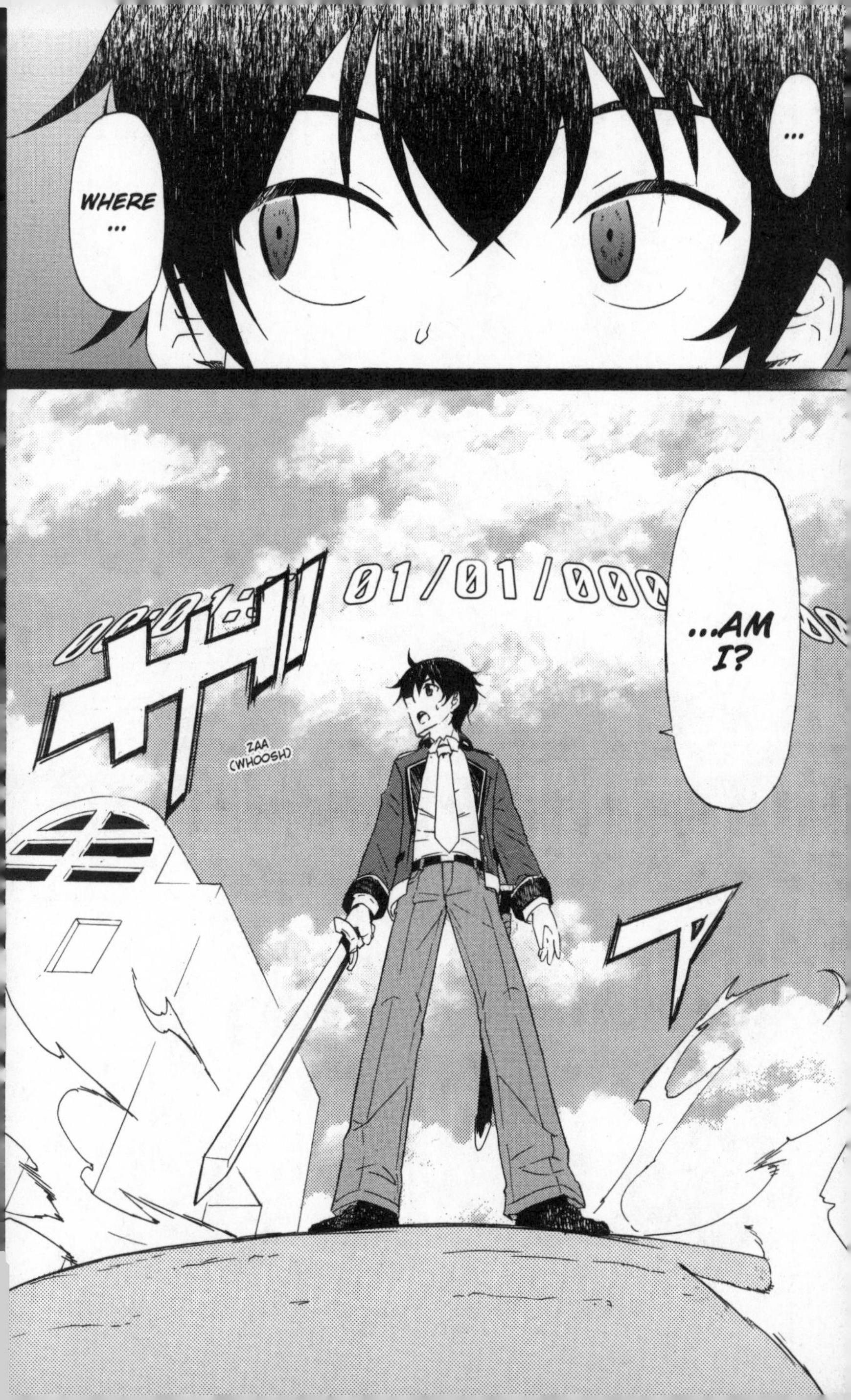
...
WHERE ...
...AM I?
01/01/000
ZAA (WHOOSH)

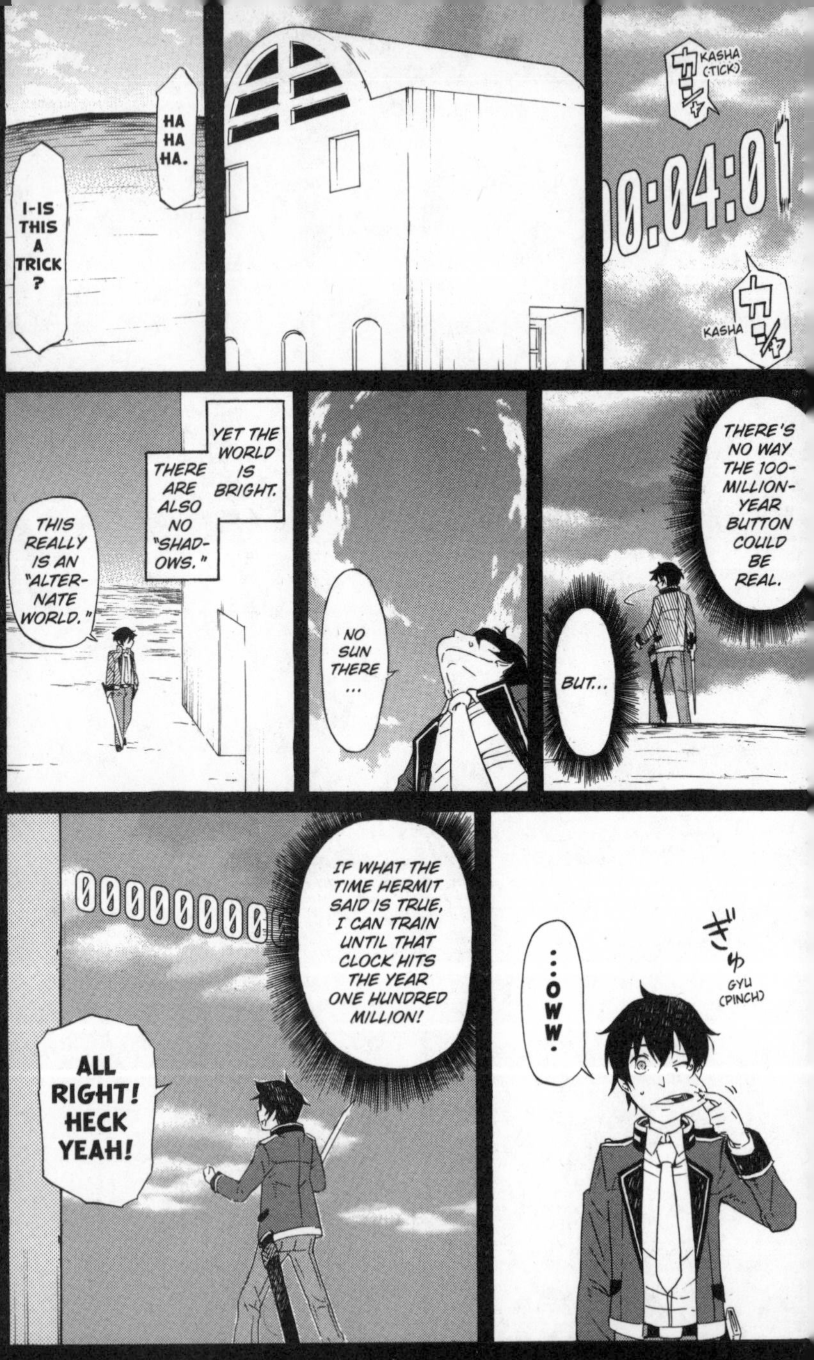
KASHA (TICK)
00:04:01
KASHA
HA HA HA.
I-IS THIS A TRICK?
THERE'S NO WAY THE 100-MILLION-YEAR BUTTON COULD BE REAL.
BUT...
NO SUN THERE...
YET THE WORLD IS BRIGHT.
THERE ARE ALSO NO "SHADOWS."
THIS REALLY IS AN "ALTERNATE WORLD."
ぎゅ
GYU (PINCH)
...OWW.
IF WHAT THE TIME HERMIT SAID IS TRUE, I CAN TRAIN UNTIL THAT CLOCK HITS THE YEAR ONE HUNDRED MILLION!
ALL RIGHT! HECK YEAH!

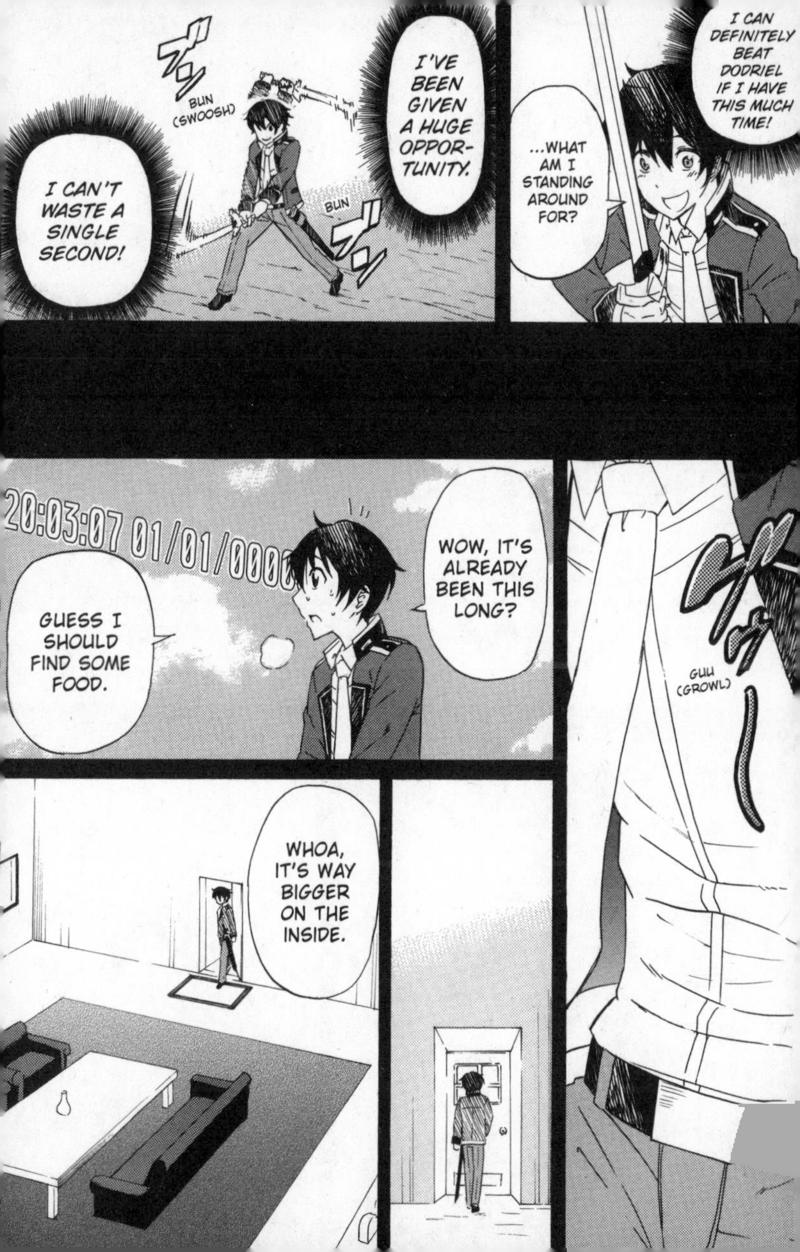
I CAN DEFINITELY BEAT DODRIEL IF I HAVE THIS MUCH TIME!
...WHAT AM I STANDING AROUND FOR?
I'VE BEEN GIVEN A HUGE OPPOR-TUNITY.
BUN (SWOOSH)
BUN
I CAN'T WASTE A SINGLE SECOND!
GUU (GROWL)
20:03:07 01/01/0000
WOW, IT'S ALREADY BEEN THIS LONG?
GUESS I SHOULD FIND SOME FOOD.
WHOA, IT'S WAY BIGGER ON THE INSIDE.

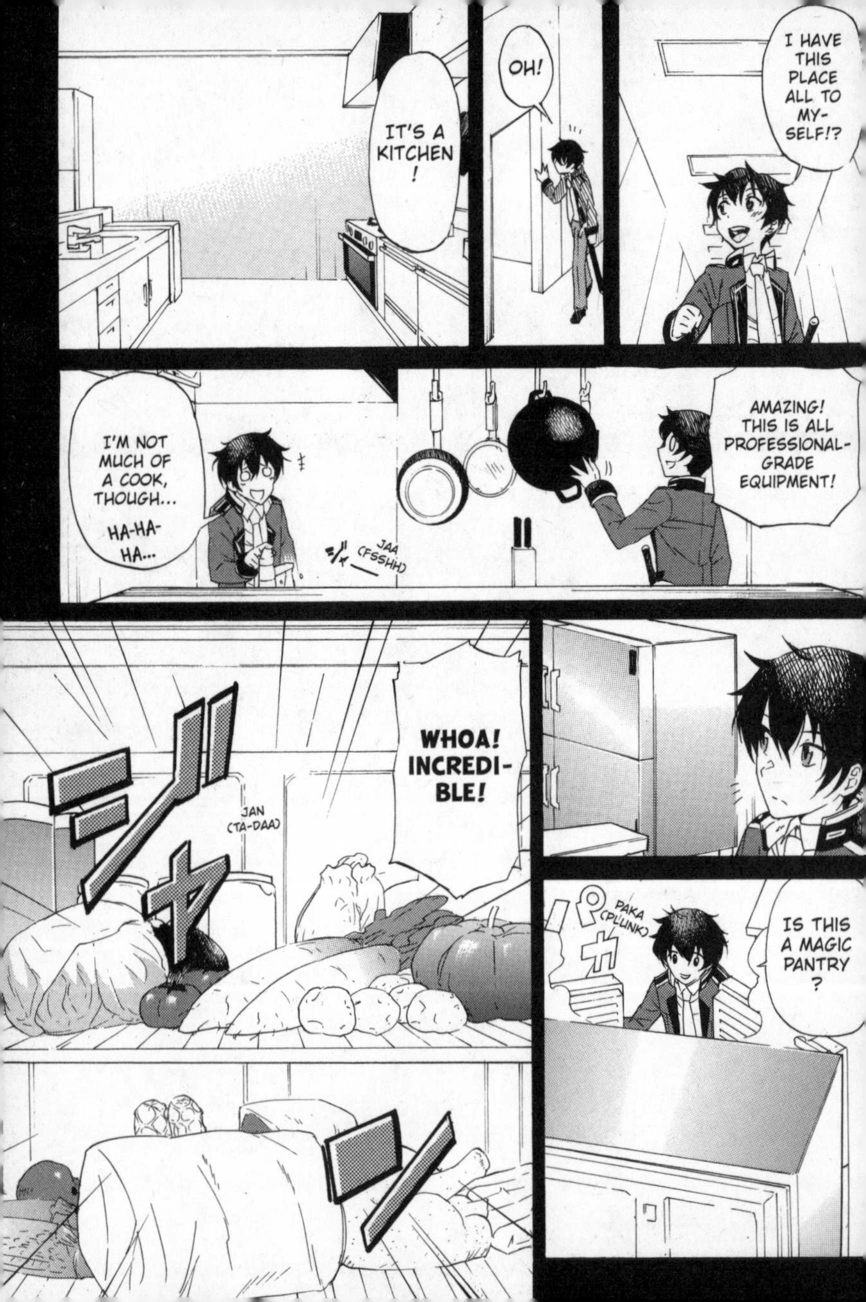

I HAVE THIS PLACE ALL TO MY-SELF!?
OH!
IT'S A KITCHEN!
AMAZING! THIS IS ALL PROFESSIONAL-GRADE EQUIPMENT!
JAA (FSSHH)
I'M NOT MUCH OF A COOK, THOUGH... HA-HA-HA...
PAKA (PLUNK)
IS THIS A MAGIC PANTRY?
WHOA! INCREDI-BLE!
JAN (TA-DAA)

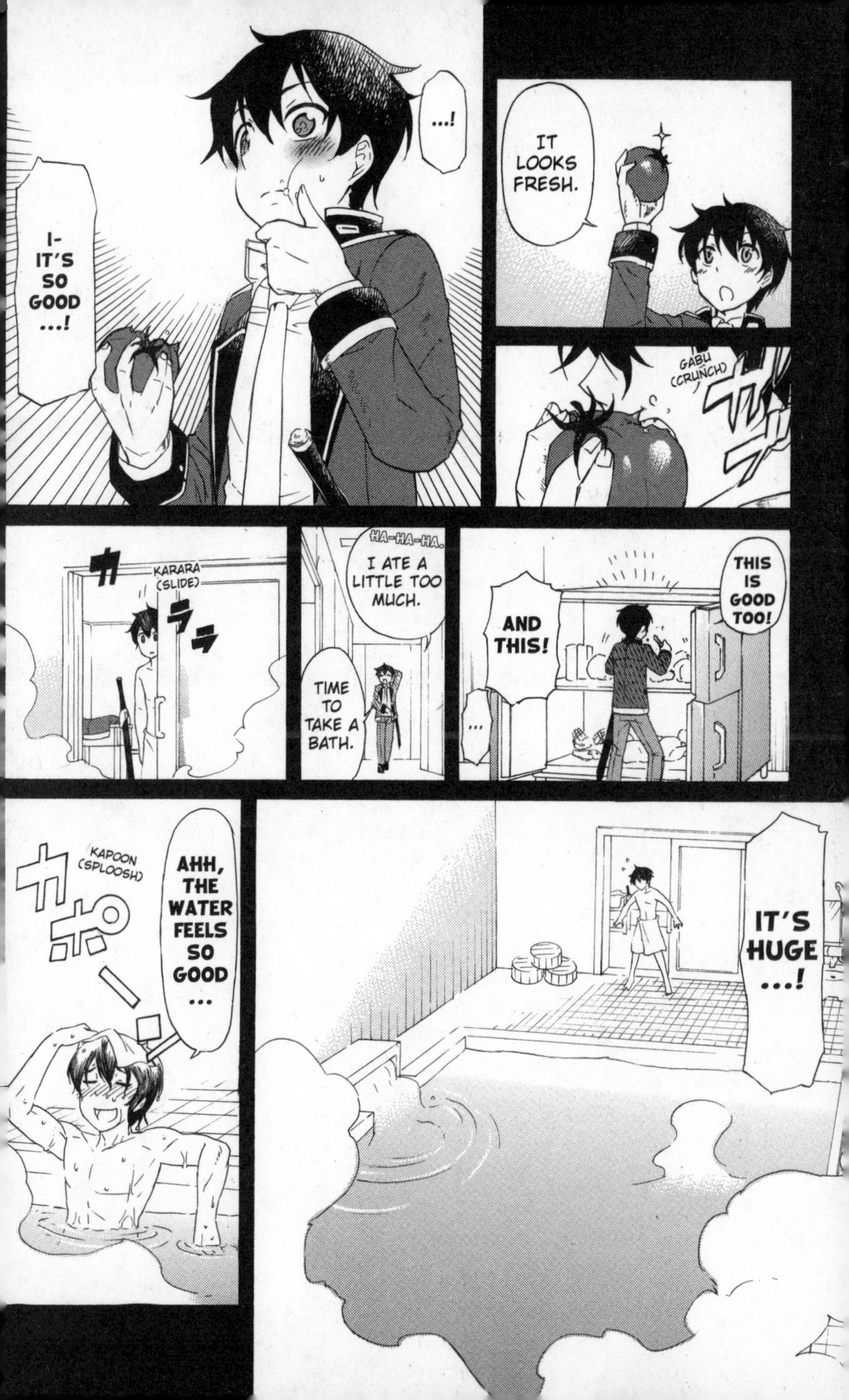
IT LOOKS FRESH.
GABU (CRUNCH)
...!
I- IT'S SO GOOD ...!
THIS IS GOOD TOO!
AND THIS!
...
HA-HA-HA.
I ATE A LITTLE TOO MUCH.
TIME TO TAKE A BATH.
KARARA (SLIDE)
IT'S HUGE ...!
AHH, THE WATER FEELS SO GOOD ...
KAPOON (SPLOOSH)

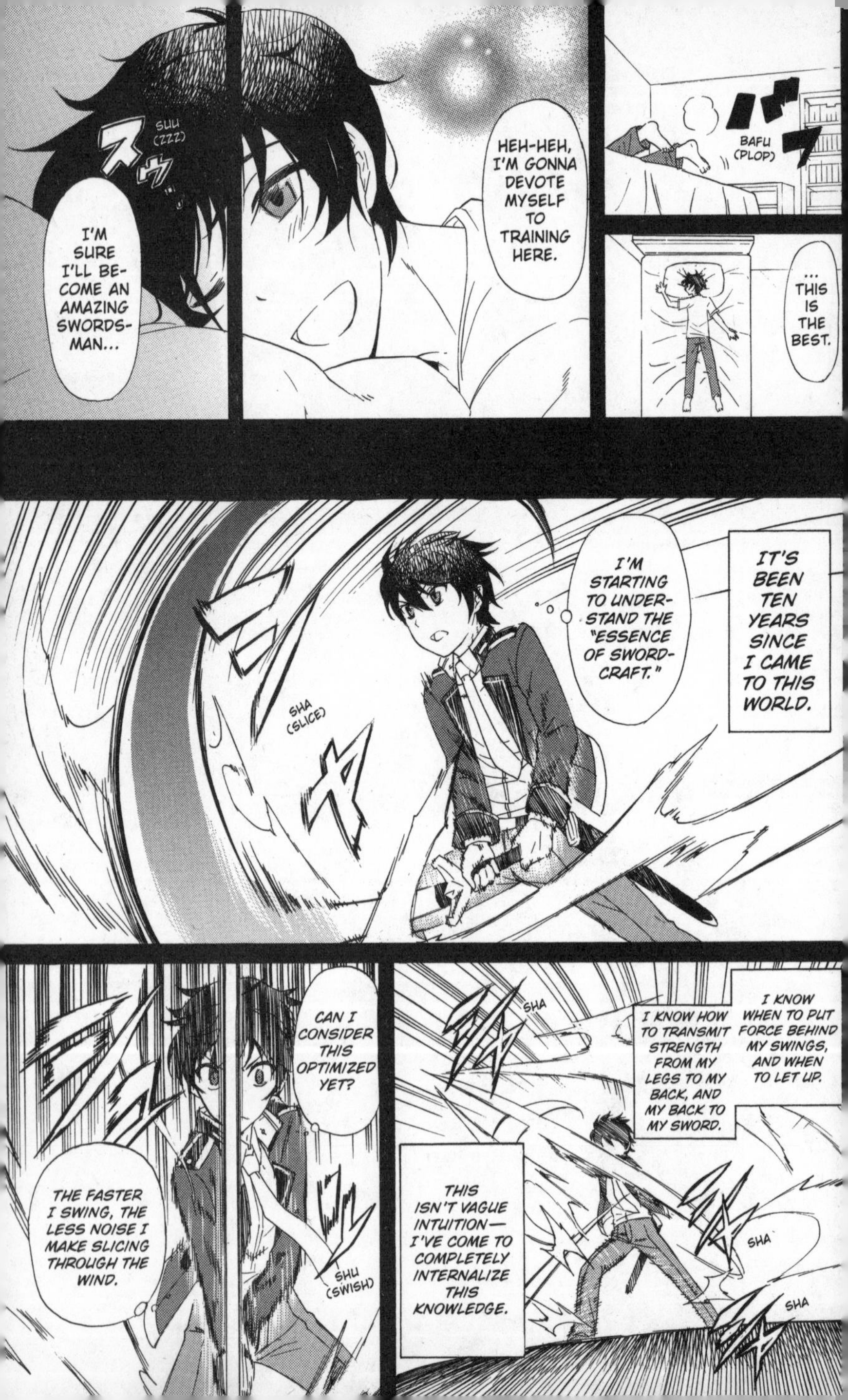
BAFU (PLOP)
...THIS IS THE BEST.
HEH-HEH, I'M GONNA DEVOTE MYSELF TO TRAINING HERE.
SUU (ZZZ)
I'M SURE I'LL BE-COME AN AMAZING SWORDS-MAN...
IT'S BEEN TEN YEARS SINCE I CAME TO THIS WORLD.
I'M STARTING TO UNDER-STAND THE "ESSENCE OF SWORD-CRAFT."
SHA (SLICE)
I KNOW WHEN TO PUT FORCE BEHIND MY SWINGS, AND WHEN TO LET UP.
I KNOW HOW TO TRANSMIT STRENGTH FROM MY LEGS TO MY BACK, AND MY BACK TO MY SWORD.
SHA
THIS ISN'T VAGUE INTUITION—I'VE COME TO COMPLETELY INTERNALIZE THIS KNOWLEDGE.
SHA
SHA
CAN I CONSIDER THIS OPTIMIZED YET?
THE FASTER I SWING, THE LESS NOISE I MAKE SLICING THROUGH THE WIND.
SHU (SWISH)

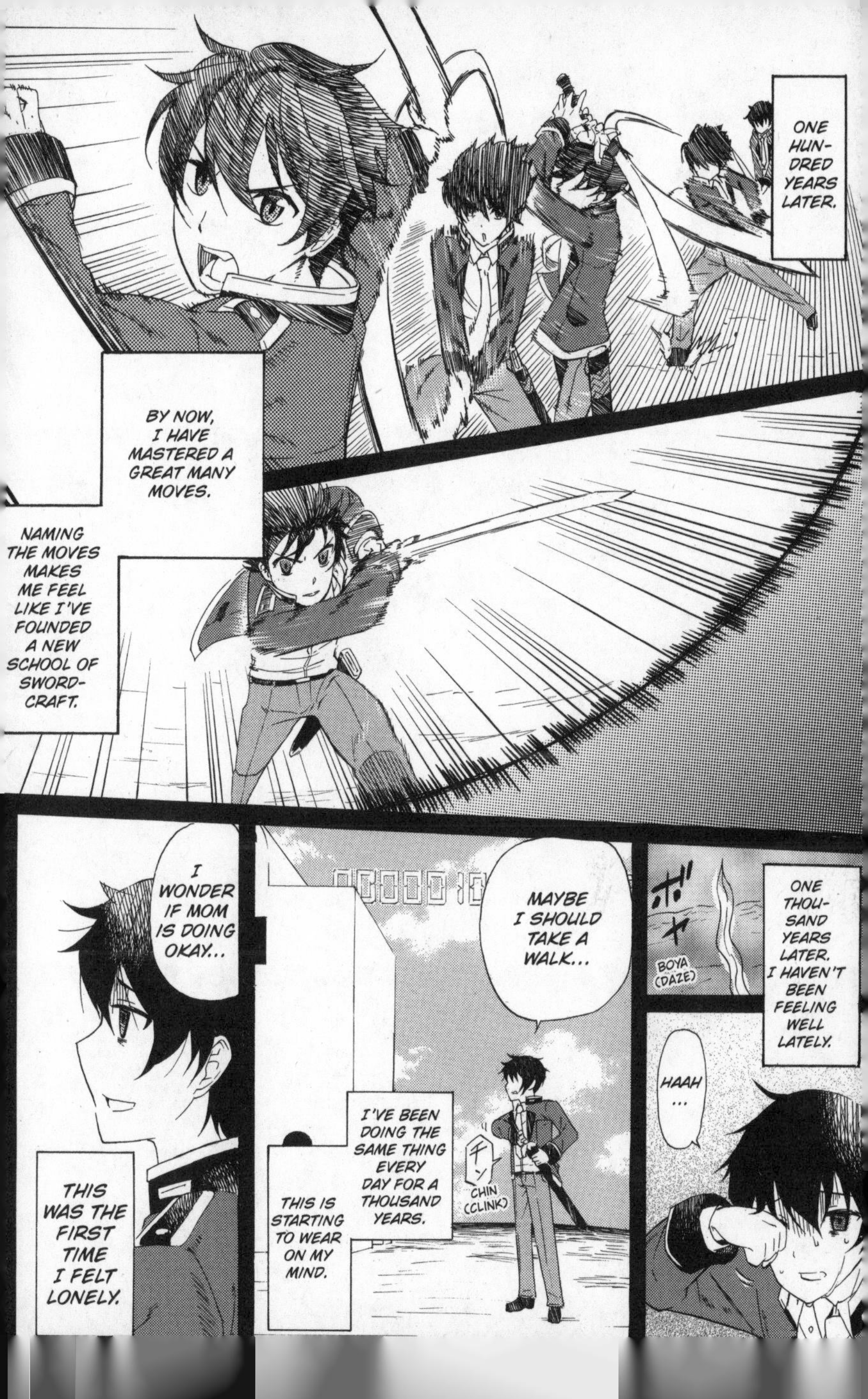
ONE HUNDRED YEARS LATER.
BY NOW, I HAVE MASTERED A GREAT MANY MOVES.
NAMING THE MOVES MAKES ME FEEL LIKE I'VE FOUNDED A NEW SCHOOL OF SWORD-CRAFT.
ONE THOUSAND YEARS LATER. I HAVEN'T BEEN FEELING WELL LATELY.
ボヤ
BOYA (DAZE)
HAAH...
MAYBE I SHOULD TAKE A WALK...
チン
CHIN (CLINK)
I'VE BEEN DOING THE SAME THING EVERY DAY FOR A THOUSAND YEARS.
THIS IS STARTING TO WEAR ON MY MIND.
I WONDER IF MOM IS DOING OKAY...
THIS WAS THE FIRST TIME I FELT LONELY.

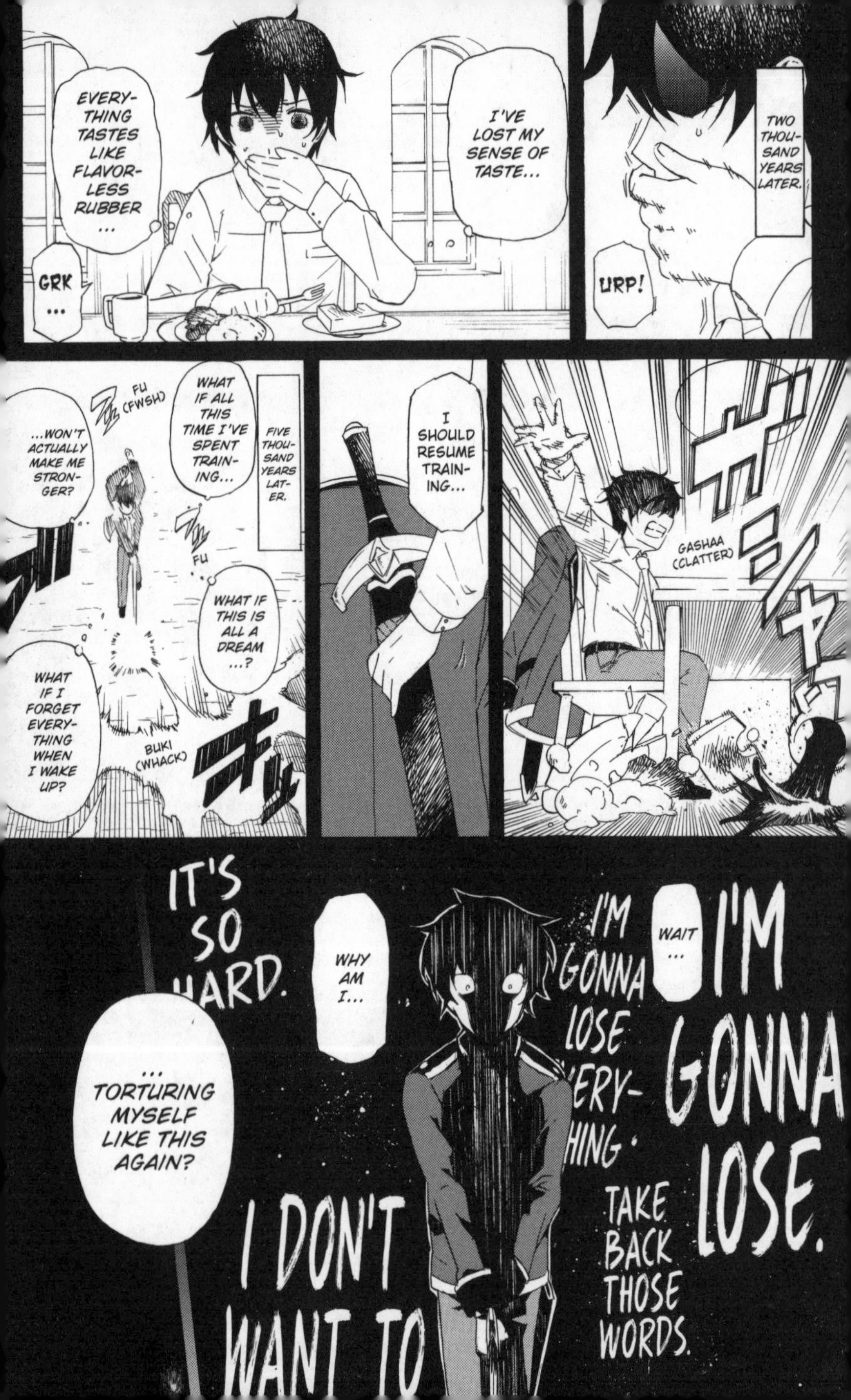
TWO THOUSAND YEARS LATER.
URP!
I'VE LOST MY SENSE OF TASTE...
EVERYTHING TASTES LIKE FLAVORLESS RUBBER...
GRK...
GASHAA (CLATTER)
I SHOULD RESUME TRAINING...
FIVE THOUSAND YEARS LATER.
WHAT IF ALL THIS TIME I'VE SPENT TRAINING...
FU (FWSH)
...WON'T ACTUALLY MAKE ME STRONGER?
FU
WHAT IF THIS IS ALL A DREAM...?
BUKI (WHACK)
WHAT IF I FORGET EVERYTHING WHEN I WAKE UP?
I'M GONNA LOSE.
WAIT...
I'M GONNA LOSE EVERYTHING.
TAKE BACK THOSE WORDS.
WHY AM I...
IT'S SO HARD.
...TORTURING MYSELF LIKE THIS AGAIN?
I DON'T WANT TO

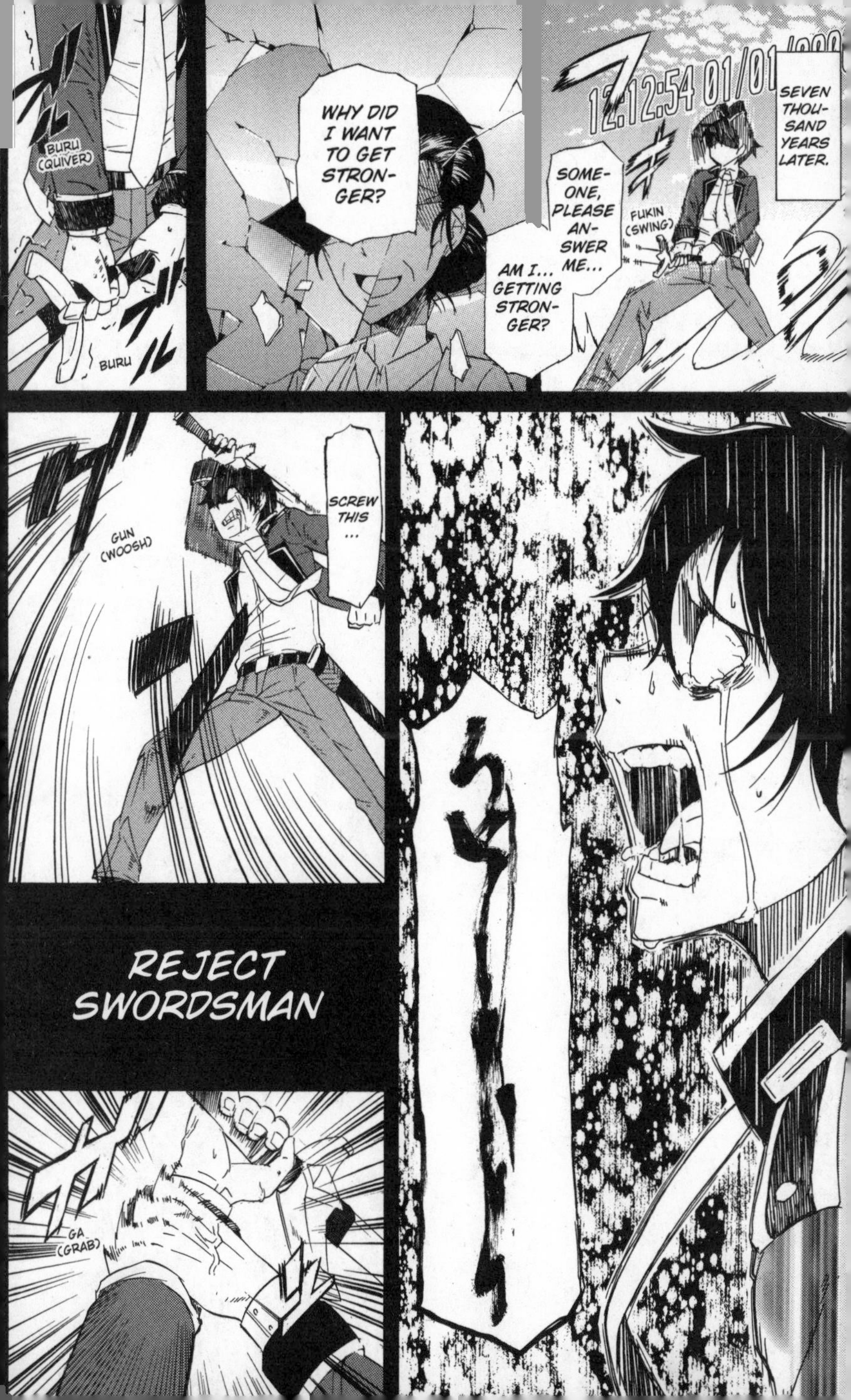
SEVEN THOUSAND YEARS LATER.
12:12:54 01/01
FUKIN (SWING)
SOME-ONE, PLEASE AN-SWER ME...
AM I... GETTING STRON-GER?
WHY DID I WANT TO GET STRON-GER?
BURU (QUIVER)
BURU
SCREW THIS ...
GUN (WOOSH)
REJECT SWORDSMAN
GA (GRAB)

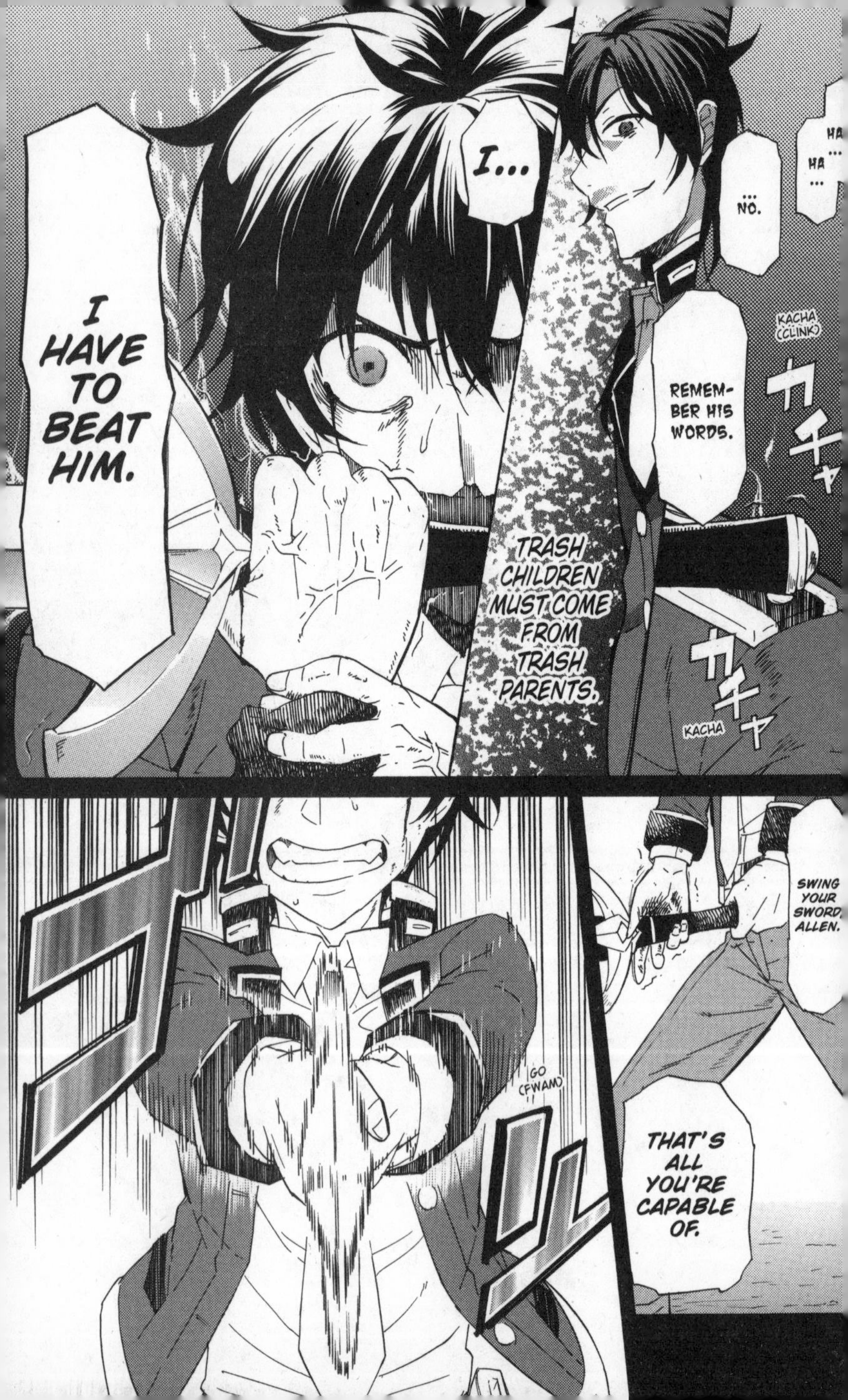
HA... HA...
...NO.
KACHA (CLINK)
カチャ
REMEMBER HIS WORDS.
カチャ
KACHA
TRASH CHILDREN MUST COME FROM TRASH PARENTS.
I...
I HAVE TO BEAT HIM.
SWING YOUR SWORD, ALLEN.
THAT'S ALL YOU'RE CAPABLE OF.
GO (FWAM)

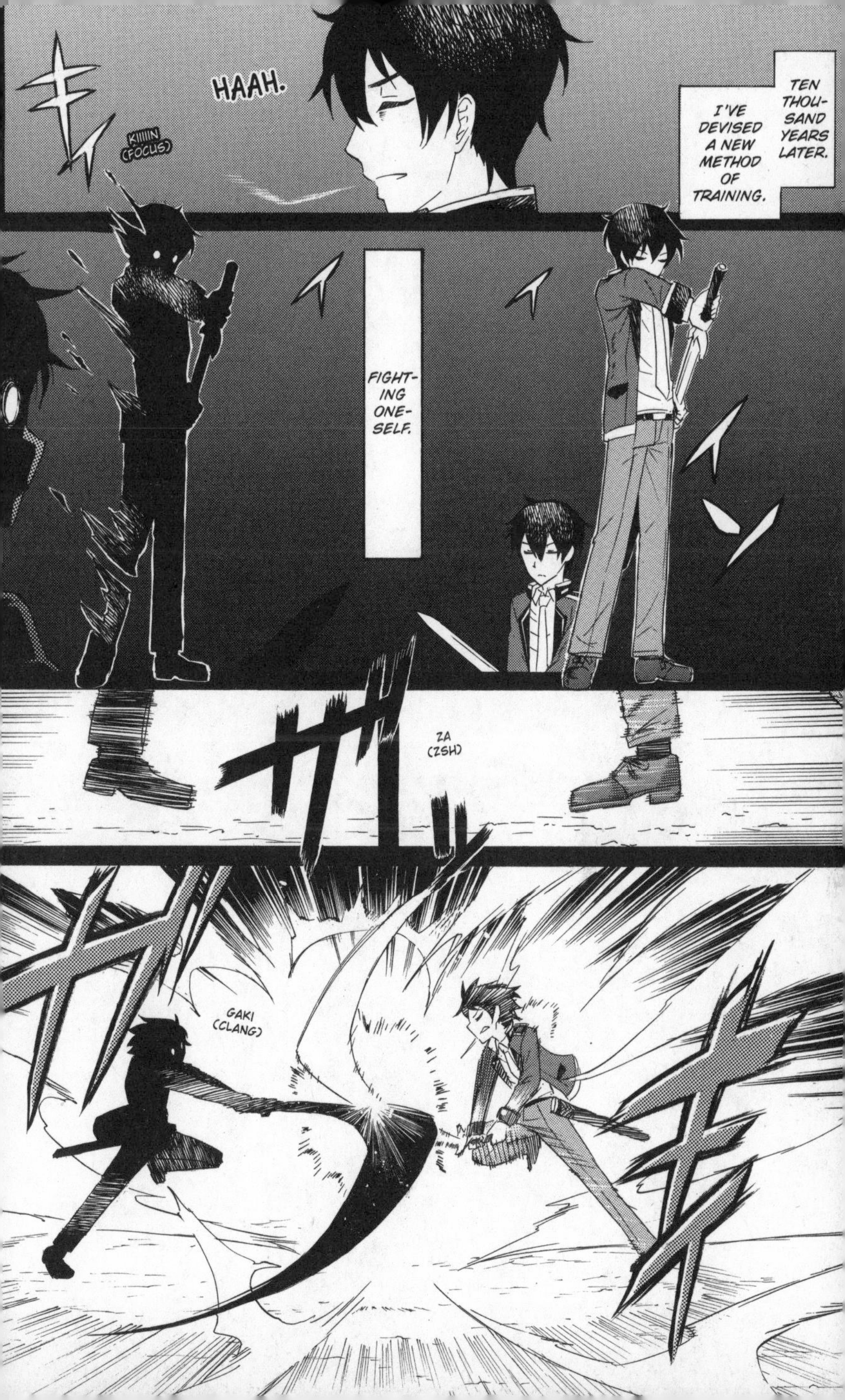
TEN THOUSAND YEARS LATER.
I'VE DEVISED A NEW METHOD OF TRAINING.
HAAH.
KIIIIN (FOCUS)
FIGHTING ONESELF.
ZA (ZSH)
GAKI (CLANG)

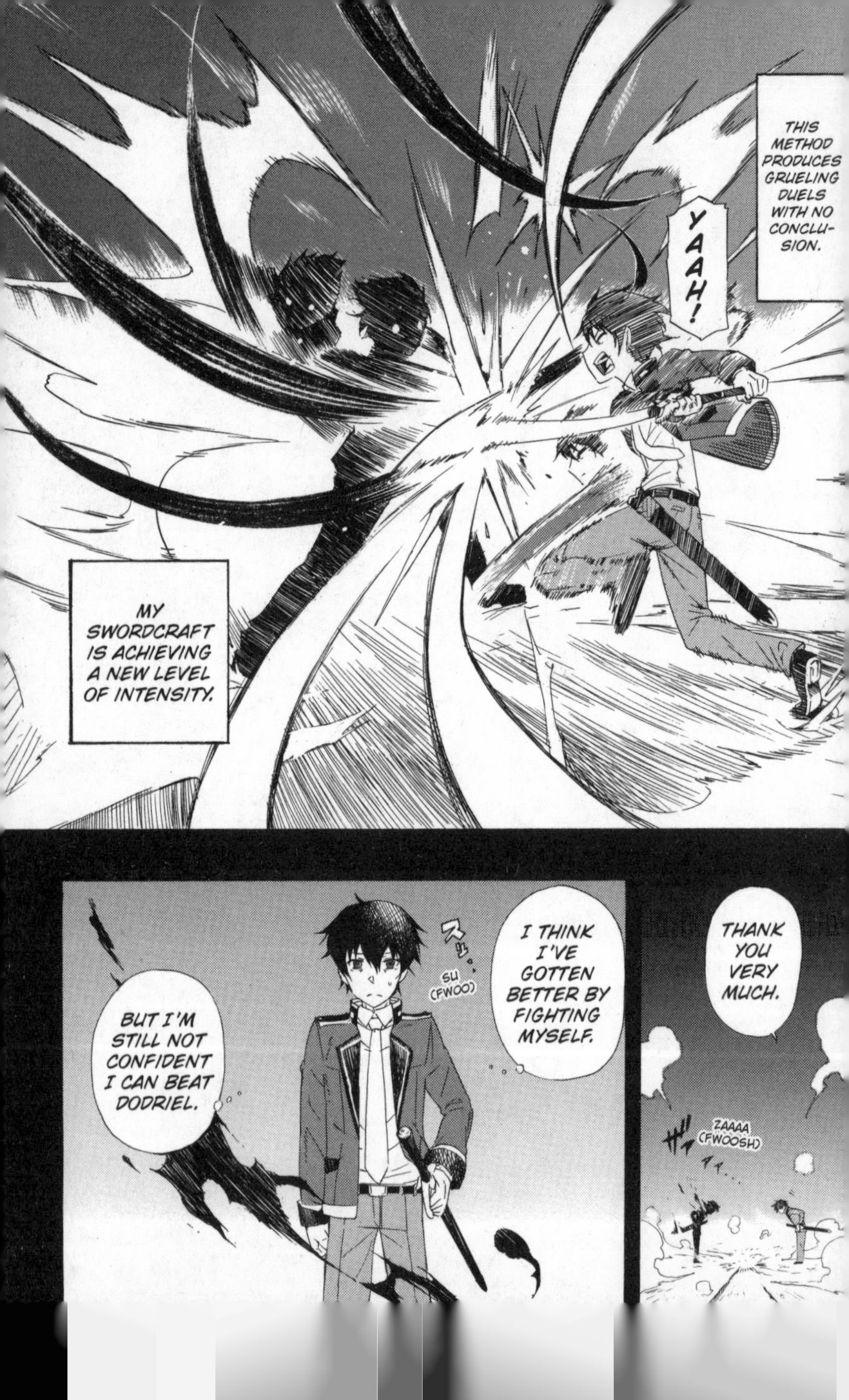
THIS METHOD PRODUCES GRUELING DUELS WITH NO CONCLUSION.
YAAH!
MY SWORDCRAFT IS ACHIEVING A NEW LEVEL OF INTENSITY.
THANK YOU VERY MUCH.
ZAAAA (FWOOSH)
SU (FWOO)
I THINK I'VE GOTTEN BETTER BY FIGHTING MYSELF.
BUT I'M STILL NOT CONFIDENT I CAN BEAT DODRIEL.

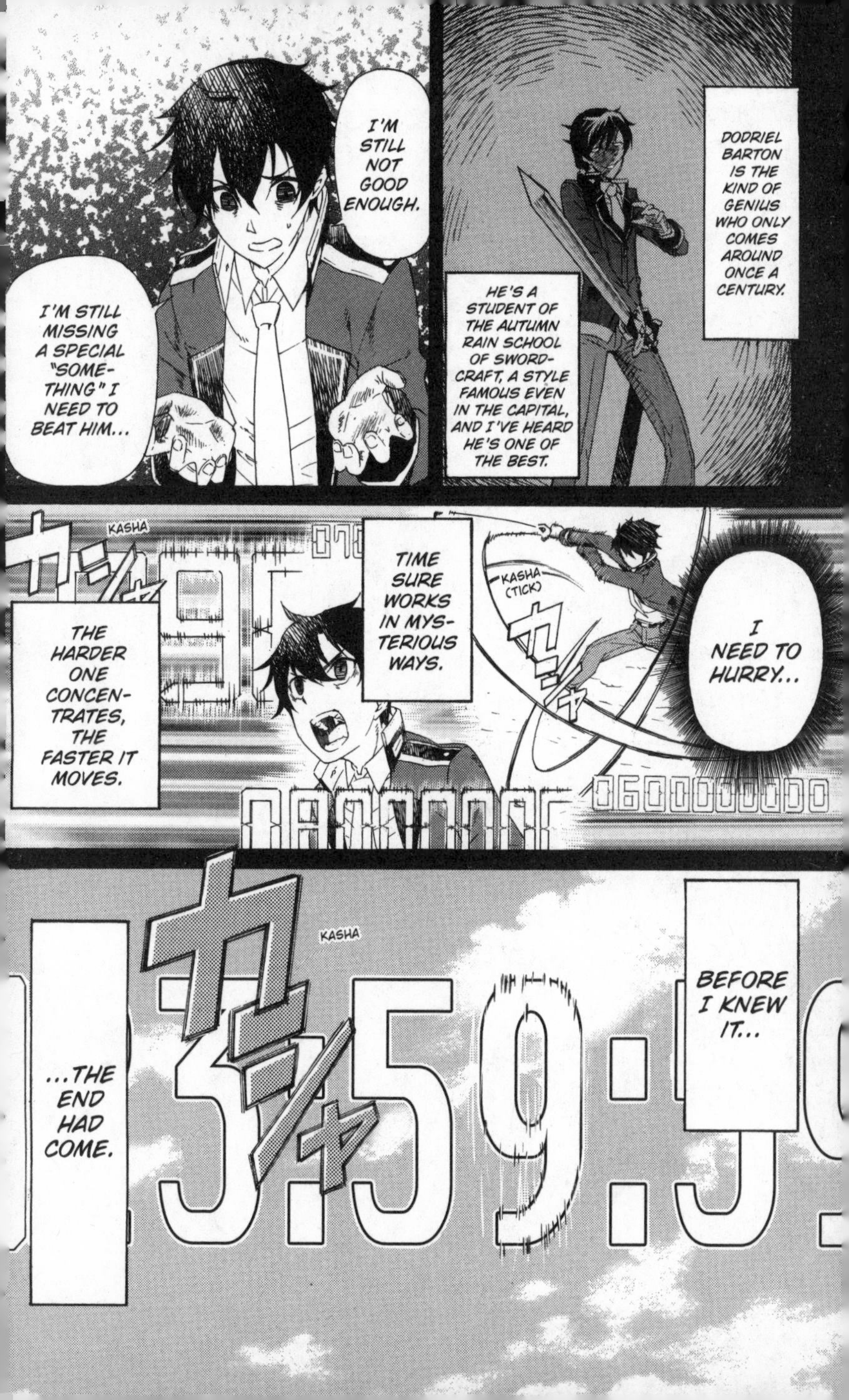
DODRIEL BARTON IS THE KIND OF GENIUS WHO ONLY COMES AROUND ONCE A CENTURY.
HE'S A STUDENT OF THE AUTUMN RAIN SCHOOL OF SWORD-CRAFT, A STYLE FAMOUS EVEN IN THE CAPITAL, AND I'VE HEARD HE'S ONE OF THE BEST.
I'M STILL NOT GOOD ENOUGH.
I'M STILL MISSING A SPECIAL "SOME-THING" I NEED TO BEAT HIM...
I NEED TO HURRY...
KASHA (TICK)
TIME SURE WORKS IN MYS-TERIOUS WAYS.
KASHA
THE HARDER ONE CONCEN-TRATES, THE FASTER IT MOVES.
BEFORE I KNEW IT...
KASHA
...THE END HAD COME.

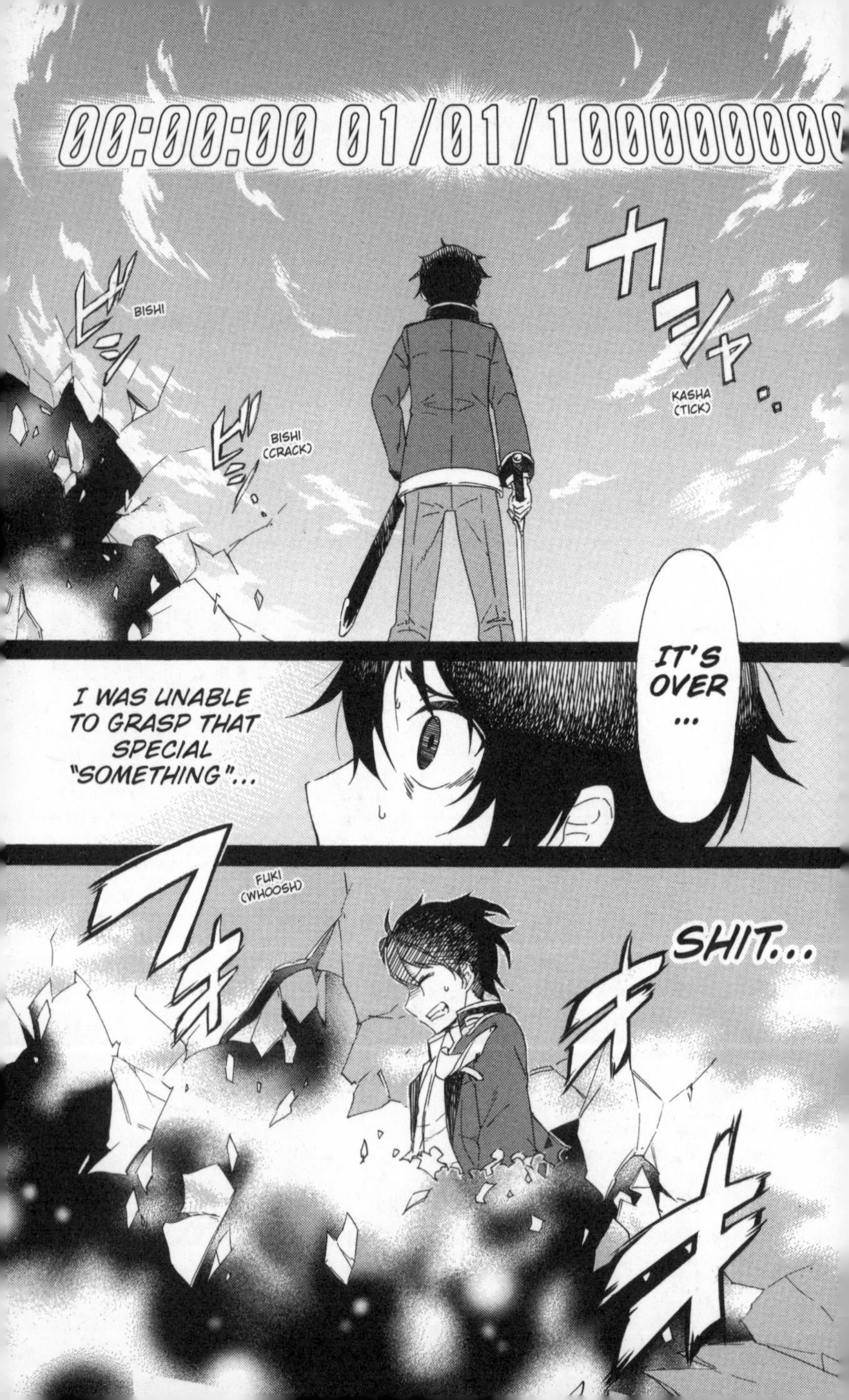
00:00:00 01/01/100000000
KASHA (TICK)
BISHI (CRACK)
BISHI
IT'S OVER...
I WAS UNABLE TO GRASP THAT SPECIAL "SOMETHING"...
SHIT...
FUKI (WHOOSH)

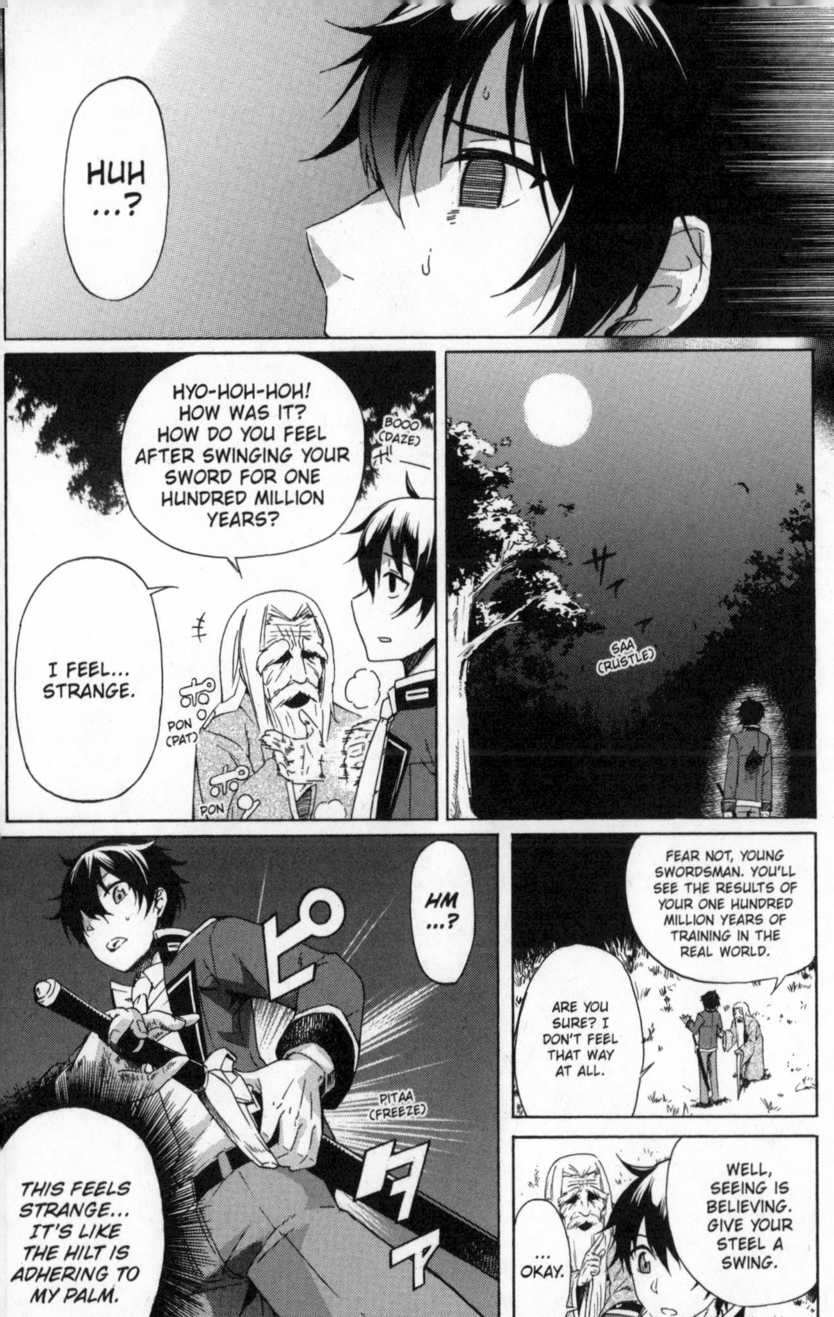
HUH ...?
SAA (RUSTLE)
HYO-HOH-HOH! HOW WAS IT? HOW DO YOU FEEL AFTER SWINGING YOUR SWORD FOR ONE HUNDRED MILLION YEARS?
BOOO (DAZE)
I FEEL... STRANGE.
PON (PAT)
PON
FEAR NOT, YOUNG SWORDSMAN. YOU'LL SEE THE RESULTS OF YOUR ONE HUNDRED MILLION YEARS OF TRAINING IN THE REAL WORLD.
ARE YOU SURE? I DON'T FEEL THAT WAY AT ALL.
WELL, SEEING IS BELIEVING. GIVE YOUR STEEL A SWING.
...OKAY.
HM ...?
PITAA (FREEZE)
THIS FEELS STRANGE... IT'S LIKE THE HILT IS ADHERING TO MY PALM.

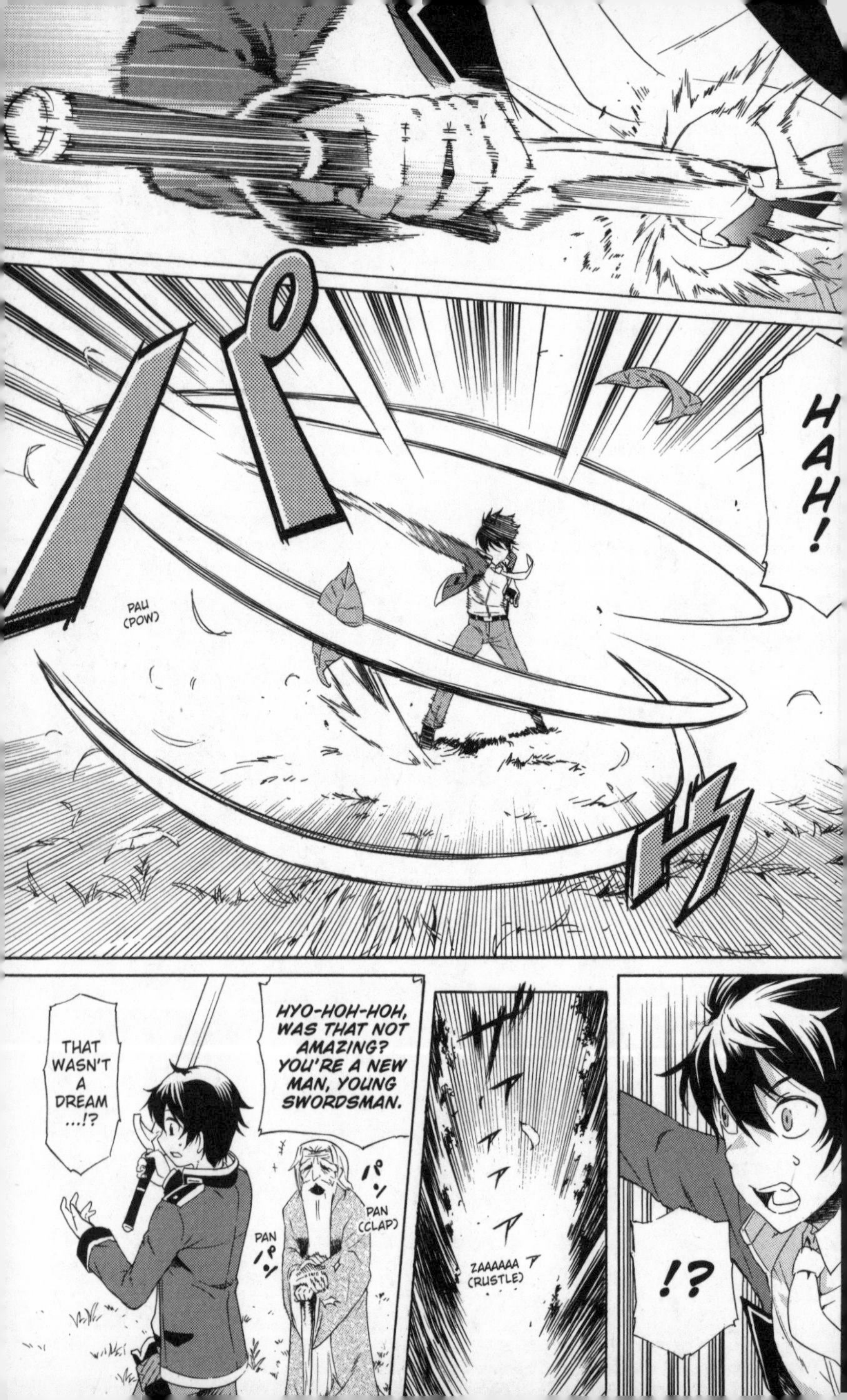
HAH!
PAU (POW)
!?
ZAAAAAA (RUSTLE)
HYO-HOH-HOH, WAS THAT NOT AMAZING? YOU'RE A NEW MAN, YOUNG SWORDSMAN.
PAN (CLAP)
PAN
THAT WASN'T A DREAM ...!?

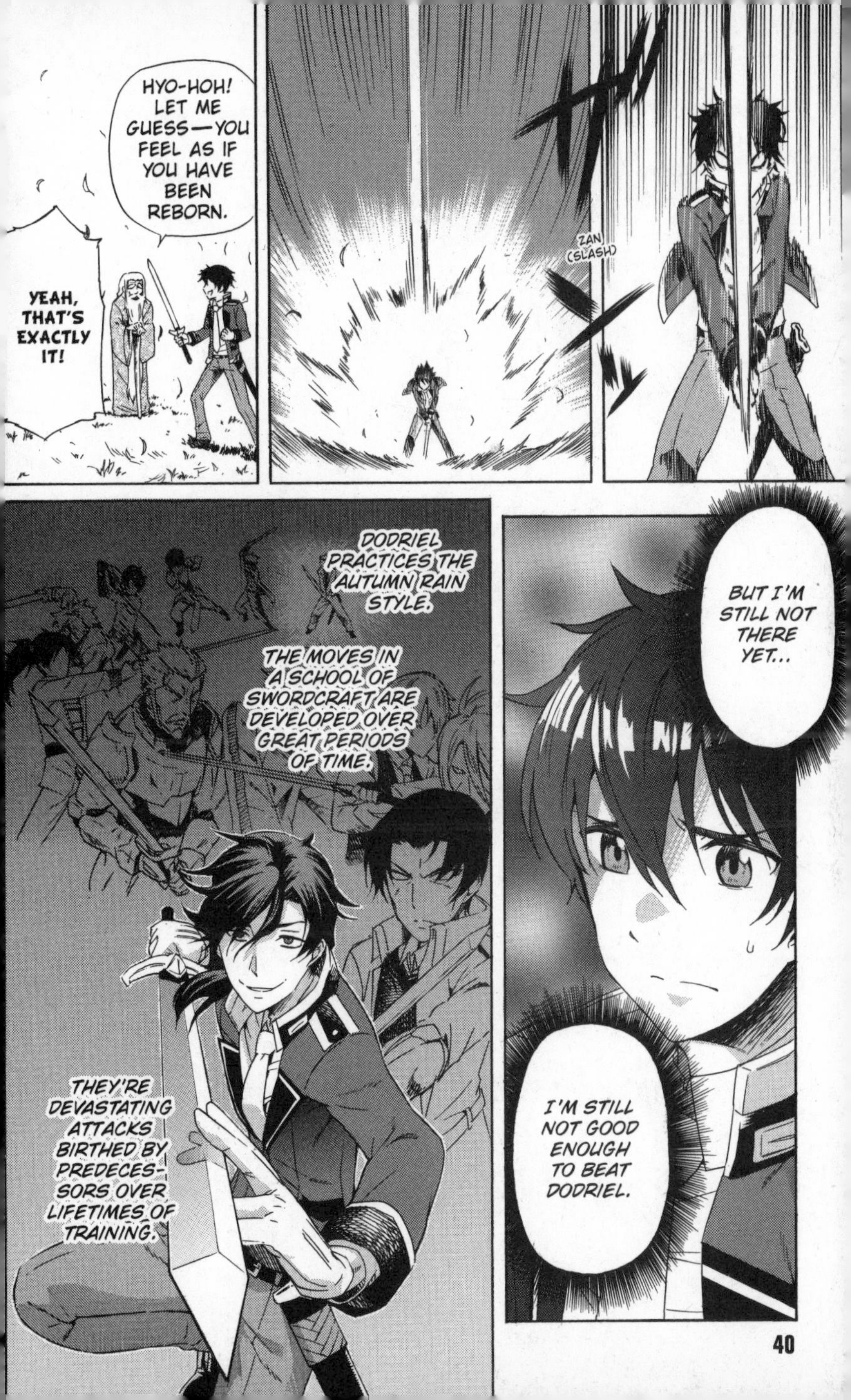
ZAN (SLASH)
HYO-HOH! LET ME GUESS—YOU FEEL AS IF YOU HAVE BEEN REBORN.
YEAH, THAT'S EXACTLY IT!
BUT I'M STILL NOT THERE YET...
I'M STILL NOT GOOD ENOUGH TO BEAT DODRIEL.
DODRIEL PRACTICES THE AUTUMN RAIN STYLE.
THE MOVES IN A SCHOOL OF SWORDCRAFT ARE DEVELOPED OVER GREAT PERIODS OF TIME.
THEY'RE DEVASTATING ATTACKS BIRTHED BY PREDECES-SORS OVER LIFETIMES OF TRAINING.

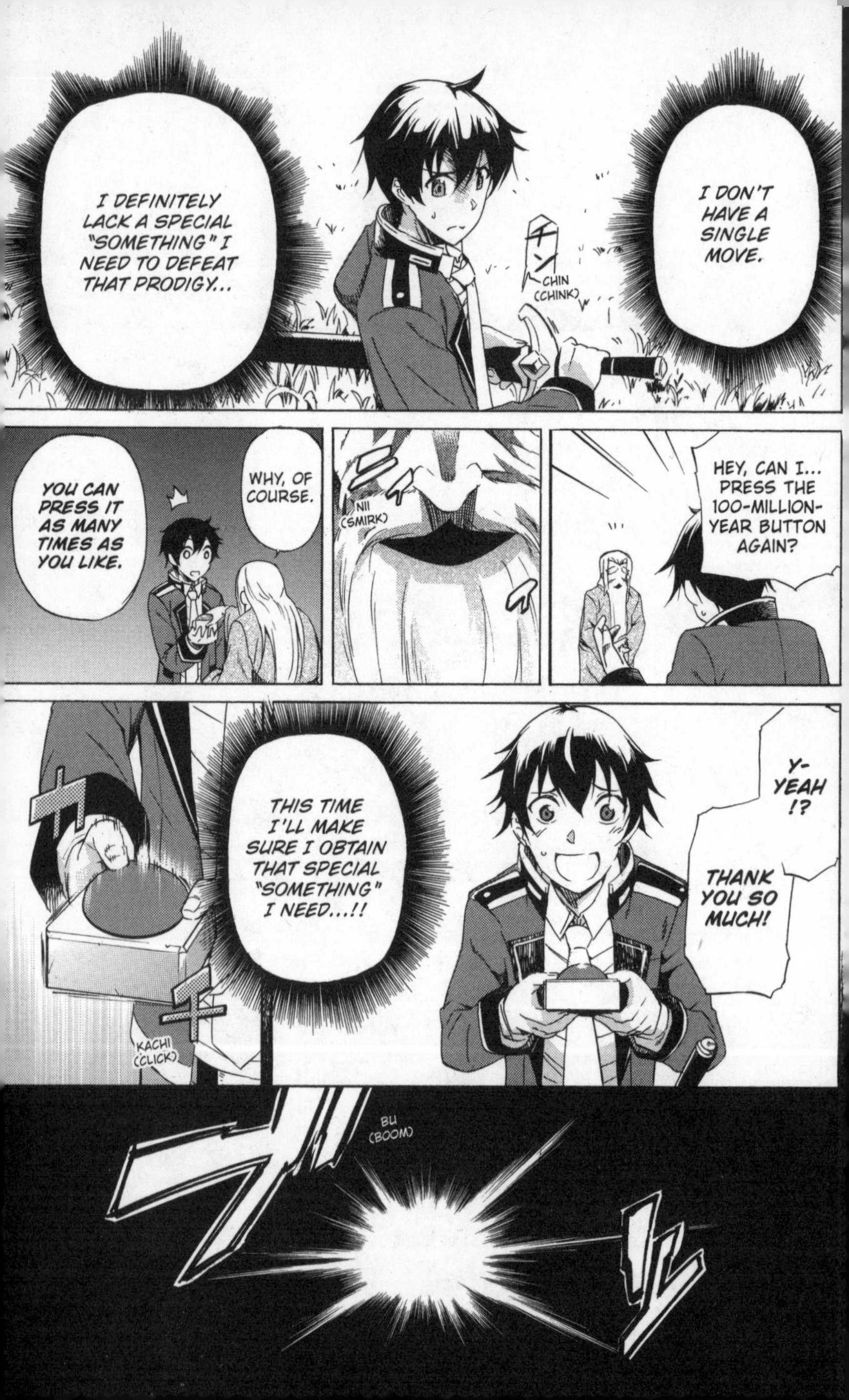
I DON'T HAVE A SINGLE MOVE.
CHIN (CHINK)
I DEFINITELY LACK A SPECIAL "SOMETHING" I NEED TO DEFEAT THAT PRODIGY...
HEY, CAN I... PRESS THE 100-MILLION-YEAR BUTTON AGAIN?
NII (SMIRK)
WHY, OF COURSE.
YOU CAN PRESS IT AS MANY TIMES AS YOU LIKE.
Y-YEAH!?
THANK YOU SO MUCH!
THIS TIME I'LL MAKE SURE I OBTAIN THAT SPECIAL "SOMETHING" I NEED...!!
KACHI (CLICK)
BU (BOOM)

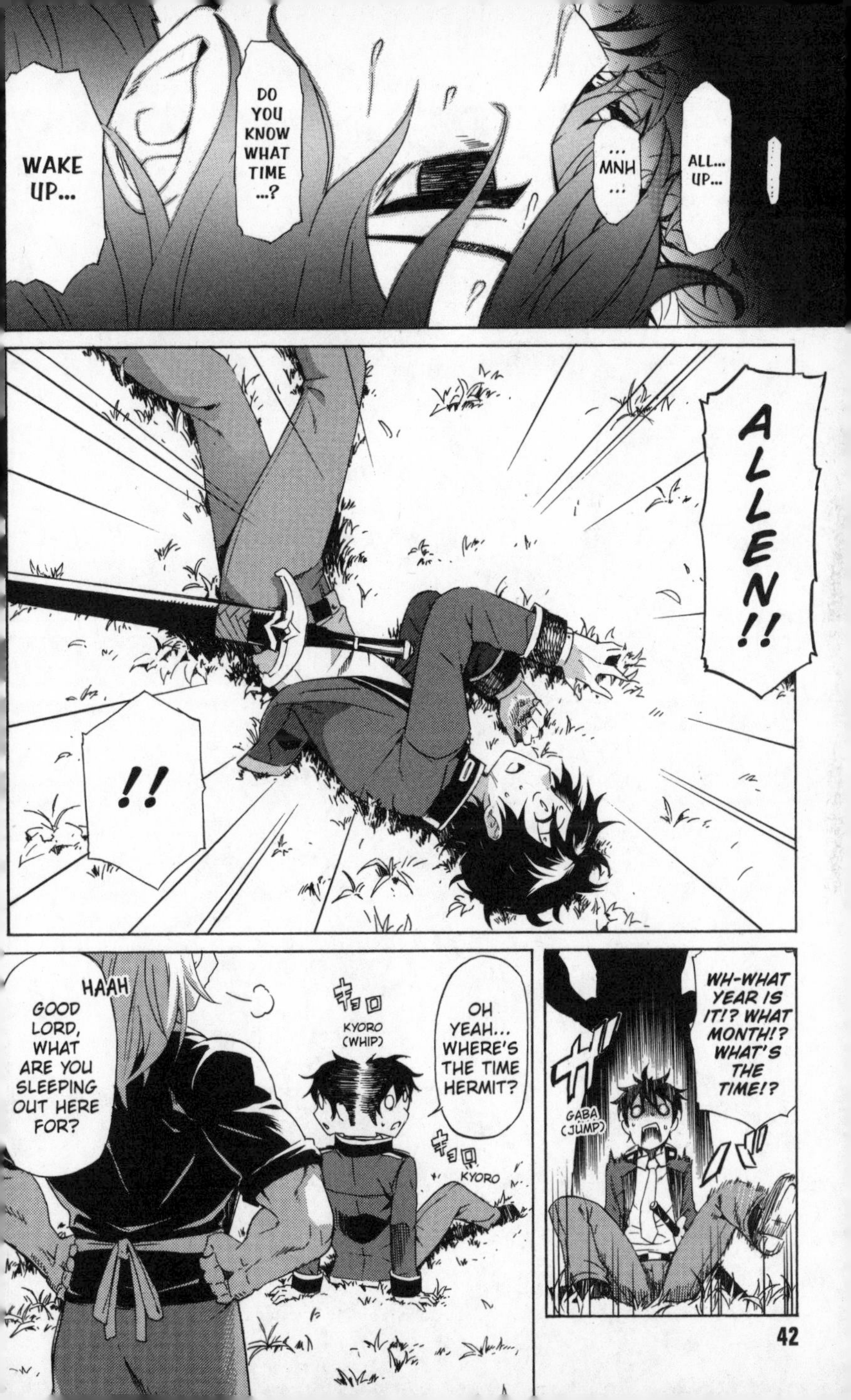
...!
ALL... UP...
... MNH ...
DO YOU KNOW WHAT TIME ...?
WAKE UP...
ALLEN!!
!!
WH-WHAT YEAR IS IT!? WHAT MONTH!? WHAT'S THE TIME!?
GABA (JUMP)
キョロ
KYORO (WHIP)
OH YEAH... WHERE'S THE TIME HERMIT?
キョロ
KYORO
HAAH
GOOD LORD, WHAT ARE YOU SLEEPING OUT HERE FOR?

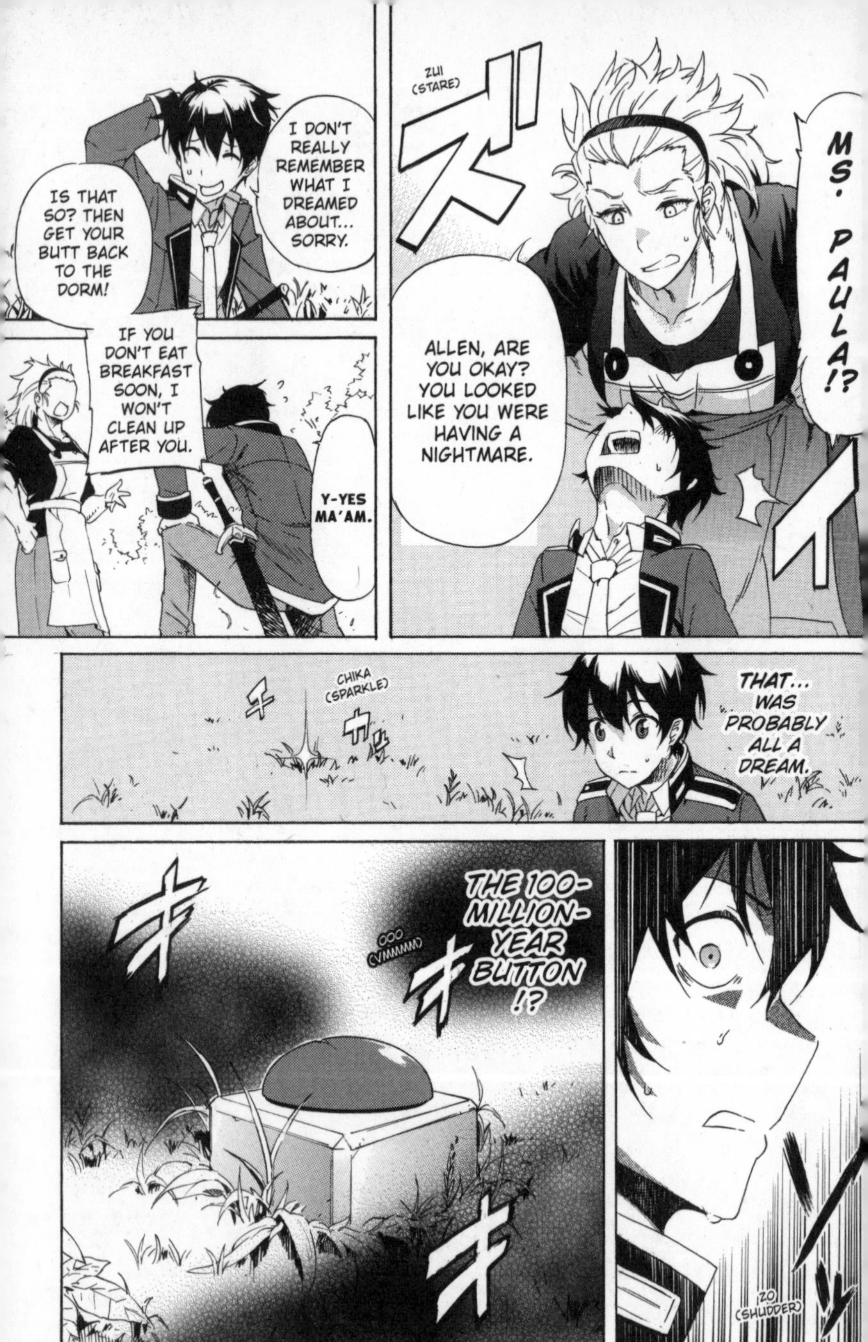

ZUI (STARE)
MS. PAULA!?
ALLEN, ARE YOU OKAY? YOU LOOKED LIKE YOU WERE HAVING A NIGHTMARE.
I DON'T REALLY REMEMBER WHAT I DREAMED ABOUT... SORRY.
IS THAT SO? THEN GET YOUR BUTT BACK TO THE DORM!
IF YOU DON'T EAT BREAKFAST SOON, I WON'T CLEAN UP AFTER YOU.
Y-YES MA'AM.
THAT... WAS PROBABLY ALL A DREAM.
CHIKA (SPARKLE)
ZO (SHUDDER)
THE 100-MILLION-YEAR BUTTON!?
OOO (VMMMMM)

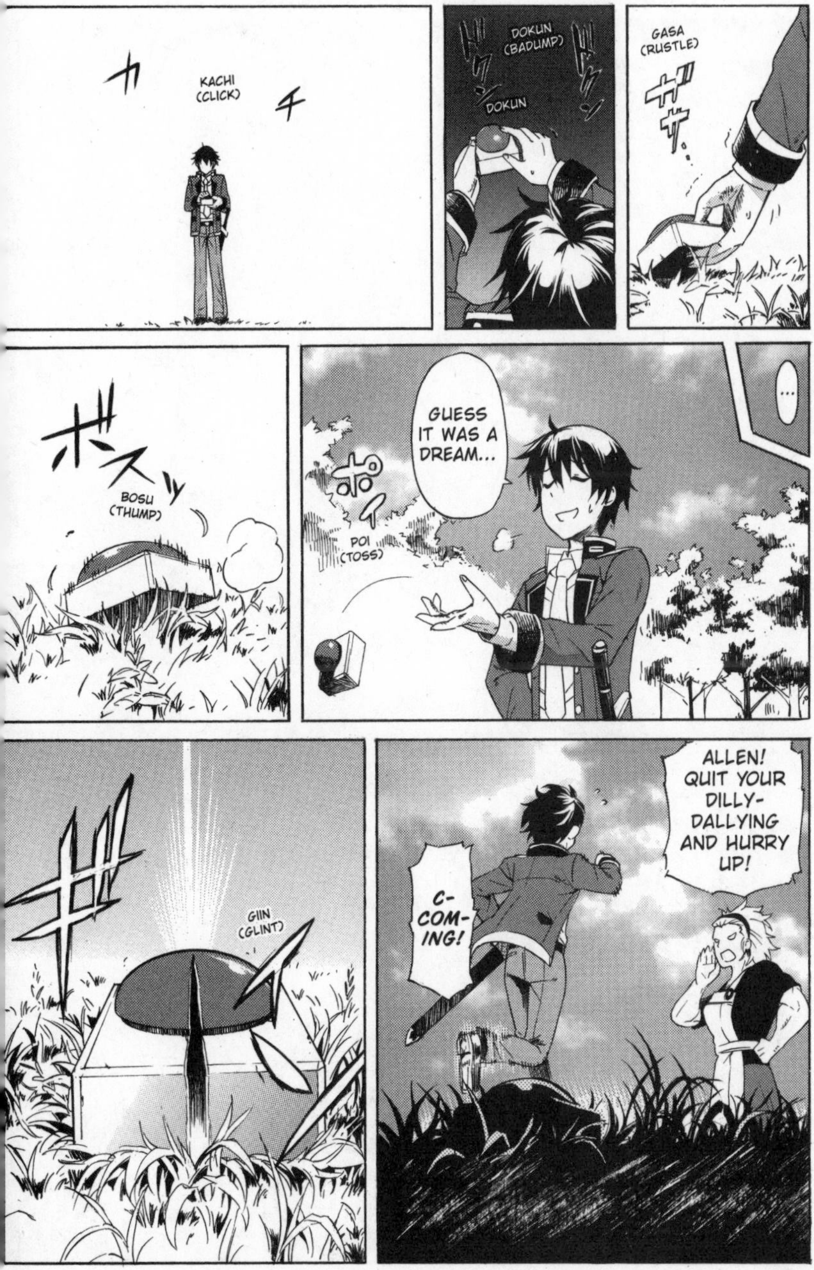
ガサ
GASA (RUSTLE)
ドクン
DOKUN (BADUMP)
ドクン
DOKUN
カチ
KACHI (CLICK)
...
GUESS IT WAS A DREAM...
ポイ
POI (TOSS)
ボスッ
BOSU (THUMP)
ALLEN! QUIT YOUR DILLY-DALLYING AND HURRY UP!
C-COMING!
ギン
GIIN (GLINT)

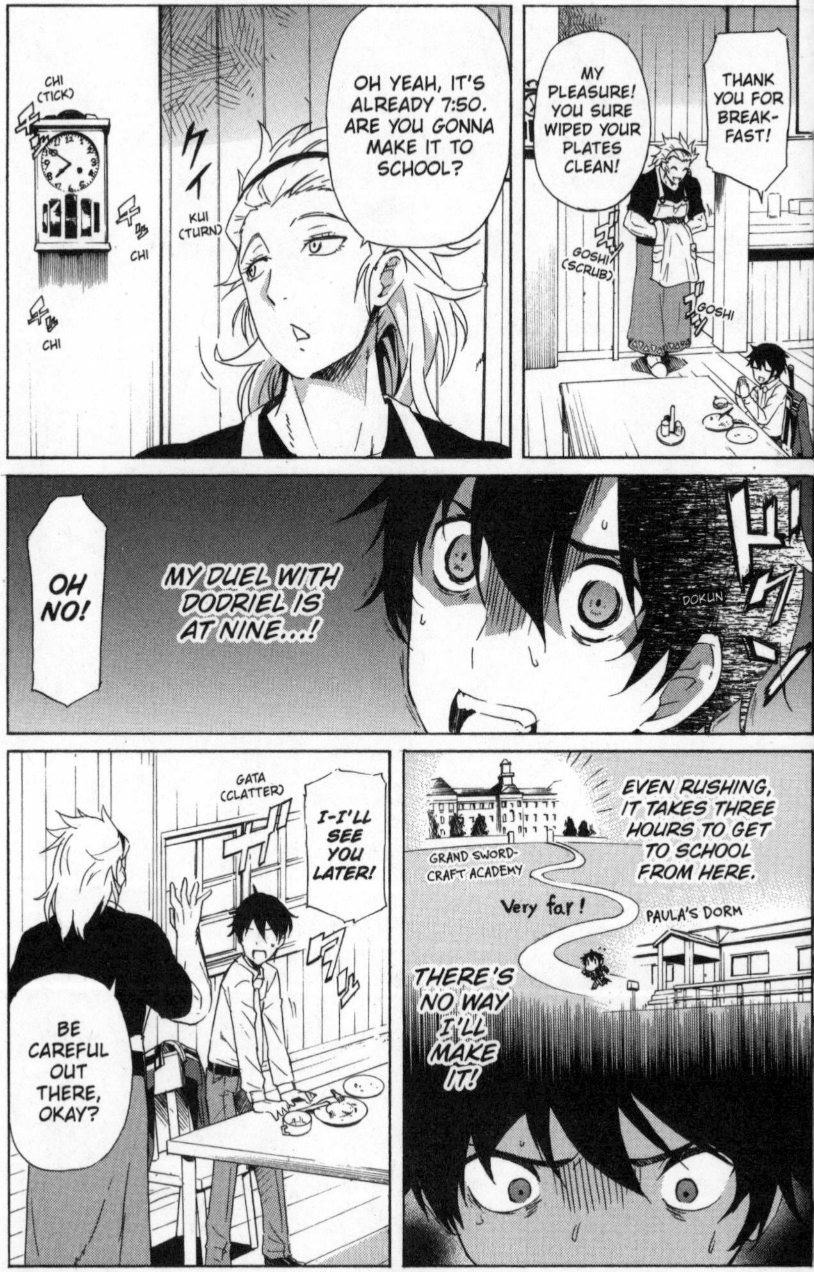
THANK YOU FOR BREAK-FAST!
MY PLEASURE! YOU SURE WIPED YOUR PLATES CLEAN!
GOSHI (SCRUB)
GOSHI
OH YEAH, IT'S ALREADY 7:50. ARE YOU GONNA MAKE IT TO SCHOOL?
KUI (TURN)
CHI (TICK)
CHI
CHI
DOKUN
MY DUEL WITH DODRIEL IS AT NINE...!
OH NO!
EVEN RUSHING, IT TAKES THREE HOURS TO GET TO SCHOOL FROM HERE.
GRAND SWORD-CRAFT ACADEMY
Very far!
PAULA'S DORM
THERE'S NO WAY I'LL MAKE IT!
GATA (CLATTER)
I-I'LL SEE YOU LATER!
BE CAREFUL OUT THERE, OKAY?

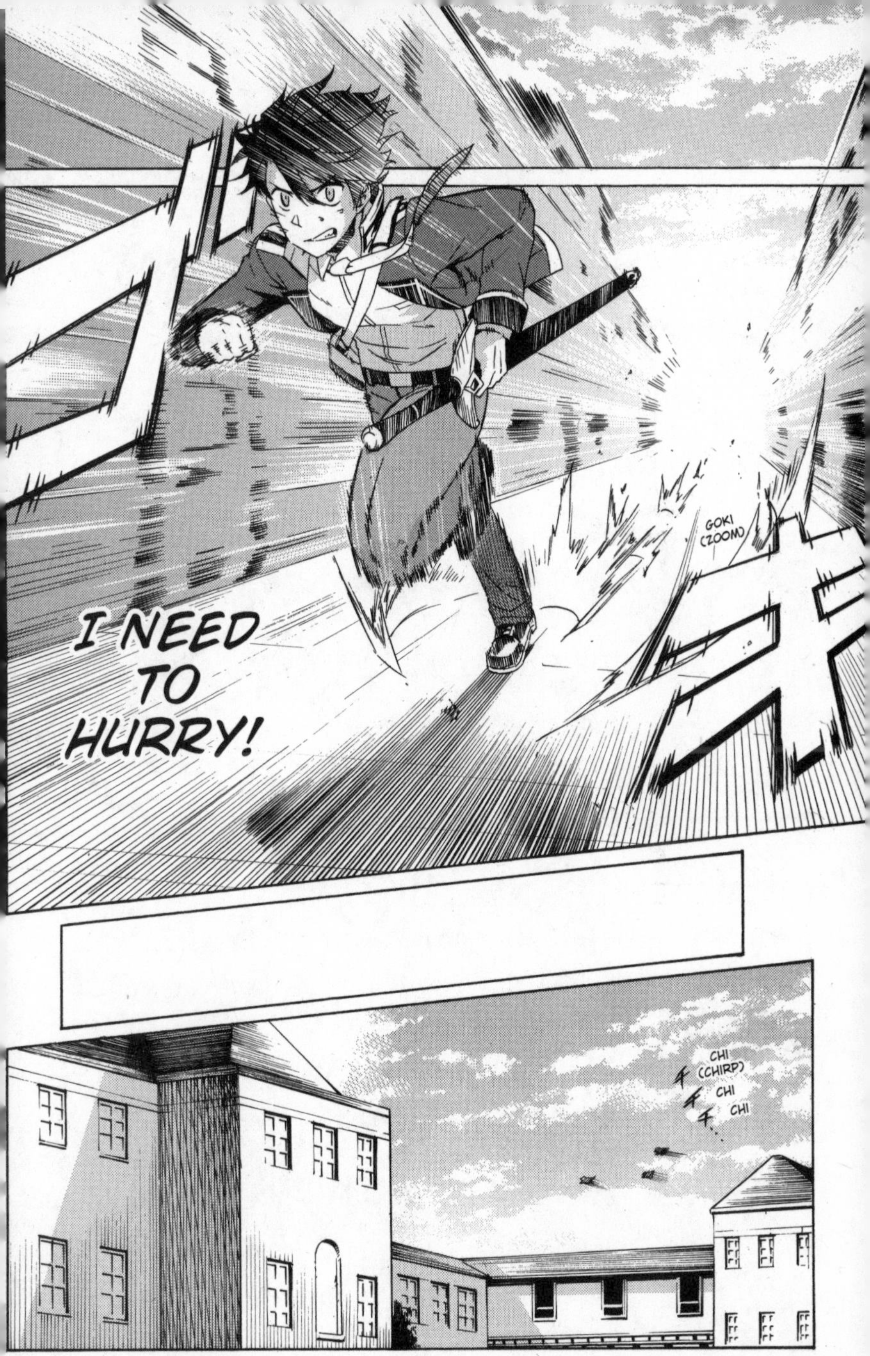
GOKI (ZOOM)
I NEED TO HURRY!
CHI (CHIRP) CHI CHI

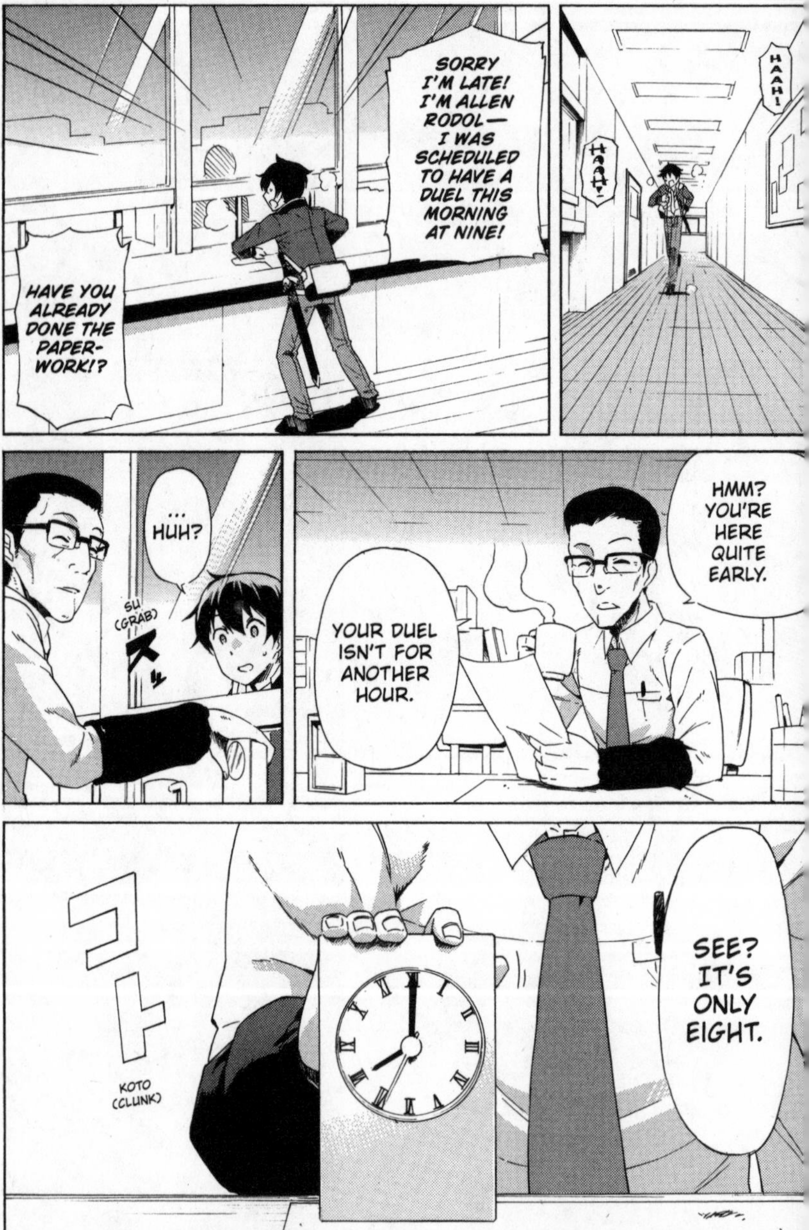
HAAAH!
HAAAH!
SORRY I'M LATE! I'M ALLEN RODOL— I WAS SCHEDULED TO HAVE A DUEL THIS MORNING AT NINE!
HAVE YOU ALREADY DONE THE PAPER-WORK!?
HMM? YOU'RE HERE QUITE EARLY.
YOUR DUEL ISN'T FOR ANOTHER HOUR.
... HUH?
SU (GRAB)
SEE? IT'S ONLY EIGHT.
KOTO (CLUNK)

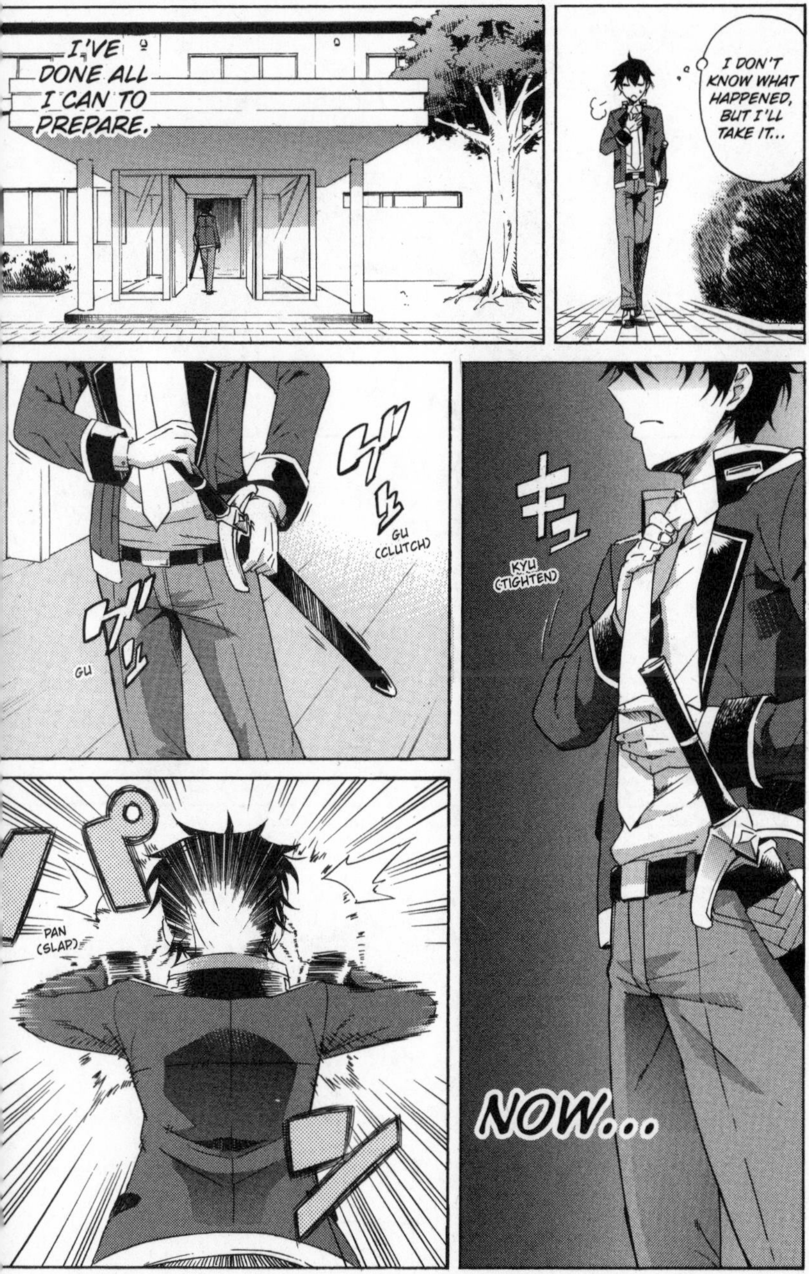
I DON'T KNOW WHAT HAPPENED, BUT I'LL TAKE IT...
I'VE DONE ALL I CAN TO PREPARE.
キュ
KYU (TIGHTEN)
NOW...
GU (CLUTCH)
GU
PAN (SLAP)

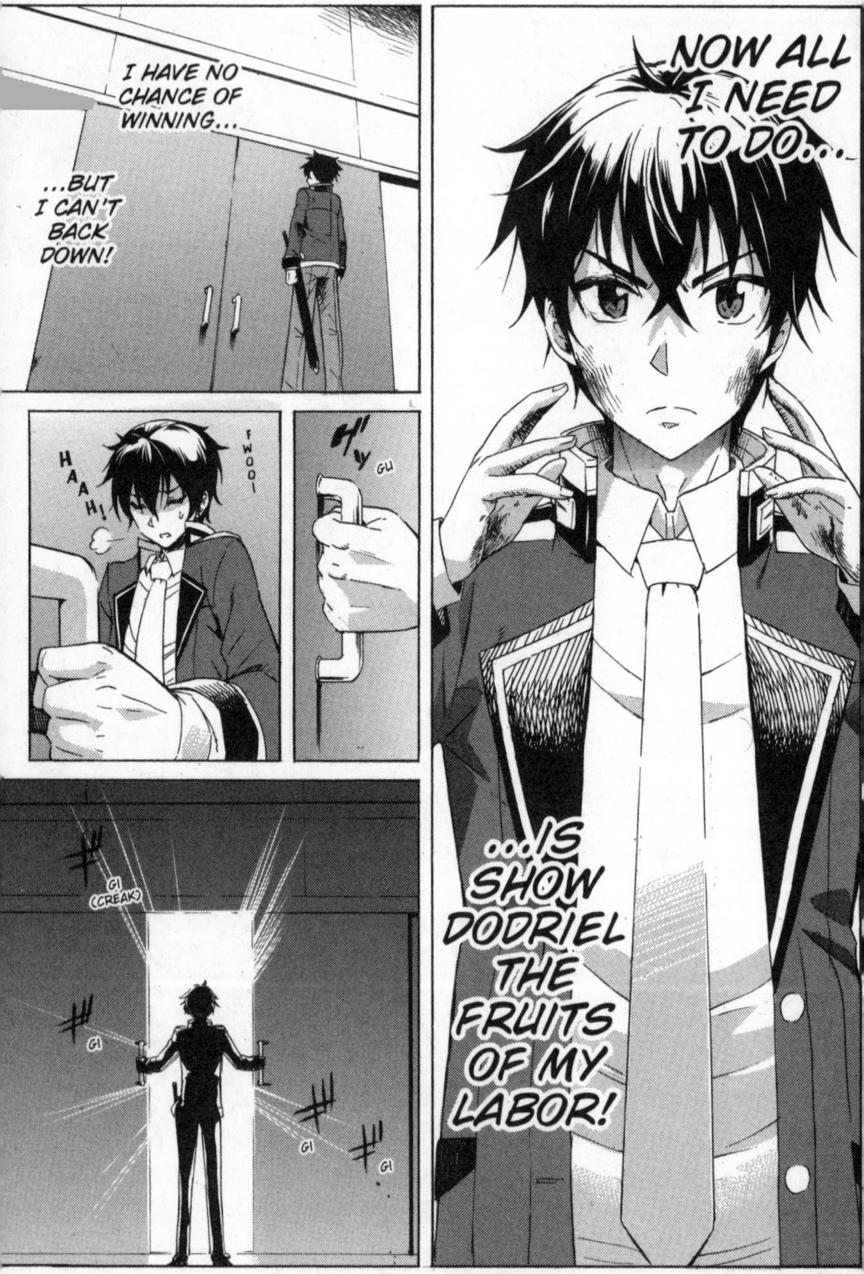
NOW ALL I NEED TO DO...
...IS SHOW DODRIEL THE FRUITS OF MY LABOR!
I HAVE NO CHANCE OF WINNING...
...BUT I CAN'T BACK DOWN!
GU
HAAAH!
FWOO!
GI (CREAK)
GI
GI
GI

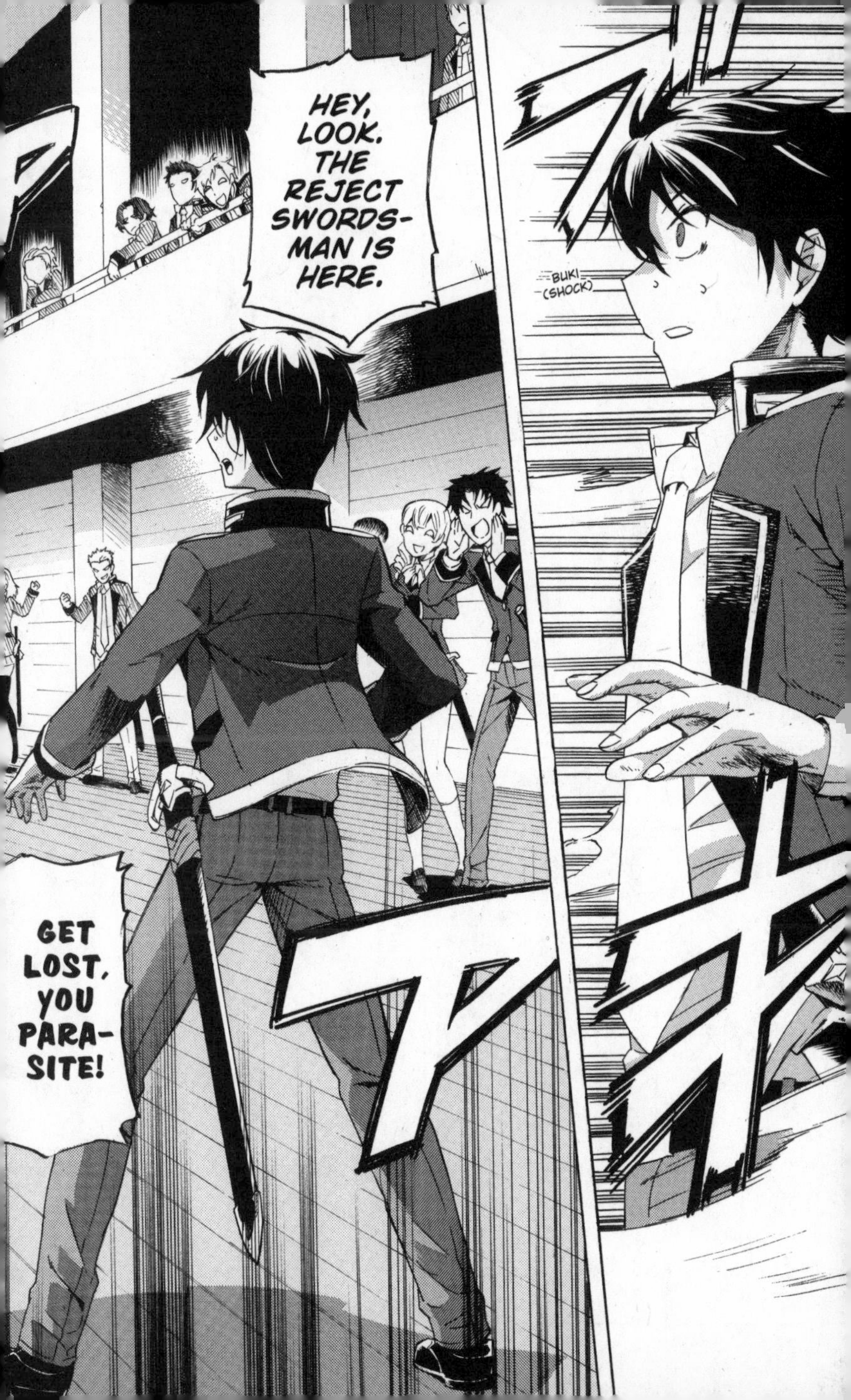
BUKI (SHOCK)
HEY, LOOK. THE REJECT SWORDS-MAN IS HERE.
GET LOST, YOU PARA-SITE!

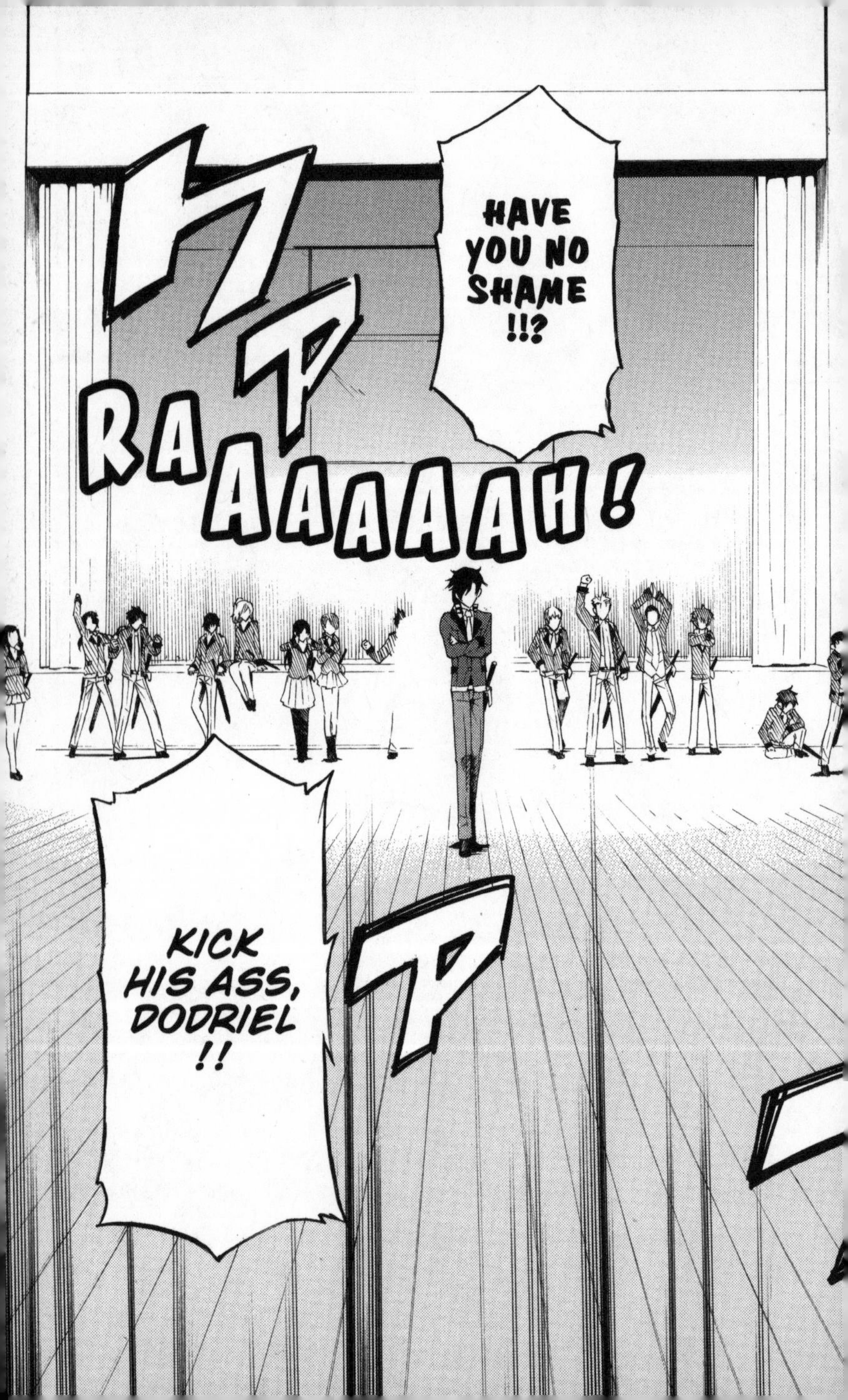
HAVE YOU NO SHAME !!?
RAAAAAAH!
KICK HIS ASS, DODRIEL !!

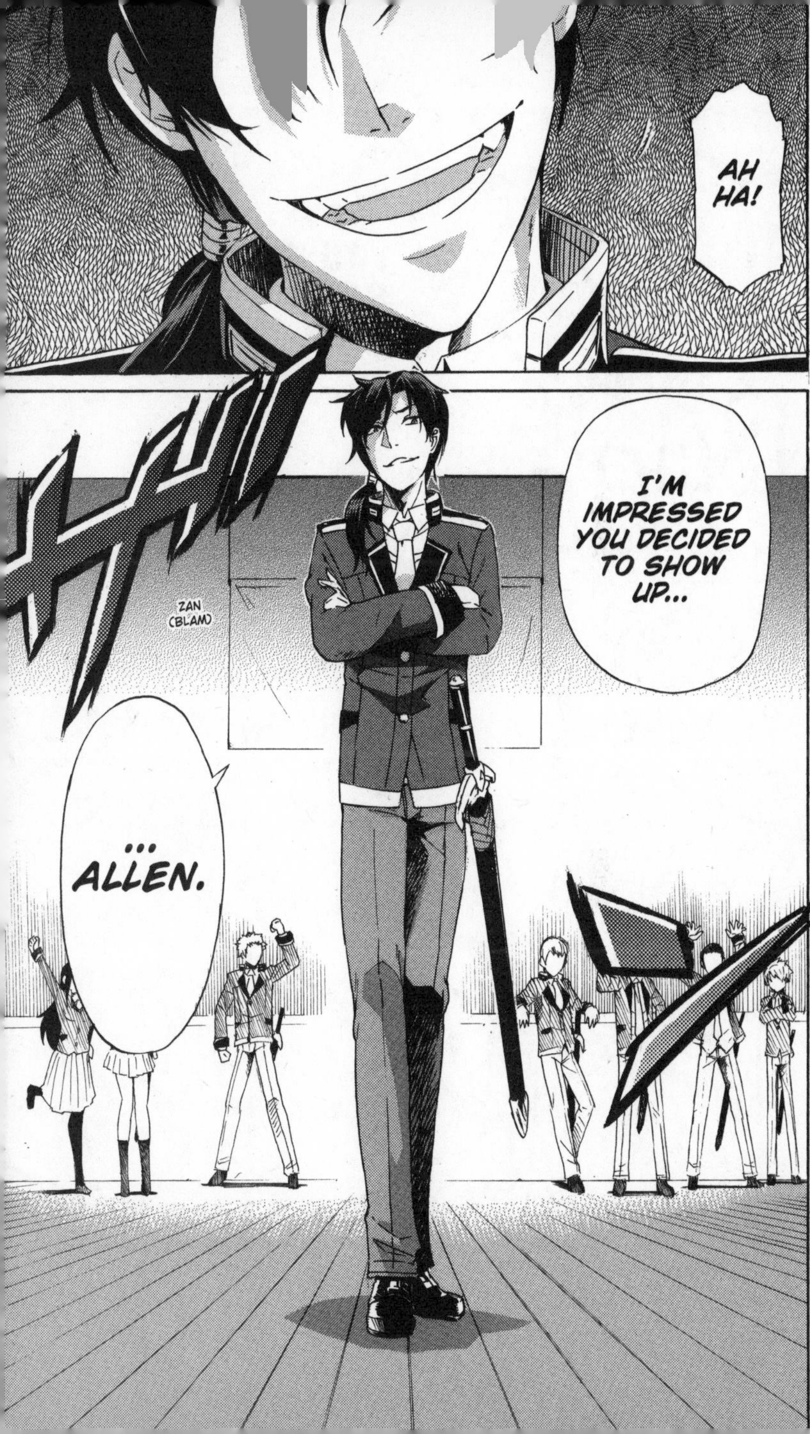
AH HA!
I'M IMPRESSED YOU DECIDED TO SHOW UP...
ZAN (BLAM)
...ALLEN.

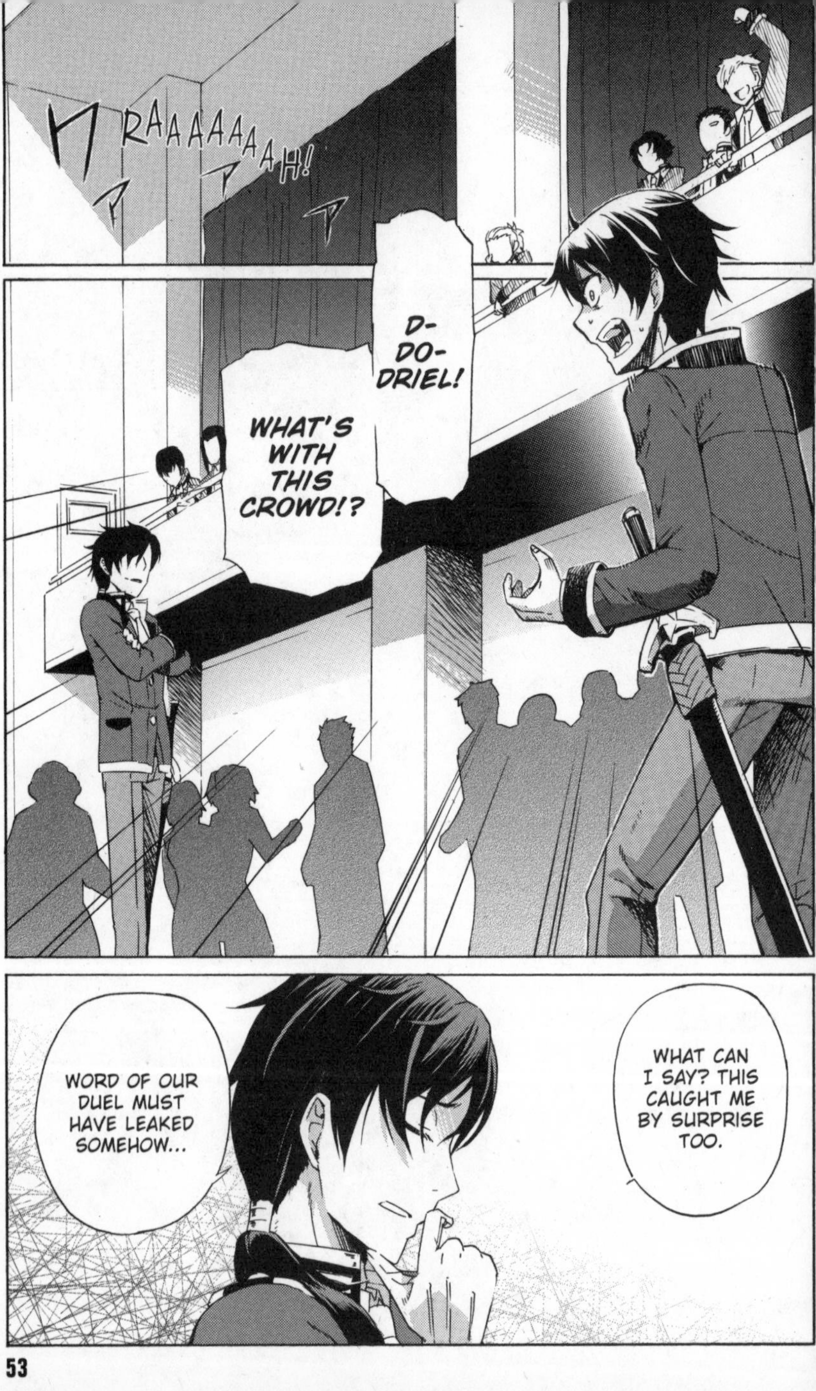
ワァァァ
RAAAAAAAAH!
D-DO-DRIEL!
WHAT'S WITH THIS CROWD!?
WHAT CAN I SAY? THIS CAUGHT ME BY SURPRISE TOO.
WORD OF OUR DUEL MUST HAVE LEAKED SOMEHOW...

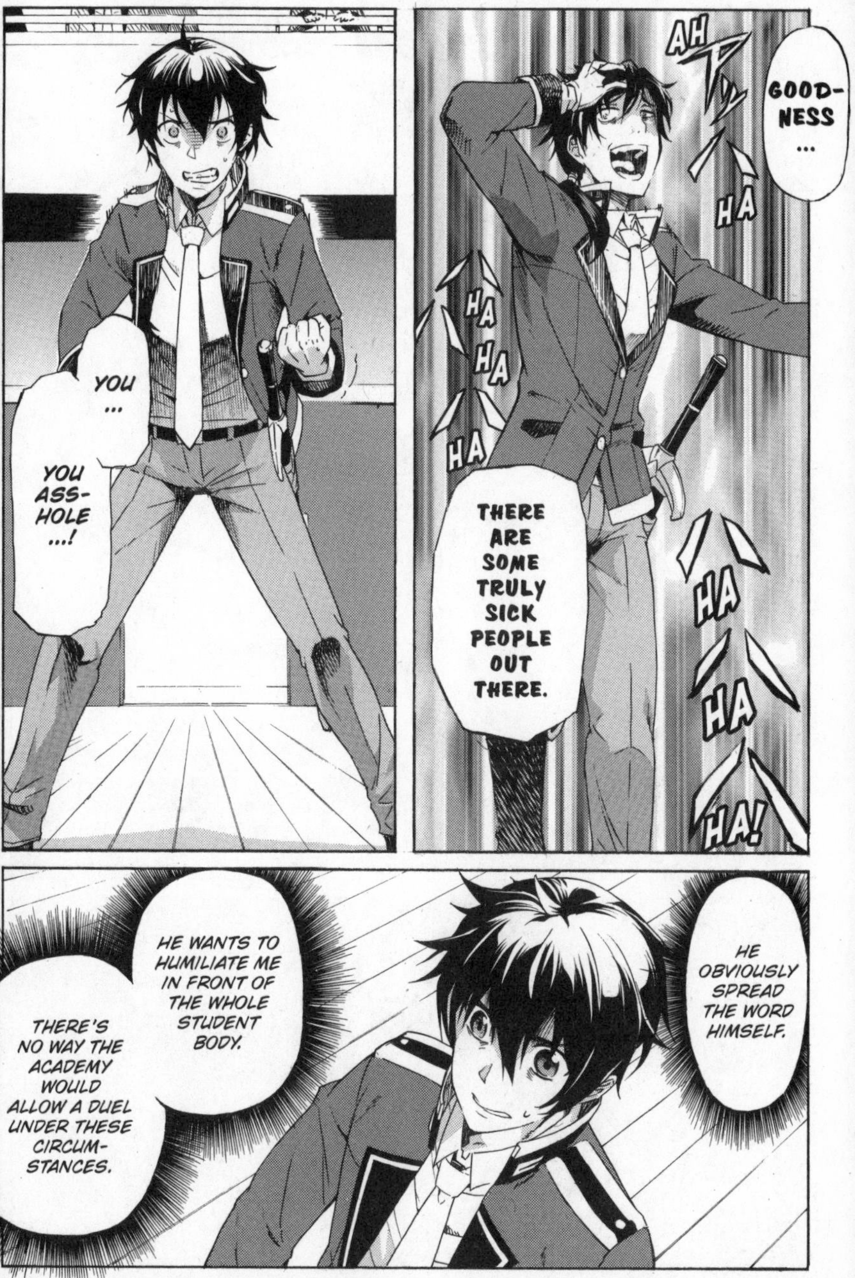
AH
GOOD-NESS ...
HA
HA
HA
HA
THERE ARE SOME TRULY SICK PEOPLE OUT THERE.
HA
HA
HA!
YOU ...
YOU ASS-HOLE ...!
HE OBVIOUSLY SPREAD THE WORD HIMSELF.
HE WANTS TO HUMILIATE ME IN FRONT OF THE WHOLE STUDENT BODY.
THERE'S NO WAY THE ACADEMY WOULD ALLOW A DUEL UNDER THESE CIRCUM-STANCES.

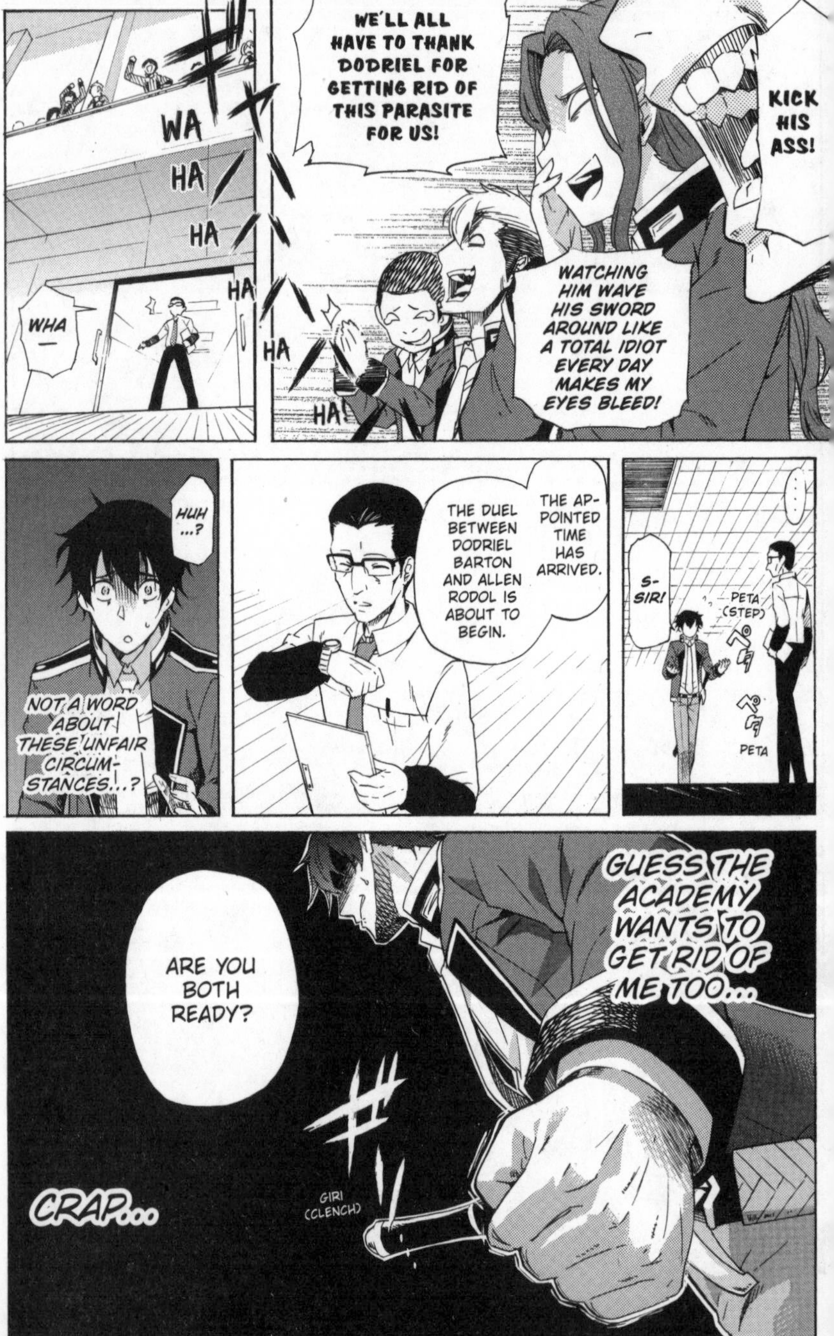
KICK HIS ASS!
WE'LL ALL HAVE TO THANK DODRIEL FOR GETTING RID OF THIS PARASITE FOR US!
WATCHING HIM WAVE HIS SWORD AROUND LIKE A TOTAL IDIOT EVERY DAY MAKES MY EYES BLEED!
WA HA HA HA HA HA HA!
WHA—
...
S-SIR!
PETA (STEP)
PETA
THE AP-POINTED TIME HAS ARRIVED.
THE DUEL BETWEEN DODRIEL BARTON AND ALLEN RODOL IS ABOUT TO BEGIN.
HUH ...?
NOT A WORD ABOUT THESE UNFAIR CIRCUM-STANCES...?
GUESS THE ACADEMY WANTS TO GET RID OF ME TOO...
ARE YOU BOTH READY?
GIRI (CLENCH)
CRAP...

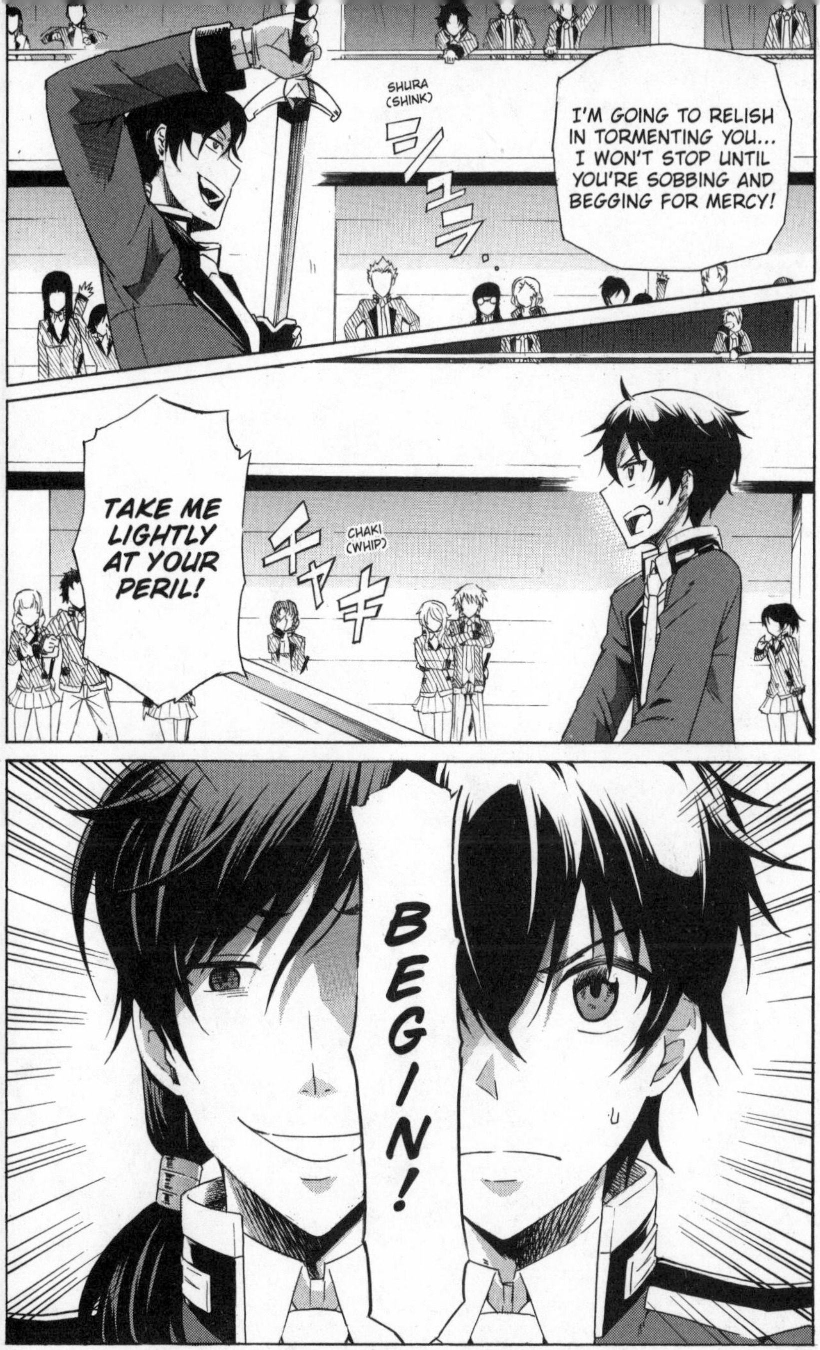
SHURA (SHINK)
シュラ
I'M GOING TO RELISH IN TORMENTING YOU... I WON'T STOP UNTIL YOU'RE SOBBING AND BEGGING FOR MERCY!
CHAKI (WHIP)
チャキ
TAKE ME LIGHTLY AT YOUR PERIL!
BEGIN!

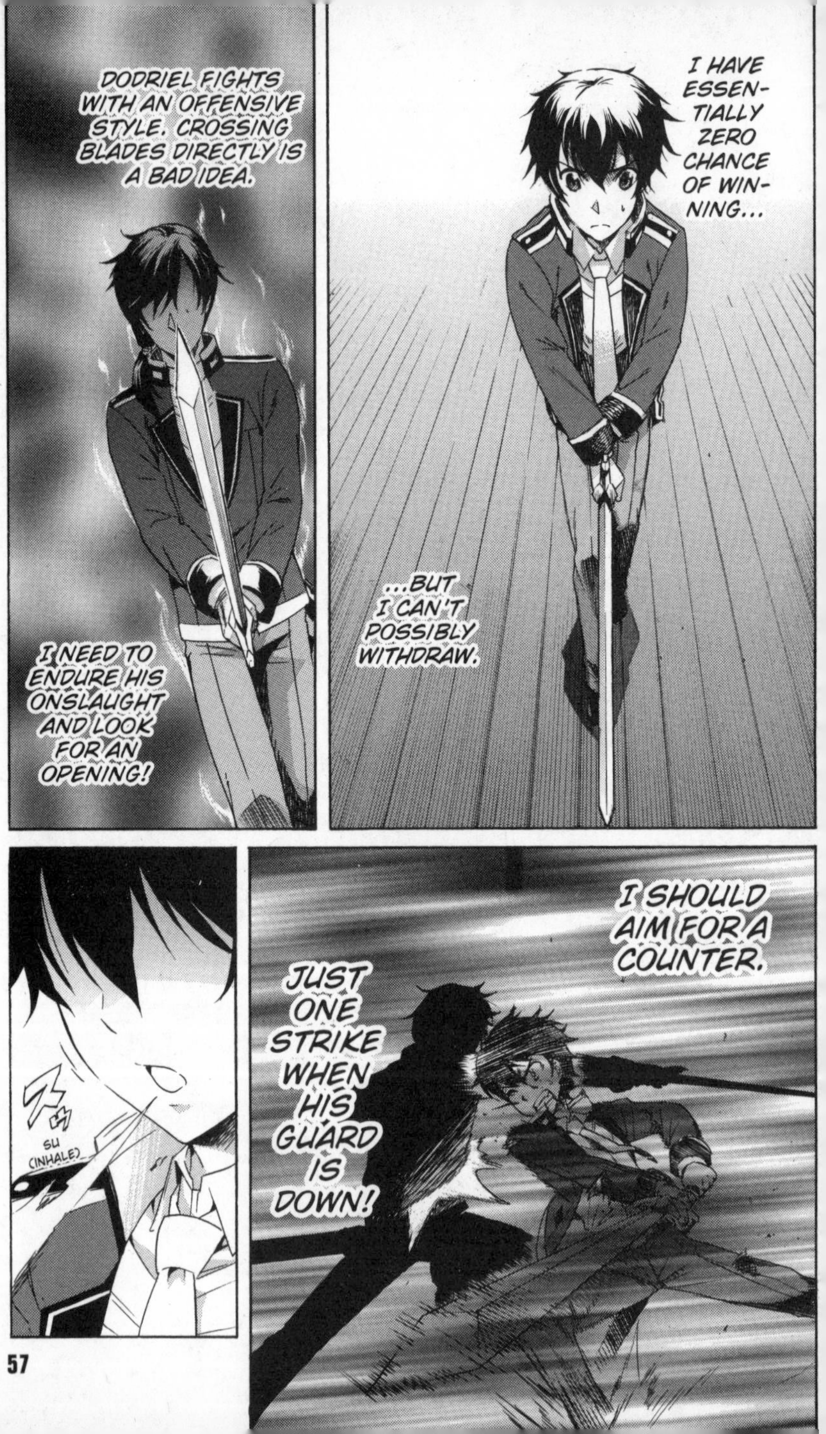
I HAVE ESSEN-TIALLY ZERO CHANCE OF WIN-NING...
...BUT I CAN'T POSSIBLY WITHDRAW.
DODRIEL FIGHTS WITH AN OFFENSIVE STYLE. CROSSING BLADES DIRECTLY IS A BAD IDEA.
I NEED TO ENDURE HIS ONSLAUGHT AND LOOK FOR AN OPENING!
I SHOULD AIM FOR A COUNTER.
JUST ONE STRIKE WHEN HIS GUARD IS DOWN!
SU (INHALE)

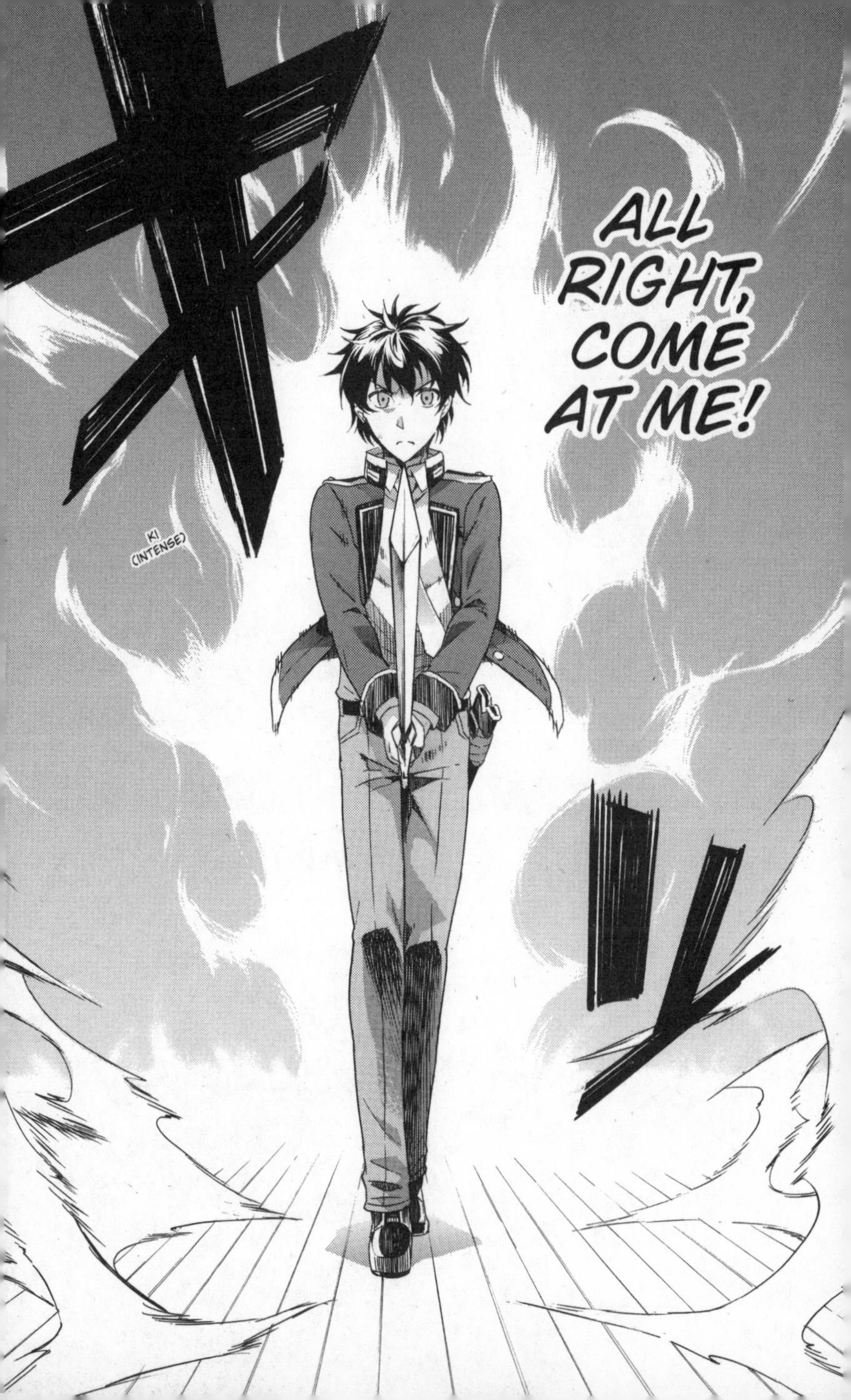
ALL RIGHT, COME AT ME!
KI (INTENSE)

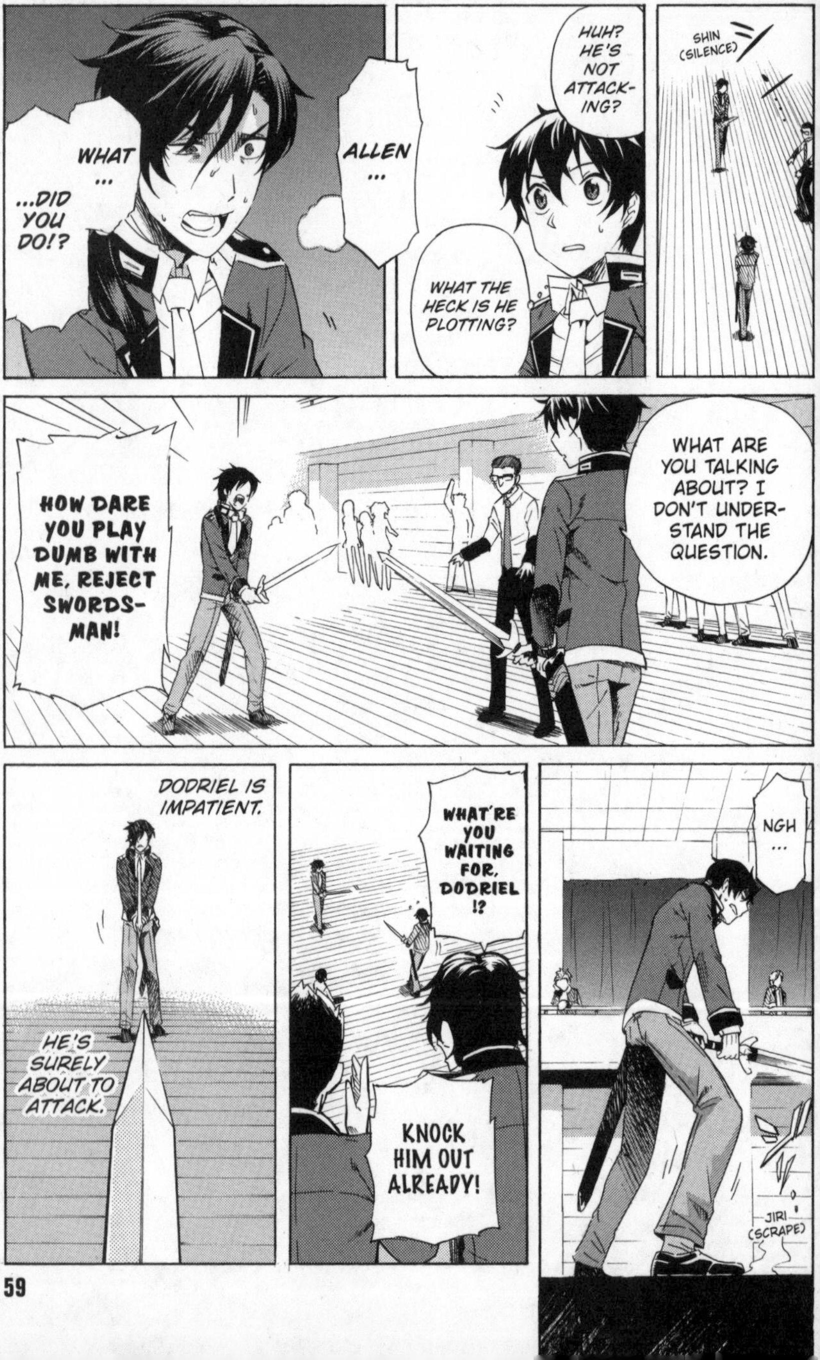
SHIN (SILENCE)
HUH? HE'S NOT ATTACK-ING?
WHAT THE HECK IS HE PLOTTING?
ALLEN ...
WHAT ...
...DID YOU DO!?
WHAT ARE YOU TALKING ABOUT? I DON'T UNDER-STAND THE QUESTION.
HOW DARE YOU PLAY DUMB WITH ME, REJECT SWORDS-MAN!
NGH ...
JIRI (SCRAPE)
WHAT'RE YOU WAITING FOR, DODRIEL !?
KNOCK HIM OUT ALREADY!
DODRIEL IS IMPATIENT.
HE'S SURELY ABOUT TO ATTACK.

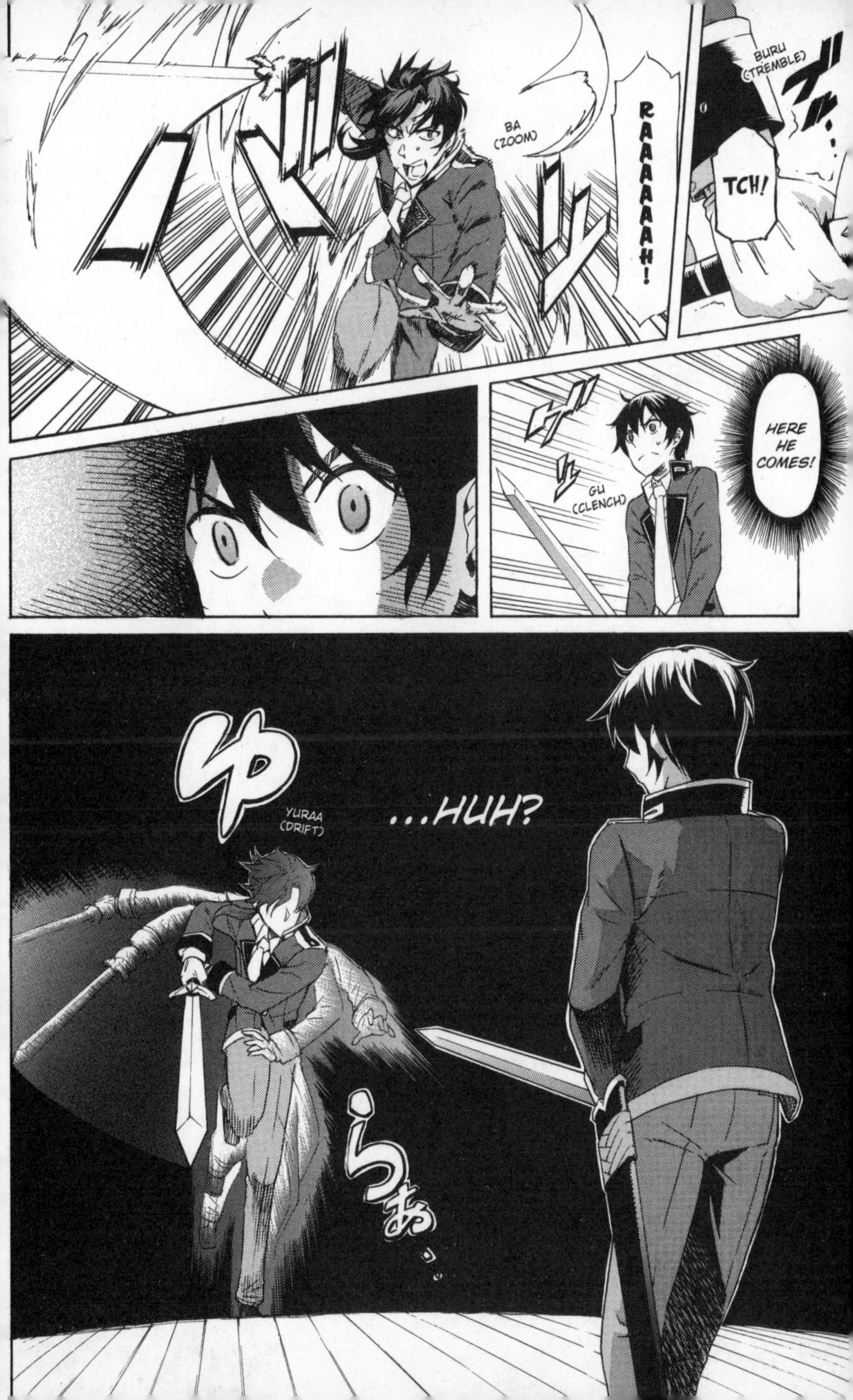
BURU (TREMBLE)
TCH!
RAAAAAAH!
BA (ZOOM)
HERE HE COMES!
GU (CLENCH)
...HUH?
YURAA (DRIFT)

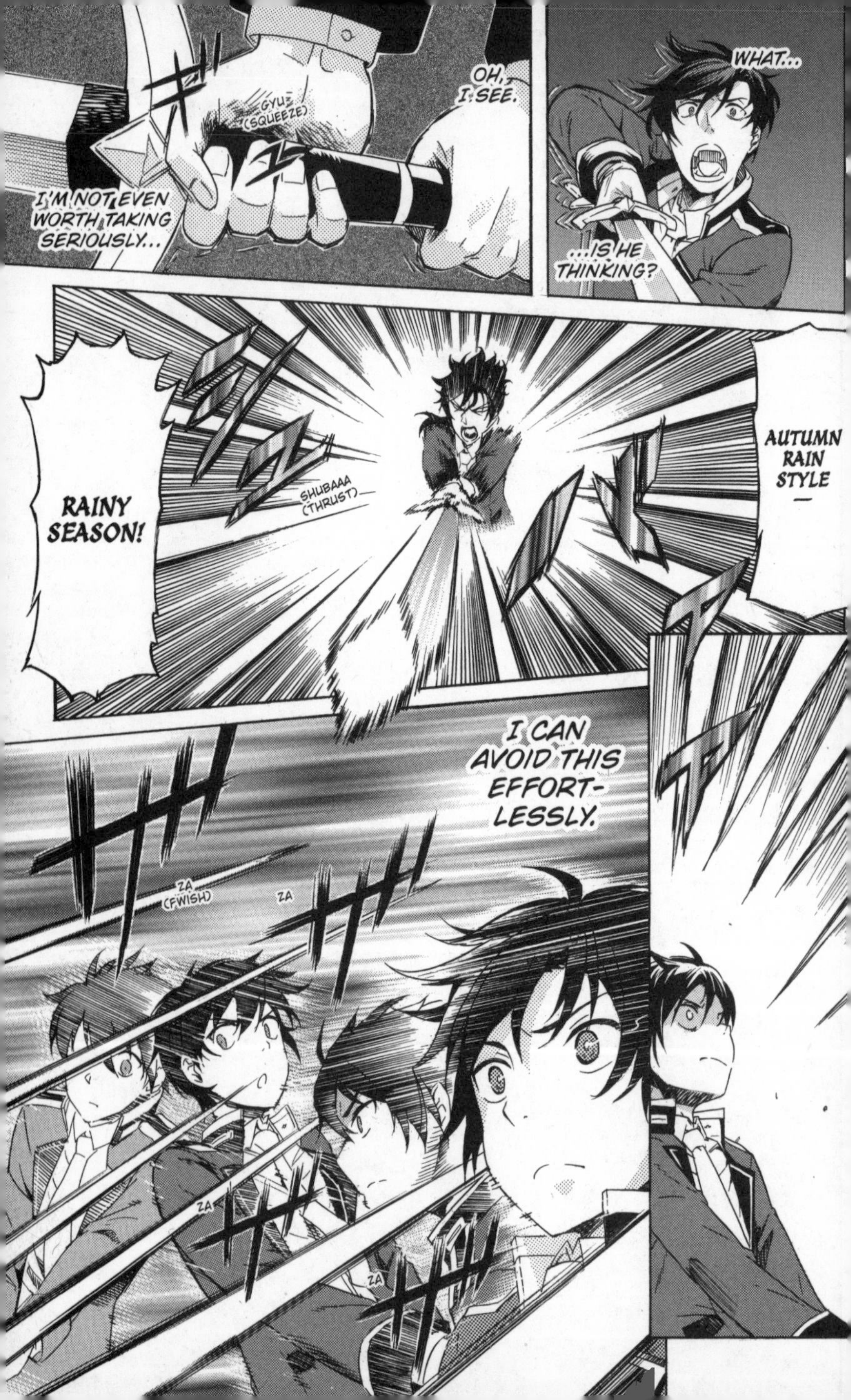
WHAT...
...IS HE THINKING?
OH, I SEE.
GYU (SQUEEZE)
I'M NOT EVEN WORTH TAKING SERIOUSLY...
AUTUMN RAIN STYLE —
SHUBAAA (THRUST)
RAINY SEASON!
I CAN AVOID THIS EFFORT-LESSLY.
ZA
ZA (FWISH)
ZA
ZA

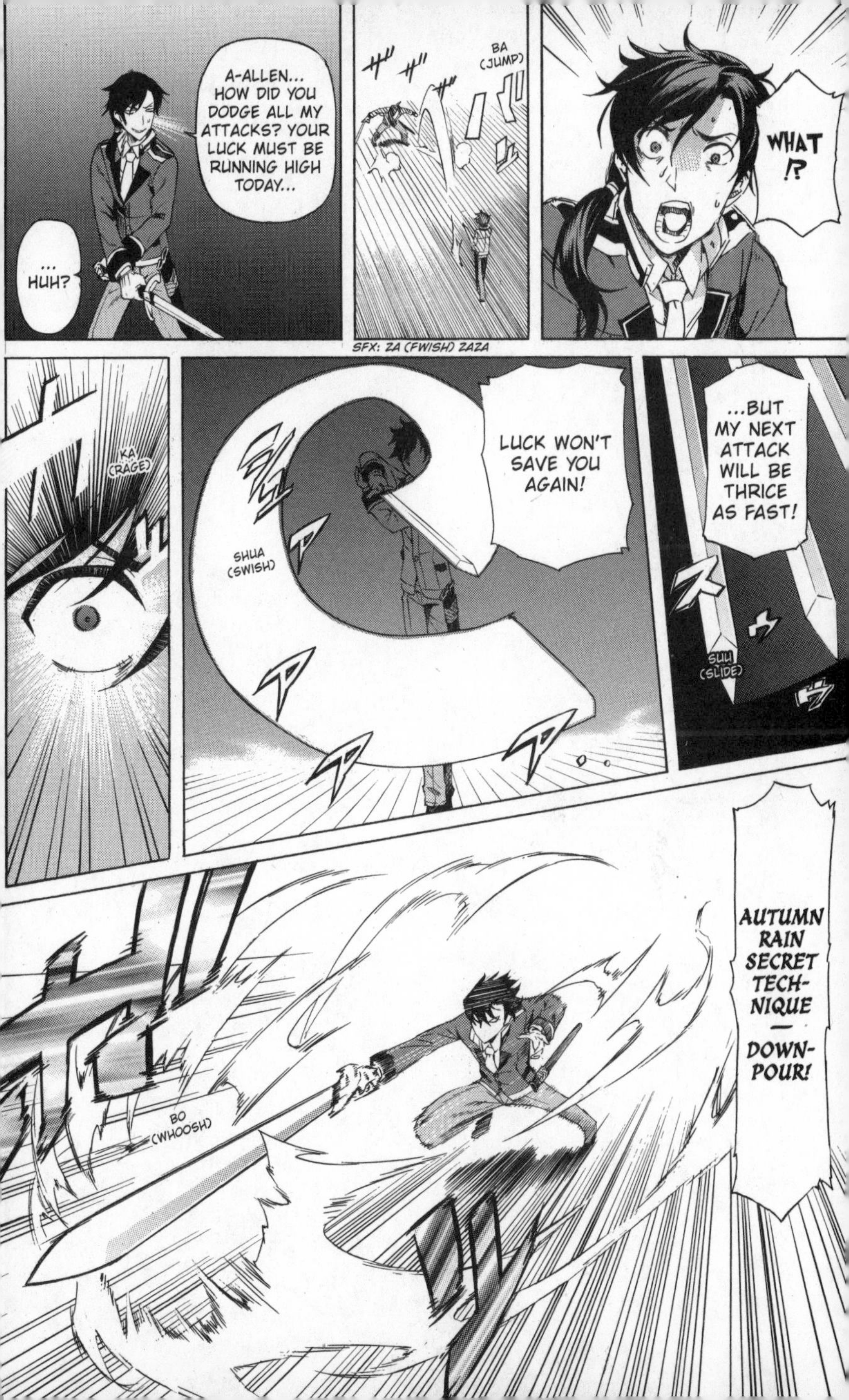
WHAT!?
BA (JUMP)
A-ALLEN... HOW DID YOU DODGE ALL MY ATTACKS? YOUR LUCK MUST BE RUNNING HIGH TODAY...
... HUH?
SFX: ZA (FWISH) ZAZA
...BUT MY NEXT ATTACK WILL BE THRICE AS FAST!
SUU (SLIDE)
LUCK WON'T SAVE YOU AGAIN!
SHUA (SWISH)
KA (RAGE)
AUTUMN RAIN SECRET TECH-NIQUE — DOWN-POUR!
BO (WHOOSH)

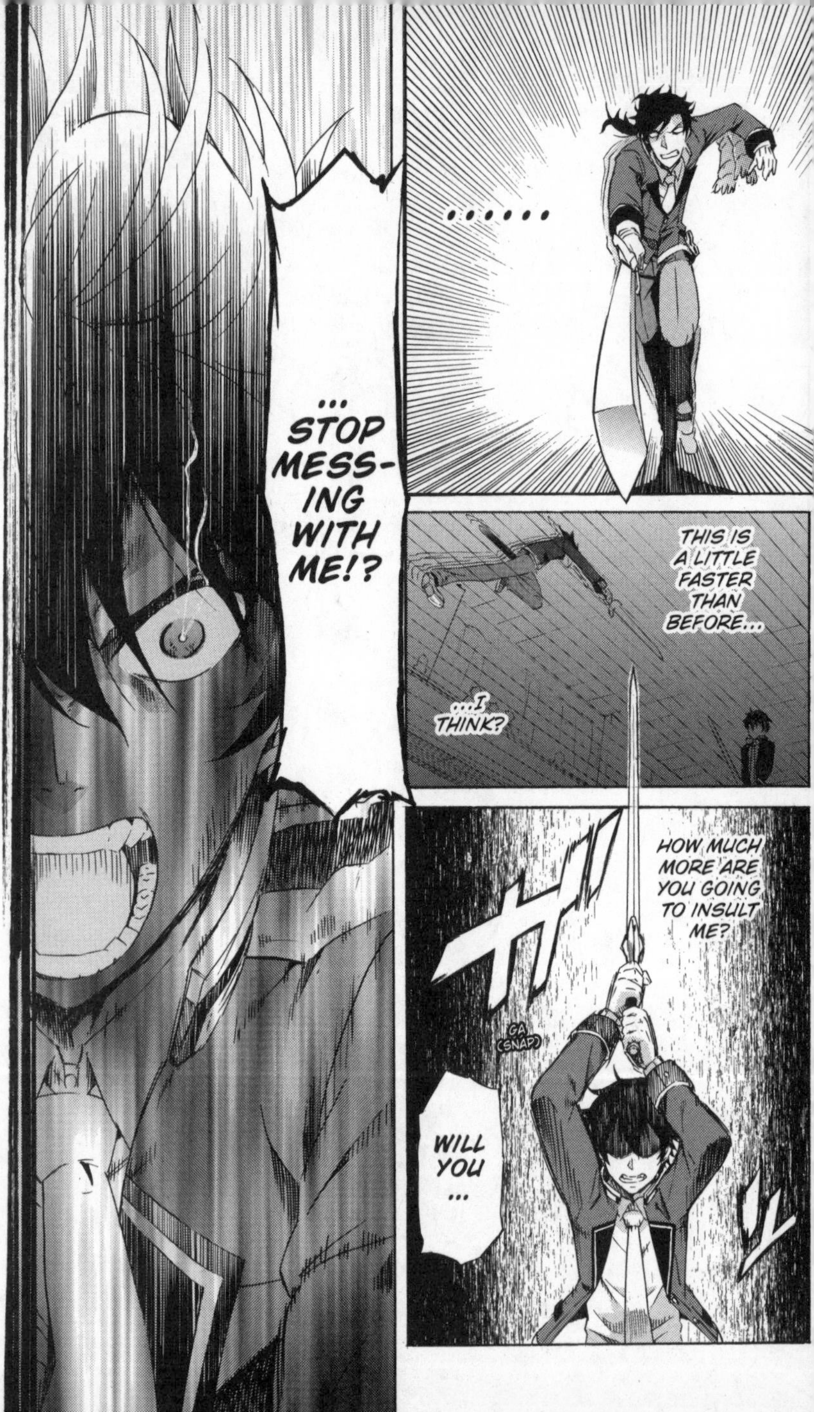
......
THIS IS A LITTLE FASTER THAN BEFORE...
...I THINK?
HOW MUCH MORE ARE YOU GOING TO INSULT ME?
GA (SNAP)
WILL YOU ...
... STOP MESS-ING WITH ME!?

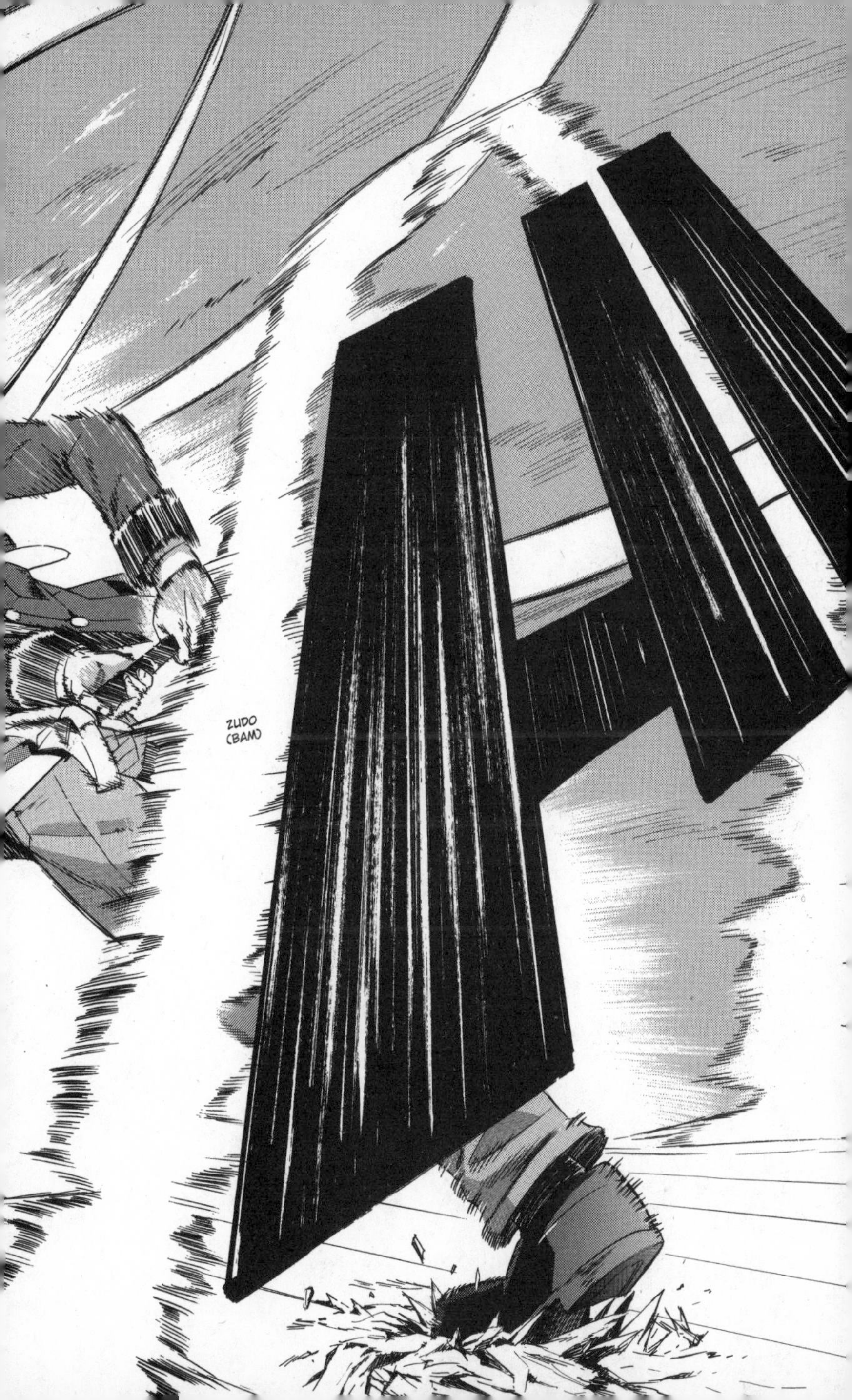
ZUDO
(BAM)

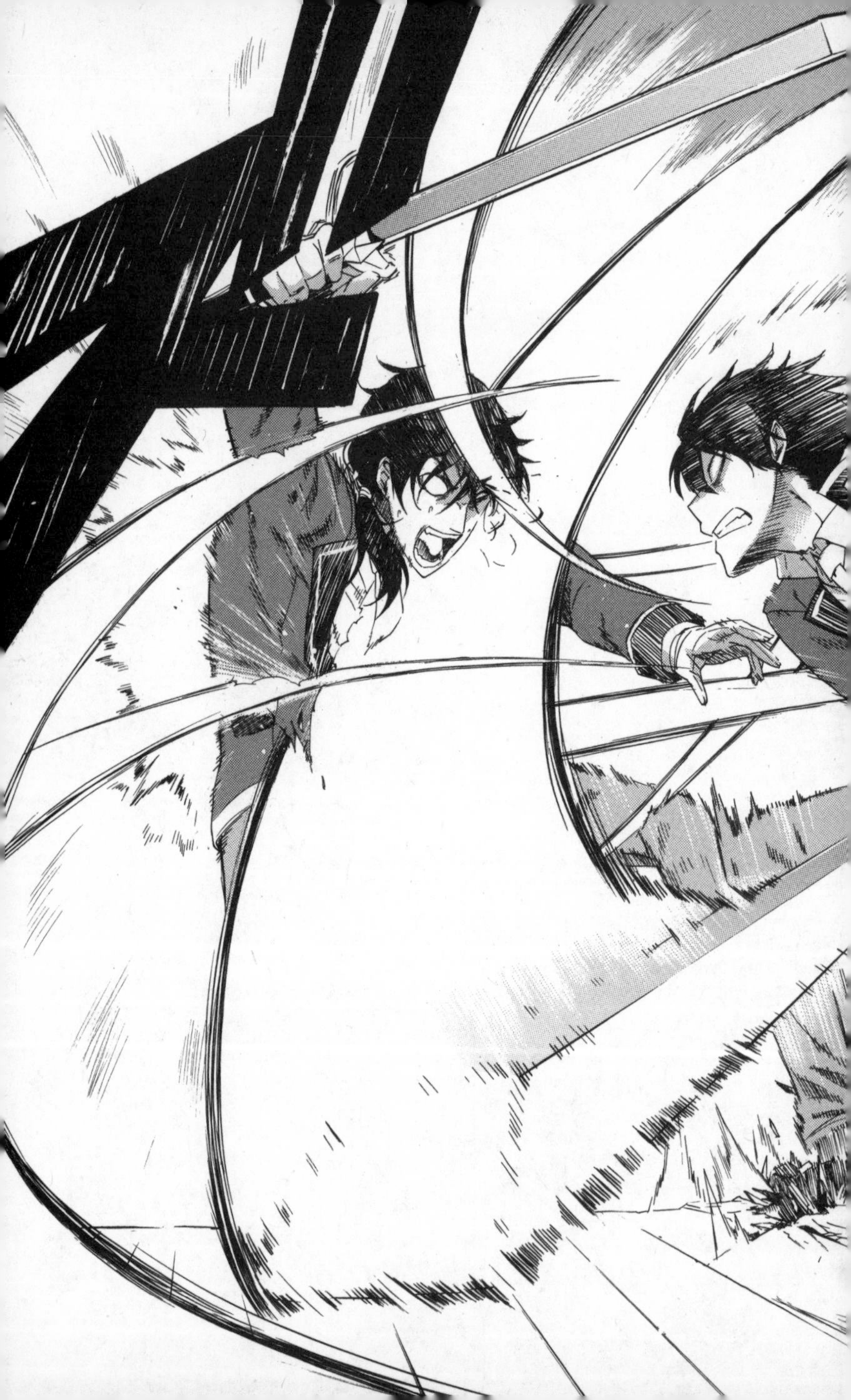

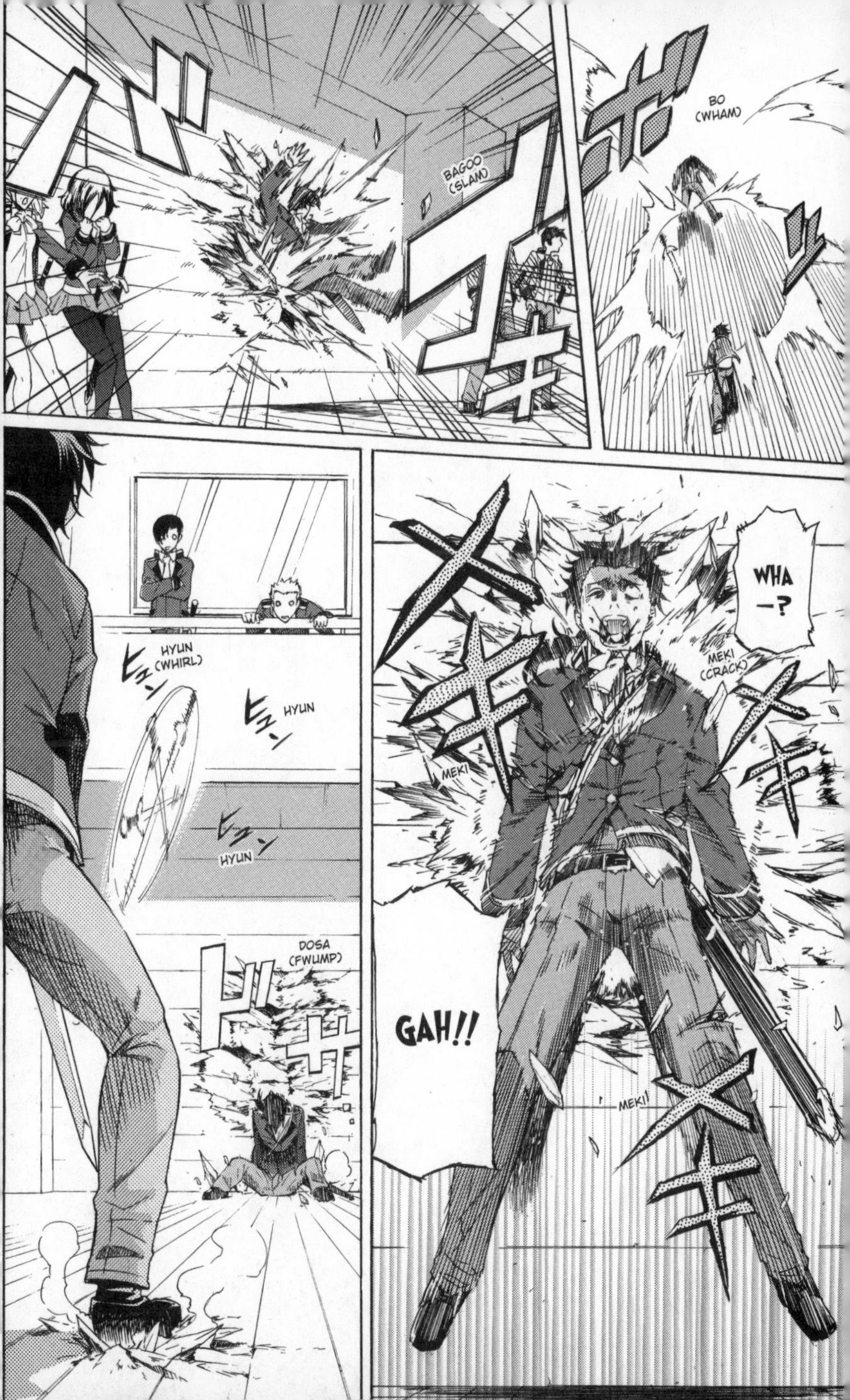
BO
(WHAM)
BAGOO
(SLAM)
WHA
—?
MEKI
(CRACK)
MEKI
MEKI!
GAH!!
HYUN
(WHIRL)
HYUN
HYUN
DOSA
(FWUMP)

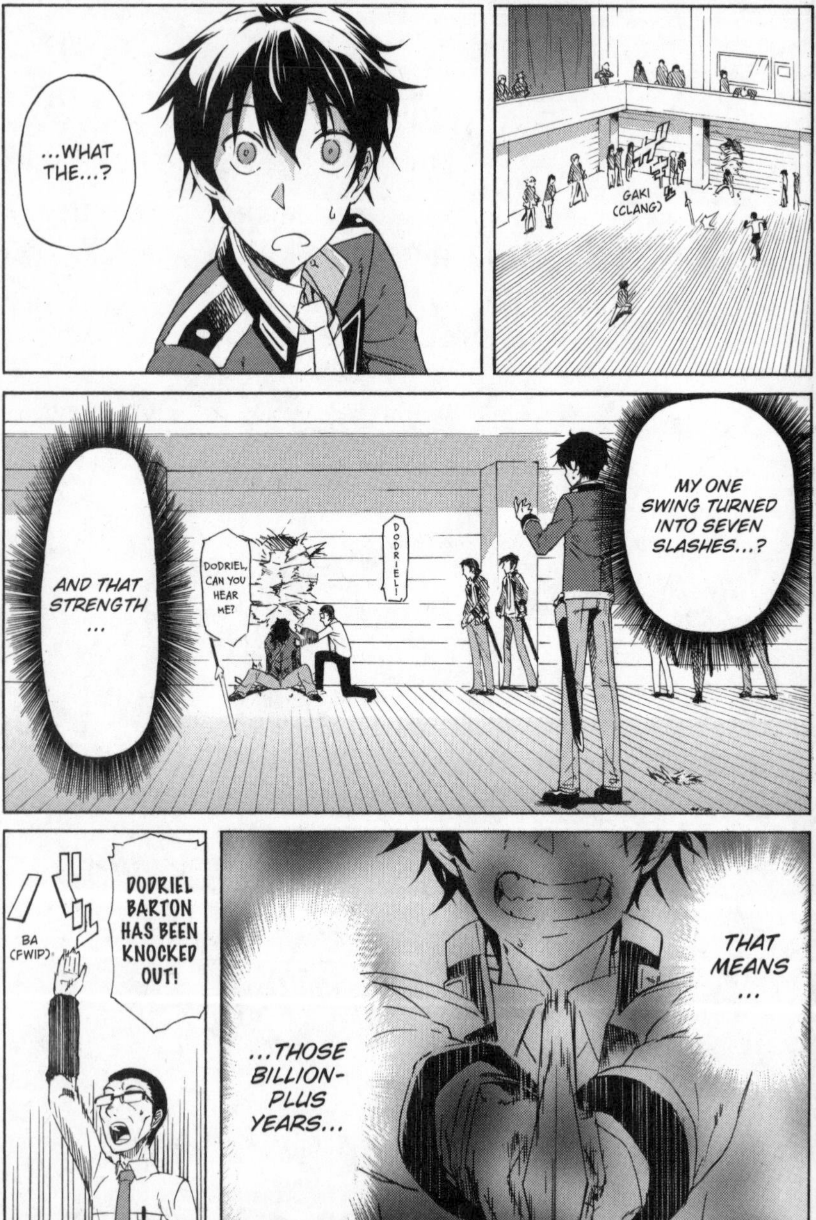
GAKI
(CLANG)
...WHAT THE...?
MY ONE SWING TURNED INTO SEVEN SLASHES...?
DODRIEL!
DODRIEL, CAN YOU HEAR ME?
AND THAT STRENGTH...
THAT MEANS...
...THOSE BILLION-PLUS YEARS...
BA
(FWIP)
DODRIEL BARTON HAS BEEN KNOCKED OUT!

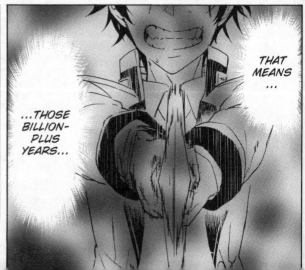

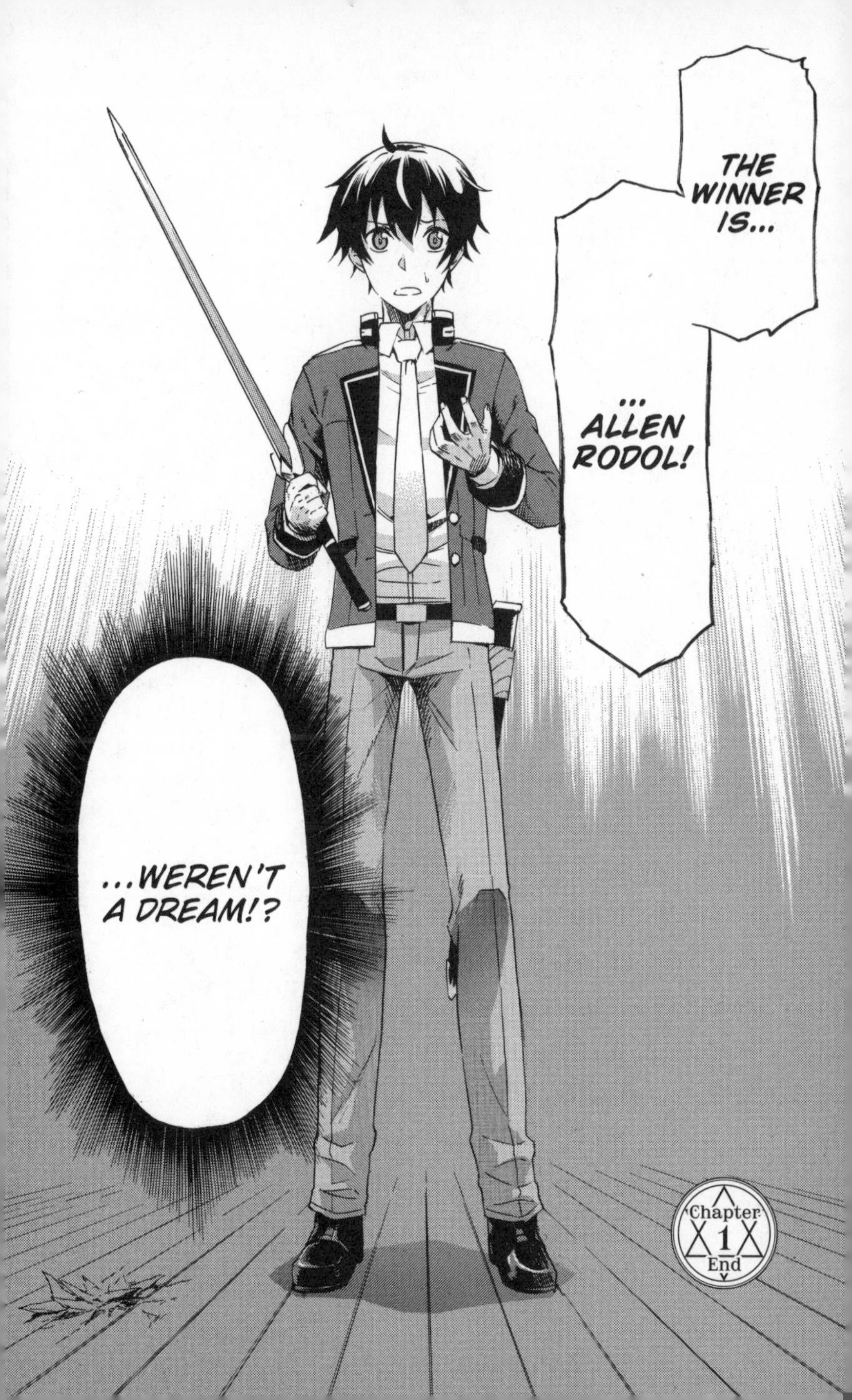
THE WINNER IS...
... ALLEN RODOL!
...WEREN'T A DREAM!?
Chapter 1 End

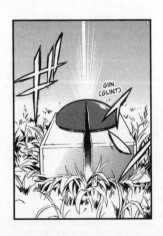

GIIN
(GLINT)

I KEPT PRESSING THE 100-MILLION-YEAR BUTTON AND CAME OUT ON TOP

~THE UNBEATABLE REJECT SWORDSMAN~

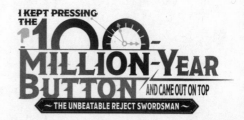

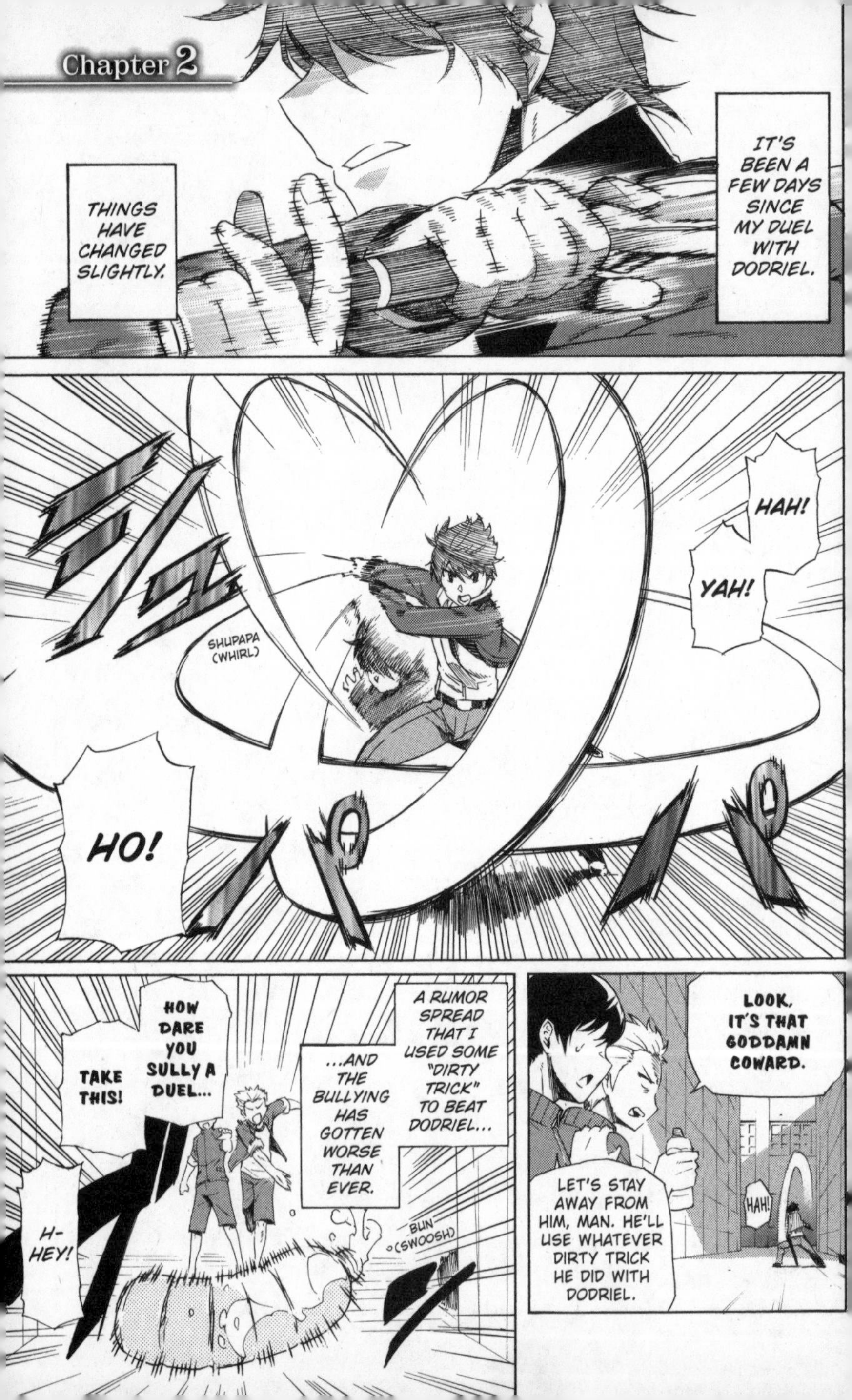
Chapter 2
IT'S BEEN A FEW DAYS SINCE MY DUEL WITH DODRIEL.
THINGS HAVE CHANGED SLIGHTLY.
HAH!
YAH!
SHUPAPA (WHIRL)
HO!
LOOK, IT'S THAT GODDAMN COWARD.
HAH!
LET'S STAY AWAY FROM HIM, MAN. HE'LL USE WHATEVER DIRTY TRICK HE DID WITH DODRIEL.
A RUMOR SPREAD THAT I USED SOME "DIRTY TRICK" TO BEAT DODRIEL...
...AND THE BULLYING HAS GOTTEN WORSE THAN EVER.
HOW DARE YOU SULLY A DUEL...
TAKE THIS!
BUN (SWOOSH)
H-HEY!

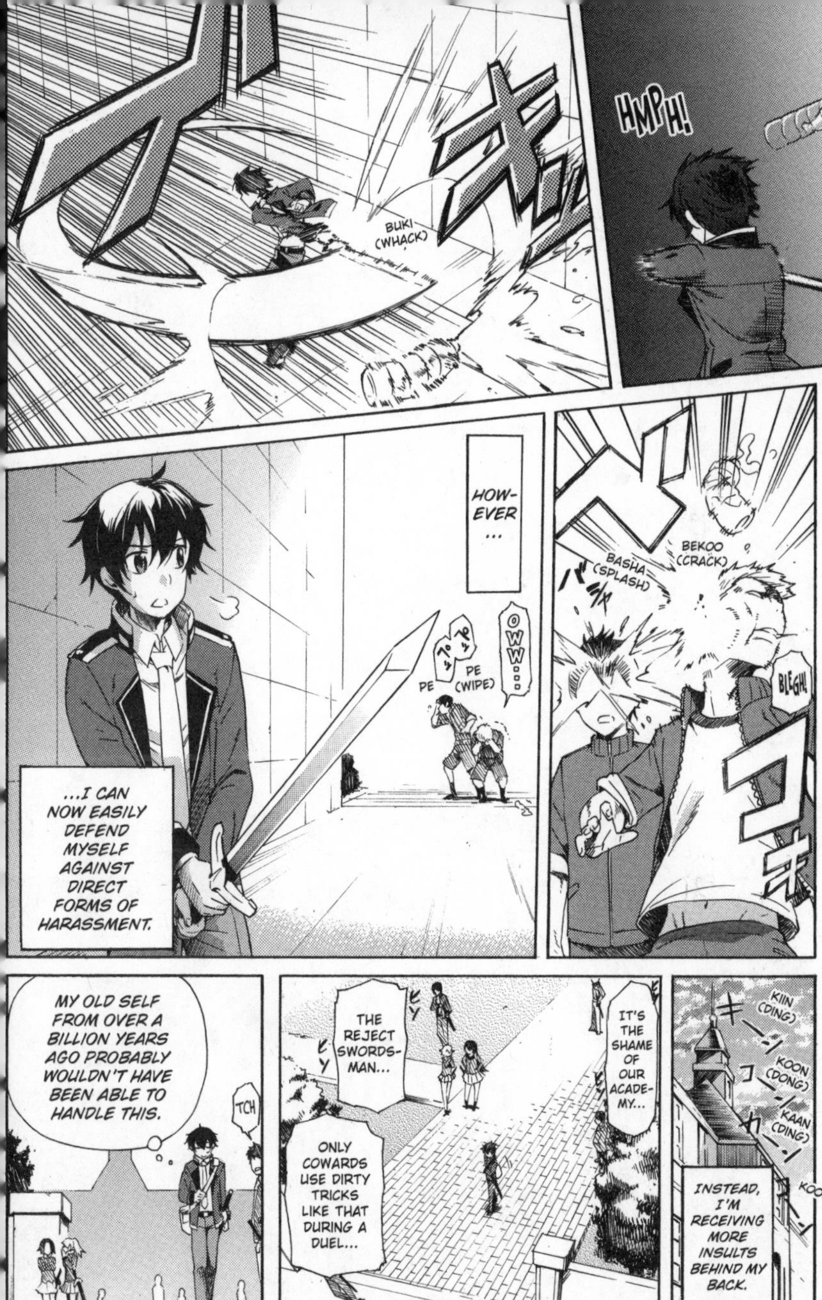
HMPH!
BUKI (WHACK)
BEKOO (CRACK)
BASHA (SPLASH)
BLEGH!
HOW-EVER...
OWW...
PE PE (WIPE)
...I CAN NOW EASILY DEFEND MYSELF AGAINST DIRECT FORMS OF HARASSMENT.
KIIN (DING)
KOON (DONG)
KAAN (DING)
KOON
INSTEAD, I'M RECEIVING MORE INSULTS BEHIND MY BACK.
IT'S THE SHAME OF OUR ACADE-MY...
THE REJECT SWORDS-MAN...
ONLY COWARDS USE DIRTY TRICKS LIKE THAT DURING A DUEL...
MY OLD SELF FROM OVER A BILLION YEARS AGO PROBABLY WOULDN'T HAVE BEEN ABLE TO HANDLE THIS.
TCH

SFX: HISO (WHISPER) HISO HISO

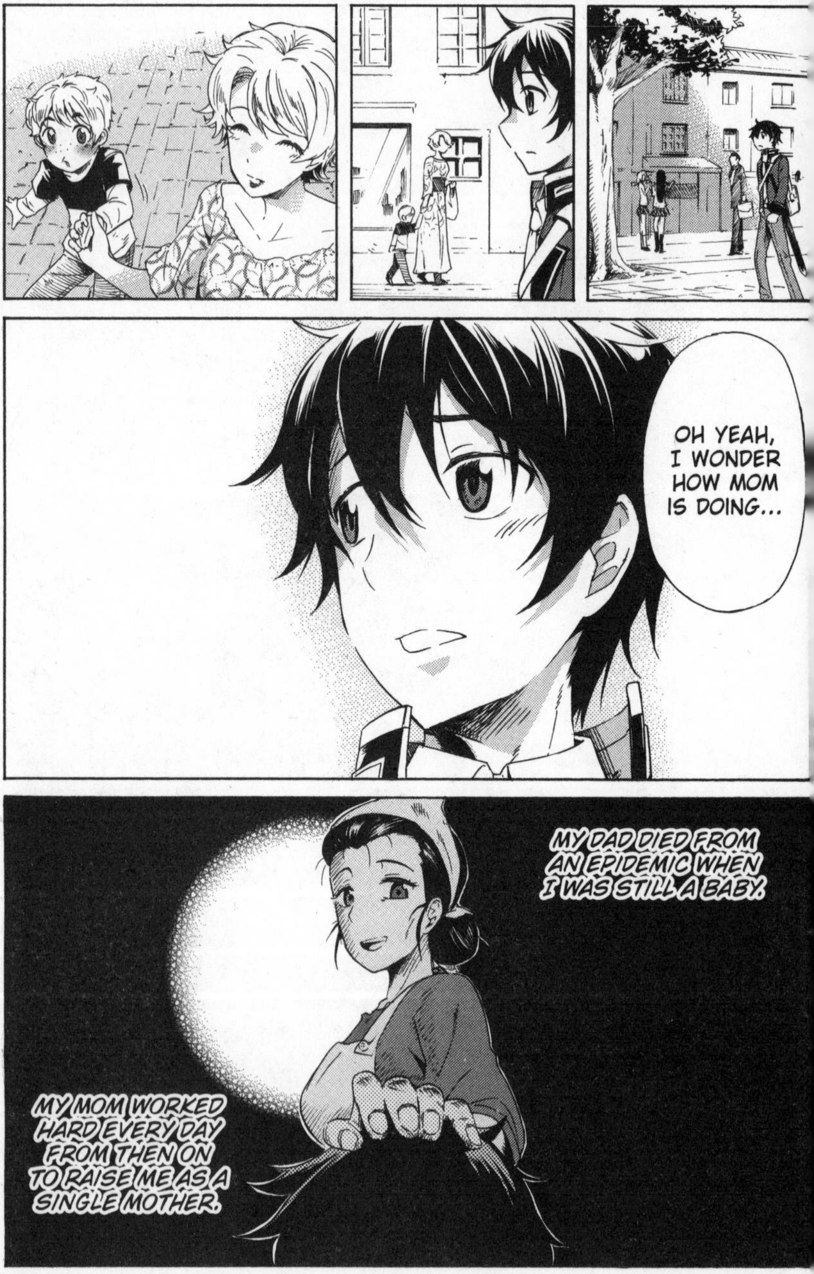
OH YEAH, I WONDER HOW MOM IS DOING...
MY DAD DIED FROM AN EPIDEMIC WHEN I WAS STILL A BABY.
MY MOM WORKED HARD EVERY DAY FROM THEN ON TO RAISE ME AS A SINGLE MOTHER.

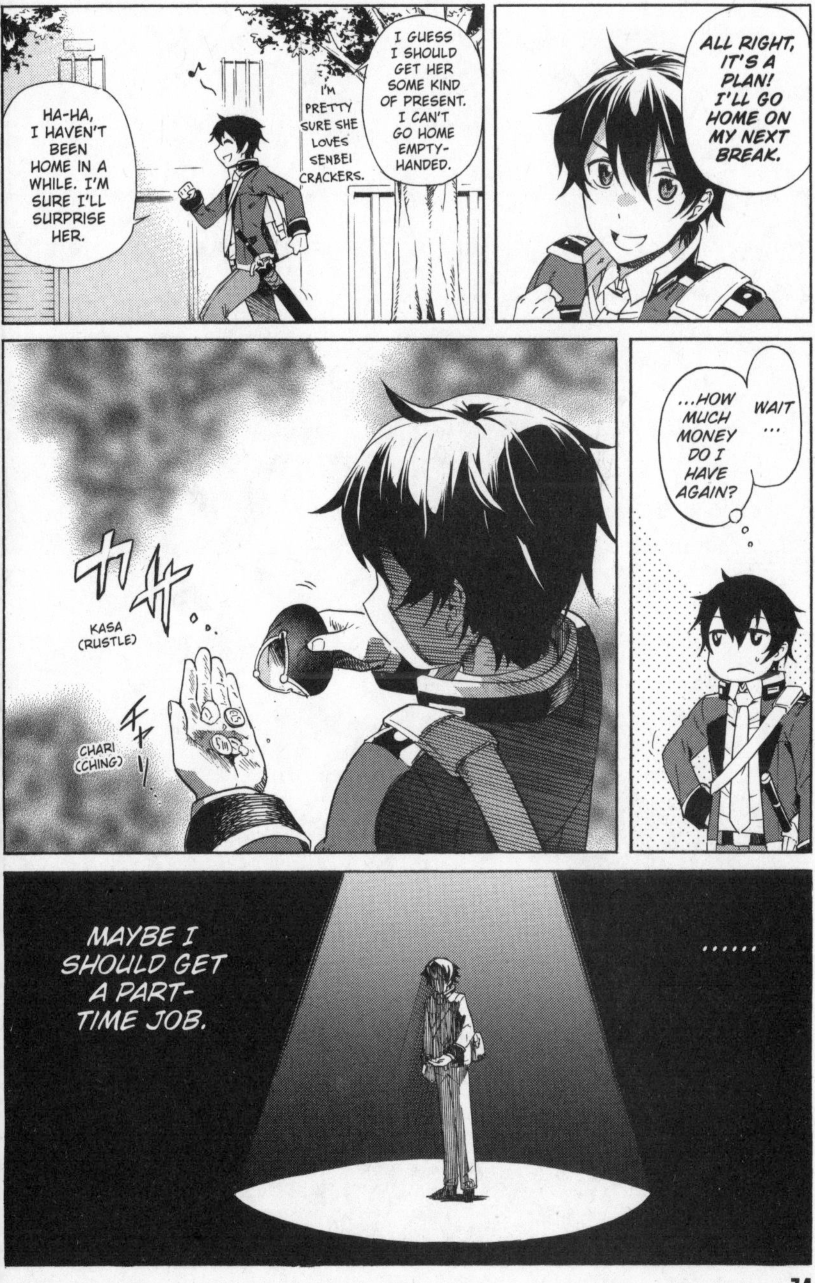
ALL RIGHT, IT'S A PLAN! I'LL GO HOME ON MY NEXT BREAK.
I GUESS I SHOULD GET HER SOME KIND OF PRESENT. I CAN'T GO HOME EMPTY-HANDED.
I'M PRETTY SURE SHE LOVES SENBEI CRACKERS.
HA-HA, I HAVEN'T BEEN HOME IN A WHILE. I'M SURE I'LL SURPRISE HER.
WAIT...
...HOW MUCH MONEY DO I HAVE AGAIN?
KASA (RUSTLE)
CHARI (CHING)
......
MAYBE I SHOULD GET A PART-TIME JOB.

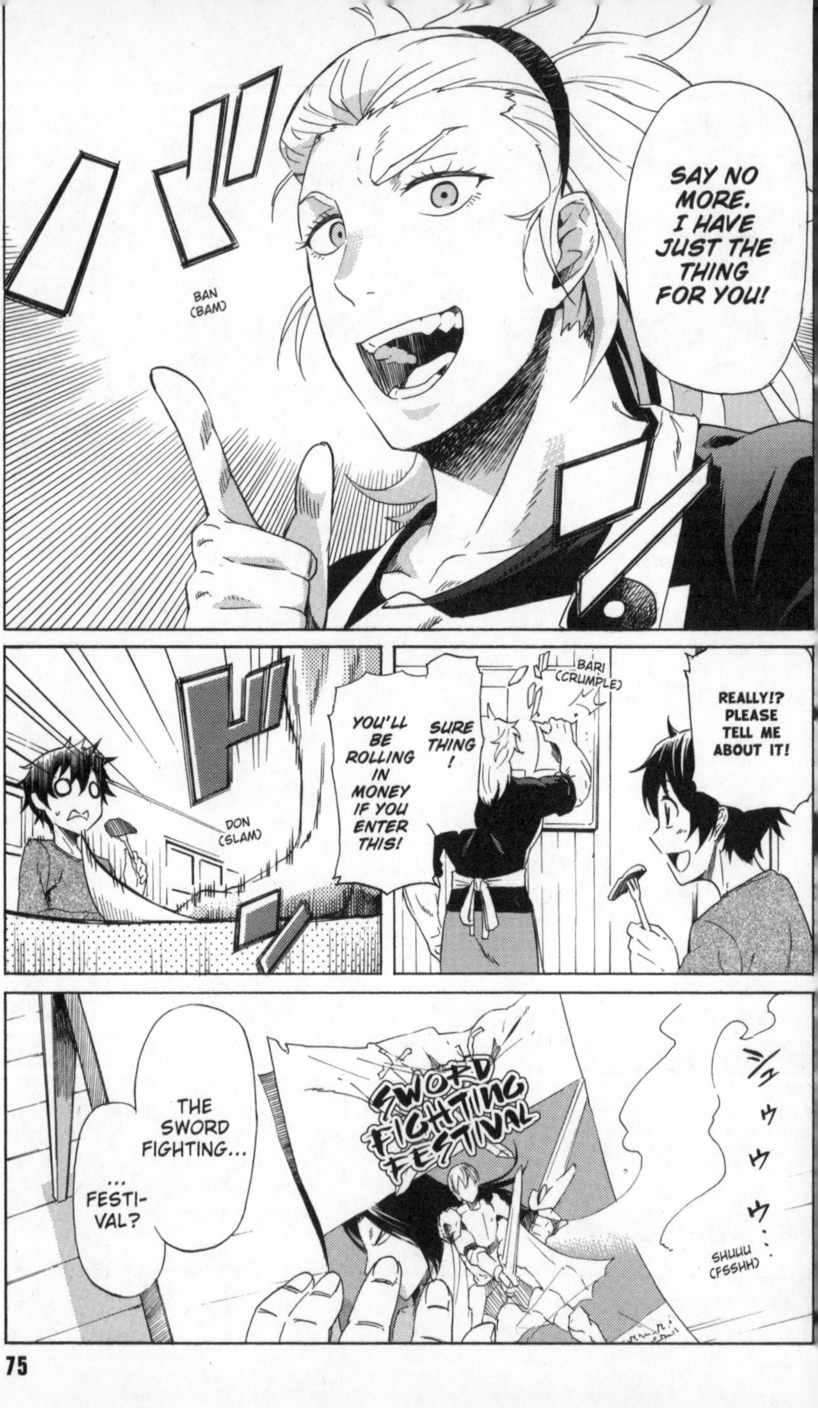
SAY NO MORE. I HAVE JUST THE THING FOR YOU!
BAN (BAM)
REALLY!? PLEASE TELL ME ABOUT IT!
BARI (CRUMPLE)
SURE THING!
YOU'LL BE ROLLING IN MONEY IF YOU ENTER THIS!
DON (SLAM)
SHUUU (FSSHH)
SWORD FIGHTING FESTIVAL
THE SWORD FIGHTING...
... FESTI-VAL?

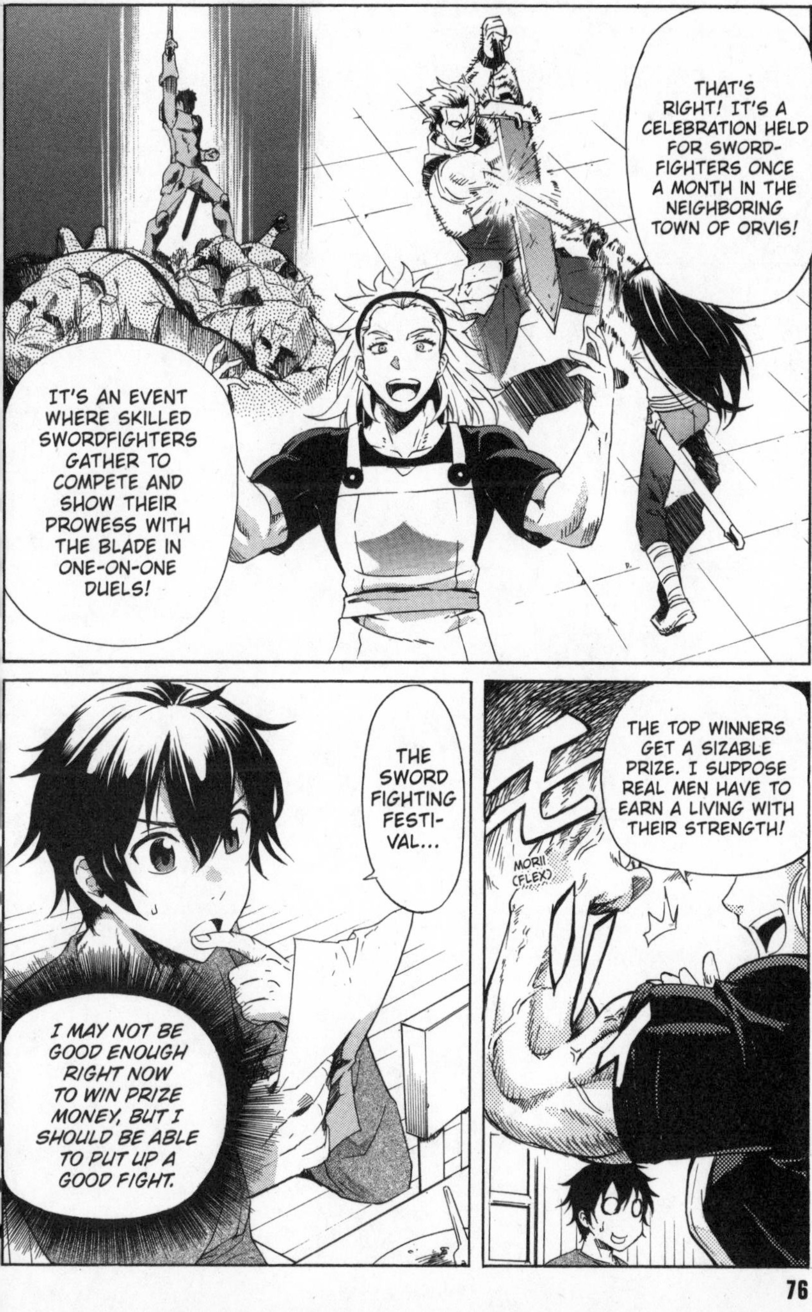
THAT'S RIGHT! IT'S A CELEBRATION HELD FOR SWORD-FIGHTERS ONCE A MONTH IN THE NEIGHBORING TOWN OF ORVIS!
IT'S AN EVENT WHERE SKILLED SWORDFIGHTERS GATHER TO COMPETE AND SHOW THEIR PROWESS WITH THE BLADE IN ONE-ON-ONE DUELS!
THE TOP WINNERS GET A SIZABLE PRIZE. I SUPPOSE REAL MEN HAVE TO EARN A LIVING WITH THEIR STRENGTH!
MORII (FLEX)
THE SWORD FIGHTING FESTI-VAL...
I MAY NOT BE GOOD ENOUGH RIGHT NOW TO WIN PRIZE MONEY, BUT I SHOULD BE ABLE TO PUT UP A GOOD FIGHT.

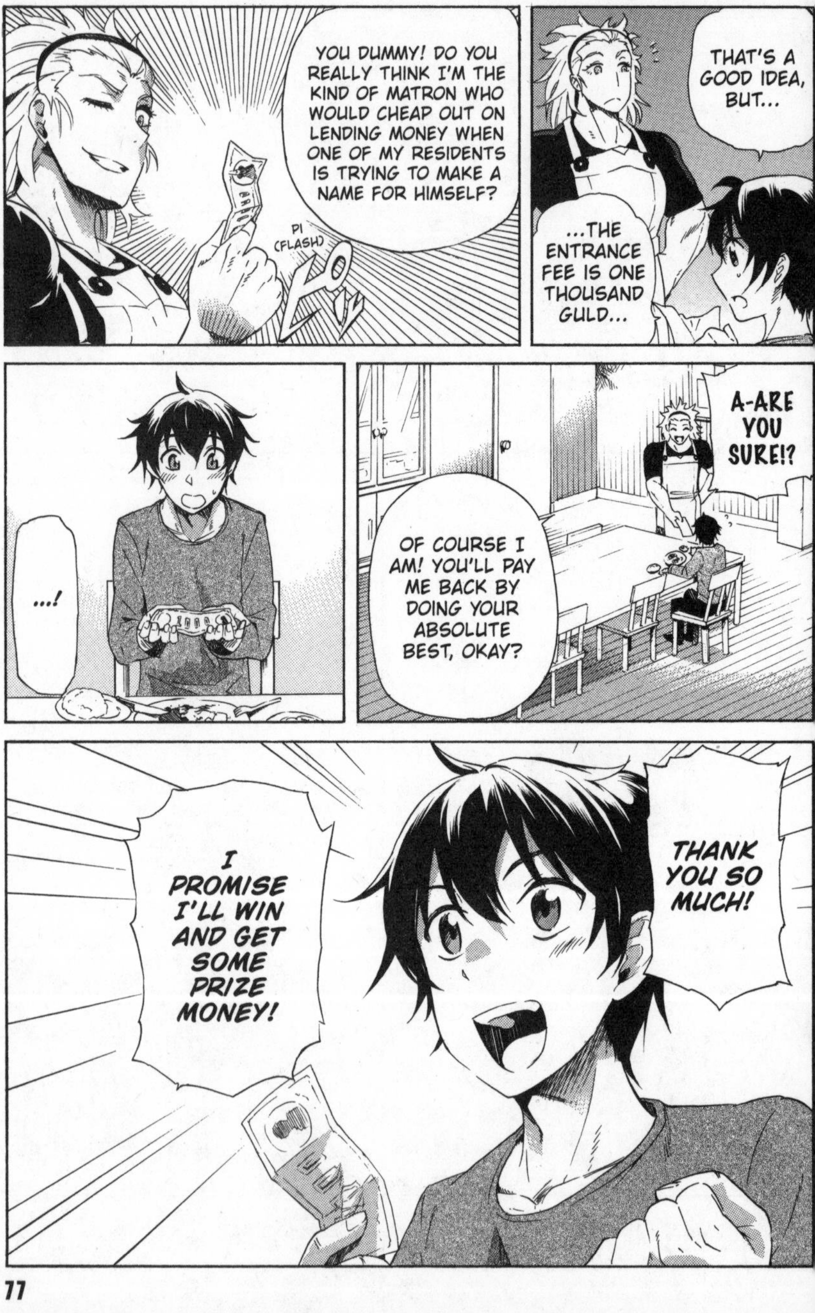
THAT'S A GOOD IDEA, BUT...
...THE ENTRANCE FEE IS ONE THOUSAND GULD...
YOU DUMMY! DO YOU REALLY THINK I'M THE KIND OF MATRON WHO WOULD CHEAP OUT ON LENDING MONEY WHEN ONE OF MY RESIDENTS IS TRYING TO MAKE A NAME FOR HIMSELF?
PI (FLASH)
A-ARE YOU SURE!?
OF COURSE I AM! YOU'LL PAY ME BACK BY DOING YOUR ABSOLUTE BEST, OKAY?
...!
THANK YOU SO MUCH!
I PROMISE I'LL WIN AND GET SOME PRIZE MONEY!

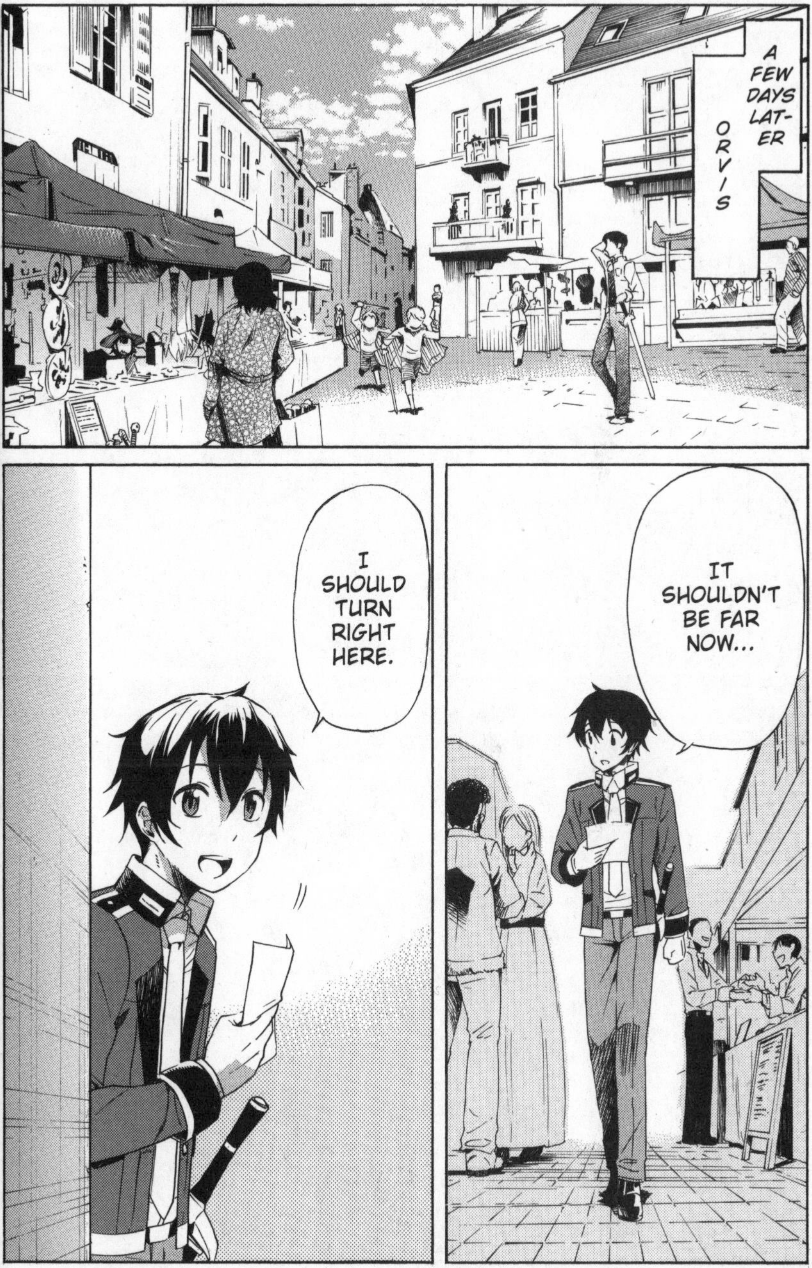
A FEW DAYS LATER-
ORVIS
IT SHOULDN'T BE FAR NOW...
I SHOULD TURN RIGHT HERE.

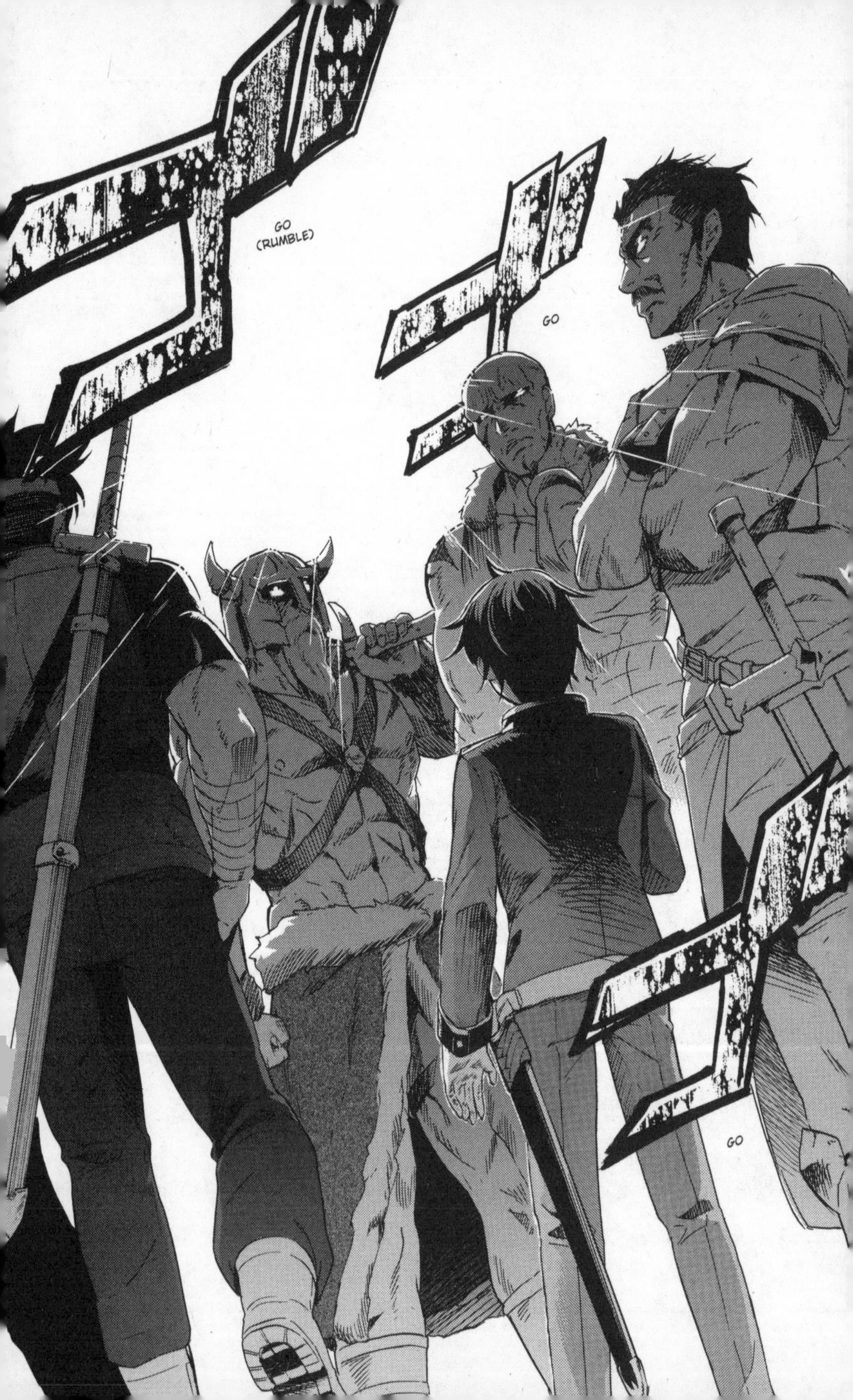
GO
(RUMBLE)
GO
GO

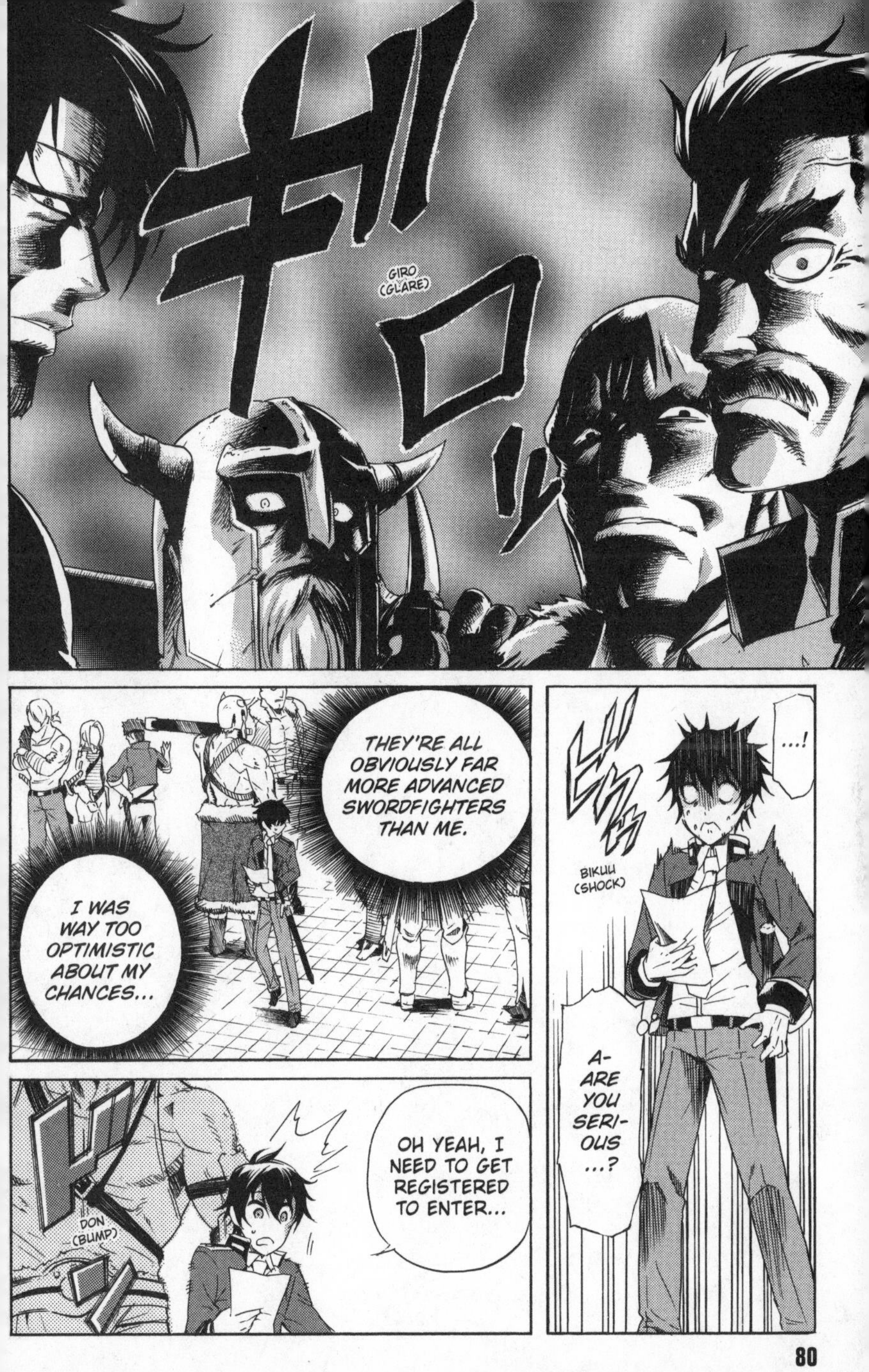
GIRO (GLARE)
...!
BIKUU (SHOCK)
A-ARE YOU SERI-OUS...?
THEY'RE ALL OBVIOUSLY FAR MORE ADVANCED SWORDFIGHTERS THAN ME.
I WAS WAY TOO OPTIMISTIC ABOUT MY CHANCES...
OH YEAH, I NEED TO GET REGISTERED TO ENTER...
DON (BUMP)

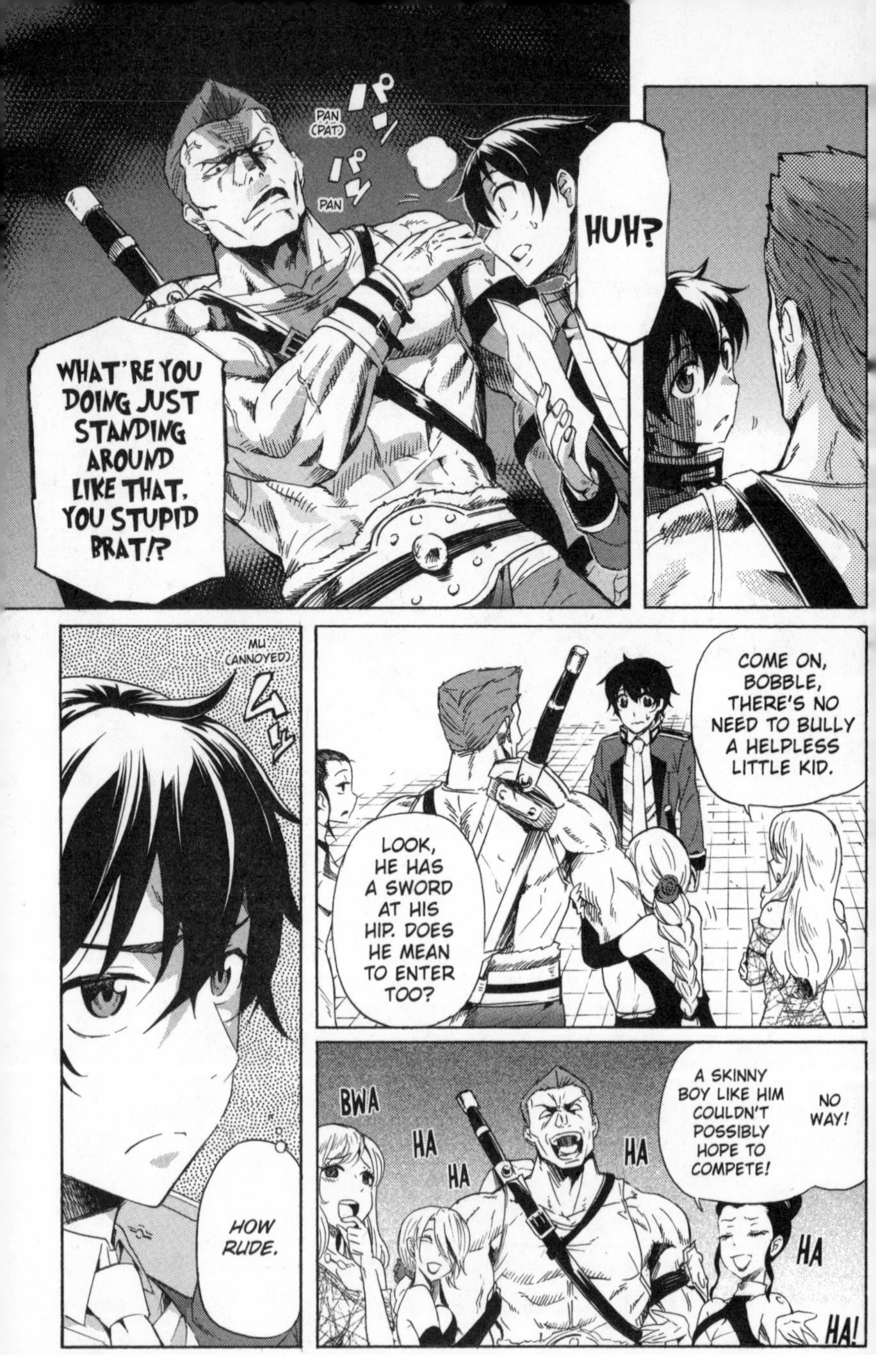
HUH?
PAN (PAT)
PAN
WHAT'RE YOU DOING JUST STANDING AROUND LIKE THAT, YOU STUPID BRAT!?
COME ON, BOBBLE, THERE'S NO NEED TO BULLY A HELPLESS LITTLE KID.
LOOK, HE HAS A SWORD AT HIS HIP. DOES HE MEAN TO ENTER TOO?
NO WAY!
A SKINNY BOY LIKE HIM COULDN'T POSSIBLY HOPE TO COMPETE!
HA
HA
HA!
HA
HA
BWA
HA
MU (ANNOYED)
HOW RUDE.

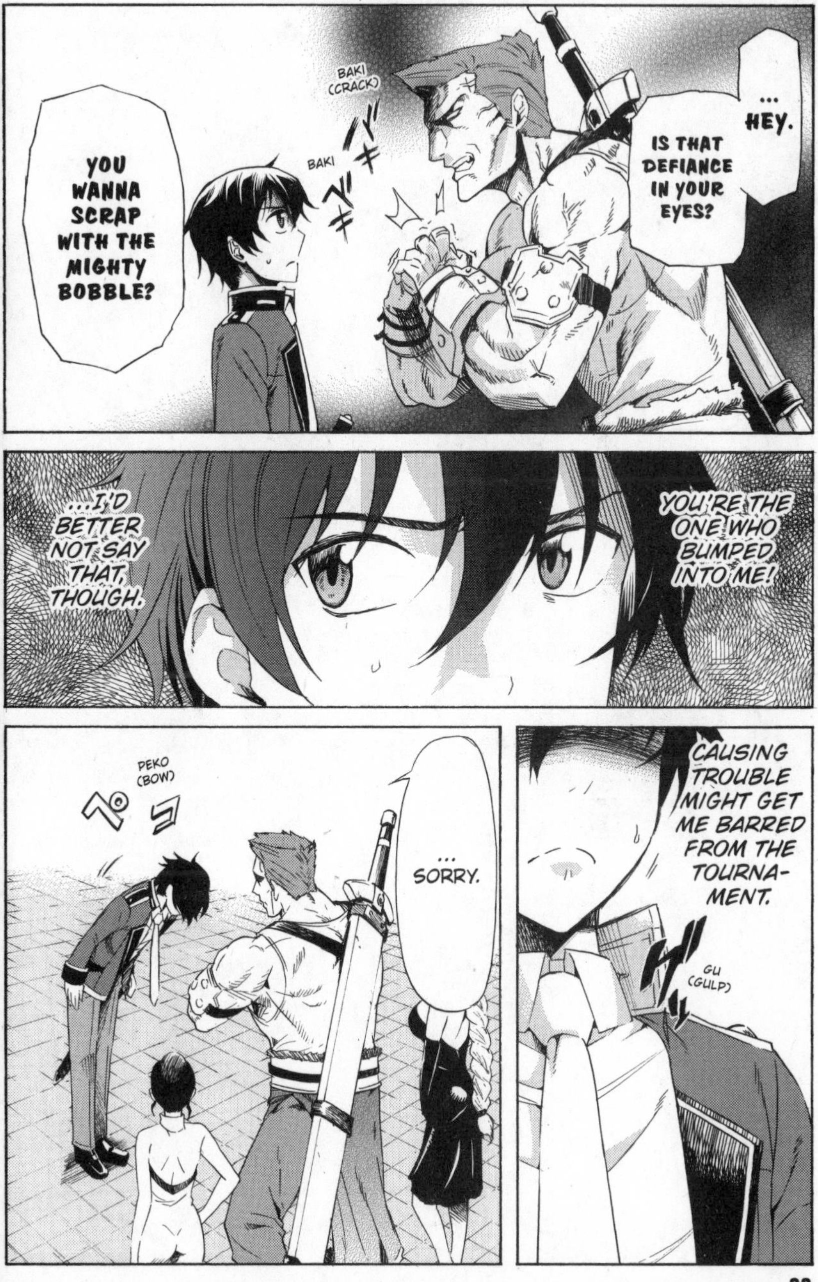
... HEY.
IS THAT DEFIANCE IN YOUR EYES?
BAKI (CRACK)
BAKI
YOU WANNA SCRAP WITH THE MIGHTY BOBBLE?
YOU'RE THE ONE WHO BUMPED INTO ME!
...I'D BETTER NOT SAY THAT, THOUGH.
CAUSING TROUBLE MIGHT GET ME BARRED FROM THE TOURNA-MENT.
GU (GULP)
... SORRY.
PEKO (BOW)

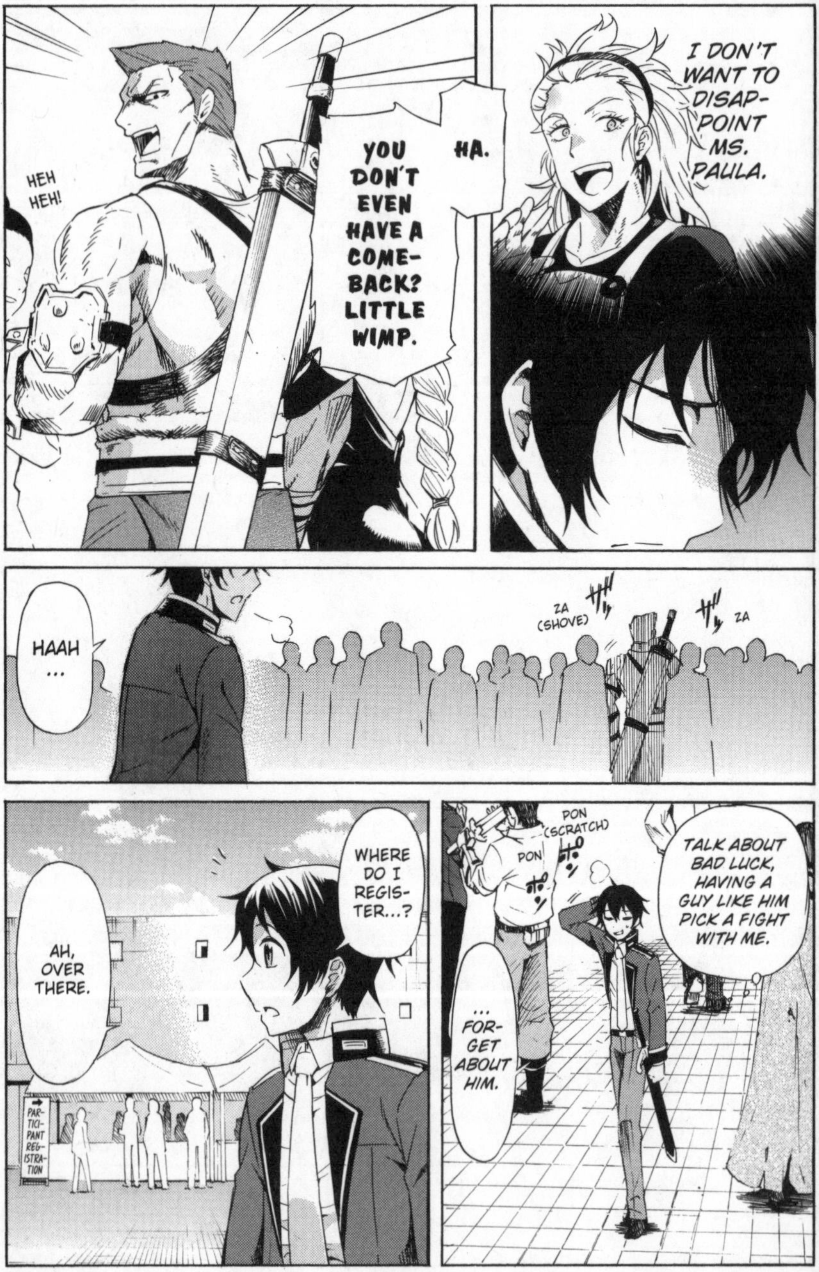
I DON'T WANT TO DISAPPOINT MS. PAULA.
HA.
YOU DON'T EVEN HAVE A COMEBACK? LITTLE WIMP.
HEH HEH!
ZA (SHOVE)
ZA
HAAH ...
PON (SCRATCH)
PON
TALK ABOUT BAD LUCK, HAVING A GUY LIKE HIM PICK A FIGHT WITH ME.
... FORGET ABOUT HIM.
WHERE DO I REGISTER...?
AH, OVER THERE.
PARTICIPANT REGISTRATION

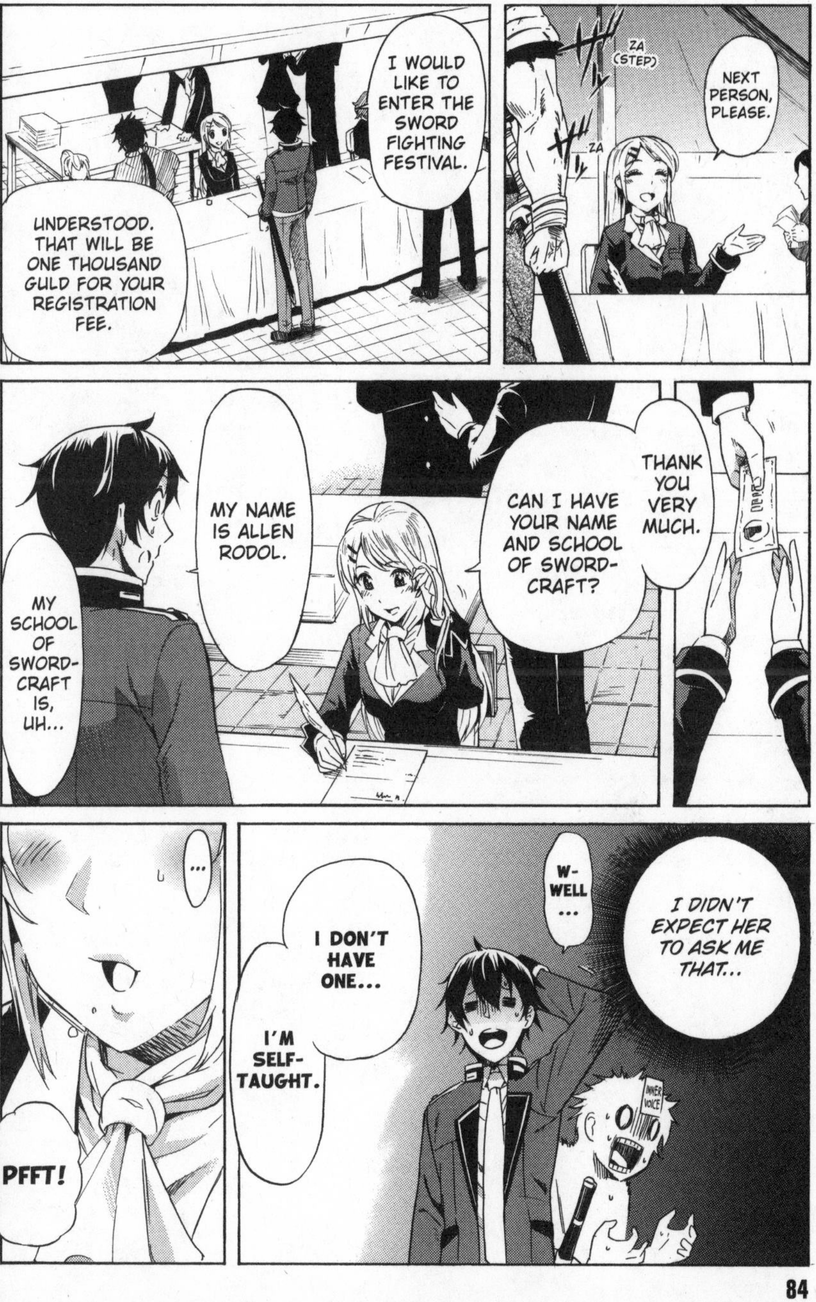
ZA (STEP)
ZA
NEXT PERSON, PLEASE.
I WOULD LIKE TO ENTER THE SWORD FIGHTING FESTIVAL.
UNDERSTOOD. THAT WILL BE ONE THOUSAND GULD FOR YOUR REGISTRATION FEE.
THANK YOU VERY MUCH.
CAN I HAVE YOUR NAME AND SCHOOL OF SWORD-CRAFT?
MY NAME IS ALLEN RODOL.
MY SCHOOL OF SWORD-CRAFT IS, UH...
I DIDN'T EXPECT HER TO ASK ME THAT...
W-WELL...
I DON'T HAVE ONE...
I'M SELF-TAUGHT.
INNER VOICE
...
PFFT!

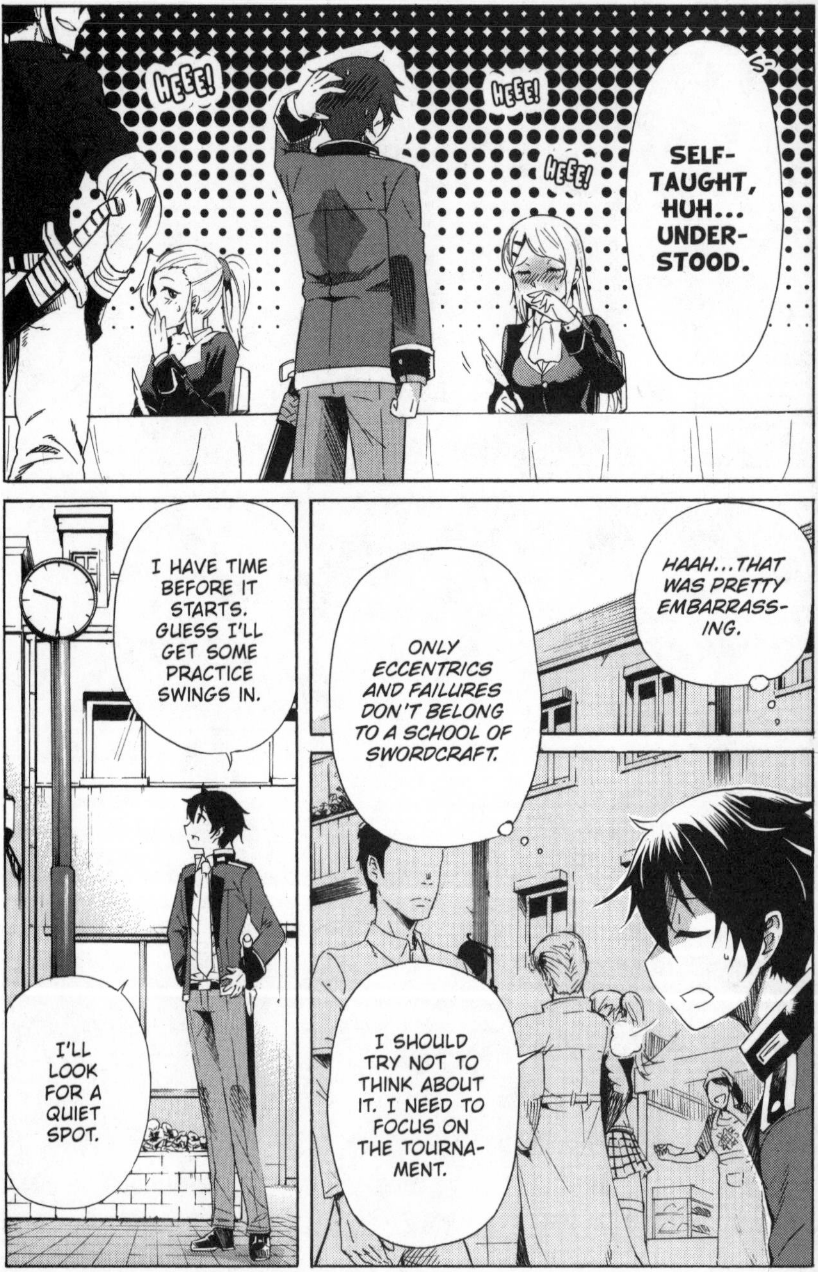
SELF-TAUGHT, HUH... UNDERSTOOD.
HEEE!
HEEE!
HEEE!
HAAH...THAT WAS PRETTY EMBARRASS-ING.
ONLY ECCENTRICS AND FAILURES DON'T BELONG TO A SCHOOL OF SWORDCRAFT.
I SHOULD TRY NOT TO THINK ABOUT IT. I NEED TO FOCUS ON THE TOURNA-MENT.
I HAVE TIME BEFORE IT STARTS. GUESS I'LL GET SOME PRACTICE SWINGS IN.
I'LL LOOK FOR A QUIET SPOT.

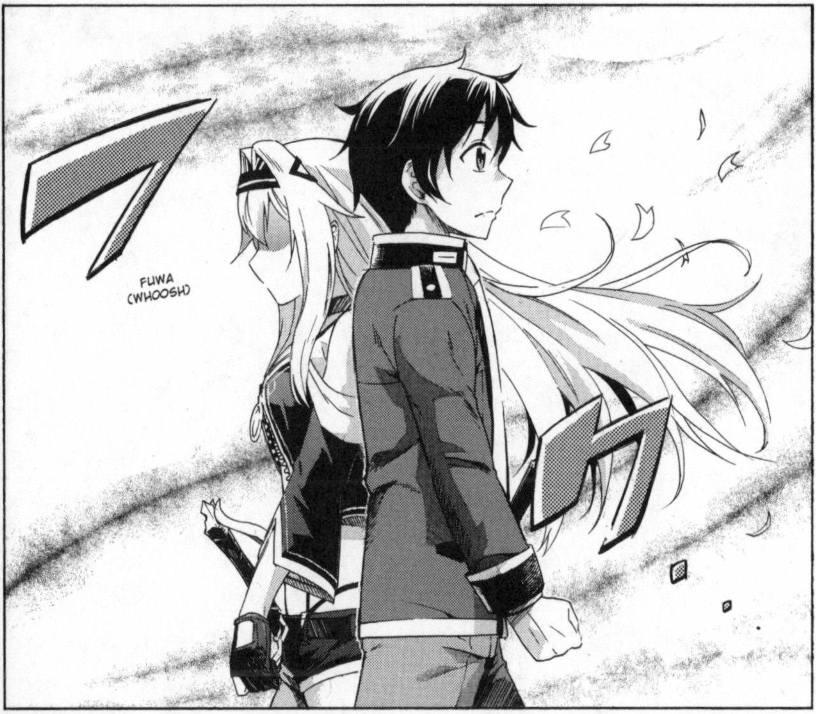
FUWA
(WHOOSH)

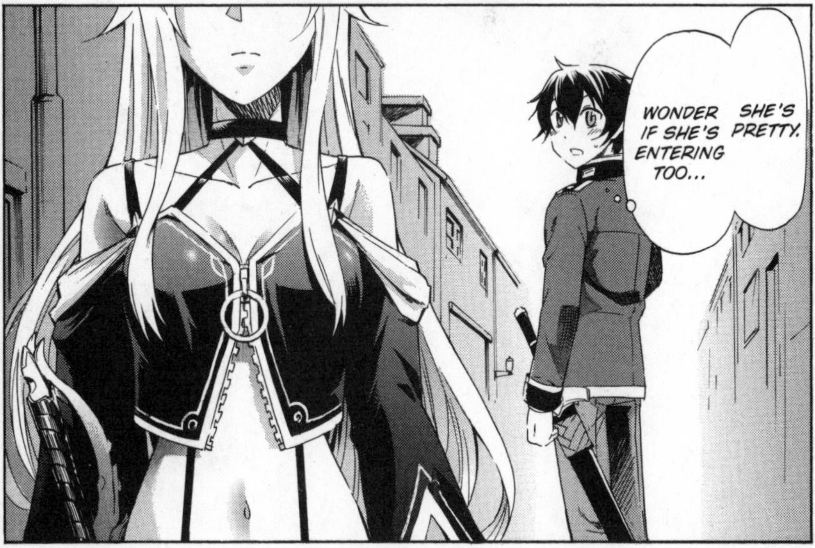
SHE'S PRETTY.
WONDER IF SHE'S ENTERING TOO...

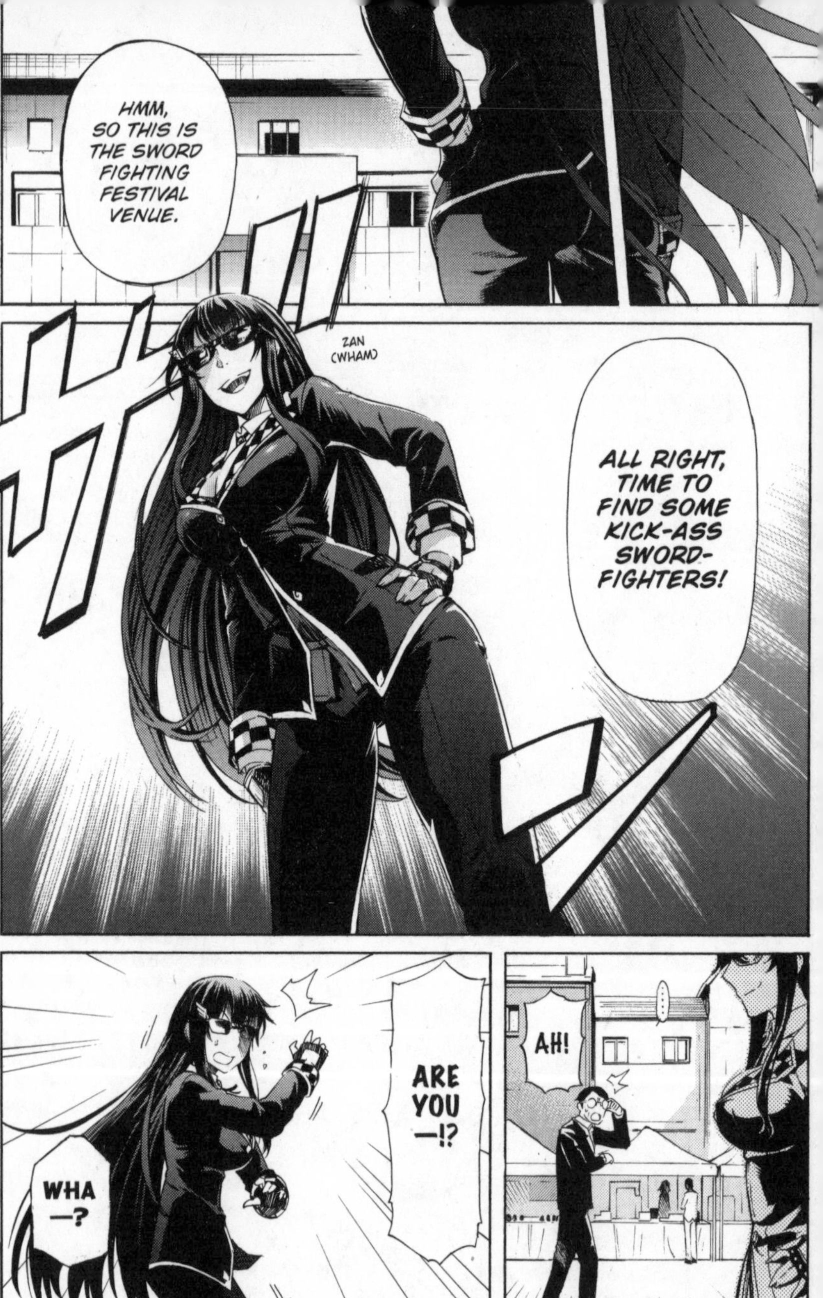
HMM, SO THIS IS THE SWORD FIGHTING FESTIVAL VENUE.
ZAN (WHAM)
ALL RIGHT, TIME TO FIND SOME KICK-ASS SWORD-FIGHTERS!
...
AH!
ARE YOU—!?
WHA—?

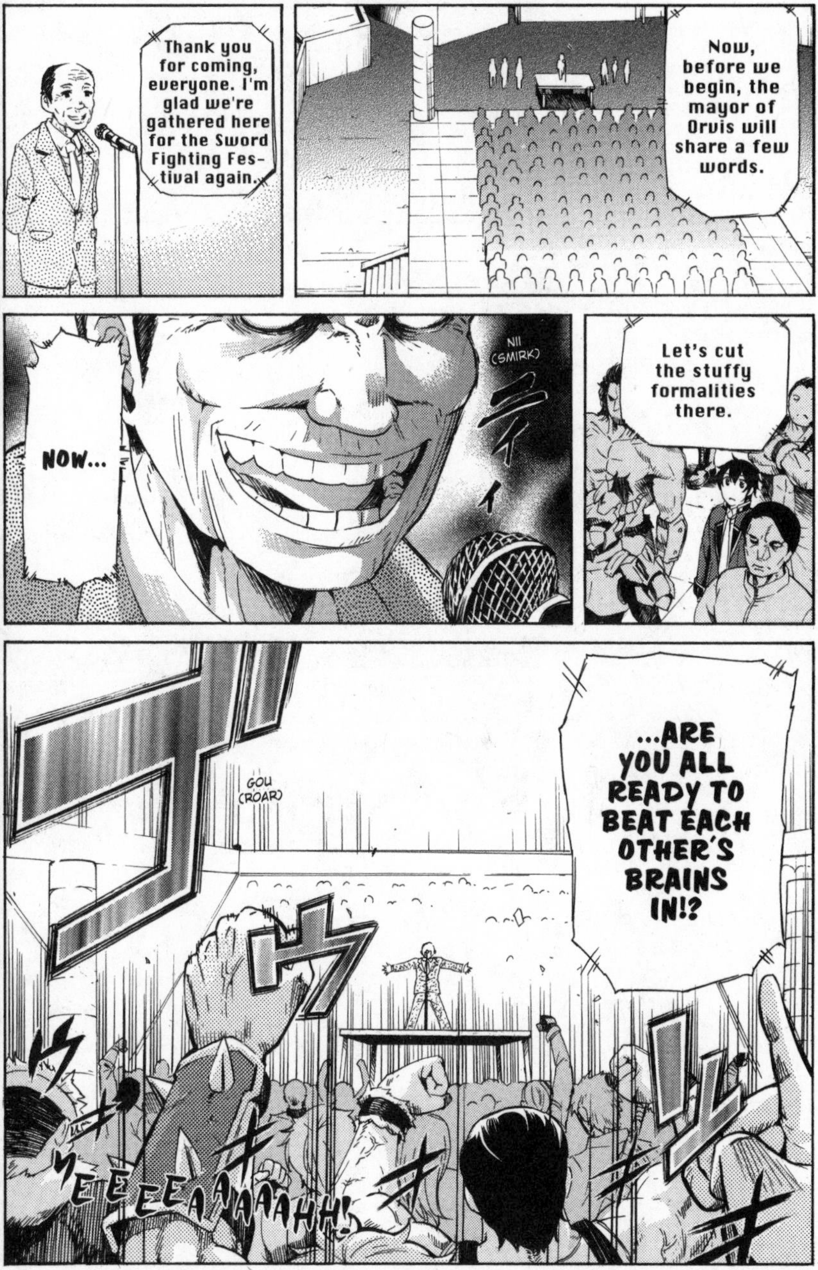
Now, before we begin, the mayor of Orvis will share a few words.
Thank you for coming, everyone. I'm glad we're gathered here for the Sword Fighting Festival again.
Let's cut the stuffy formalities there.
NII (SMIRK)
NOW...
...ARE YOU ALL READY TO BEAT EACH OTHER'S BRAINS IN!?
GOU (ROAR)
YEEEEAAAAAAHH!

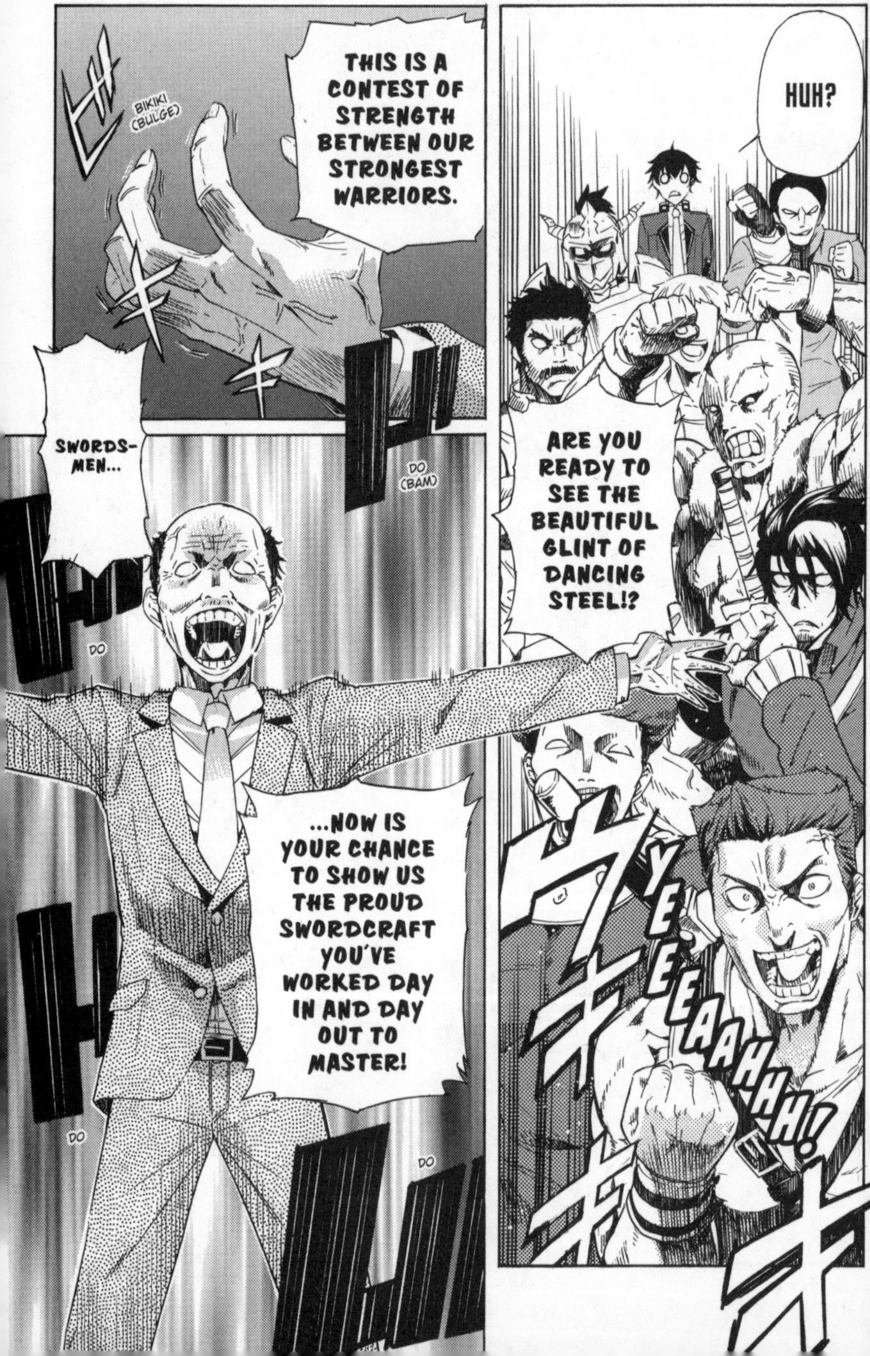
HUH?
ARE YOU READY TO SEE THE BEAUTIFUL GLINT OF DANCING STEEL!?
YEEEAAHHHH!
BIKIKI (BULGE)
THIS IS A CONTEST OF STRENGTH BETWEEN OUR STRONGEST WARRIORS.
SWORDS-MEN...
DO (BAM)
DO
...NOW IS YOUR CHANCE TO SHOW US THE PROUD SWORDCRAFT YOU'VE WORKED DAY IN AND DAY OUT TO MASTER!
DO
DO

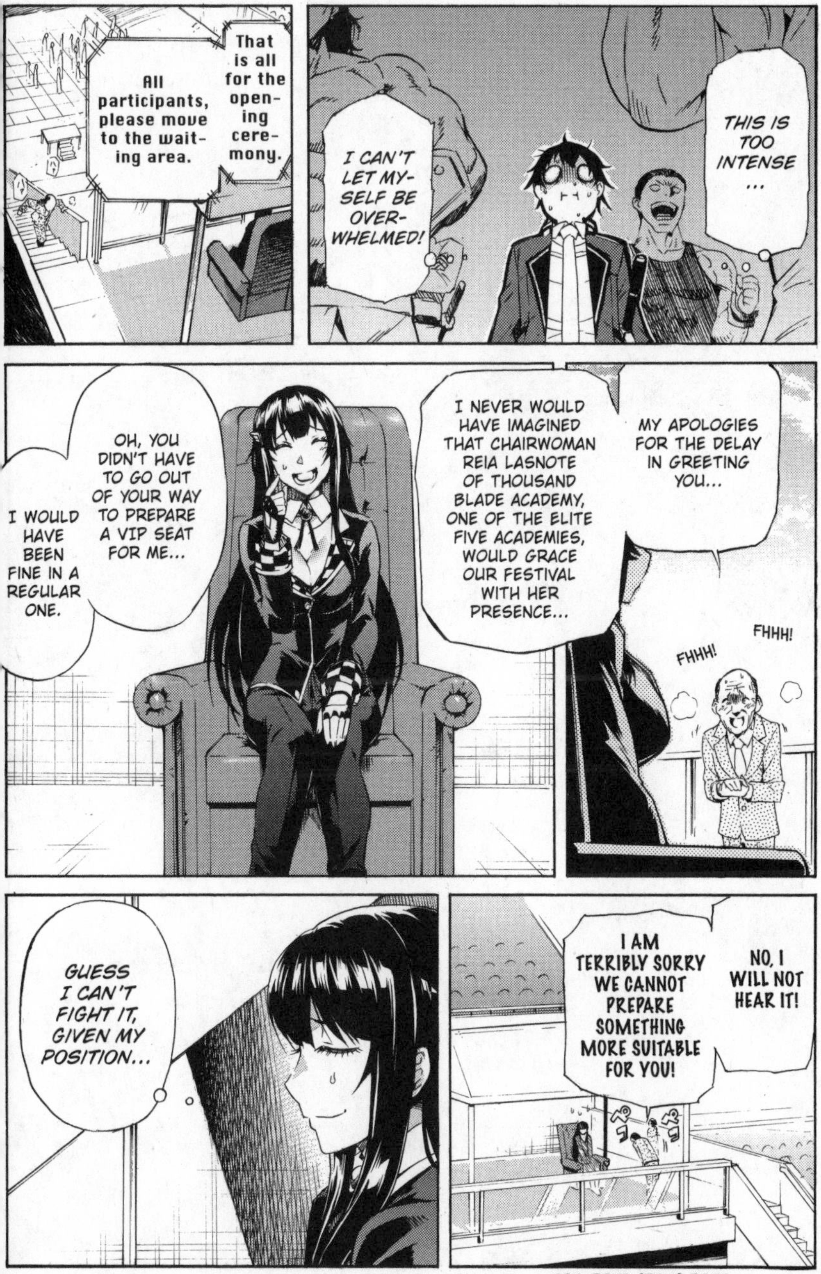
THIS IS TOO INTENSE...
I CAN'T LET MYSELF BE OVERWHELMED!
That is all for the opening ceremony.
All participants, please move to the waiting area.
MY APOLOGIES FOR THE DELAY IN GREETING YOU...
I NEVER WOULD HAVE IMAGINED THAT CHAIRWOMAN REIA LASNOTE OF THOUSAND BLADE ACADEMY, ONE OF THE ELITE FIVE ACADEMIES, WOULD GRACE OUR FESTIVAL WITH HER PRESENCE...
FHHH!
FHHH!
OH, YOU DIDN'T HAVE TO GO OUT OF YOUR WAY TO PREPARE A VIP SEAT FOR ME...
I WOULD HAVE BEEN FINE IN A REGULAR ONE.
NO, I WILL NOT HEAR IT!
I AM TERRIBLY SORRY WE CANNOT PREPARE SOMETHING MORE SUITABLE FOR YOU!
ペコ
ペコ
GUESS I CAN'T FIGHT IT, GIVEN MY POSITION...

SFX: PEKO (BOW) PEKO

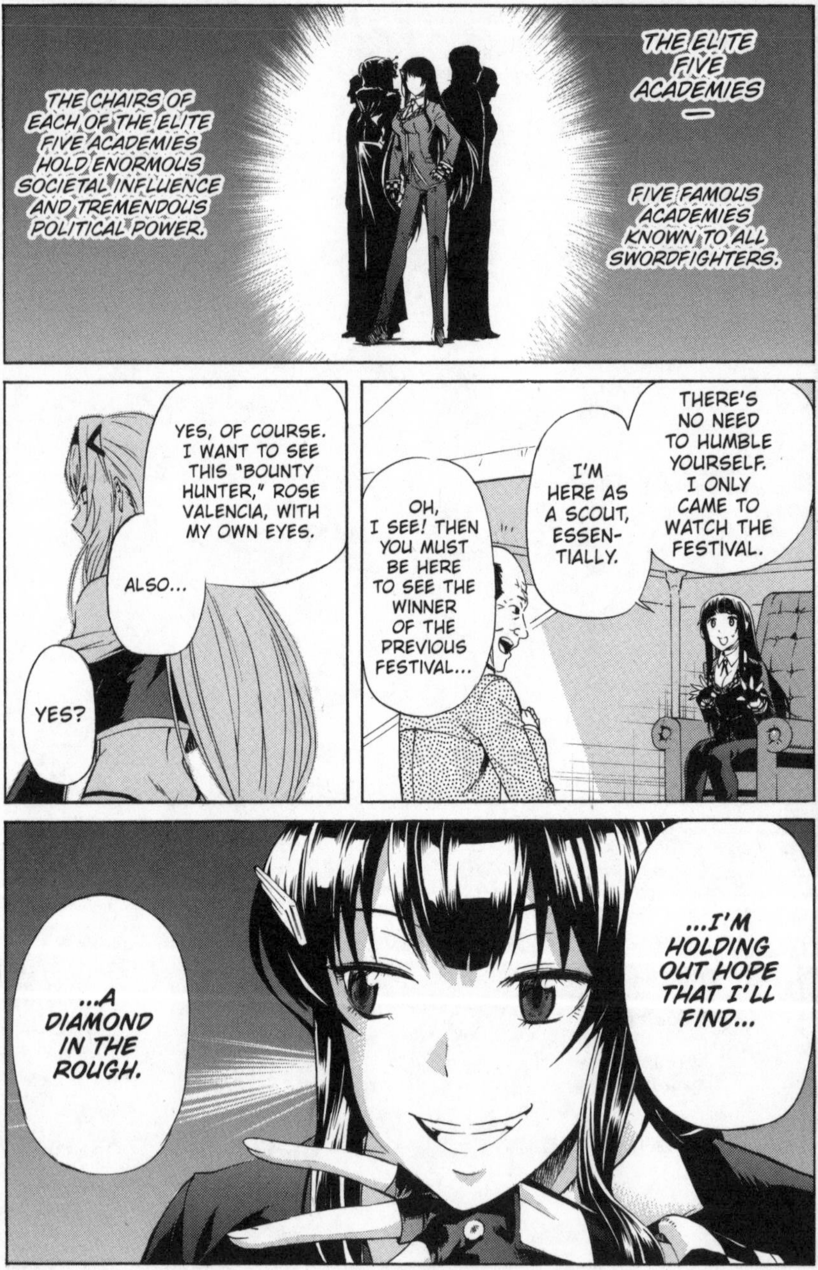
THE ELITE FIVE ACADEMIES—
FIVE FAMOUS ACADEMIES KNOWN TO ALL SWORDFIGHTERS.
THE CHAIRS OF EACH OF THE ELITE FIVE ACADEMIES HOLD ENORMOUS SOCIETAL INFLUENCE AND TREMENDOUS POLITICAL POWER.
THERE'S NO NEED TO HUMBLE YOURSELF. I ONLY CAME TO WATCH THE FESTIVAL.
I'M HERE AS A SCOUT, ESSENTIALLY.
OH, I SEE! THEN YOU MUST BE HERE TO SEE THE WINNER OF THE PREVIOUS FESTIVAL...
YES, OF COURSE. I WANT TO SEE THIS "BOUNTY HUNTER," ROSE VALENCIA, WITH MY OWN EYES.
ALSO...
YES?
...I'M HOLDING OUT HOPE THAT I'LL FIND...
...A DIAMOND IN THE ROUGH.

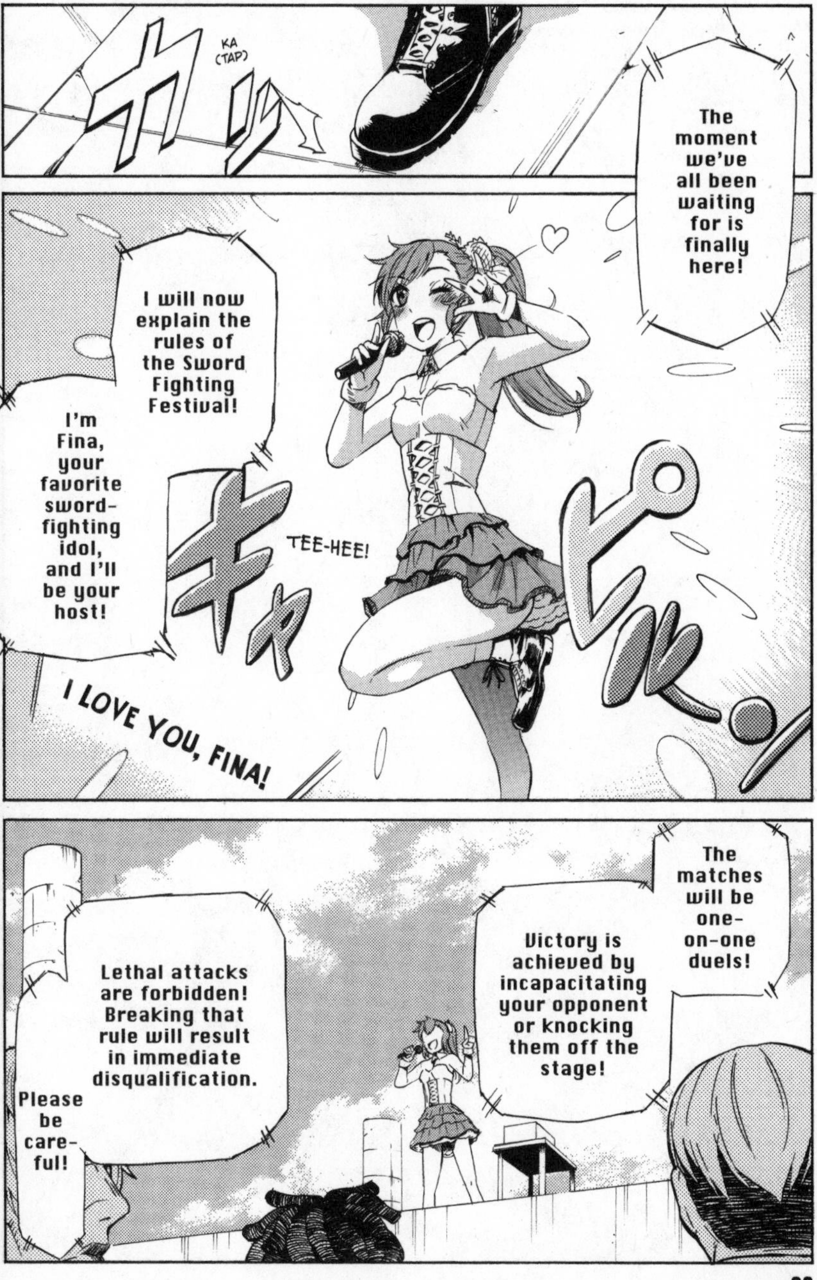
KA (TAP)
The moment we've all been waiting for is finally here!
I will now explain the rules of the Sword Fighting Festival!
I'm Fina, your favorite sword-fighting idol, and I'll be your host!
TEE-HEE!
I LOVE YOU, FINA!
The matches will be one-on-one duels!
Victory is achieved by incapacitating your opponent or knocking them off the stage!
Lethal attacks are forbidden! Breaking that rule will result in immediate disqualification.
Please be care-ful!

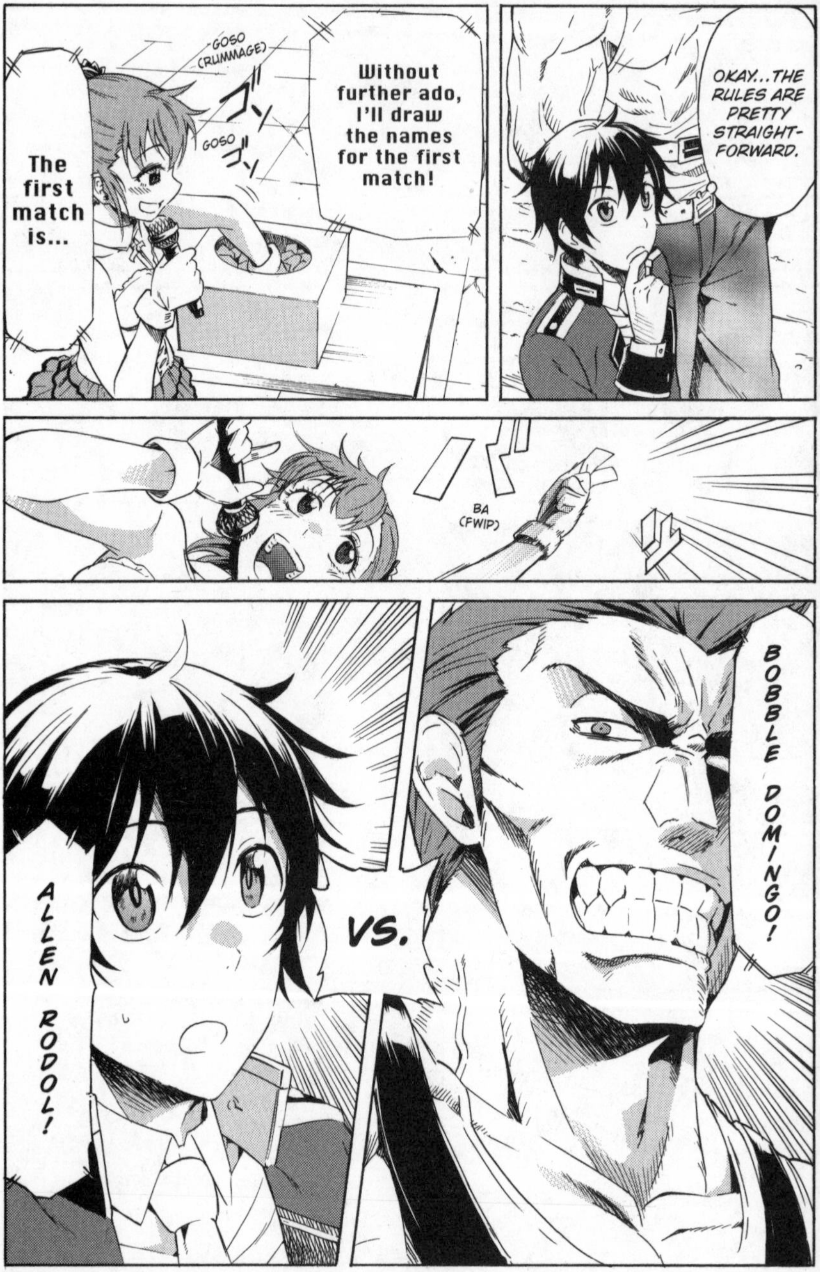
OKAY...THE RULES ARE PRETTY STRAIGHT-FORWARD.
GOSO (RUMMAGE)
Without further ado, I'll draw the names for the first match!
GOSO
The first match is...
BA (FWIP)
BOBBLE DOMINGO!
VS.
ALLEN RODOL!

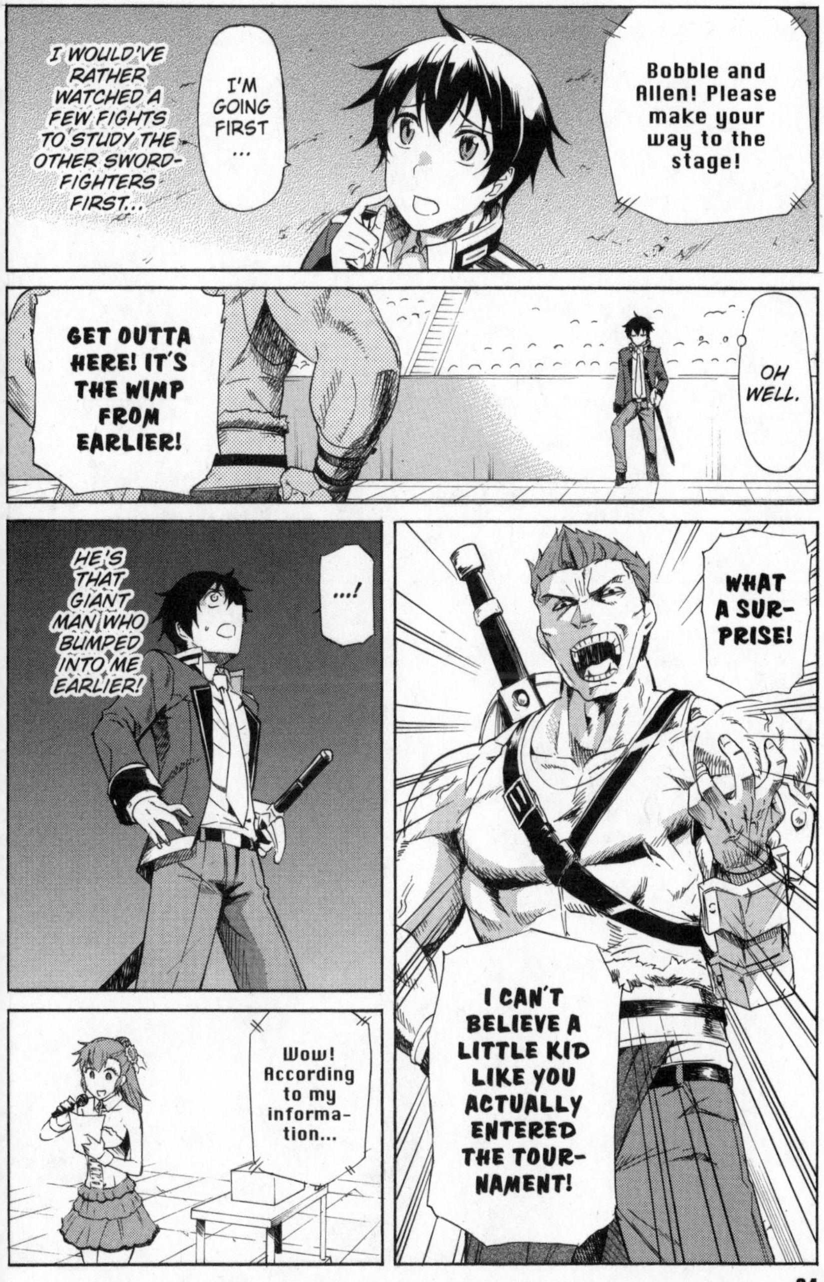
Bobble and Allen! Please make your way to the stage!
I'M GOING FIRST...
I WOULD'VE RATHER WATCHED A FEW FIGHTS TO STUDY THE OTHER SWORD-FIGHTERS FIRST...
OH WELL.
GET OUTTA HERE! IT'S THE WIMP FROM EARLIER!
WHAT A SUR-PRISE!
I CAN'T BELIEVE A LITTLE KID LIKE YOU ACTUALLY ENTERED THE TOUR-NAMENT!
...!
HE'S THAT GIANT MAN WHO BUMPED INTO ME EARLIER!
Wow! According to my informa-tion...

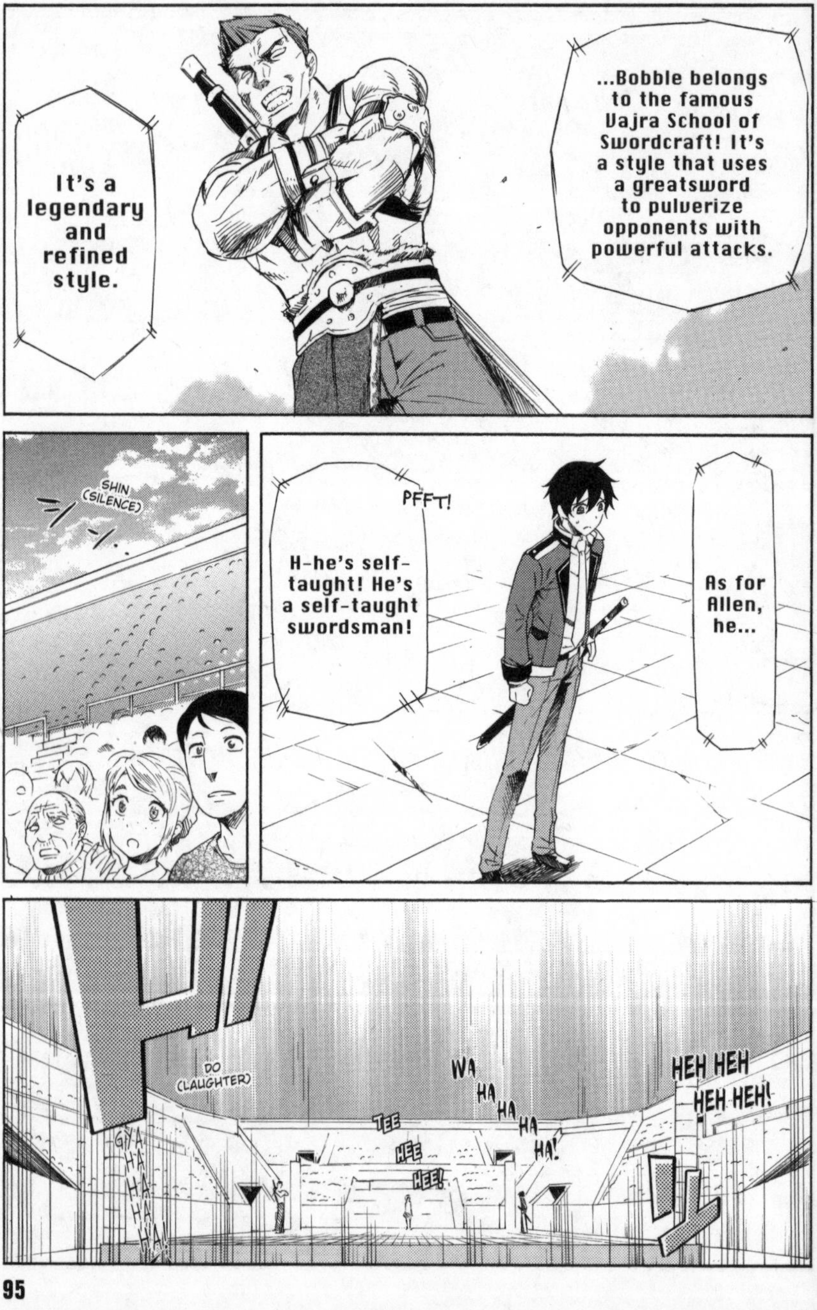
...Bobble belongs to the famous Vajra School of Swordcraft! It's a style that uses a greatsword to pulverize opponents with powerful attacks.
It's a legendary and refined style.
As for Allen, he...
PFFT!
H-he's self-taught! He's a self-taught swordsman!
SHIN (SILENCE)
HEH HEH HEH HEH!
WA HA HA HA HA!
TEE HEE HEE!
DO (LAUGHTER)
GYA HA HA HA HA HA!

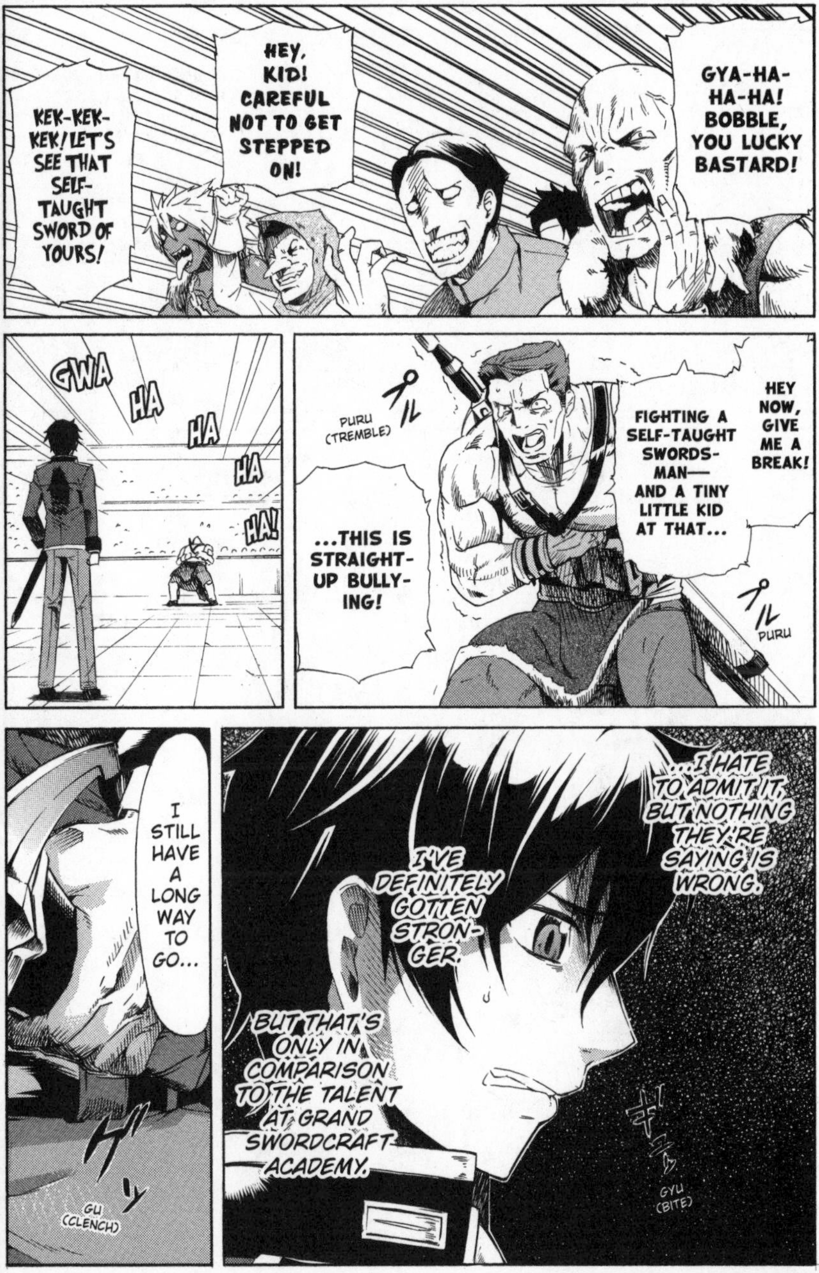
GYA-HA-HA-HA! BOBBLE, YOU LUCKY BASTARD!
HEY, KID! CAREFUL NOT TO GET STEPPED ON!
KEK-KEK-KEK! LET'S SEE THAT SELF-TAUGHT SWORD OF YOURS!
HEY NOW, GIVE ME A BREAK!
FIGHTING A SELF-TAUGHT SWORDSMAN— AND A TINY LITTLE KID AT THAT...
PURU (TREMBLE)
...THIS IS STRAIGHT-UP BULLYING!
PURU
GWA HA HA HA HA!
...I HATE TO ADMIT IT, BUT NOTHING THEY'RE SAYING IS WRONG.
I'VE DEFINITELY GOTTEN STRONGER.
BUT THAT'S ONLY IN COMPARISON TO THE TALENT AT GRAND SWORDCRAFT ACADEMY.
GYU (BITE)
I STILL HAVE A LONG WAY TO GO...
GU (CLENCH)

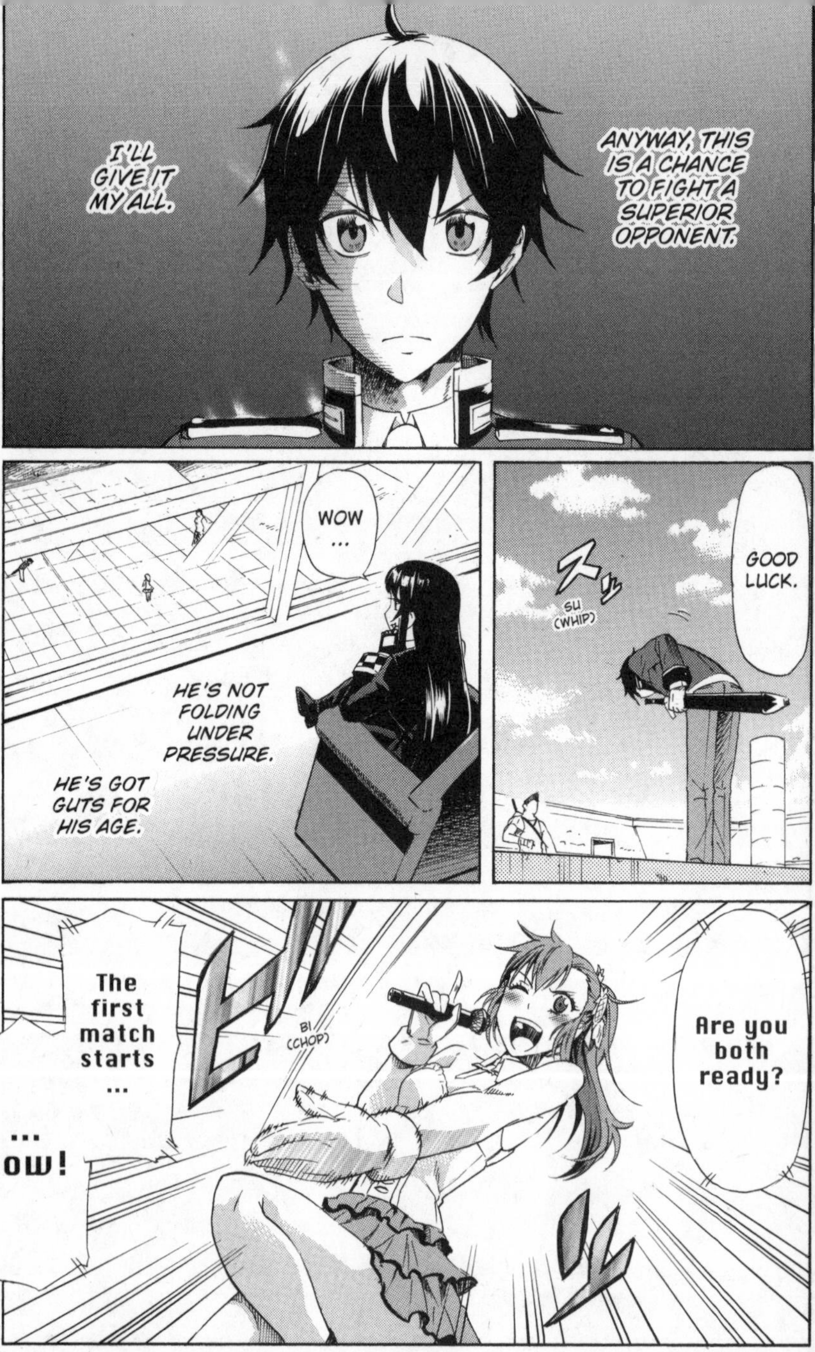
ANYWAY, THIS IS A CHANCE TO FIGHT A SUPERIOR OPPONENT.
I'LL GIVE IT MY ALL.
GOOD LUCK.
SU (WHIP)
WOW ...
HE'S NOT FOLDING UNDER PRESSURE.
HE'S GOT GUTS FOR HIS AGE.
Are you both ready?
BI (CHOP)
The first match starts ...
... now!

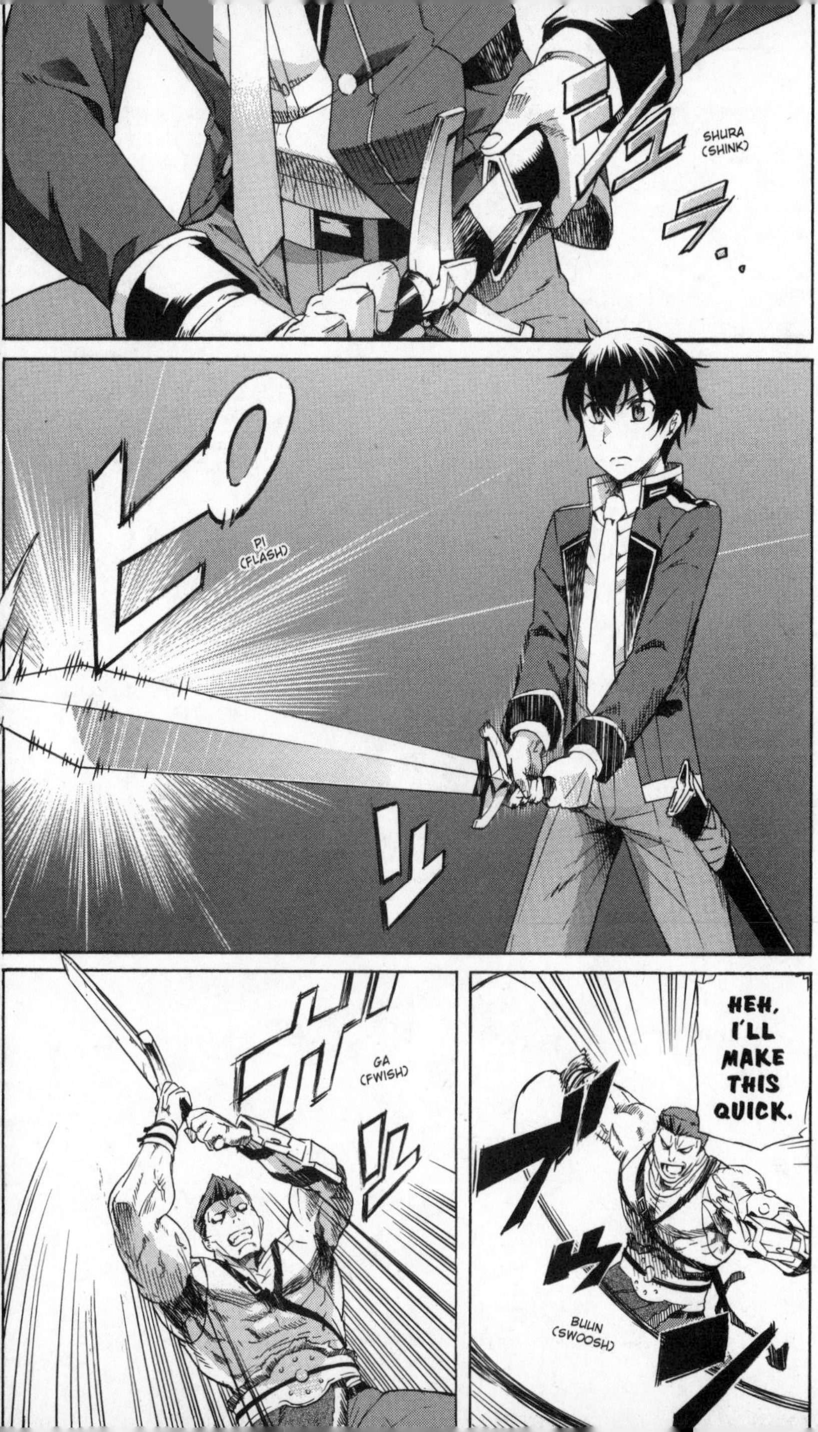
SHURA
(SHINK)
PI
(FLASH)
HEH, I'LL MAKE THIS QUICK.
BUUN
(SWOOSH)
GA
(FWISH)

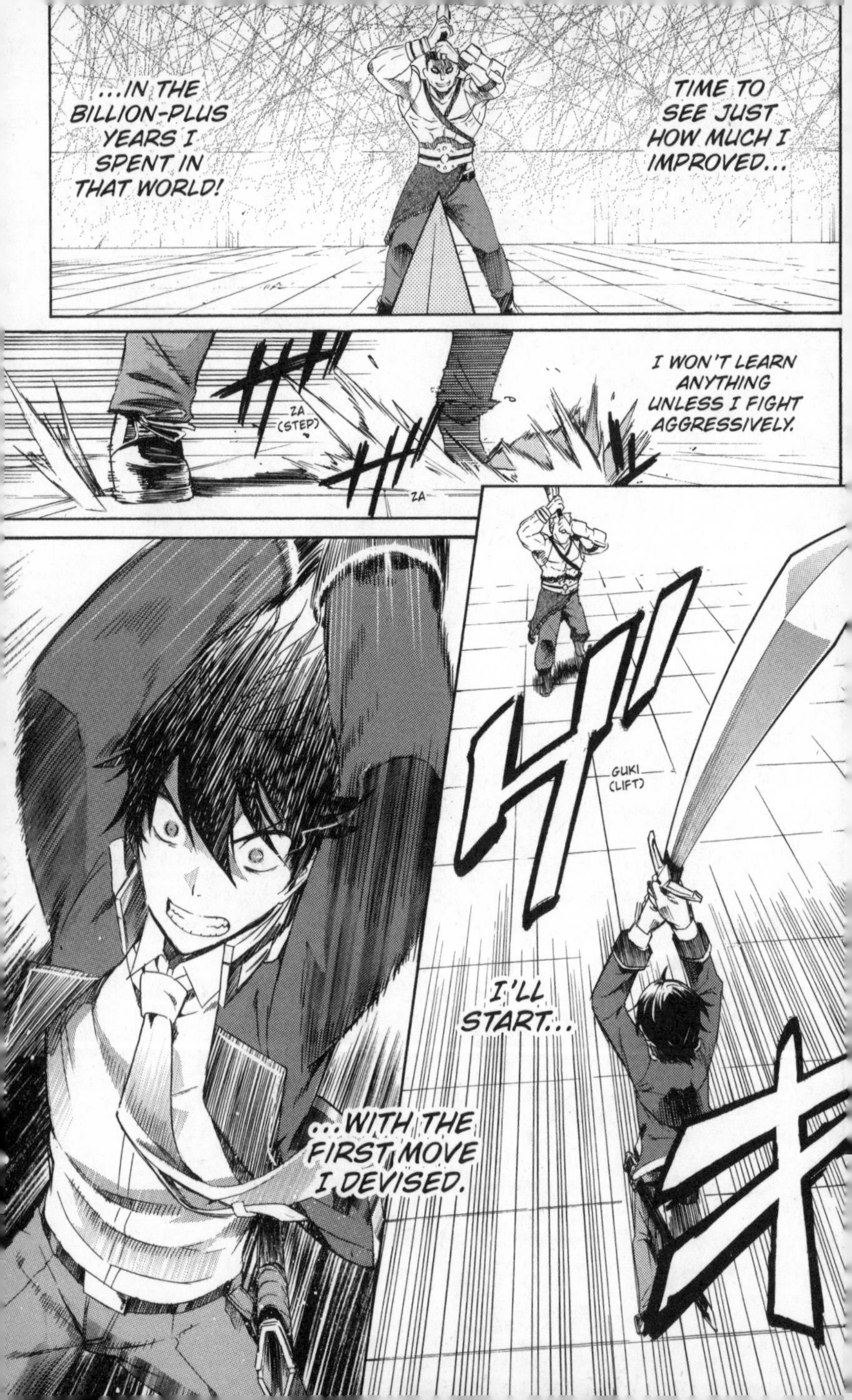
TIME TO SEE JUST HOW MUCH I IMPROVED...
...IN THE BILLION-PLUS YEARS I SPENT IN THAT WORLD!
I WON'T LEARN ANYTHING UNLESS I FIGHT AGGRESSIVELY.
ZA (STEP)
ZA
GUKI (LIFT)
I'LL START...
...WITH THE FIRST MOVE I DEVISED.

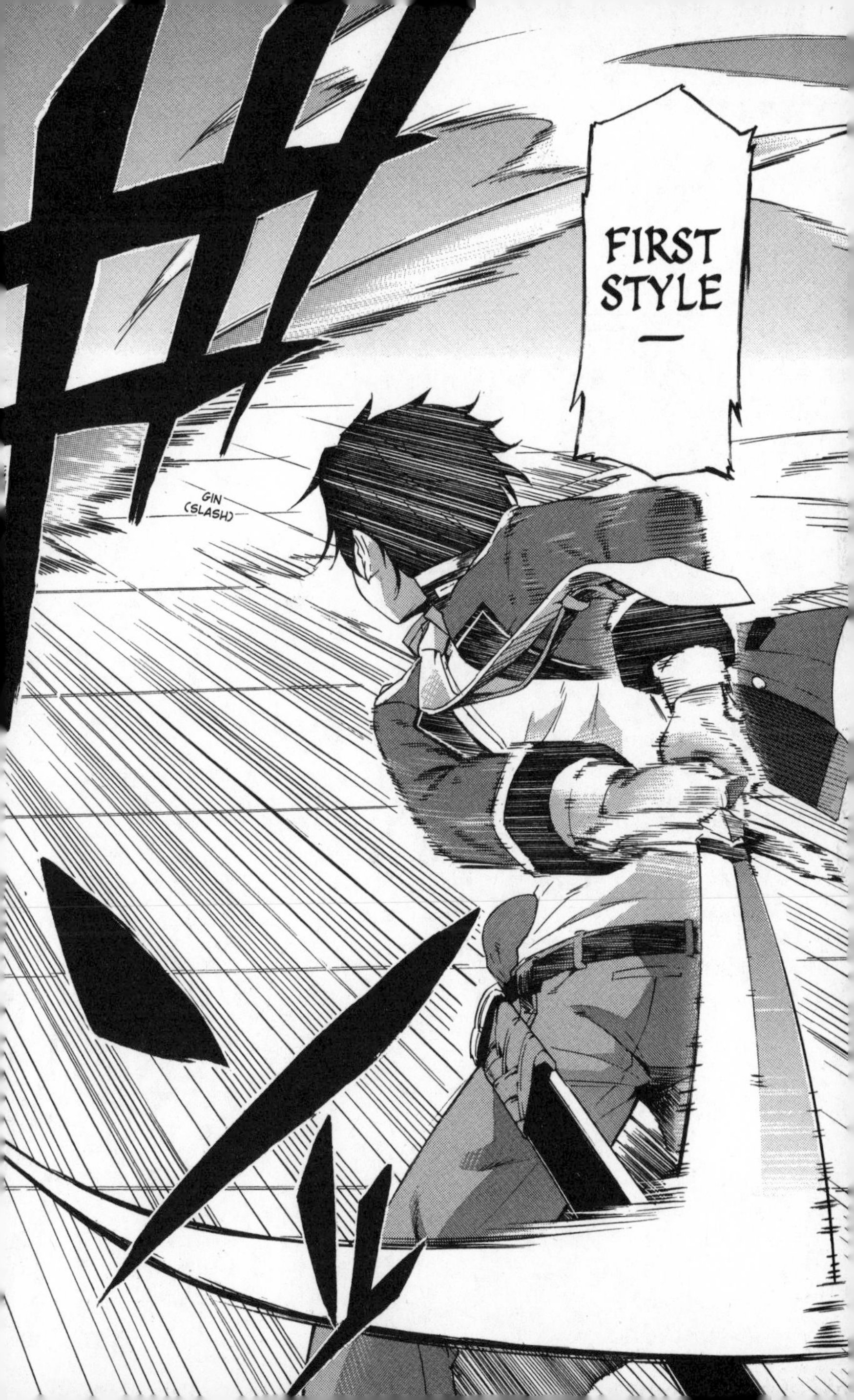
FIRST STYLE —
GIN (SLASH)

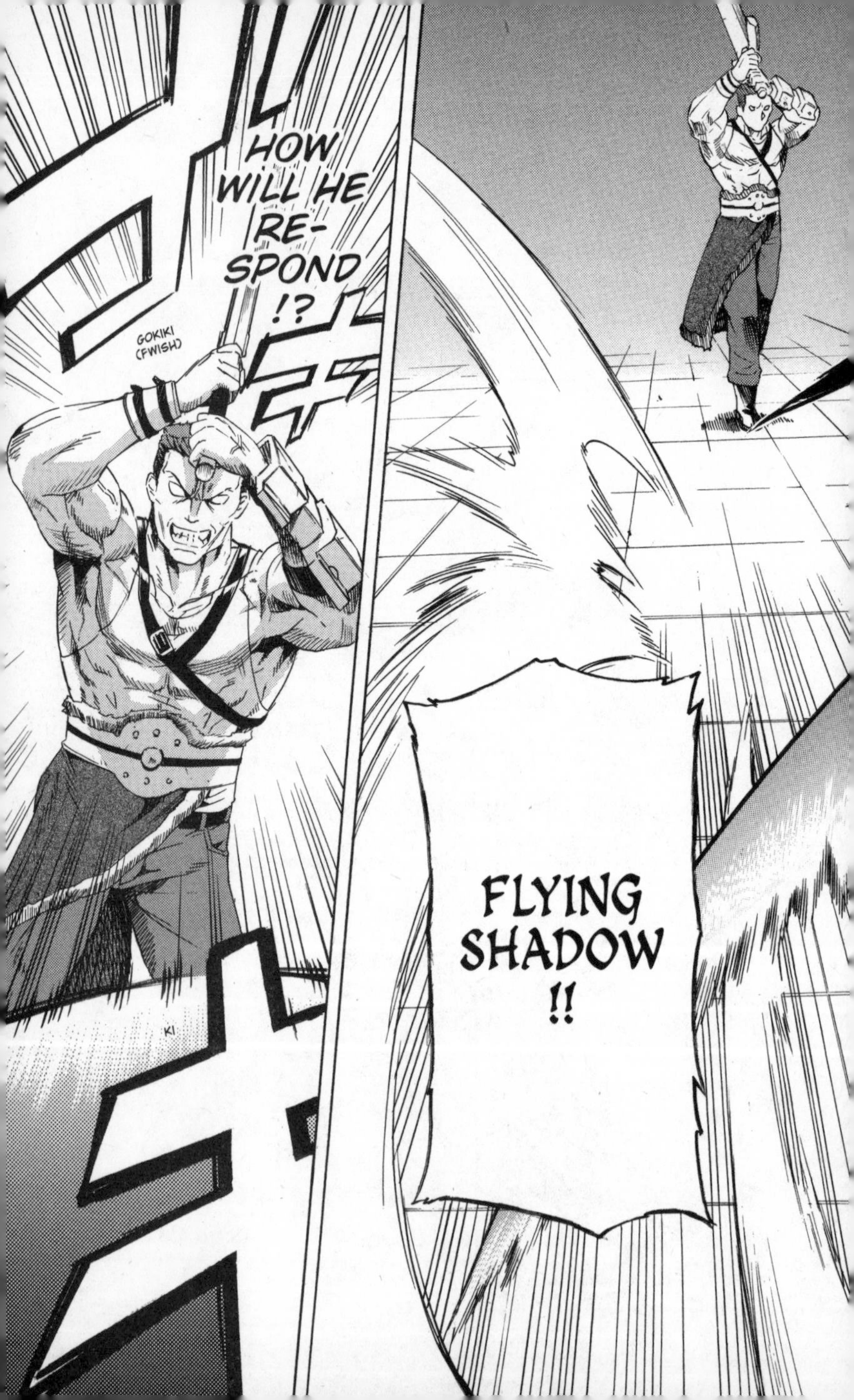
FLYING SHADOW !!
HOW WILL HE RE-SPOND !?
GOKIKI (FWISH)
KI

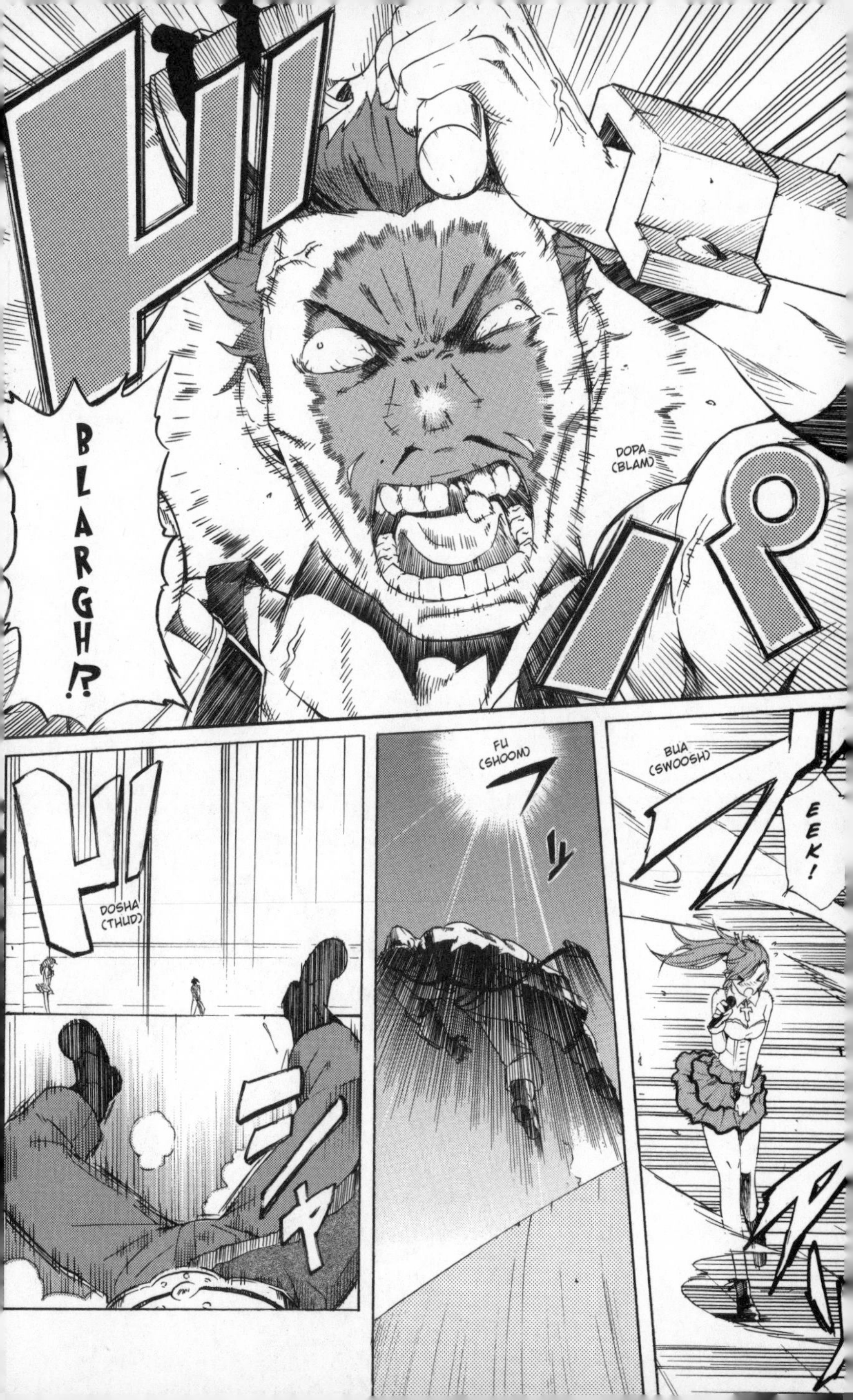
DOPA (BLAM)
BLARGH!?
BUA (SWOOSH)
EEK!
FU (SHOOM)
DOSHA (THUD)

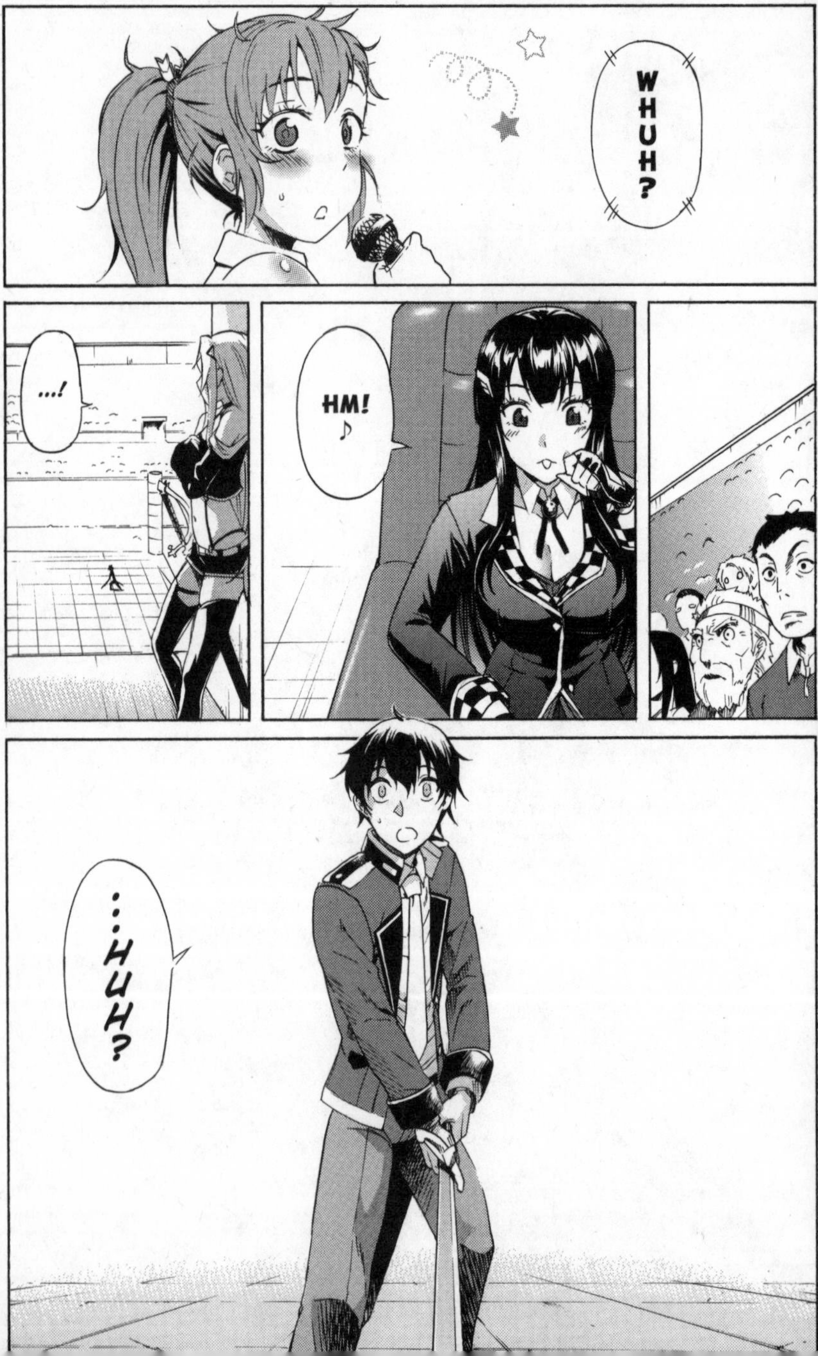
WHUH?
HM! ♪
...!
...HUH?

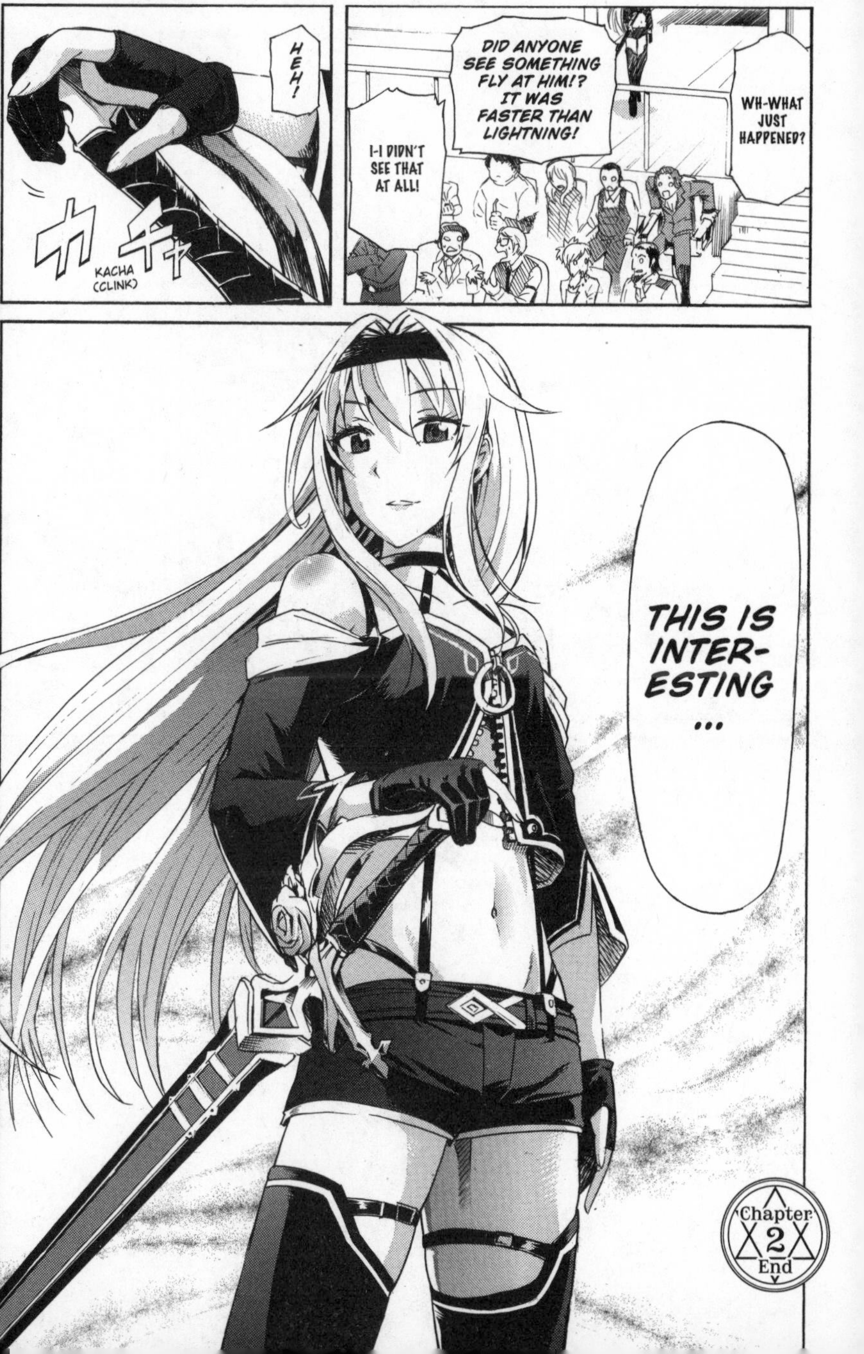
WH-WHAT JUST HAPPENED?
DID ANYONE SEE SOMETHING FLY AT HIM!? IT WAS FASTER THAN LIGHTNING!
I-I DIDN'T SEE THAT AT ALL!
HEH!
KACHA (CLINK)
THIS IS INTER-ESTING ...
Chapter 2 End

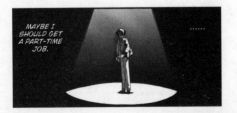

MAYBE I
SHOULD GET
A PART-TIME
JOB.

......

I KEPT PRESSING THE 100-MILLION-YEAR BUTTON AND CAME OUT ON TOP

~THE UNBEATABLE REJECT SWORDSMAN~

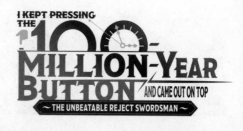

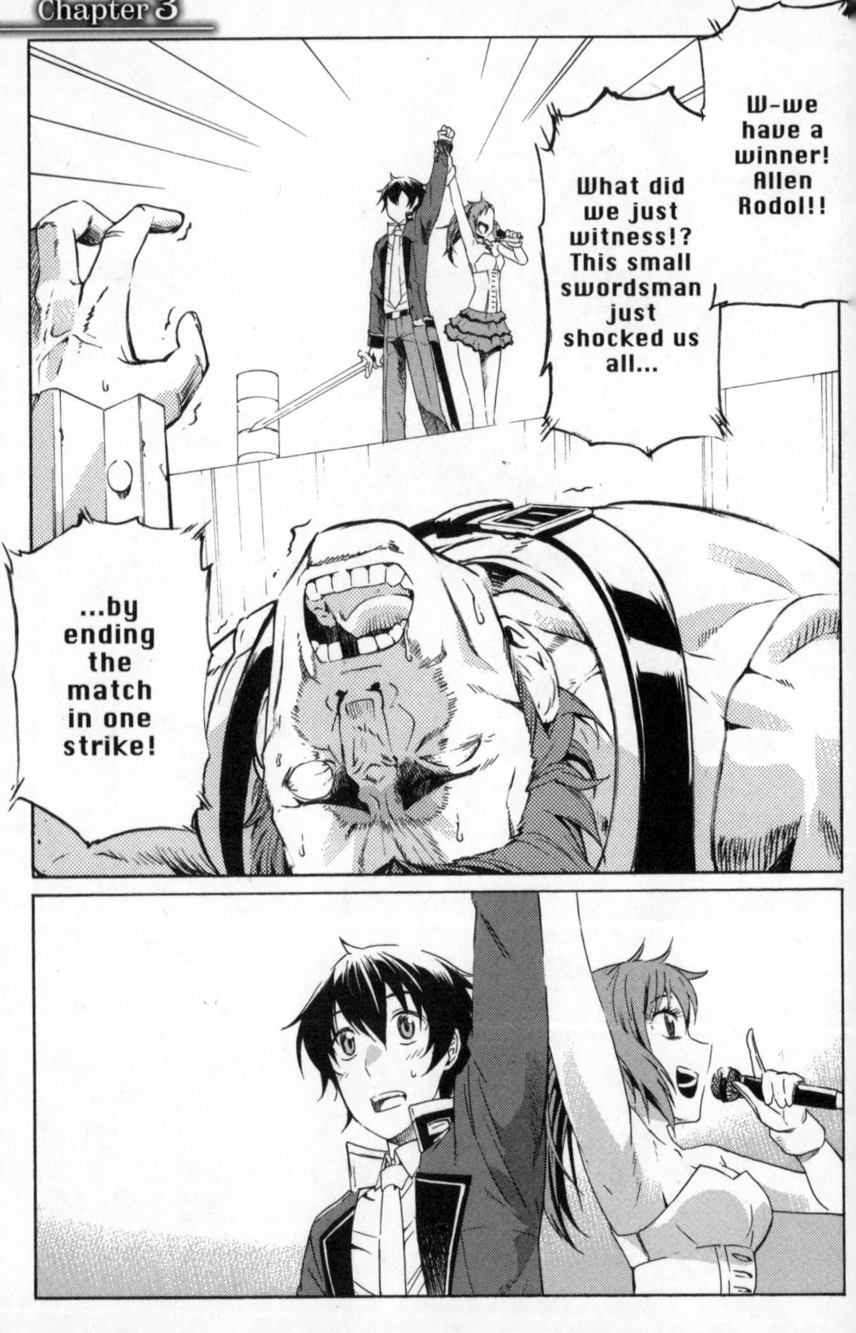
W-we have a winner! Allen Rodol!!
What did we just witness!? This small swordsman just shocked us all...
...by ending the match in one strike!

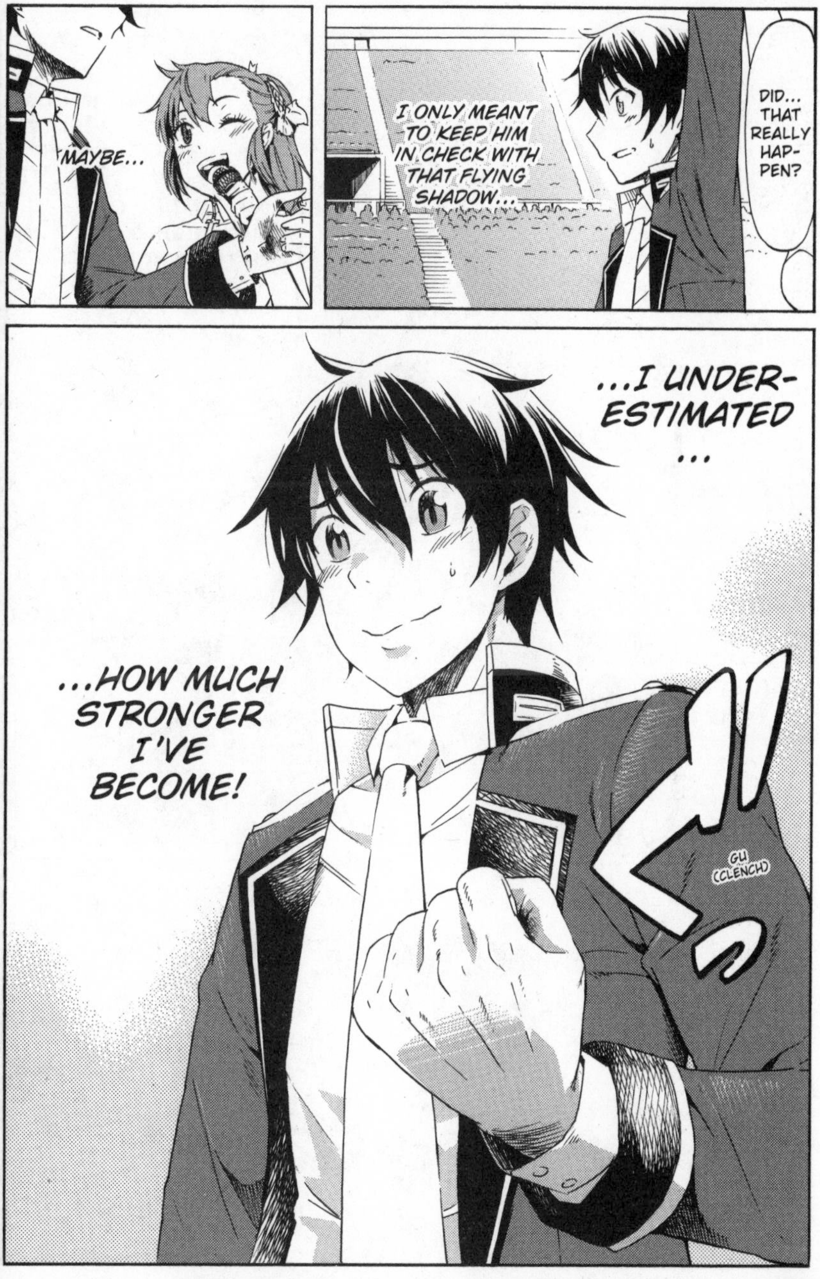
DID... THAT REALLY HAP-PEN?
I ONLY MEANT TO KEEP HIM IN CHECK WITH THAT FLYING SHADOW...
MAYBE...
...I UNDER-ESTIMATED...
GU (CLENCH)
...HOW MUCH STRONGER I'VE BECOME!

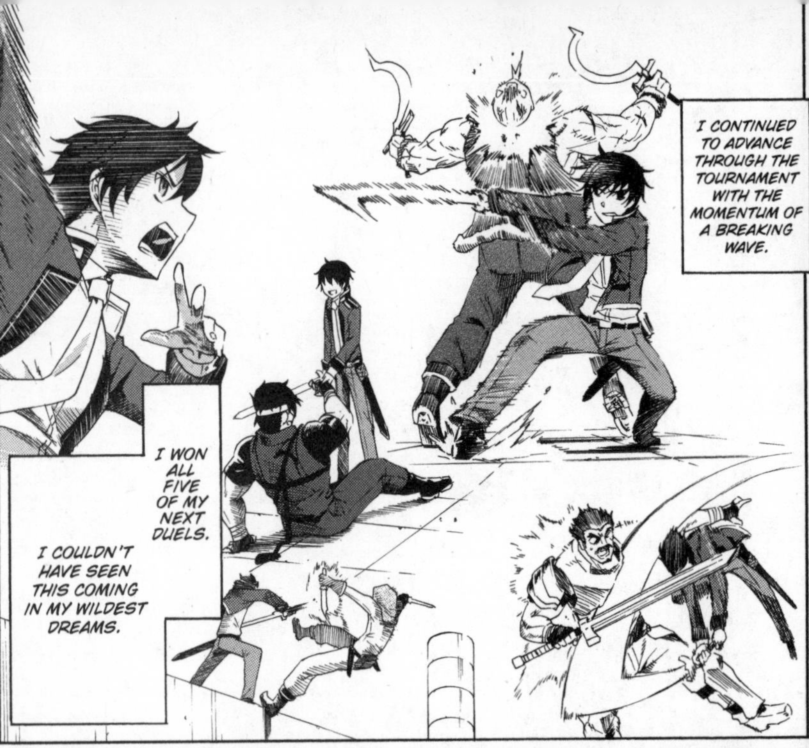
I CONTINUED TO ADVANCE THROUGH THE TOURNAMENT WITH THE MOMENTUM OF A BREAKING WAVE.
I WON ALL FIVE OF MY NEXT DUELS.
I COULDN'T HAVE SEEN THIS COMING IN MY WILDEST DREAMS.

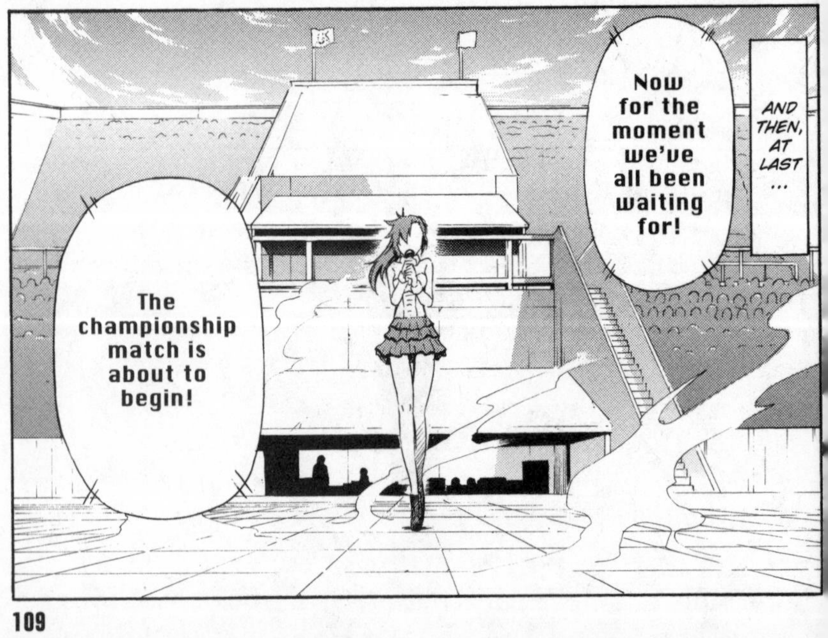
AND THEN, AT LAST ...
Now for the moment we've all been waiting for!
The championship match is about to begin!

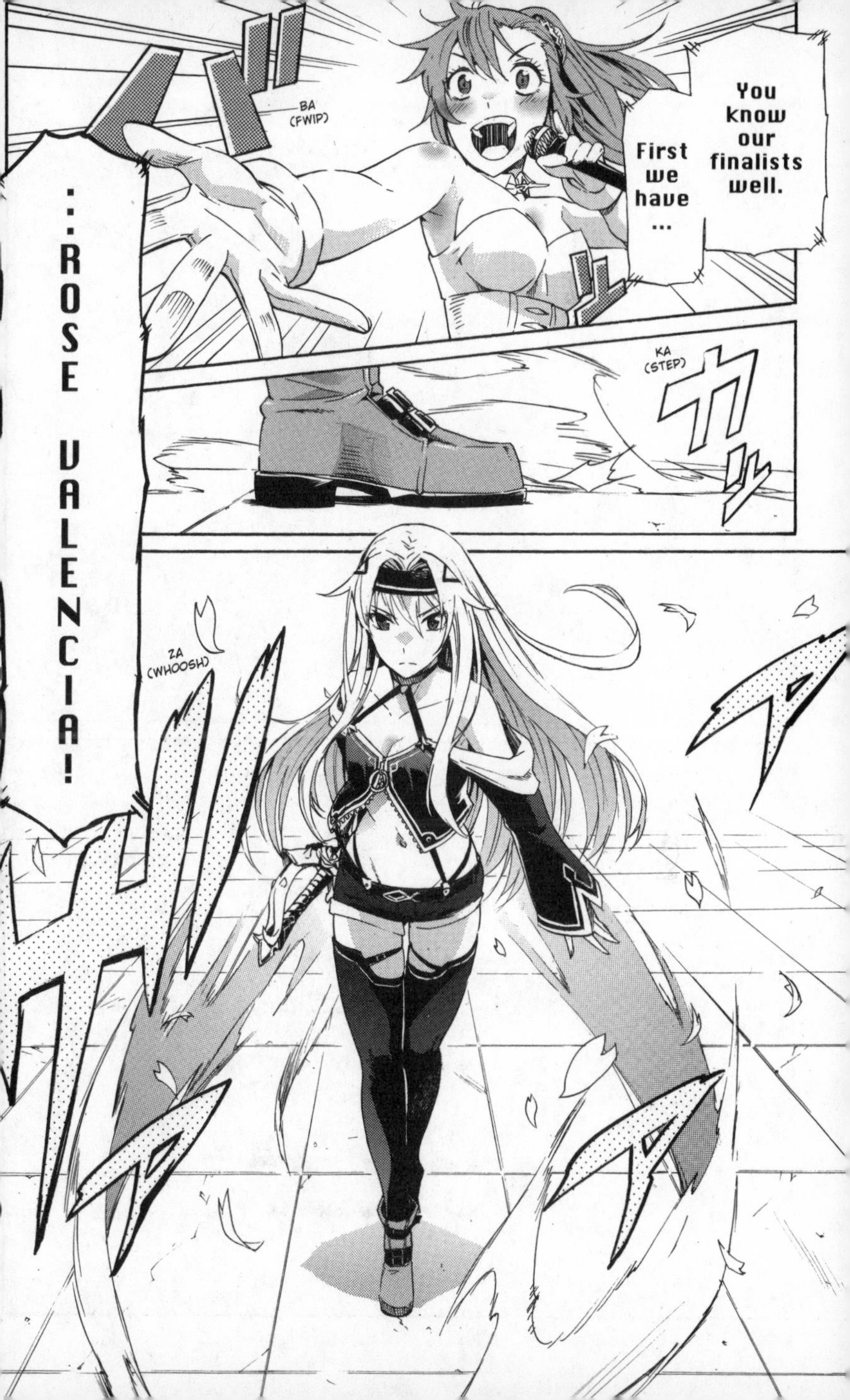
You know our finalists well.
First we have ...
BA (FWIP)
...ROSE VALENCIA!
KA (STEP)
ZA (WHOOSH)

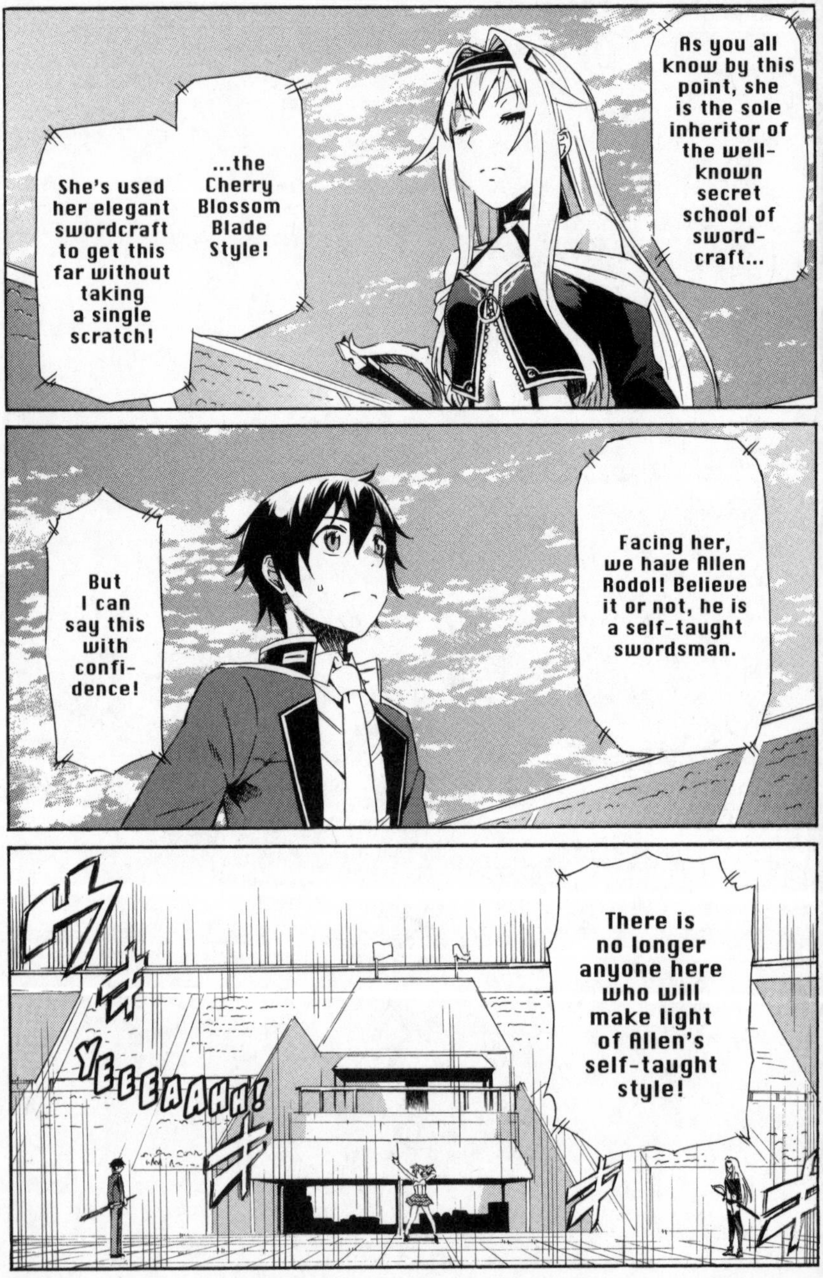
As you all know by this point, she is the sole inheritor of the well-known secret school of sword-craft...
...the Cherry Blossom Blade Style!
She's used her elegant swordcraft to get this far without taking a single scratch!
Facing her, we have Allen Rodol! Believe it or not, he is a self-taught swordsman.
But I can say this with confidence!
There is no longer anyone here who will make light of Allen's self-taught style!
YEEEAAHH!

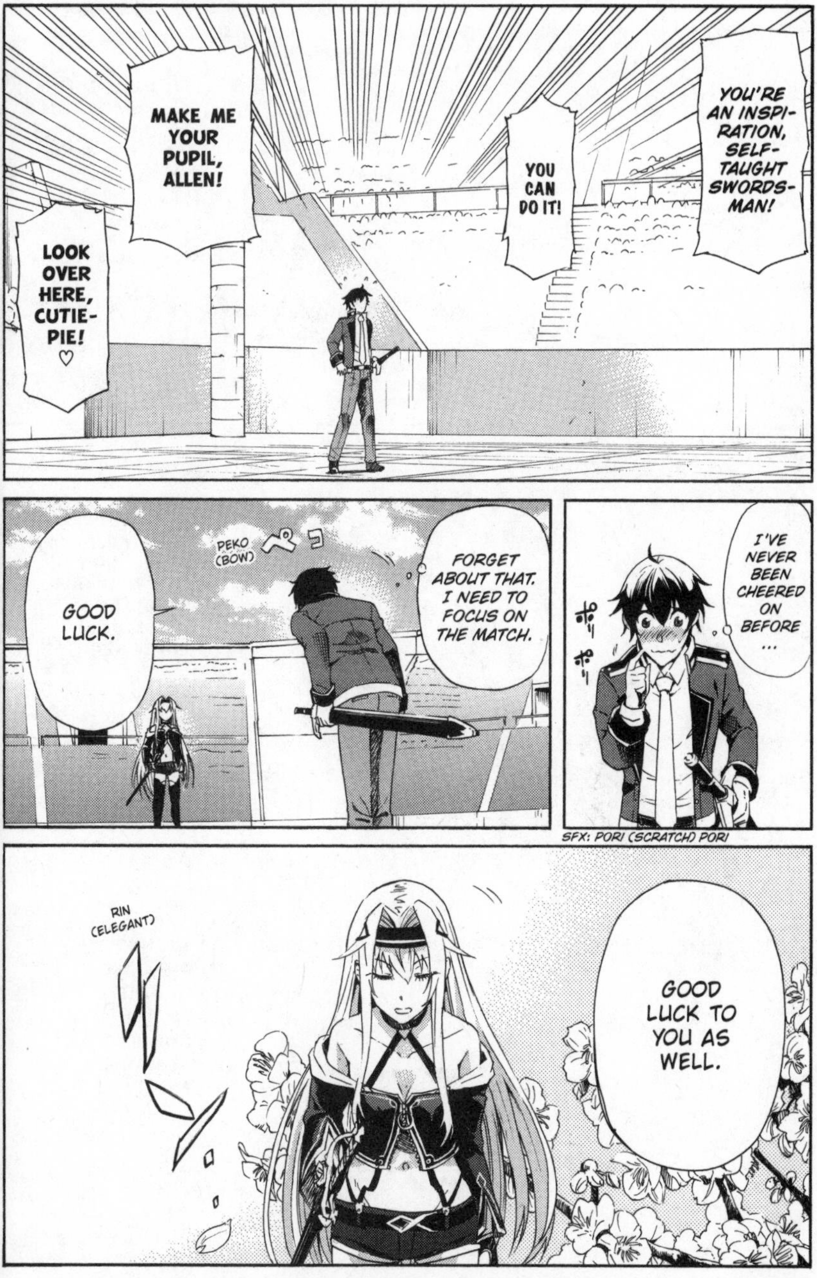
YOU'RE AN INSPIRATION, SELF-TAUGHT SWORDSMAN!
YOU CAN DO IT!
MAKE ME YOUR PUPIL, ALLEN!
LOOK OVER HERE, CUTIE-PIE! ♡
I'VE NEVER BEEN CHEERED ON BEFORE...
SFX: PORI (SCRATCH) PORI
FORGET ABOUT THAT. I NEED TO FOCUS ON THE MATCH.
PEKO (BOW)
GOOD LUCK.
GOOD LUCK TO YOU AS WELL.
RIN (ELEGANT)

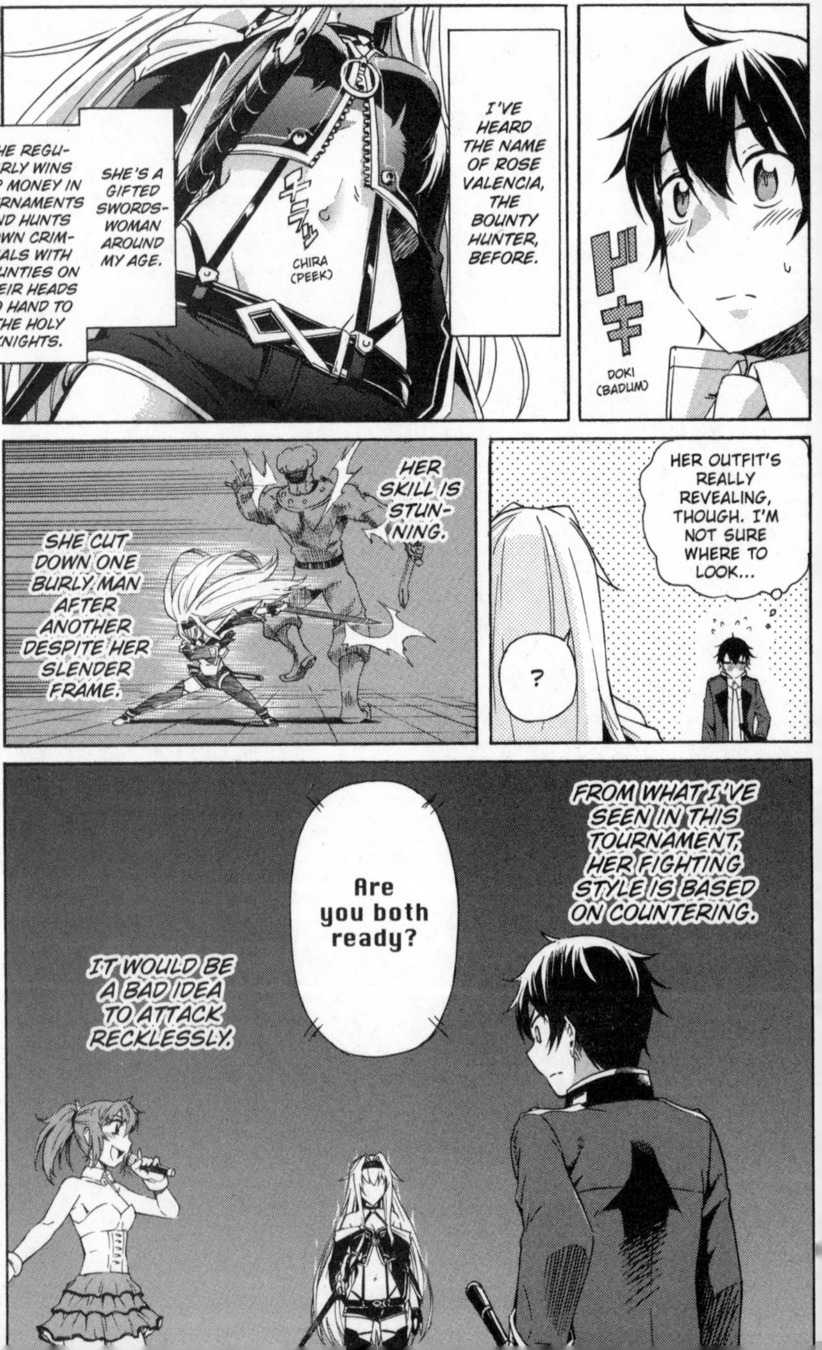
DOKI (BADUM)
I'VE HEARD THE NAME OF ROSE VALENCIA, THE BOUNTY HUNTER, BEFORE.
CHIRA (PEEK)
SHE'S A GIFTED SWORDS-WOMAN AROUND MY AGE.
SHE REGU-LARLY WINS TOP MONEY IN TOURNAMENTS AND HUNTS DOWN CRIM-INALS WITH BOUNTIES ON THEIR HEADS TO HAND TO THE HOLY KNIGHTS.
HER OUTFIT'S REALLY REVEALING, THOUGH. I'M NOT SURE WHERE TO LOOK...
?
HER SKILL IS STUN-NING.
SHE CUT DOWN ONE BURLY MAN AFTER ANOTHER DESPITE HER SLENDER FRAME.
FROM WHAT I'VE SEEN IN THIS TOURNAMENT, HER FIGHTING STYLE IS BASED ON COUNTERING.
Are you both ready?
IT WOULD BE A BAD IDEA TO ATTACK RECKLESSLY.

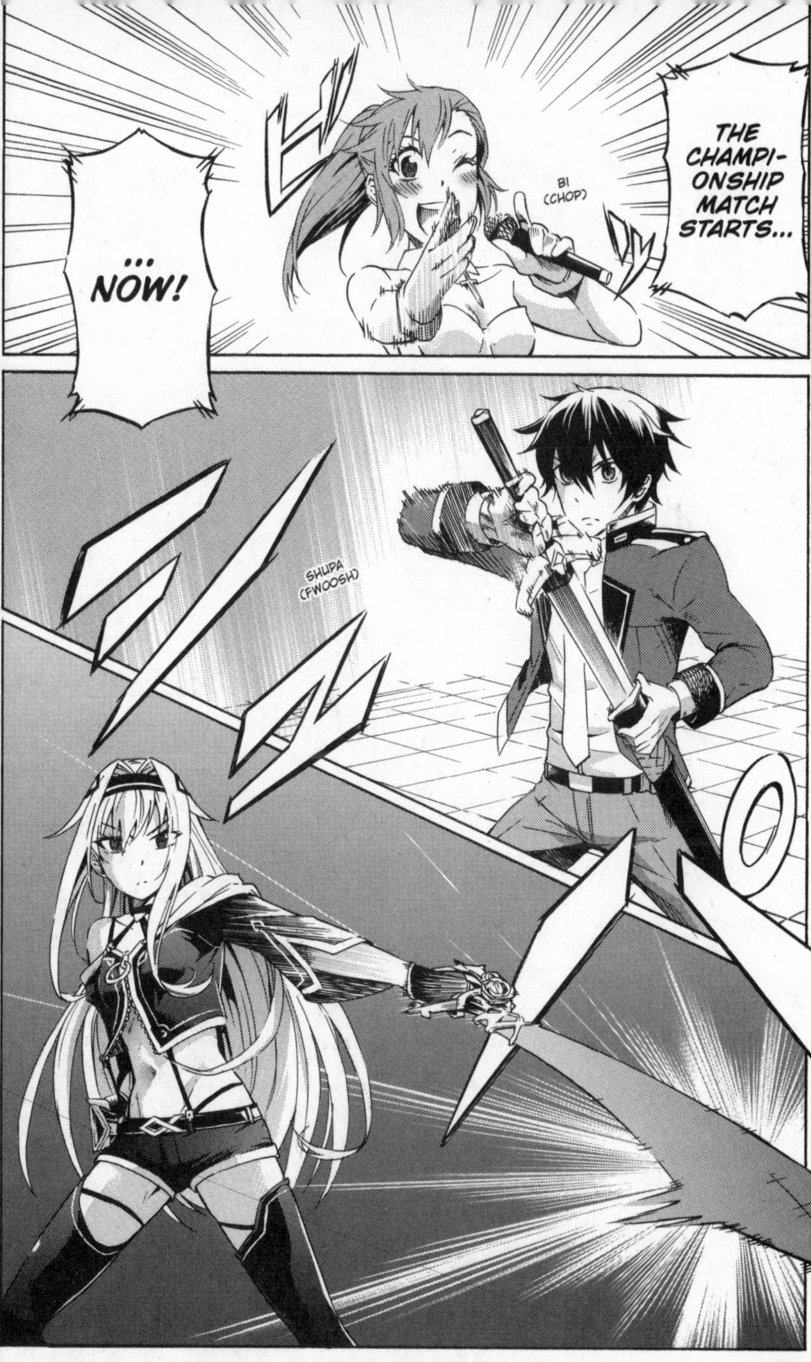
THE CHAMPI-ONSHIP MATCH STARTS...
BI (CHOP)
... NOW!
SHUPA (FWOOSH)

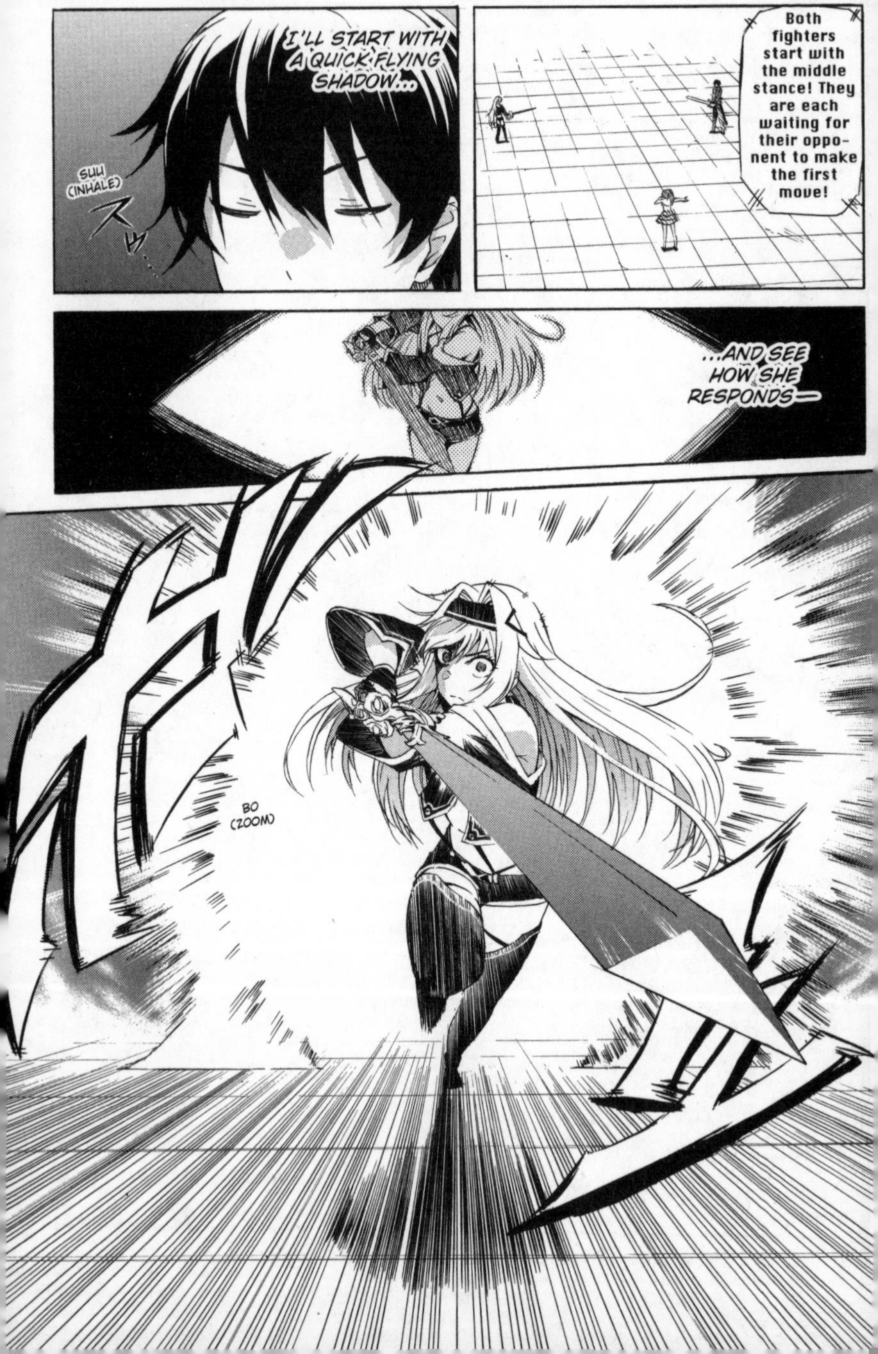
Both fighters start with the middle stance! They are each waiting for their opponent to make the first move!
I'LL START WITH A QUICK FLYING SHADOW...
SUU (INHALE)
スゥ…
...AND SEE HOW SHE RESPONDS—
BO (ZOOM)

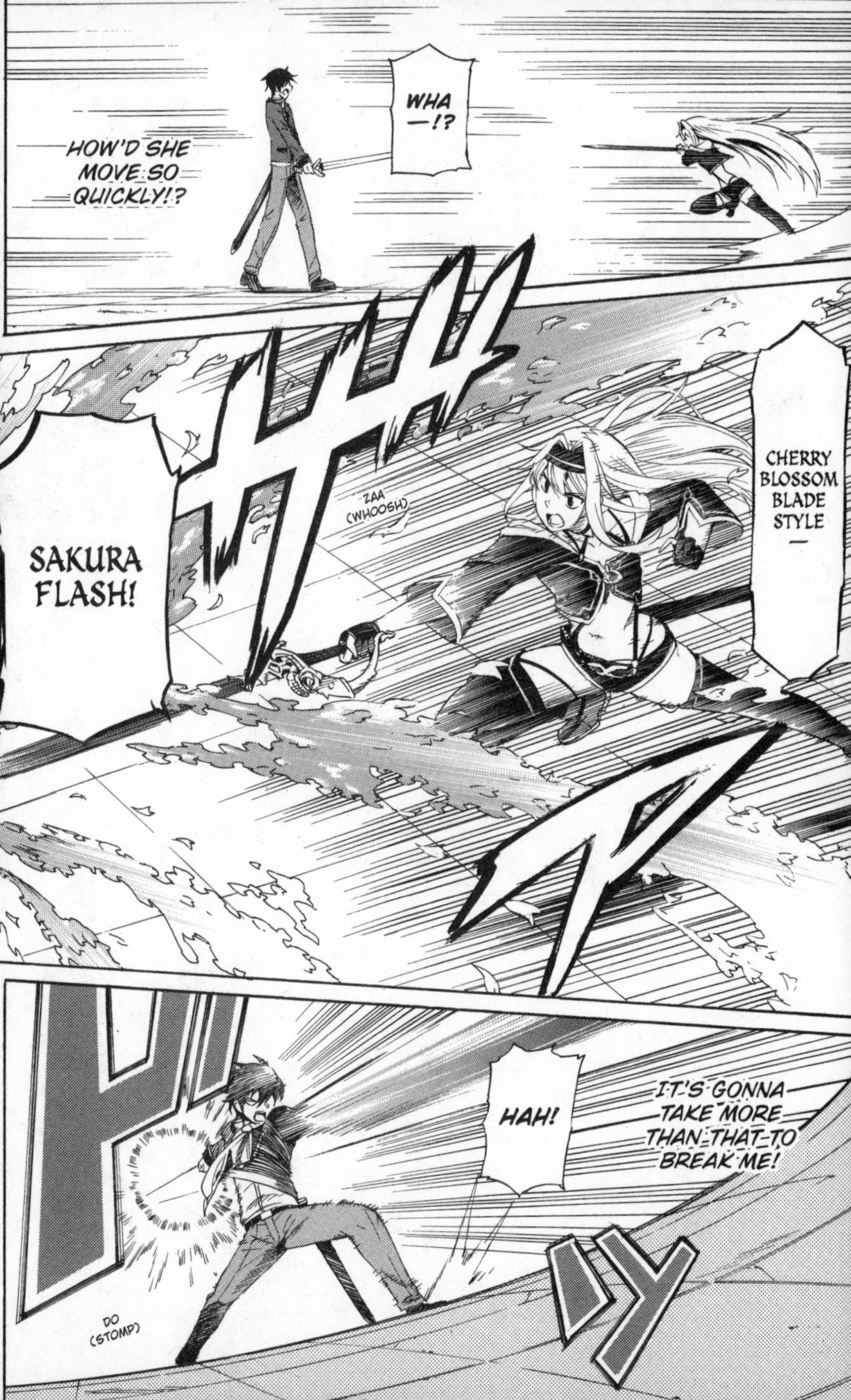
WHA—!?
HOW'D SHE MOVE SO QUICKLY!?
CHERRY BLOSSOM BLADE STYLE—
ZAA (WHOOSH)
SAKURA FLASH!
IT'S GONNA TAKE MORE THAN THAT TO BREAK ME!
HAH!
DO (STOMP)

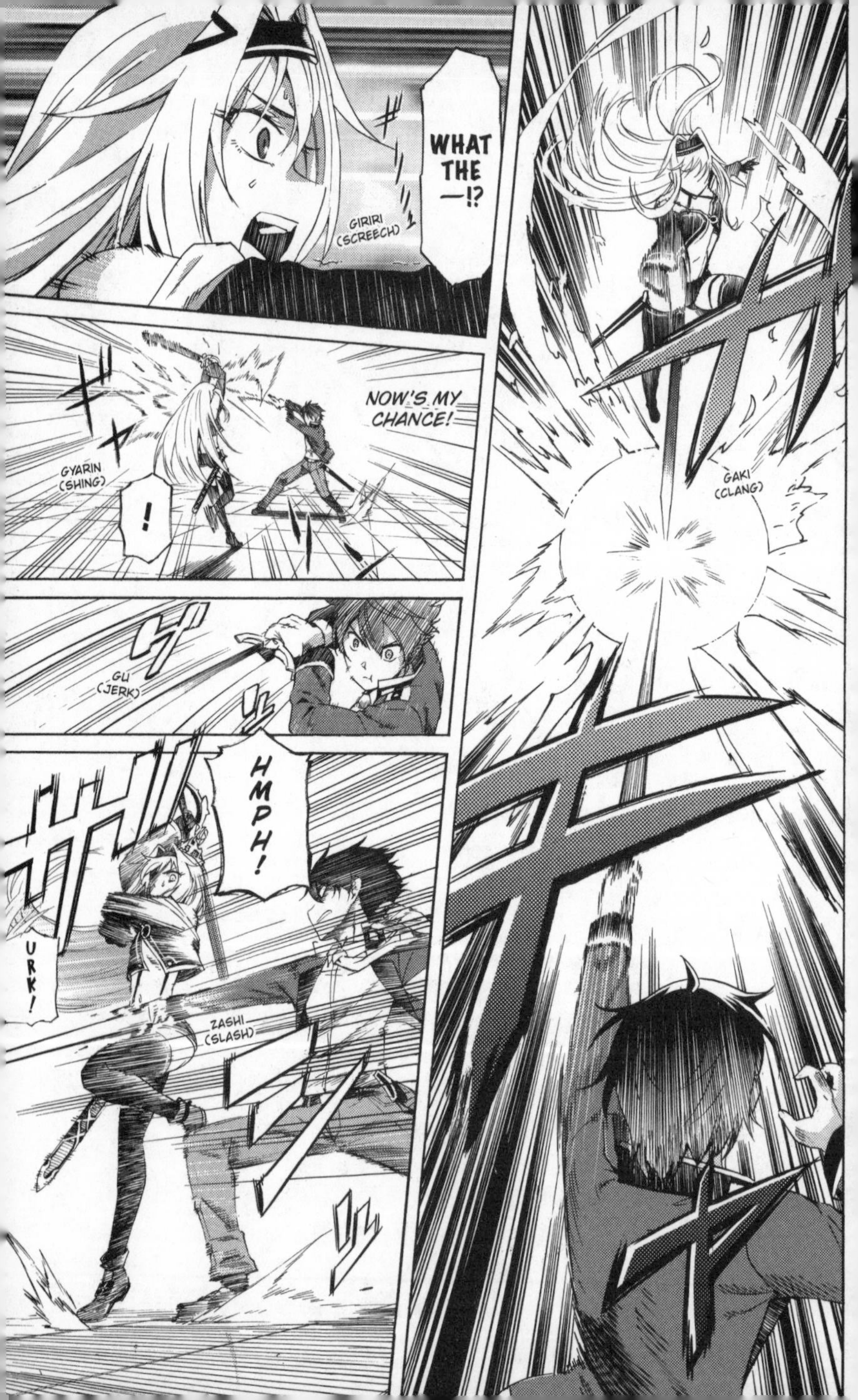
GAKI (CLANG)
WHAT THE—!?
GIRIRI (SCREECH)
NOW'S MY CHANCE!
GYARIN (SHING)
!
GU (JERK)
HMPH!
URK!
ZASHI (SLASH)

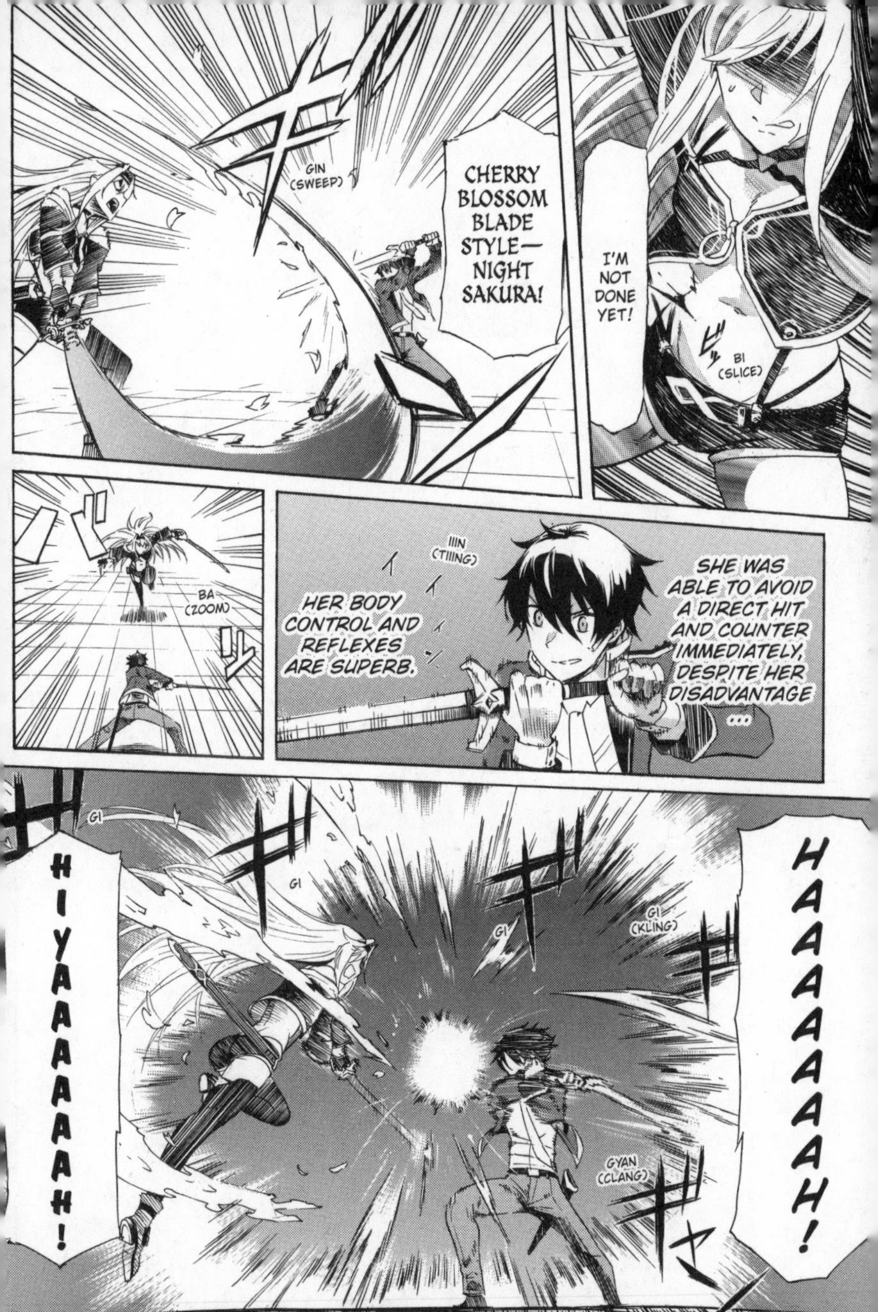
I'M NOT DONE YET!
BI (SLICE)
GIN (SWEEP)
CHERRY BLOSSOM BLADE STYLE— NIGHT SAKURA!
IIIN (TIIING)
SHE WAS ABLE TO AVOID A DIRECT HIT AND COUNTER IMMEDIATELY, DESPITE HER DISADVANTAGE ...
HER BODY CONTROL AND REFLEXES ARE SUPERB.
BA (ZOOM)
HAAAAAAAAAH!
GI (KLING)
GYAN (CLANG)
GI
GI
GI
HIYAAAAAAAAH!

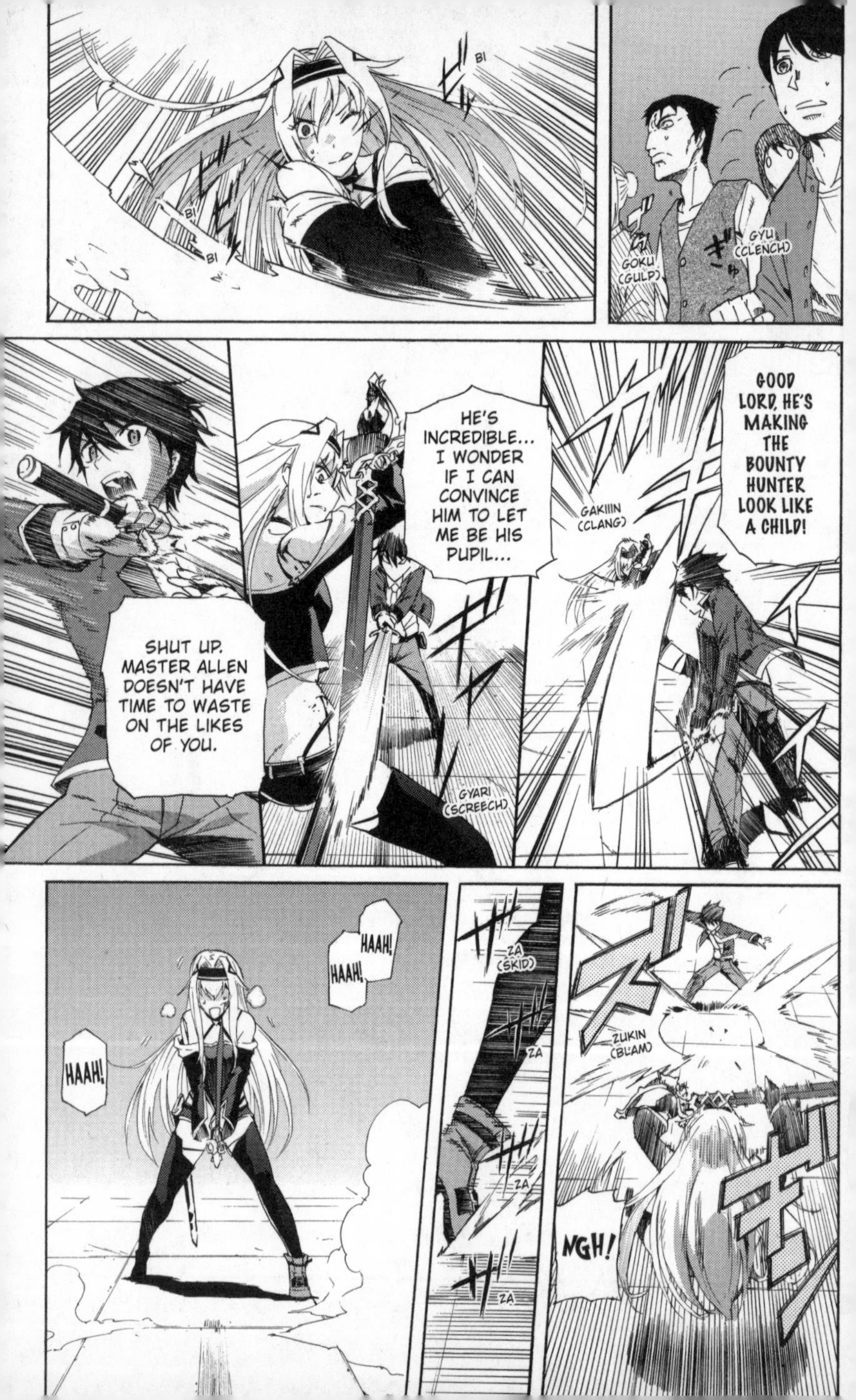
GYU (CLENCH)
GOKU (GULP)
BI
BI
BI
GOOD LORD, HE'S MAKING THE BOUNTY HUNTER LOOK LIKE A CHILD!
GAKIIIN (CLANG)
HE'S INCREDIBLE... I WONDER IF I CAN CONVINCE HIM TO LET ME BE HIS PUPIL...
GYARI (SCREECH)
SHUT UP. MASTER ALLEN DOESN'T HAVE TIME TO WASTE ON THE LIKES OF YOU.
ZUKIN (BLAM)
NGH!
ZA (SKID)
ZA
ZA
ZA
HAAH!
HAAH!
HAAH!

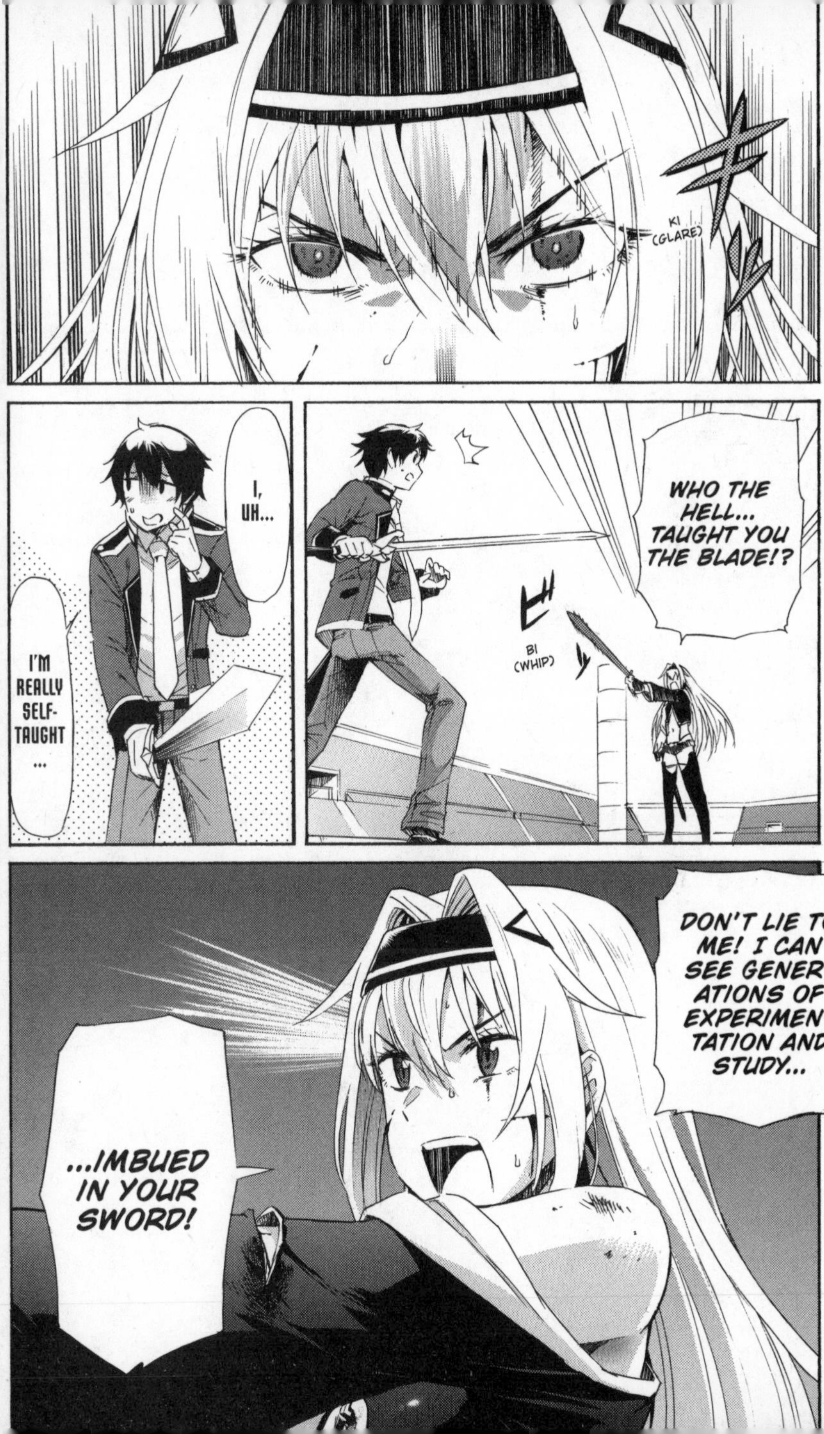
KI (GLARE)
WHO THE HELL... TAUGHT YOU THE BLADE!?
BI (WHIP)
I, UH...
I'M REALLY SELF-TAUGHT...
DON'T LIE TO ME! I CAN SEE GENER-ATIONS OF EXPERIMEN-TATION AND STUDY...
...IMBUED IN YOUR SWORD!

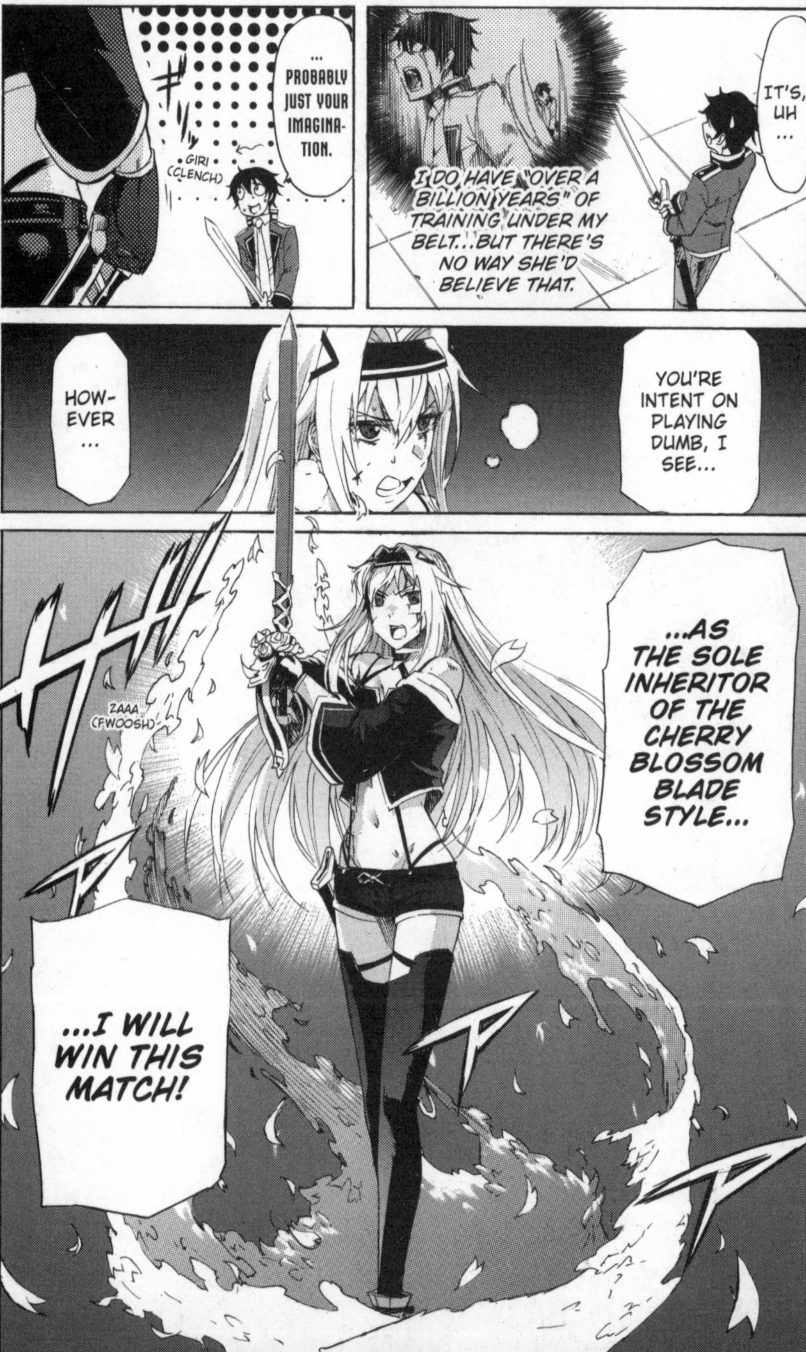
IT'S, UH ...
I DO HAVE "OVER A BILLION YEARS" OF TRAINING UNDER MY BELT...BUT THERE'S NO WAY SHE'D BELIEVE THAT.
... PROBABLY JUST YOUR IMAGINA-TION.
GIRI (CLENCH)
YOU'RE INTENT ON PLAYING DUMB, I SEE...
HOW-EVER ...
...AS THE SOLE INHERITOR OF THE CHERRY BLOSSOM BLADE STYLE...
ZAAA (FWOOSH)
...I WILL WIN THIS MATCH!

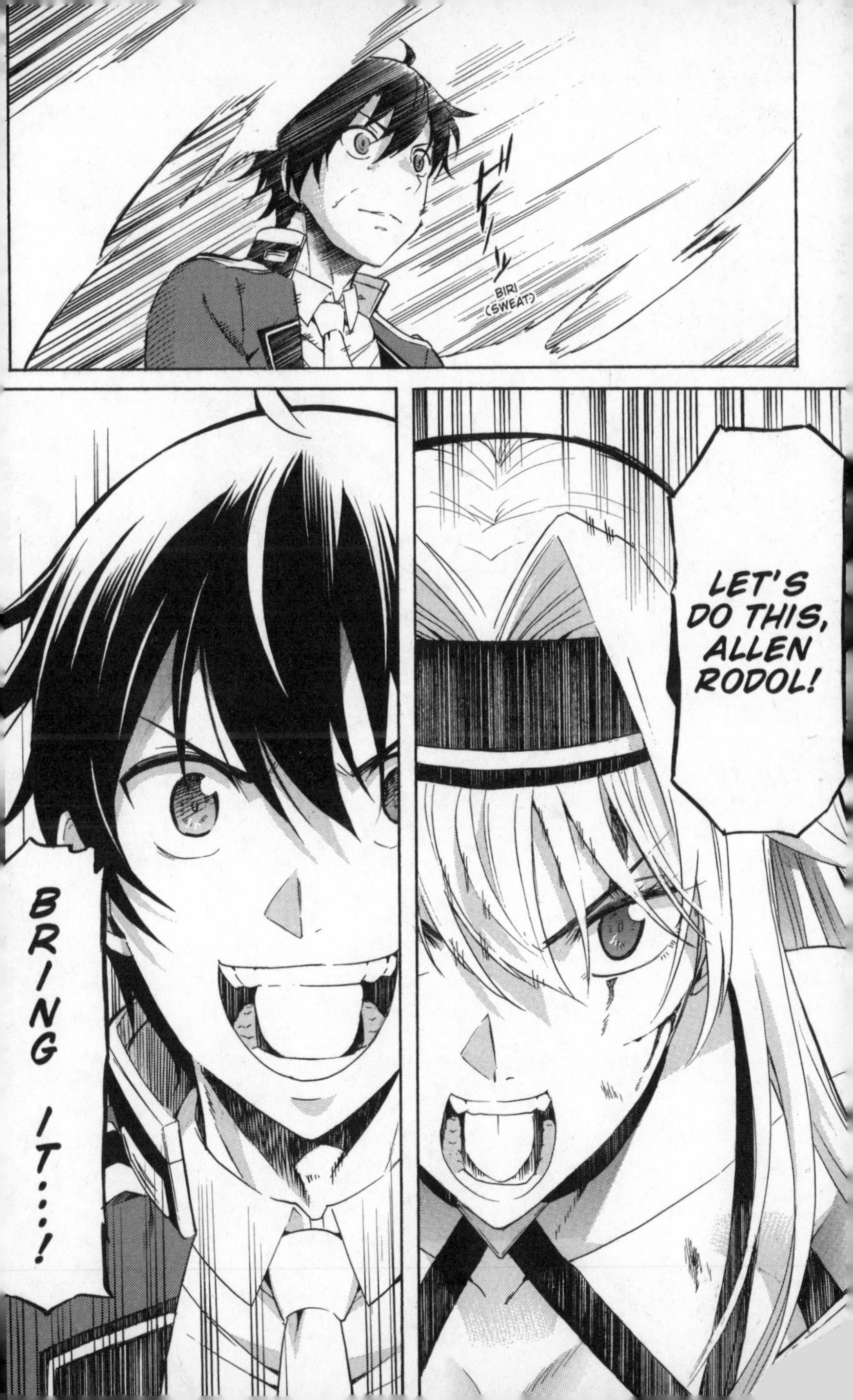
BIRI
(SWEAT)
LET'S DO THIS, ALLEN RODOL!
BRING IT...!

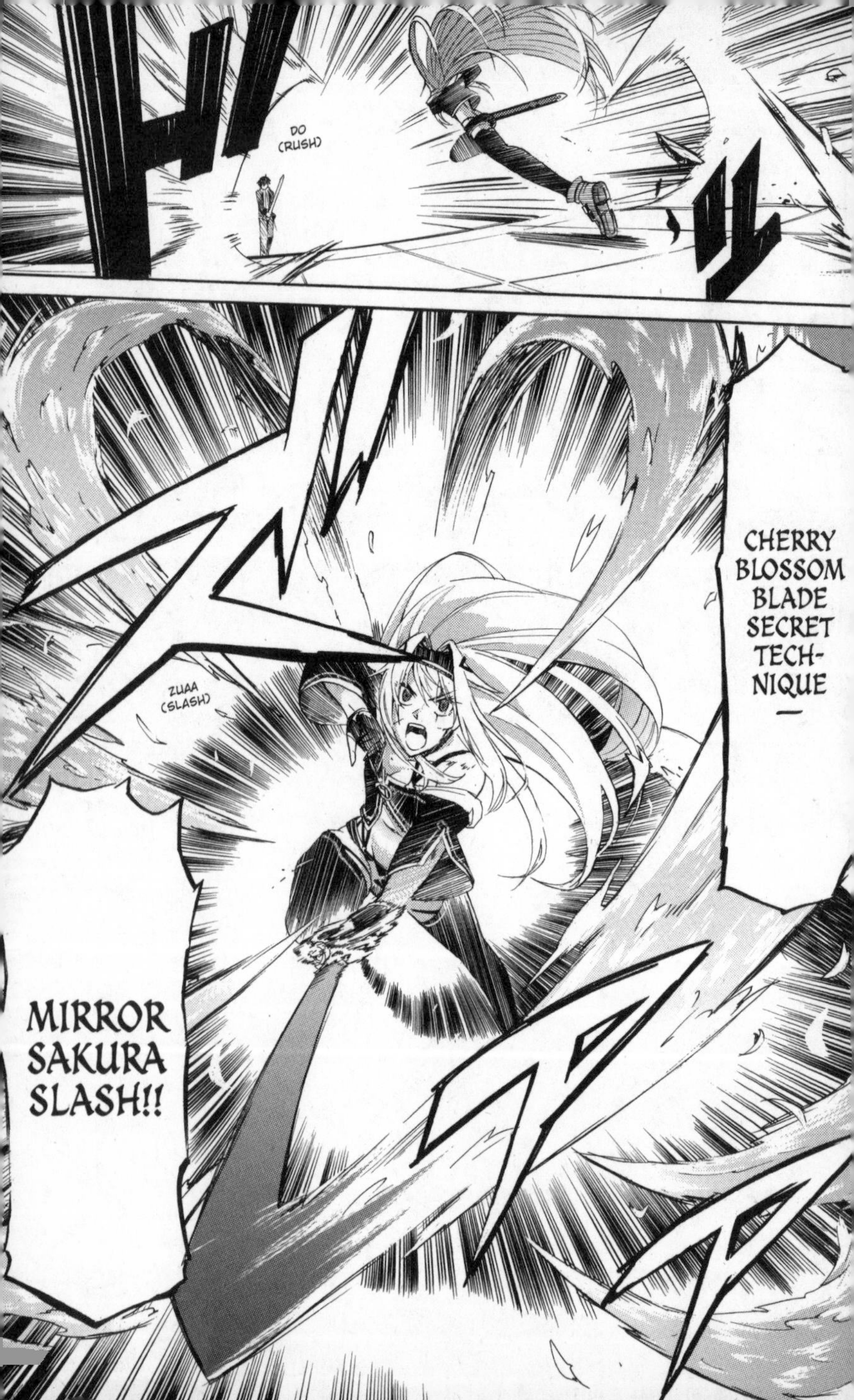
DO
(RUSH)
CHERRY BLOSSOM BLADE SECRET TECH-NIQUE —
ZUAA
(SLASH)
MIRROR SAKURA SLASH!!

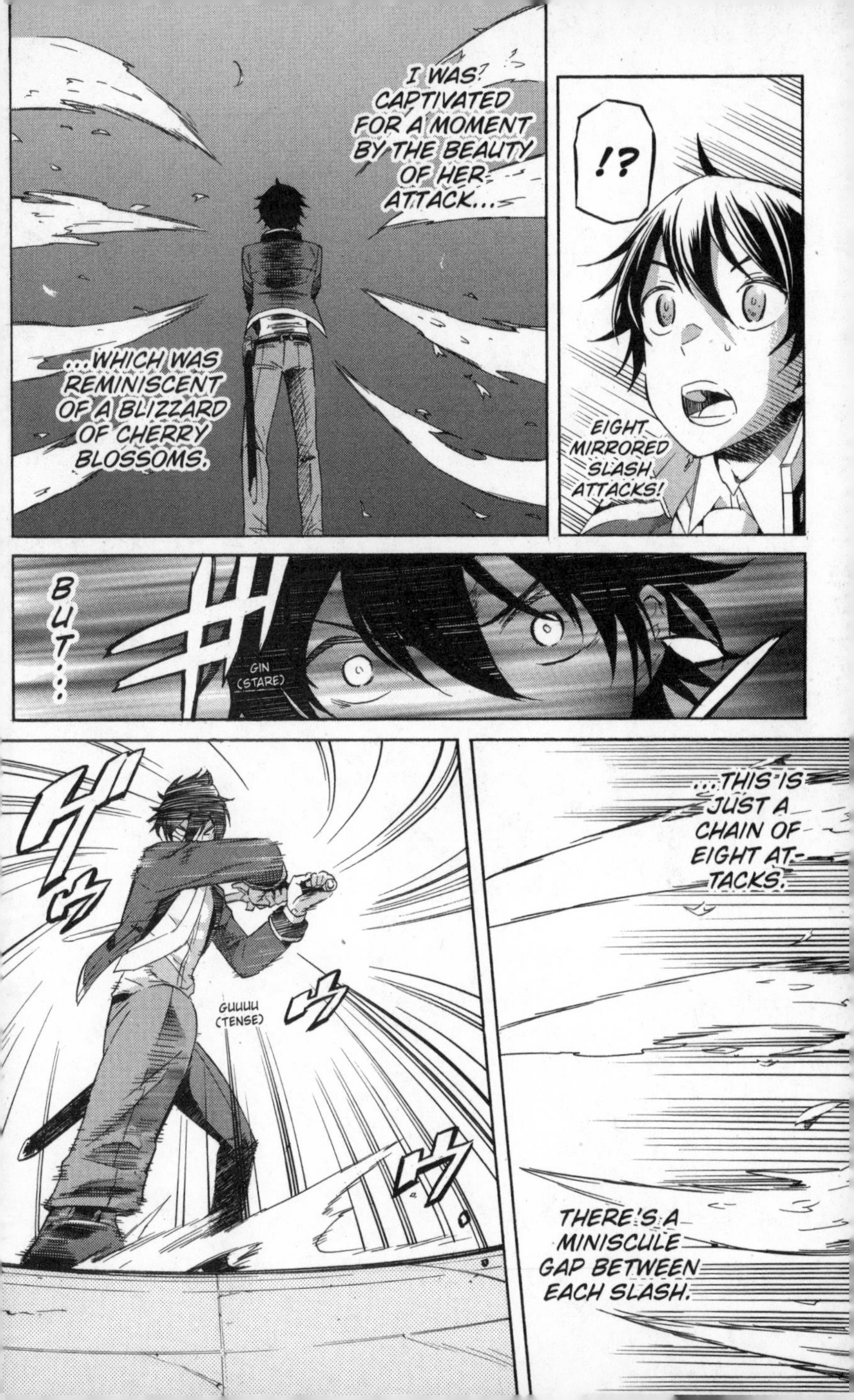
!?
EIGHT MIRRORED SLASH ATTACKS!
I WAS CAPTIVATED FOR A MOMENT BY THE BEAUTY OF HER ATTACK...
...WHICH WAS REMINISCENT OF A BLIZZARD OF CHERRY BLOSSOMS.
BUT...
GIN (STARE)
...THIS IS JUST A CHAIN OF EIGHT AT-TACKS.
THERE'S A MINISCULE GAP BETWEEN EACH SLASH.
GUUUU (TENSE)

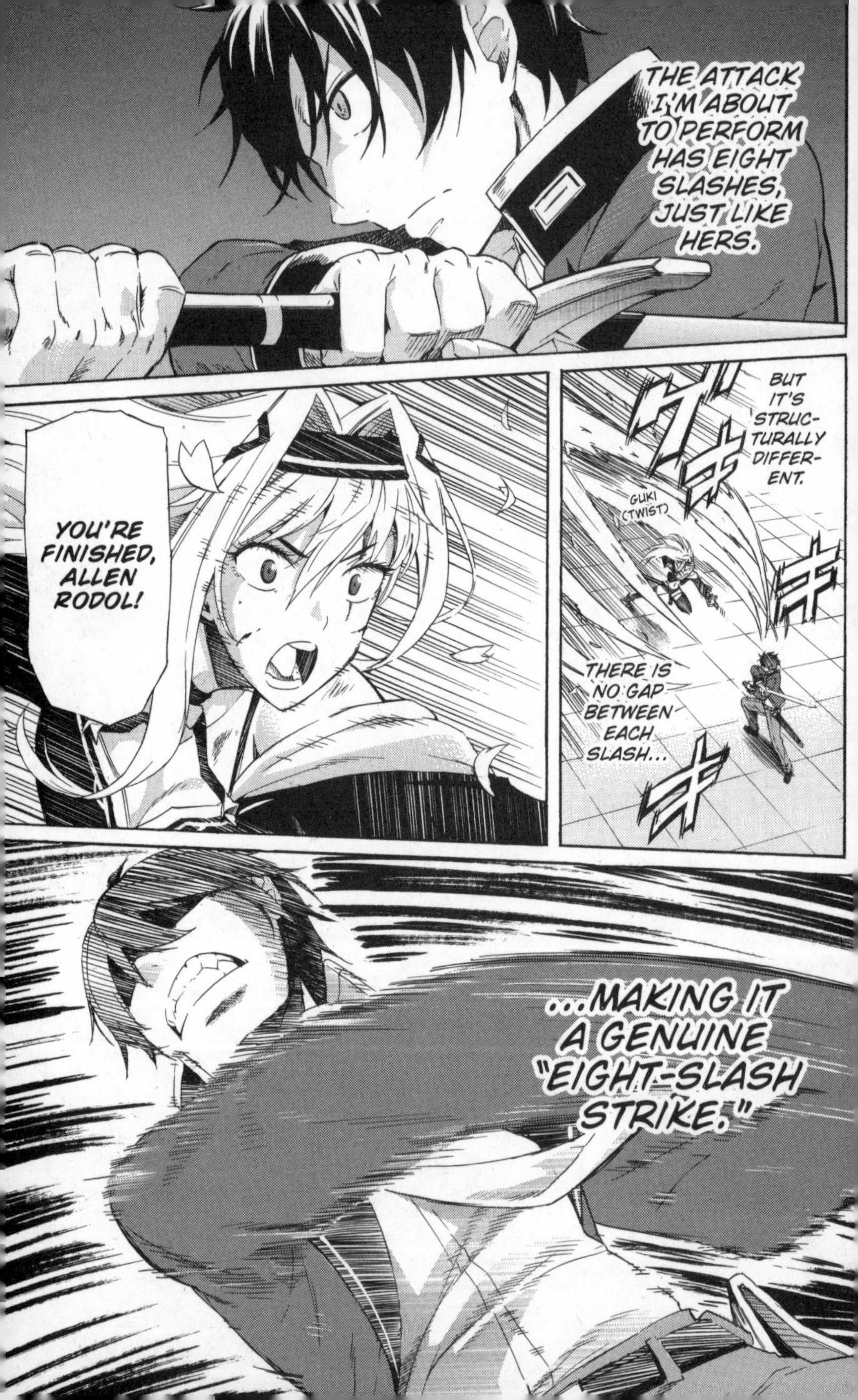
THE ATTACK I'M ABOUT TO PERFORM HAS EIGHT SLASHES, JUST LIKE HERS.
BUT IT'S STRUC-TURALLY DIFFER-ENT.
GUKI (TWIST)
THERE IS NO GAP BETWEEN EACH SLASH...
YOU'RE FINISHED, ALLEN RODOL!
...MAKING IT A GENUINE "EIGHT-SLASH STRIKE."

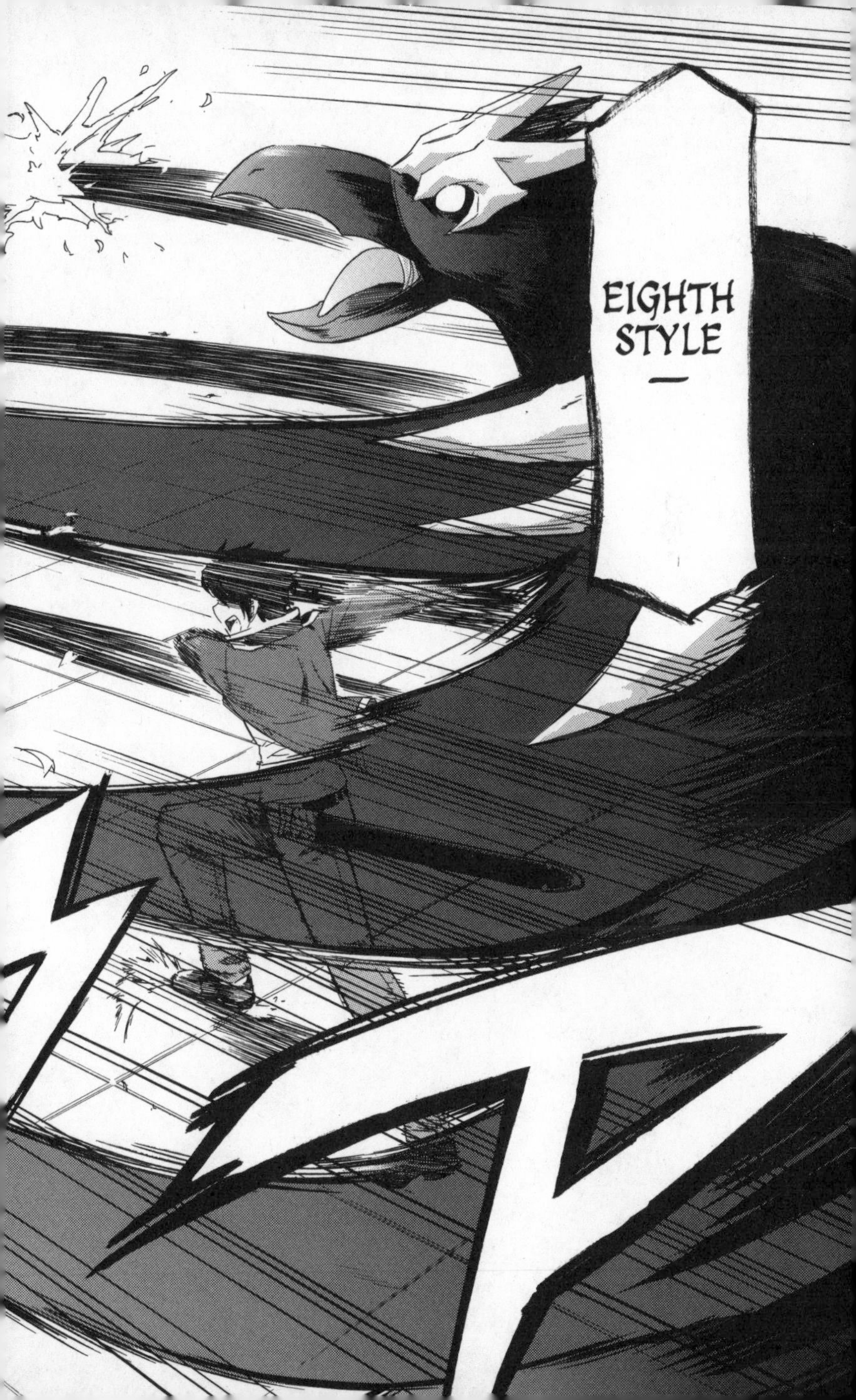
EIGHTH STYLE—

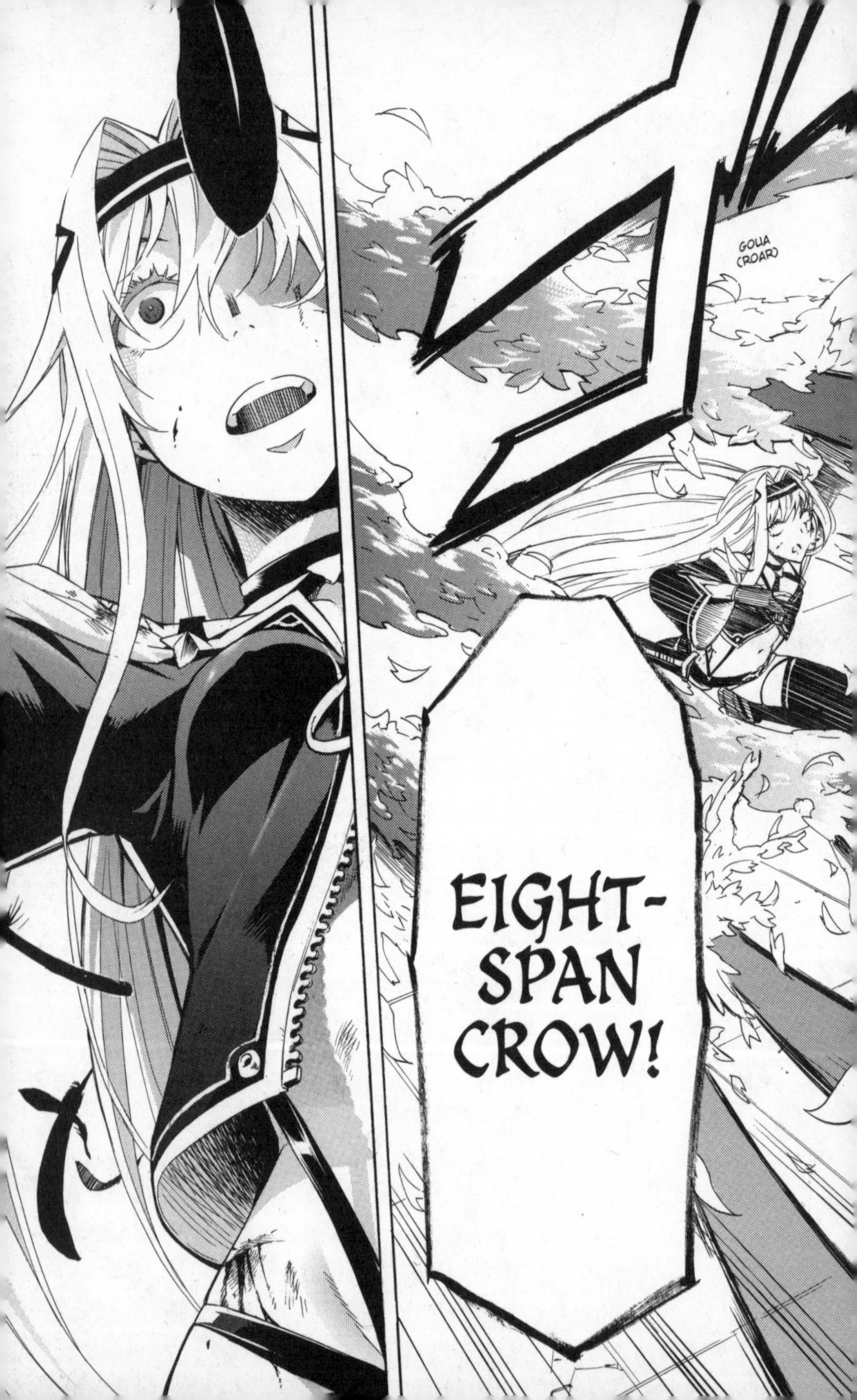
GOUA (ROAR)
EIGHT-SPAN CROW!

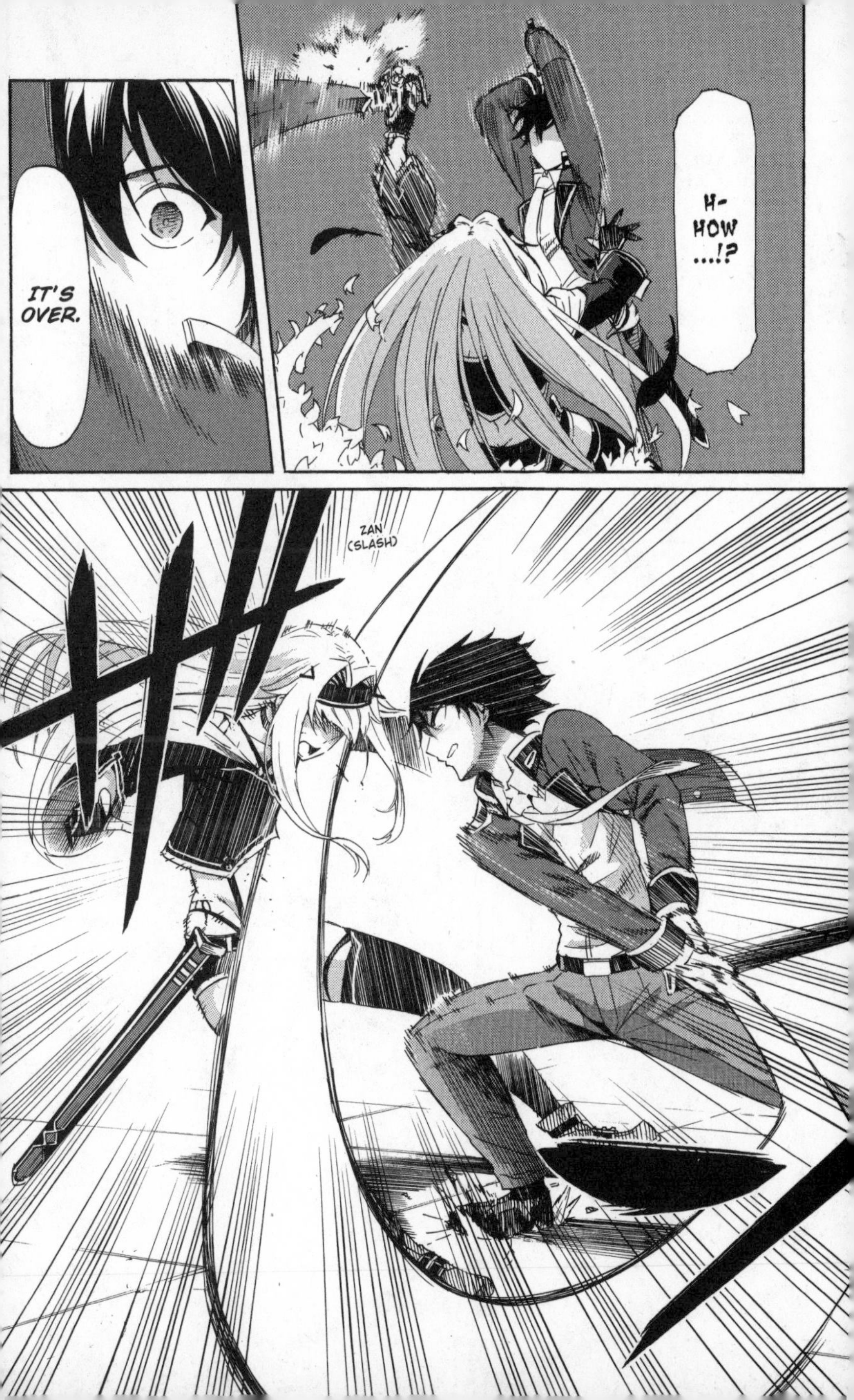
H-HOW ....!?
IT'S OVER.
ZAN (SLASH)

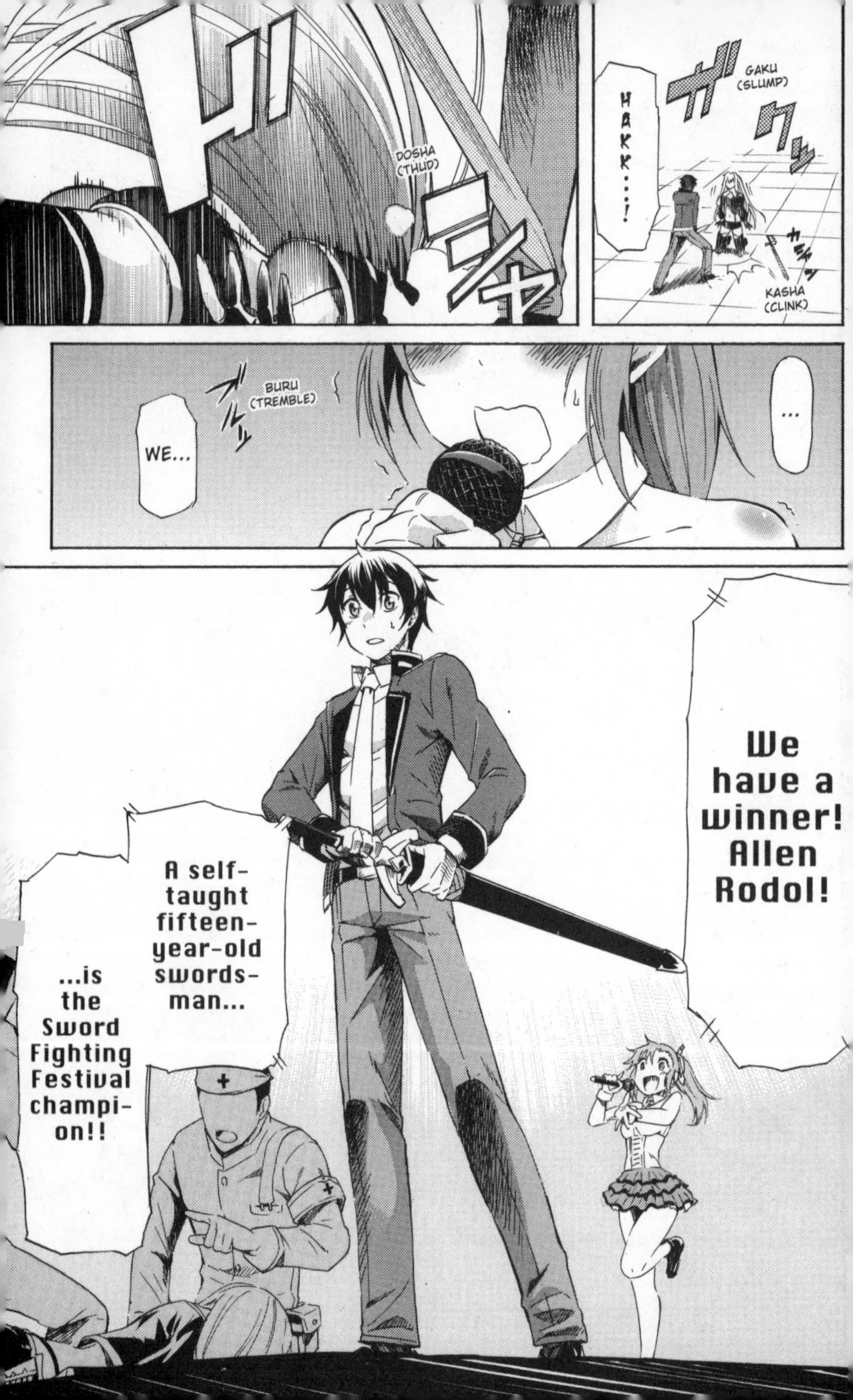
GAKU (SLUMP)
HAKK...!
KASHA (CLINK)
DOSHA (THUD)
...
BURU (TREMBLE)
WE...
We have a winner! Allen Rodol!
A self-taught fifteen-year-old swordsman...
...is the Sword Fighting Festival champion!!

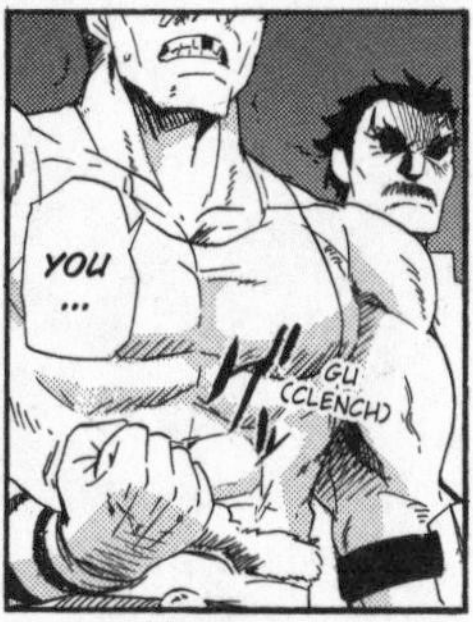
YOU ...
GU
(CLENCH)

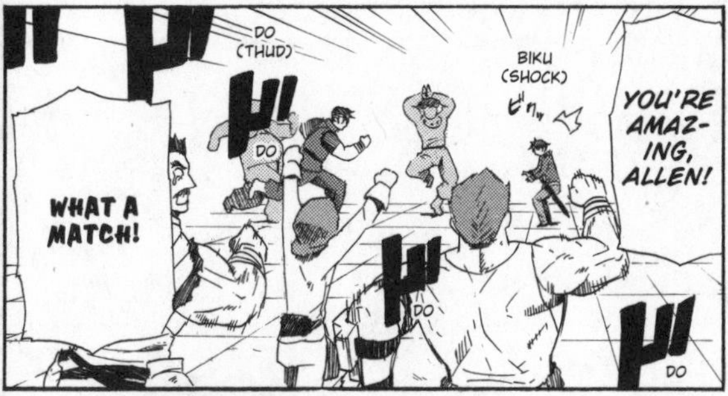
YOU'RE AMAZ-ING, ALLEN!
BIKU
(SHOCK)
DO
(THUD)
DO
WHAT A MATCH!
DO
DO

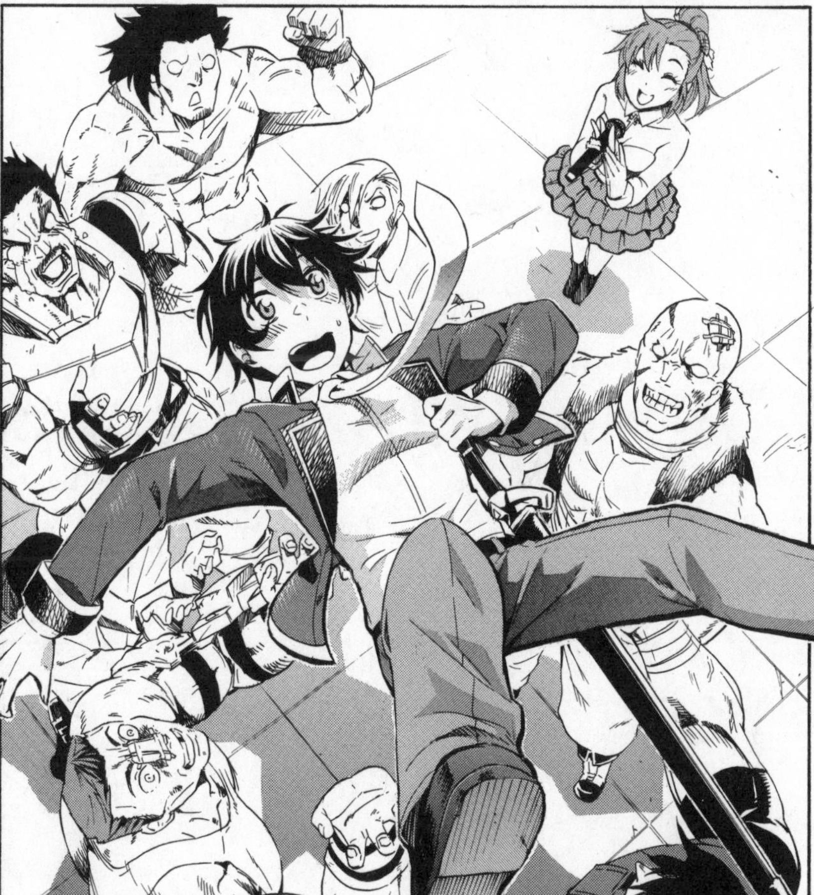

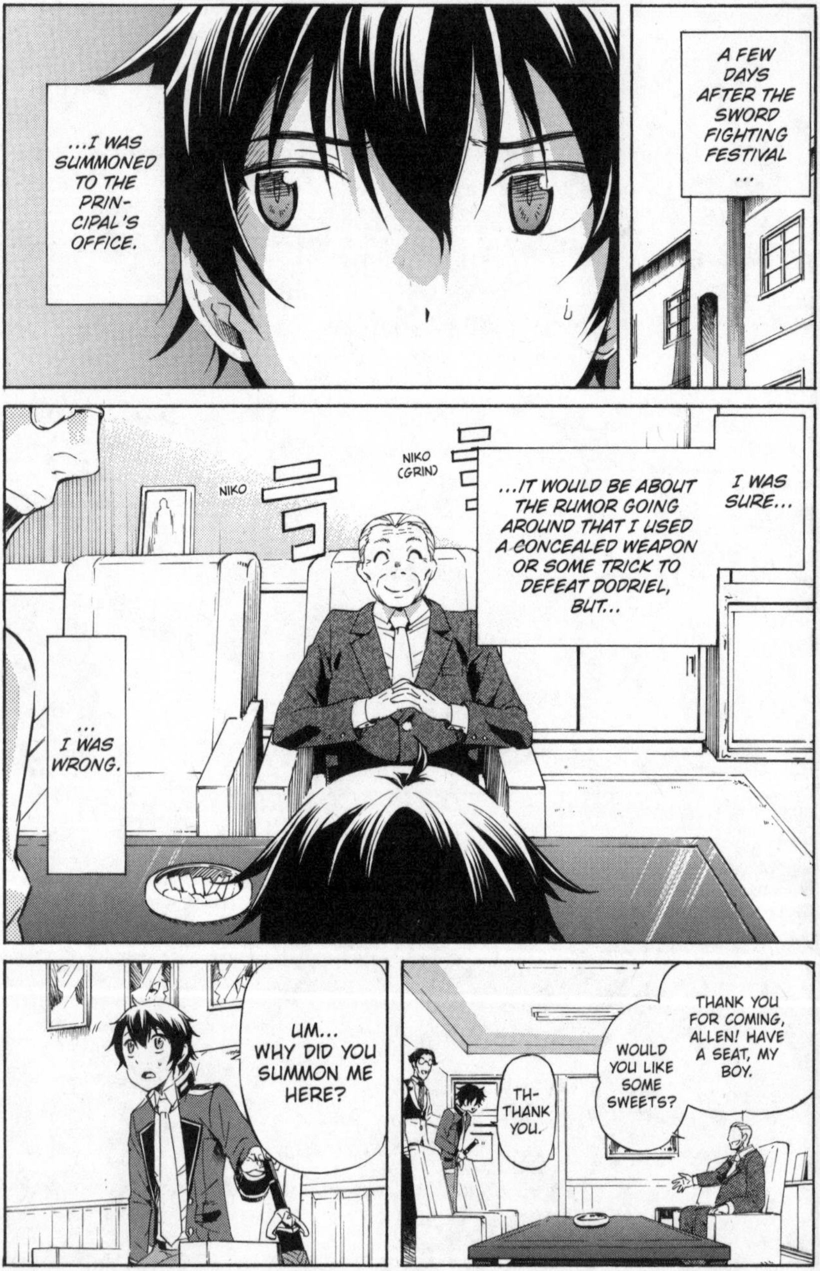
A FEW DAYS AFTER THE SWORD FIGHTING FESTIVAL...
...I WAS SUMMONED TO THE PRIN-CIPAL'S OFFICE.
I WAS SURE...
...IT WOULD BE ABOUT THE RUMOR GOING AROUND THAT I USED A CONCEALED WEAPON OR SOME TRICK TO DEFEAT DODRIEL, BUT...
NIKO (GRIN)
NIKO
... I WAS WRONG.
THANK YOU FOR COMING, ALLEN! HAVE A SEAT, MY BOY.
WOULD YOU LIKE SOME SWEETS?
TH-THANK YOU.
UM... WHY DID YOU SUMMON ME HERE?

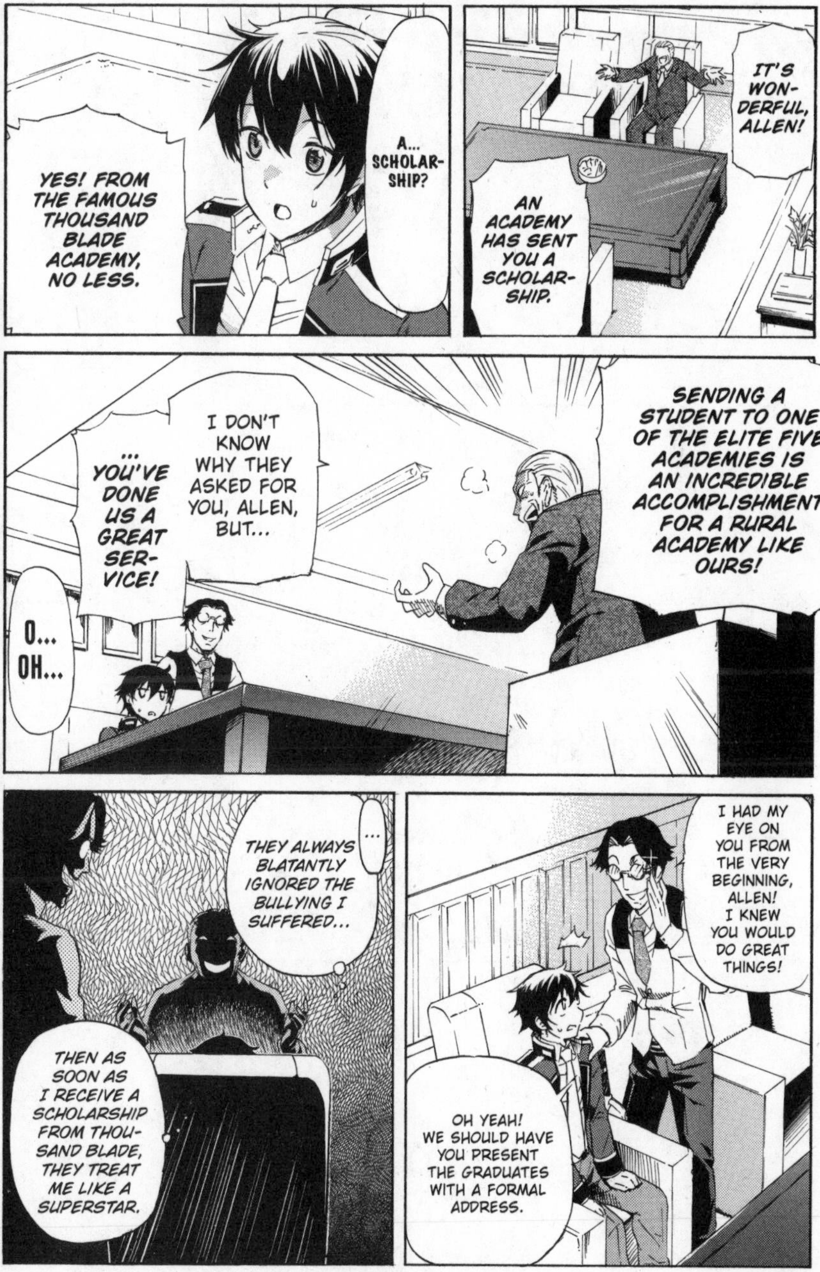
IT'S WONDERFUL, ALLEN!
AN ACADEMY HAS SENT YOU A SCHOLARSHIP.
A... SCHOLARSHIP?
YES! FROM THE FAMOUS THOUSAND BLADE ACADEMY, NO LESS.
SENDING A STUDENT TO ONE OF THE ELITE FIVE ACADEMIES IS AN INCREDIBLE ACCOMPLISHMENT FOR A RURAL ACADEMY LIKE OURS!
I DON'T KNOW WHY THEY ASKED FOR YOU, ALLEN, BUT...
...YOU'VE DONE US A GREAT SERVICE!
O... OH...
I HAD MY EYE ON YOU FROM THE VERY BEGINNING, ALLEN! I KNEW YOU WOULD DO GREAT THINGS!
OH YEAH! WE SHOULD HAVE YOU PRESENT THE GRADUATES WITH A FORMAL ADDRESS.
...
THEY ALWAYS BLATANTLY IGNORED THE BULLYING I SUFFERED...
THEN AS SOON AS I RECEIVE A SCHOLARSHIP FROM THOUSAND BLADE, THEY TREAT ME LIKE A SUPERSTAR.

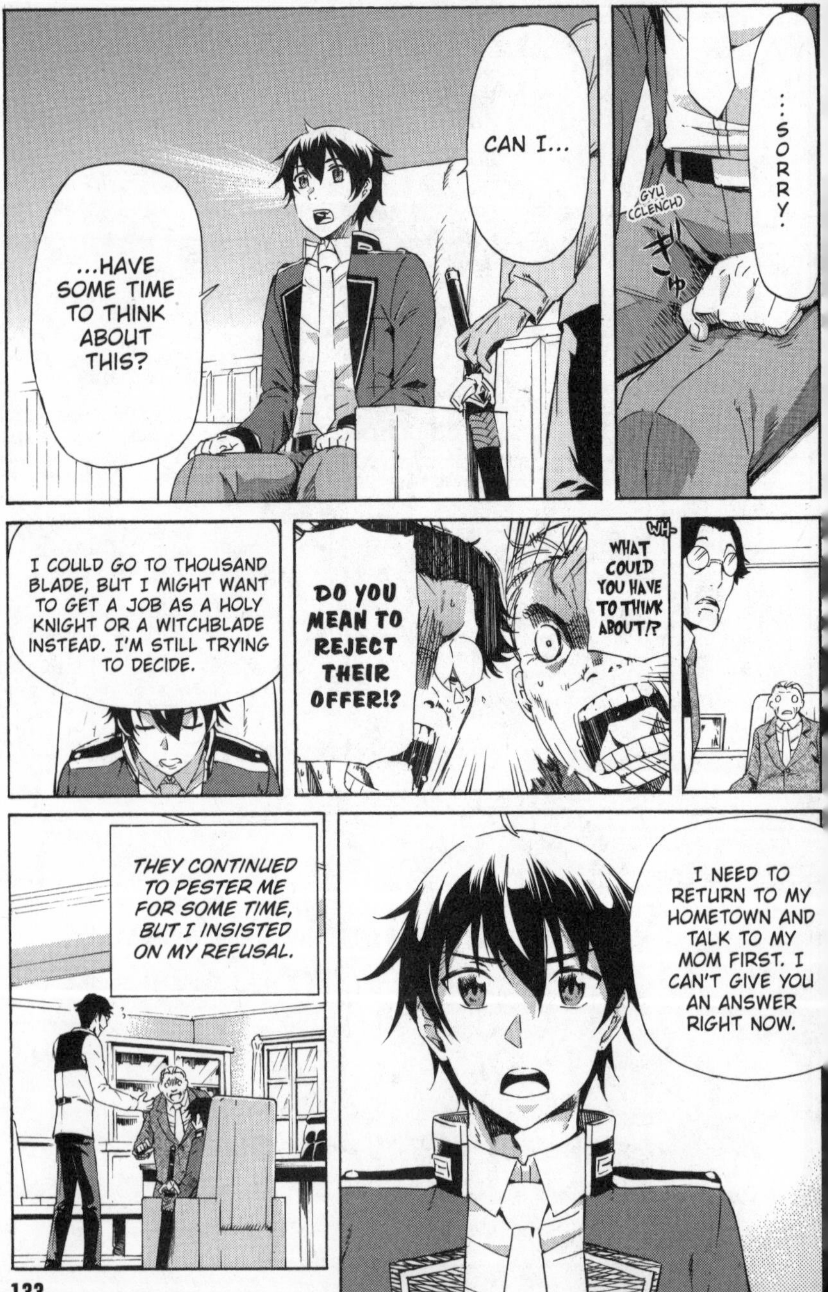
...SORRY.
GYU (CLENCH)
CAN I...
...HAVE SOME TIME TO THINK ABOUT THIS?
WH-
WHAT COULD YOU HAVE TO THINK ABOUT!?
DO YOU MEAN TO REJECT THEIR OFFER!?
I COULD GO TO THOUSAND BLADE, BUT I MIGHT WANT TO GET A JOB AS A HOLY KNIGHT OR A WITCHBLADE INSTEAD. I'M STILL TRYING TO DECIDE.
I NEED TO RETURN TO MY HOMETOWN AND TALK TO MY MOM FIRST. I CAN'T GIVE YOU AN ANSWER RIGHT NOW.
THEY CONTINUED TO PESTER ME FOR SOME TIME, BUT I INSISTED ON MY REFUSAL.

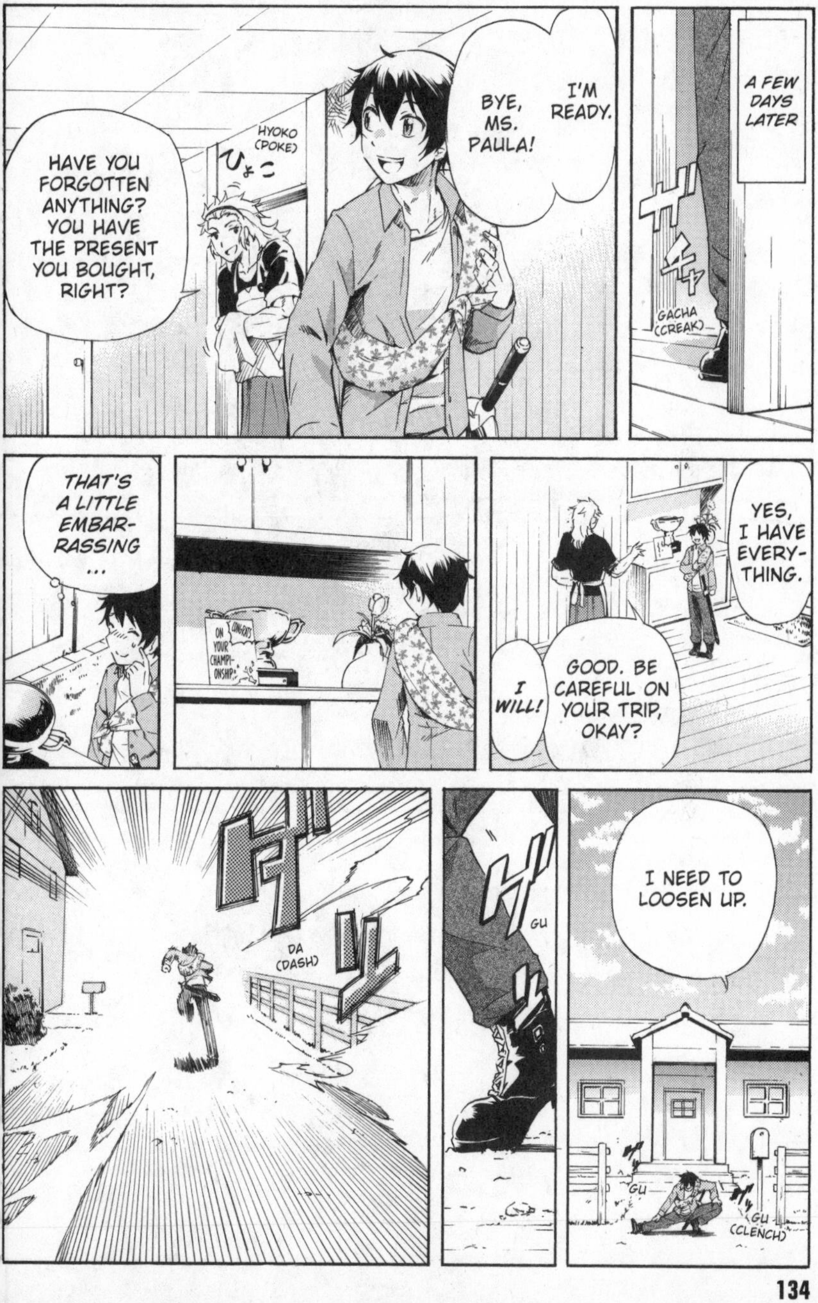
A FEW DAYS LATER
GACHA (CREAK)
I'M READY.
BYE, MS. PAULA!
ひょこ
HYOKO (POKE)
HAVE YOU FORGOTTEN ANYTHING? YOU HAVE THE PRESENT YOU BOUGHT, RIGHT?
YES, I HAVE EVERYTHING.
GOOD. BE CAREFUL ON YOUR TRIP, OKAY?
I WILL!
CONGRATS ON YOUR CHAMPIONSHIP!
THAT'S A LITTLE EMBARRASSING...
I NEED TO LOOSEN UP.
GU
GU (CLENCH)
GU
DA (DASH)

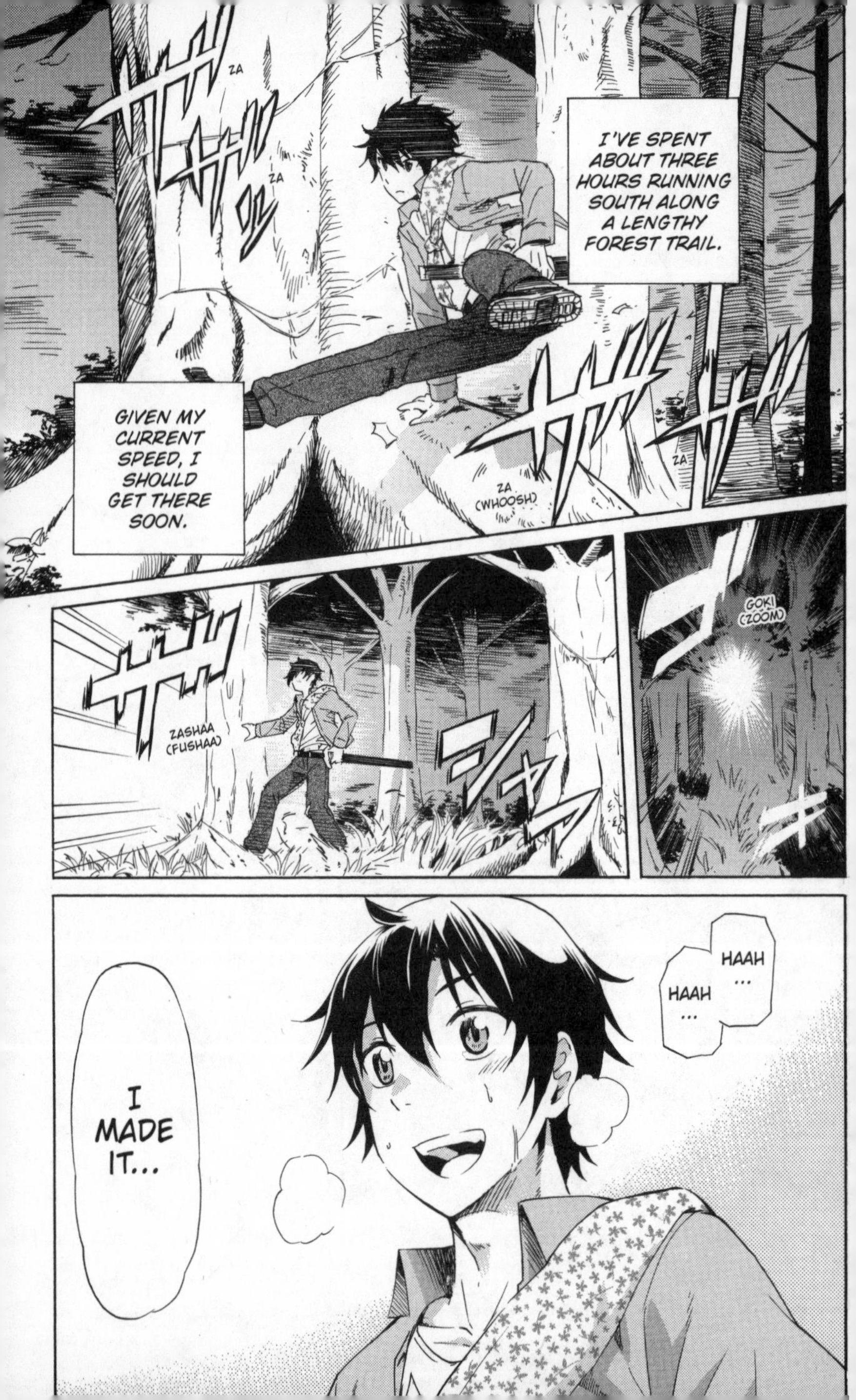
I'VE SPENT ABOUT THREE HOURS RUNNING SOUTH ALONG A LENGTHY FOREST TRAIL.
ZA
ZA
ZA
ZA (WHOOSH)
GIVEN MY CURRENT SPEED, I SHOULD GET THERE SOON.
GOKI (ZOOM)
ZASHAA (FUSHAA)
HAAH ... HAAH ...
I MADE IT...

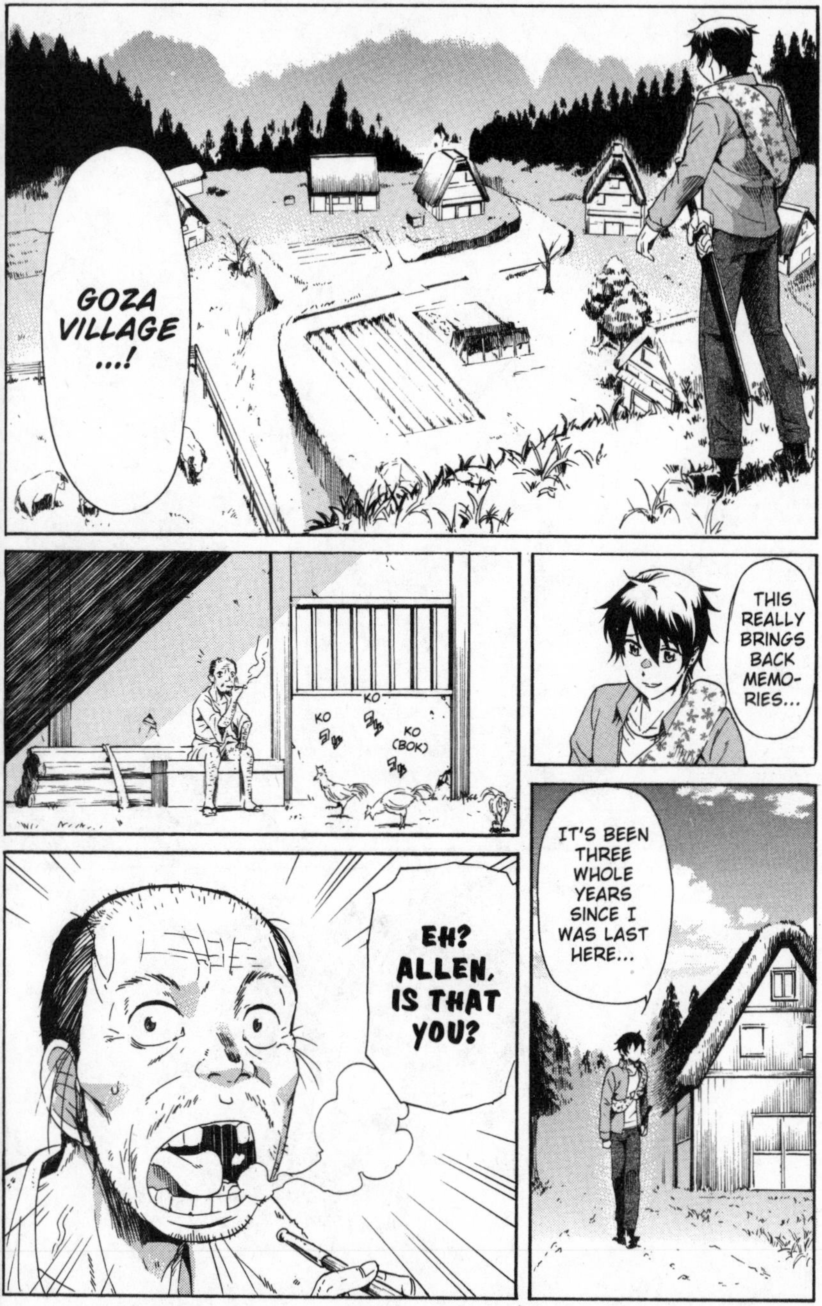
GOZA VILLAGE ...!
THIS REALLY BRINGS BACK MEMORIES...
IT'S BEEN THREE WHOLE YEARS SINCE I WAS LAST HERE...
KO KO KO (BOK)
EH? ALLEN, IS THAT YOU?

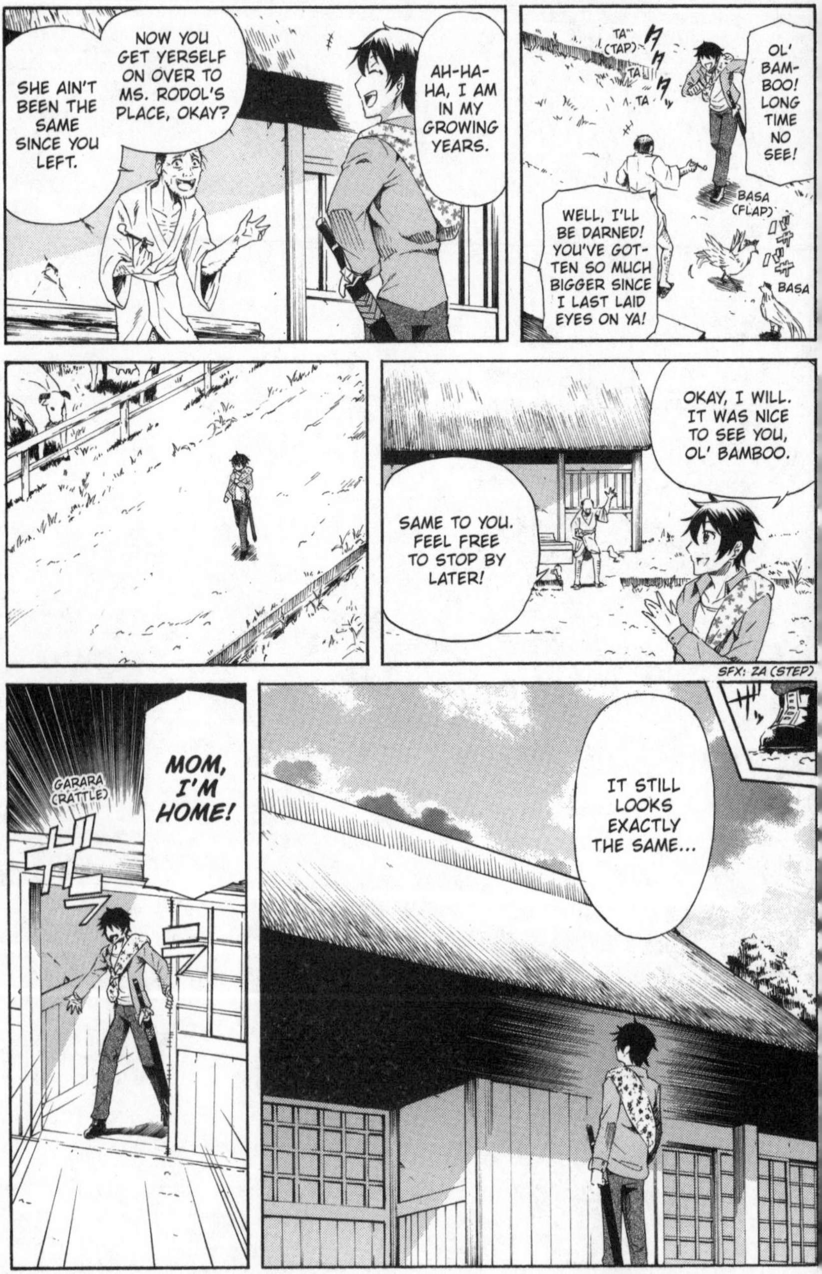
OL' BAMBOO! LONG TIME NO SEE!
TA' (TAP)
TA
TA
WELL, I'LL BE DARNED! YOU'VE GOTTEN SO MUCH BIGGER SINCE I LAST LAID EYES ON YA!
BASA (FLAP)
BASA
AH-HA-HA, I AM IN MY GROWING YEARS.
NOW YOU GET YERSELF ON OVER TO MS. RODOL'S PLACE, OKAY?
SHE AIN'T BEEN THE SAME SINCE YOU LEFT.
OKAY, I WILL. IT WAS NICE TO SEE YOU, OL' BAMBOO.
SAME TO YOU. FEEL FREE TO STOP BY LATER!
SFX: ZA (STEP)
IT STILL LOOKS EXACTLY THE SAME...
MOM, I'M HOME!
GARARA (RATTLE)

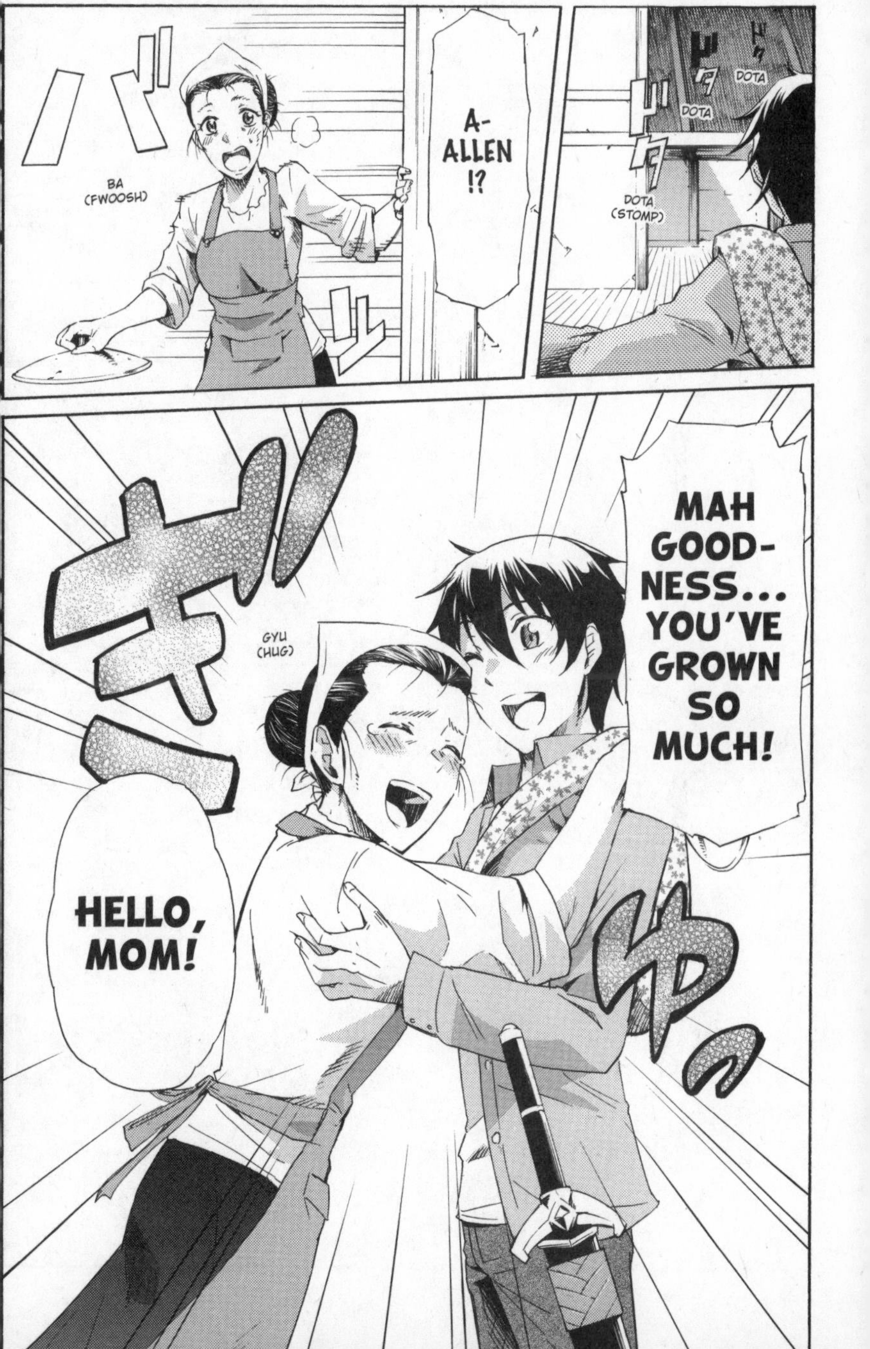
DOTA
DOTA
DOTA (STOMP)
A-ALLEN!?
BA (FWOOSH)
MAH GOODNESS... YOU'VE GROWN SO MUCH!
GYU (HUG)
HELLO, MOM!

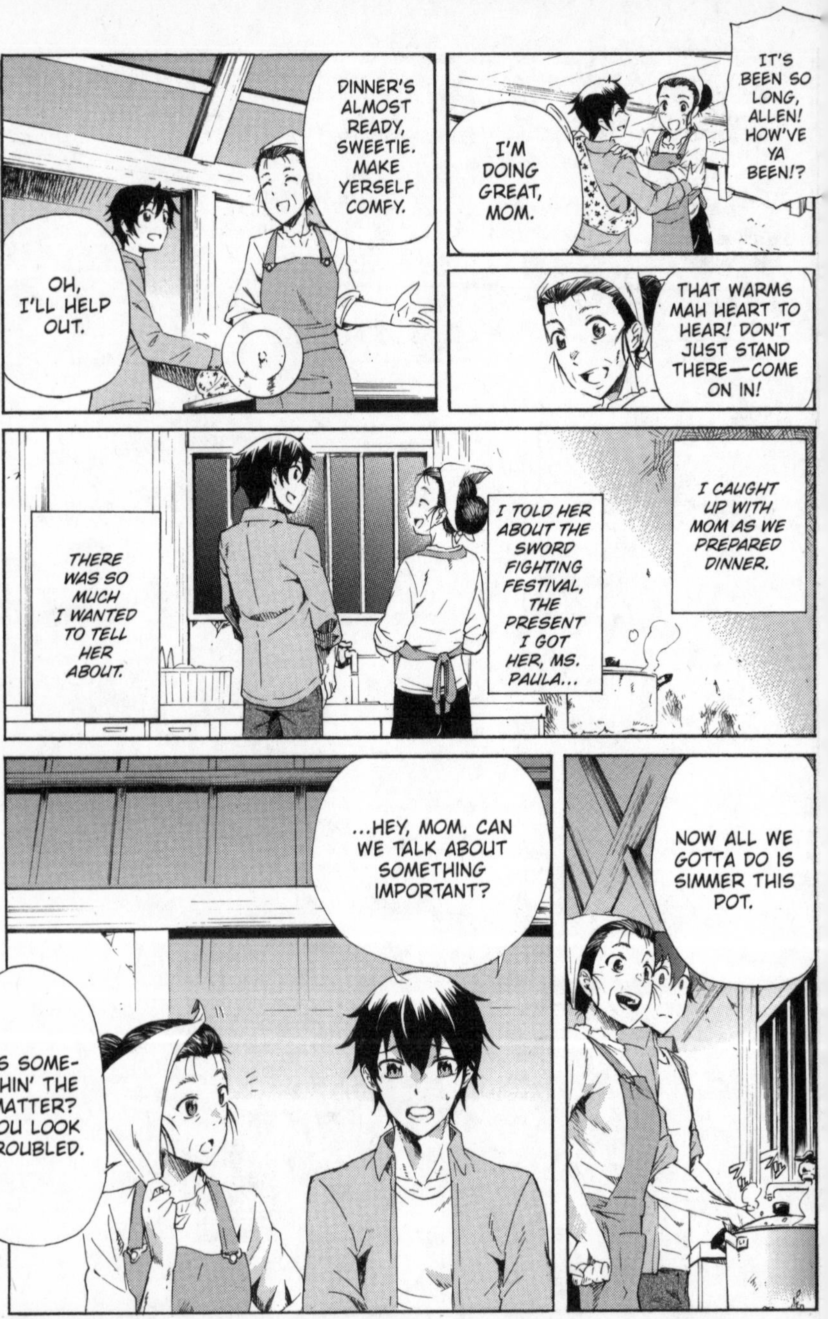
IT'S BEEN SO LONG, ALLEN! HOW'VE YA BEEN!?
I'M DOING GREAT, MOM.
THAT WARMS MAH HEART TO HEAR! DON'T JUST STAND THERE—COME ON IN!
DINNER'S ALMOST READY, SWEETIE. MAKE YERSELF COMFY.
OH, I'LL HELP OUT.
I CAUGHT UP WITH MOM AS WE PREPARED DINNER.
I TOLD HER ABOUT THE SWORD FIGHTING FESTIVAL, THE PRESENT I GOT HER, MS. PAULA...
THERE WAS SO MUCH I WANTED TO TELL HER ABOUT.
NOW ALL WE GOTTA DO IS SIMMER THIS POT.
...HEY, MOM. CAN WE TALK ABOUT SOMETHING IMPORTANT?
IS SOME-THIN' THE MATTER? YOU LOOK TROUBLED.

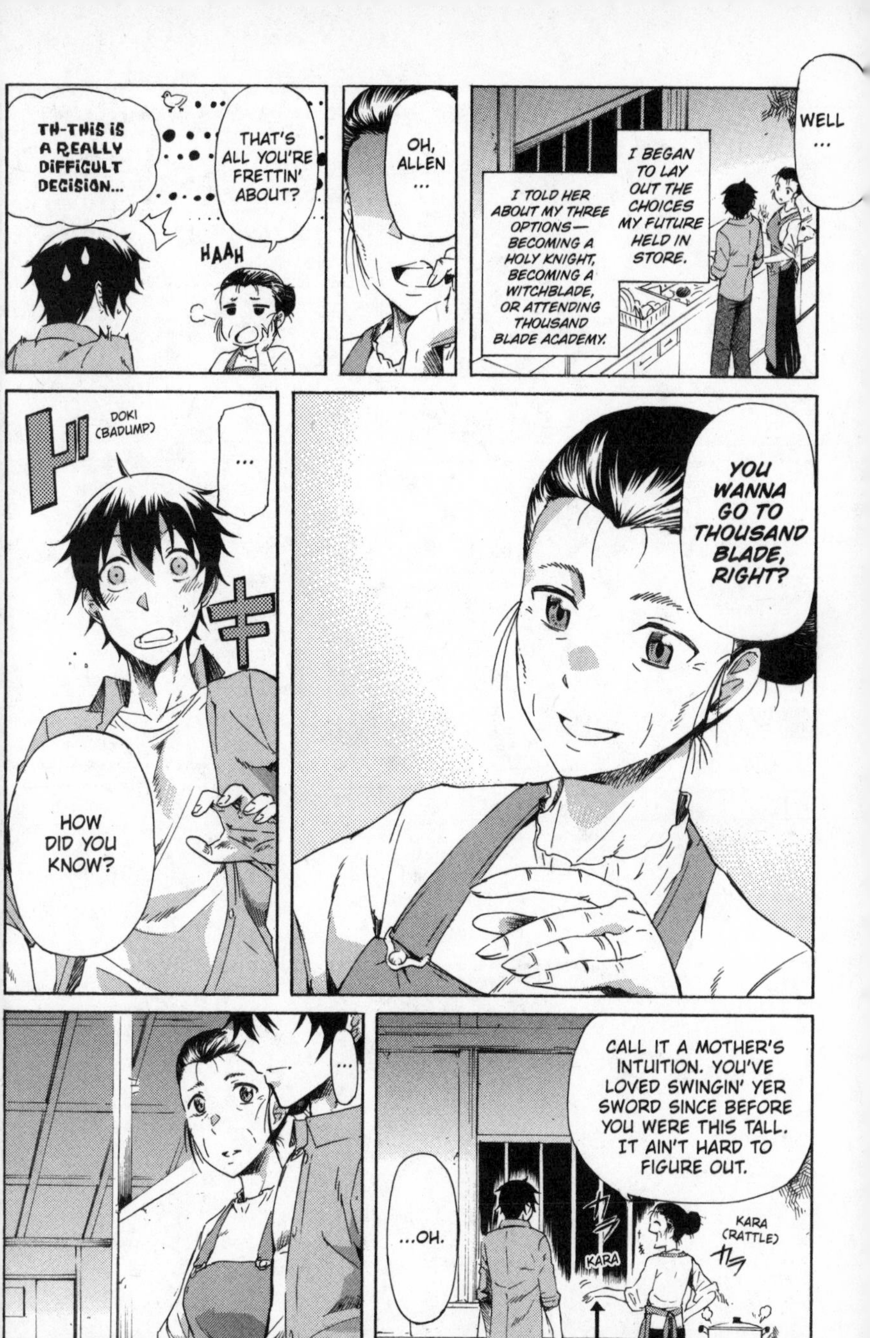

WELL ...
I BEGAN TO LAY OUT THE CHOICES MY FUTURE HELD IN STORE.
I TOLD HER ABOUT MY THREE OPTIONS—BECOMING A HOLY KNIGHT, BECOMING A WITCHBLADE, OR ATTENDING THOUSAND BLADE ACADEMY.
OH, ALLEN ...
THAT'S ALL YOU'RE FRETTIN' ABOUT?
HAAH
TH-THIS IS A REALLY DIFFICULT DECISION...
YOU WANNA GO TO THOUSAND BLADE, RIGHT?
...
DOKI (BADUMP)
HOW DID YOU KNOW?
CALL IT A MOTHER'S INTUITION. YOU'VE LOVED SWINGIN' YER SWORD SINCE BEFORE YOU WERE THIS TALL. IT AIN'T HARD TO FIGURE OUT.
KARA (RATTLE)
KARA
...OH.
...

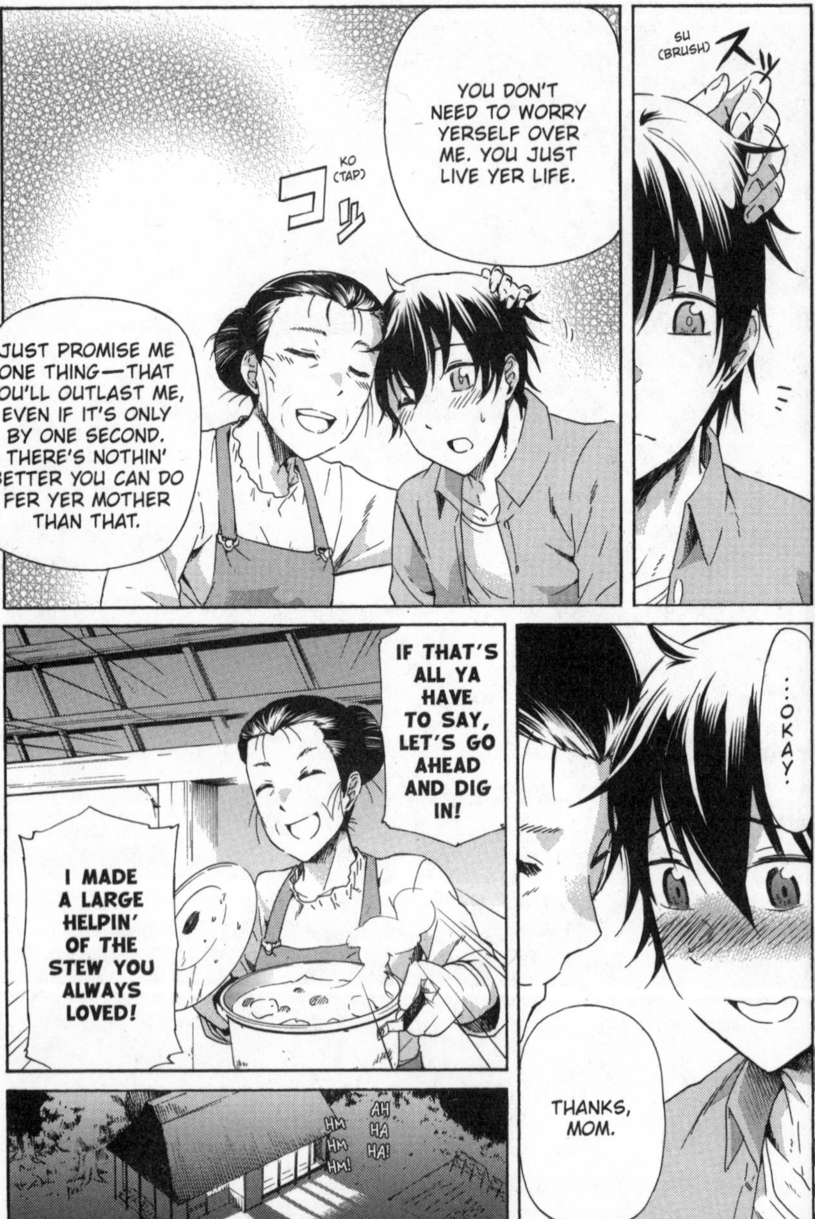
SU (BRUSH)
YOU DON'T NEED TO WORRY YERSELF OVER ME. YOU JUST LIVE YER LIFE.
KO (TAP)
JUST PROMISE ME ONE THING—THAT YOU'LL OUTLAST ME, EVEN IF IT'S ONLY BY ONE SECOND. THERE'S NOTHIN' BETTER YOU CAN DO FER YER MOTHER THAN THAT.
...OKAY.
THANKS, MOM.
IF THAT'S ALL YA HAVE TO SAY, LET'S GO AHEAD AND DIG IN!
I MADE A LARGE HELPIN' OF THE STEW YOU ALWAYS LOVED!
AH HA HA!
HM HM HM!

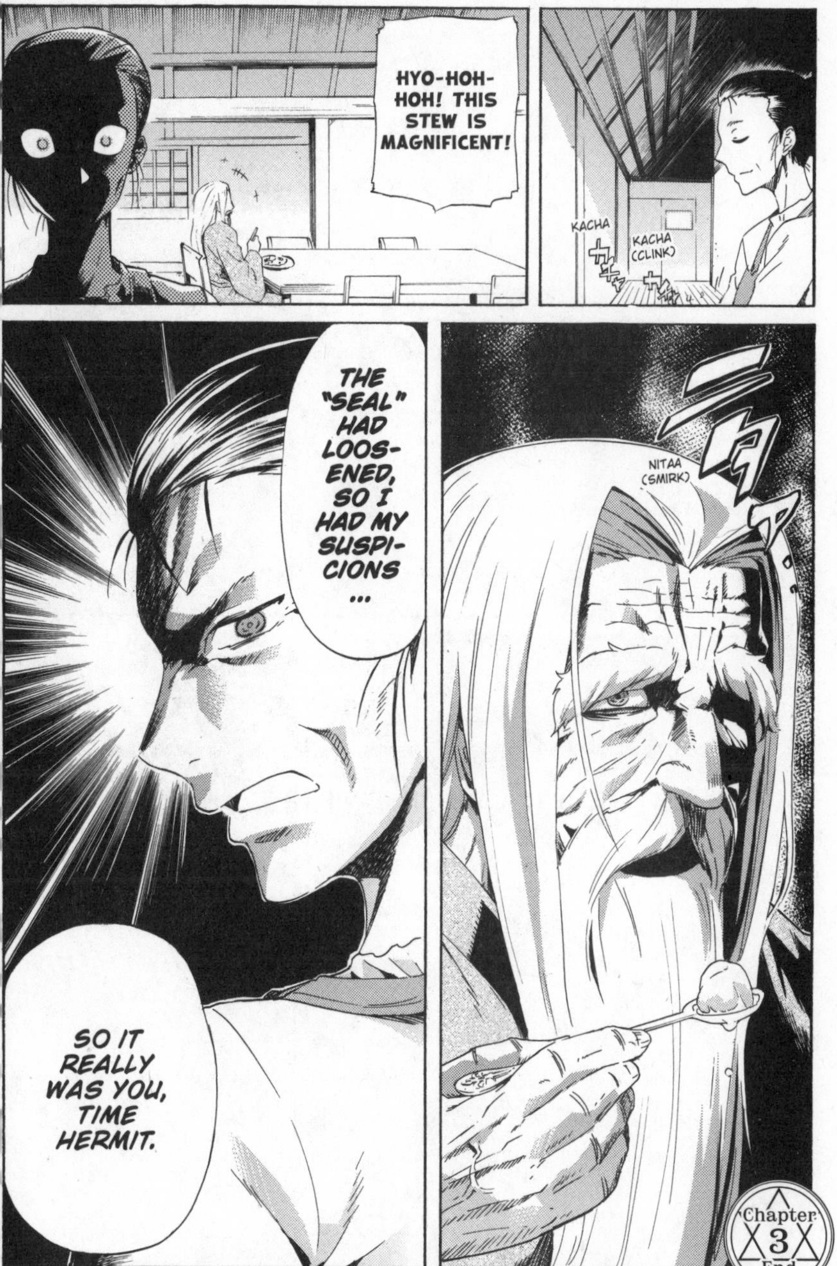
KACHA
KACHA (CLINK)
HYO-HOH-HOH! THIS STEW IS MAGNIFICENT!
NITAA (SMIRK)
THE "SEAL" HAD LOOSENED, SO I HAD MY SUSPICIONS ...
SO IT REALLY WAS YOU, TIME HERMIT.
Chapter 3 End

YOU'RE AMAZ-ING, ALLEN!
BIKU (SHOCK)
DO (THUD)
DO
DO
DO
WHAT A MATCH!

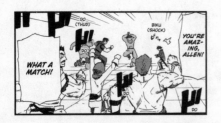

I KEPT PRESSING THE 100-MILLION-YEAR BUTTON AND CAME OUT ON TOP

~THE UNBEATABLE REJECT SWORDSMAN~

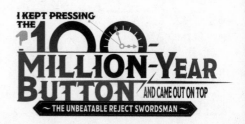

Chapter 4

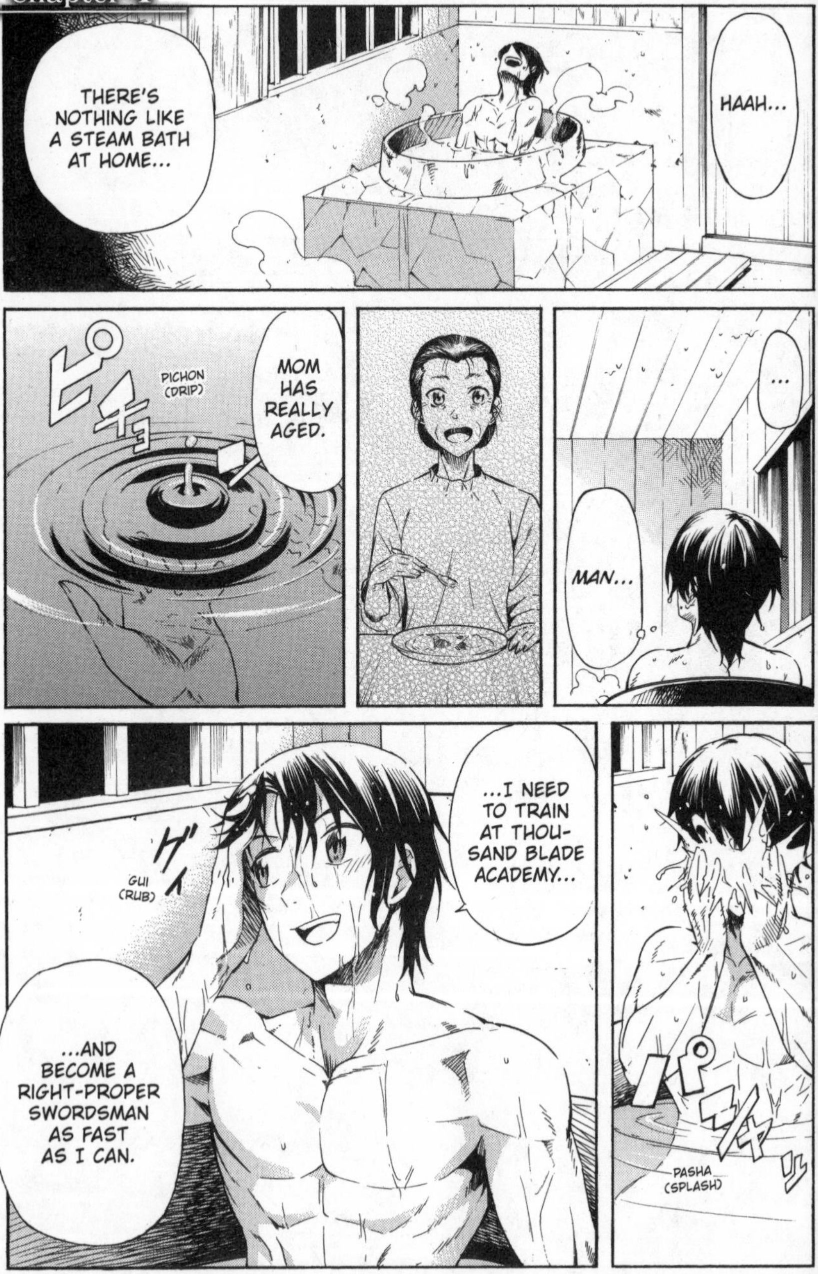
HAAH...
THERE'S NOTHING LIKE A STEAM BATH AT HOME...
...
MAN...
MOM HAS REALLY AGED.
PICHON (DRIP)
PASHA (SPLASH)
...I NEED TO TRAIN AT THOU-SAND BLADE ACADEMY...
GUI (RUB)
...AND BECOME A RIGHT-PROPER SWORDSMAN AS FAST AS I CAN.

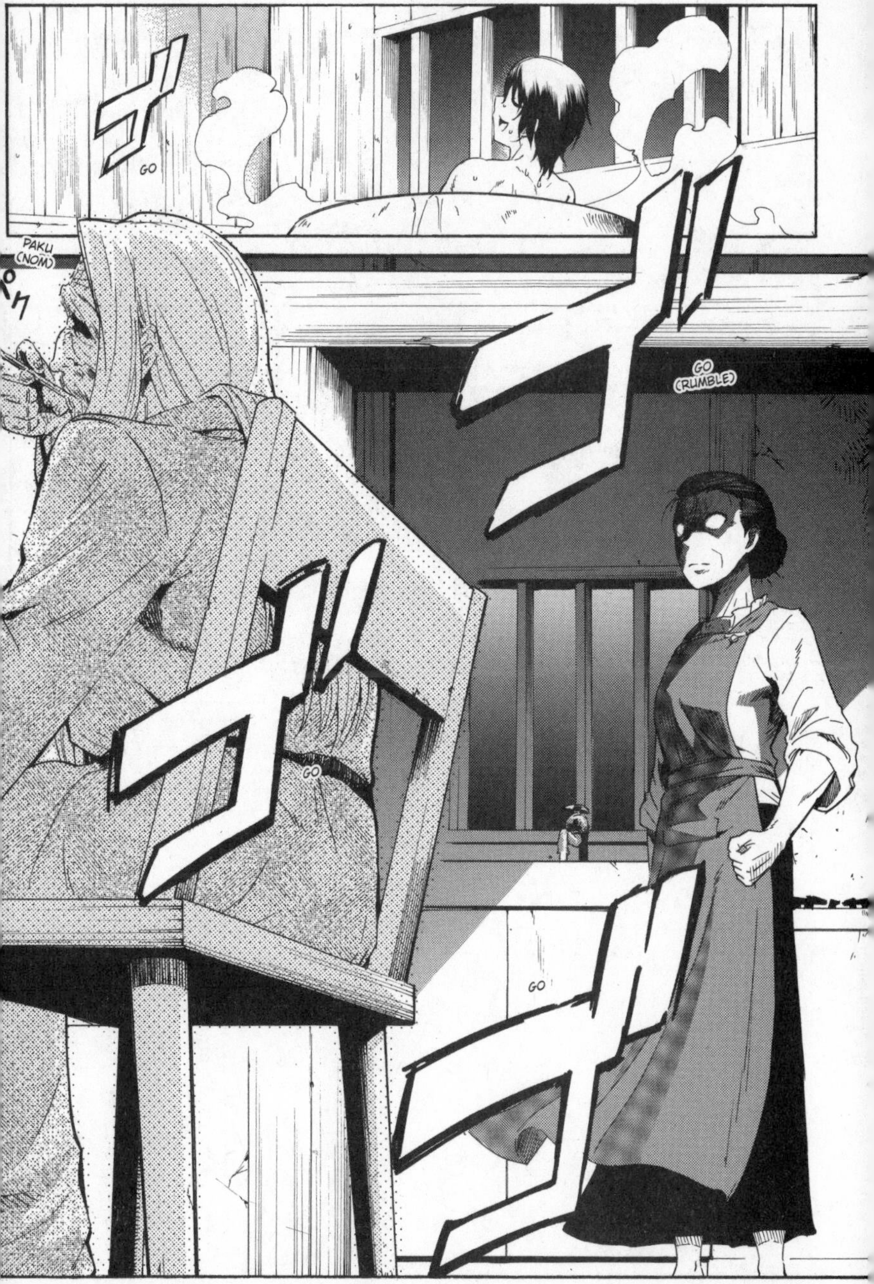
GO
GO
(RUMBLE)
PAKU
(NOM)
GO
GO

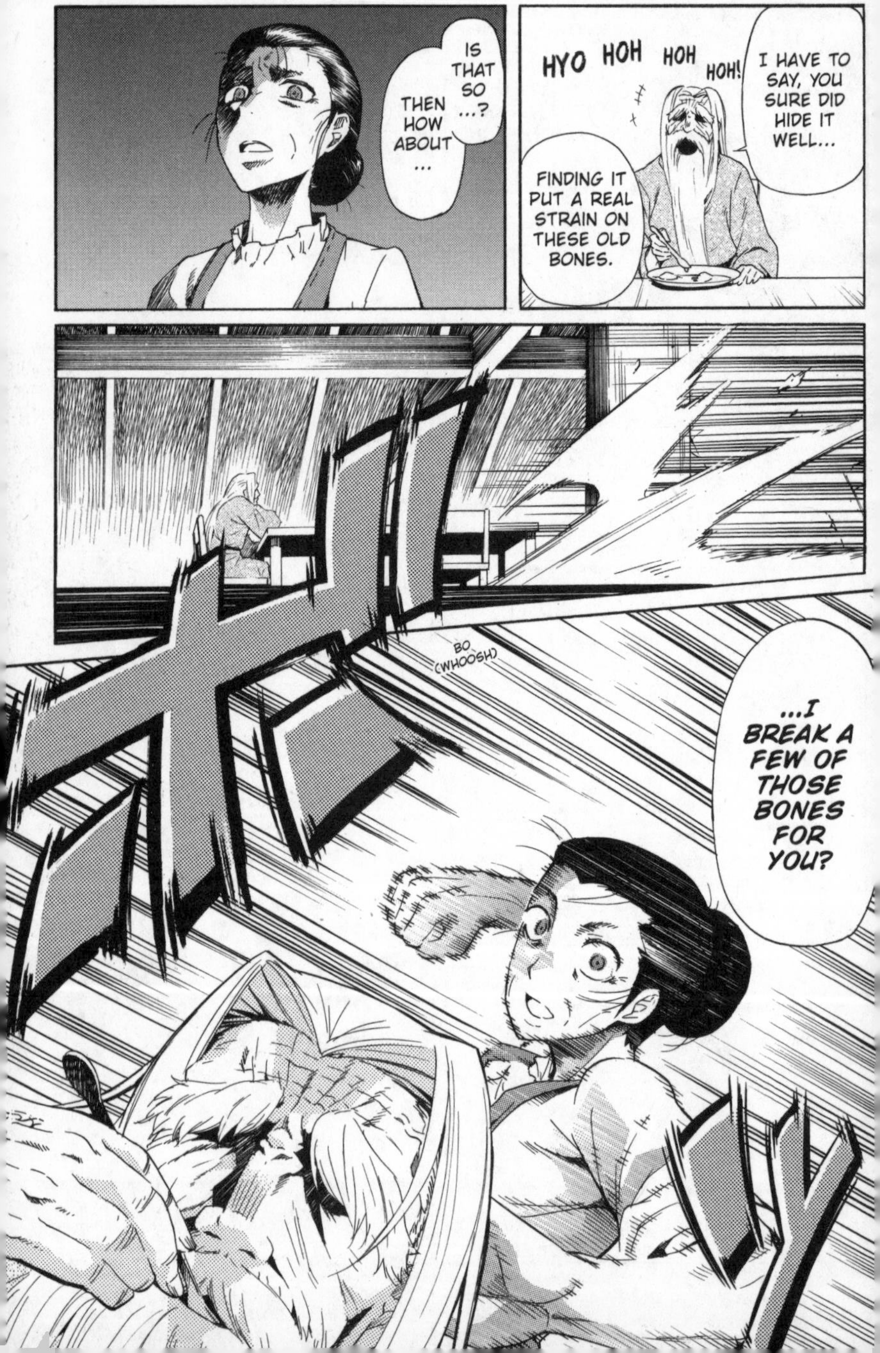
I HAVE TO SAY, YOU SURE DID HIDE IT WELL...
HYO HOH HOH HOH!
FINDING IT PUT A REAL STRAIN ON THESE OLD BONES.
IS THAT SO ...?
THEN HOW ABOUT ...
BO (WHOOSH)
...I BREAK A FEW OF THOSE BONES FOR YOU?

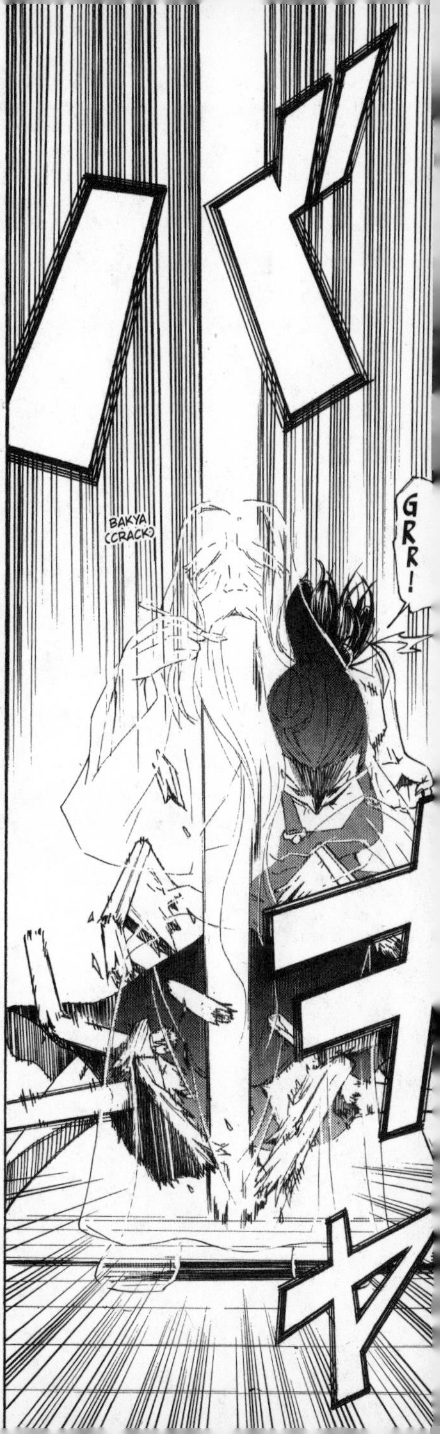
GRR!
BAKYA (CRACK)

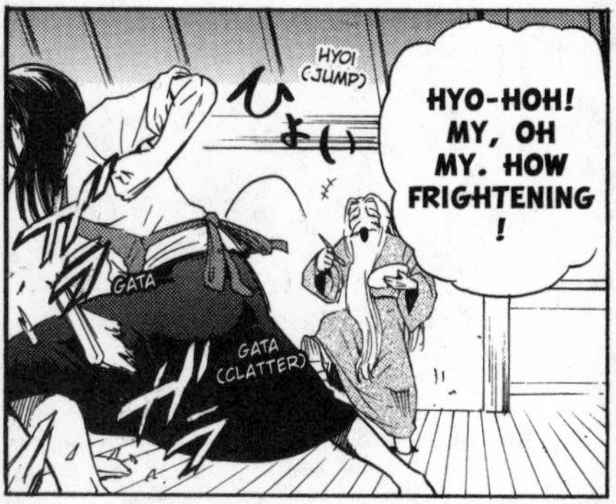
HYO-HOH! MY, OH MY. HOW FRIGHTENING!
HYOI (JUMP)
GATA
GATA (CLATTER)

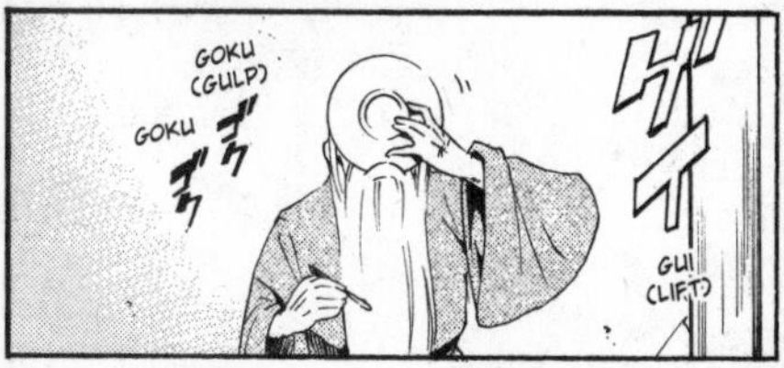
GUI (LIFT)
GOKU (GULP)
GOKU

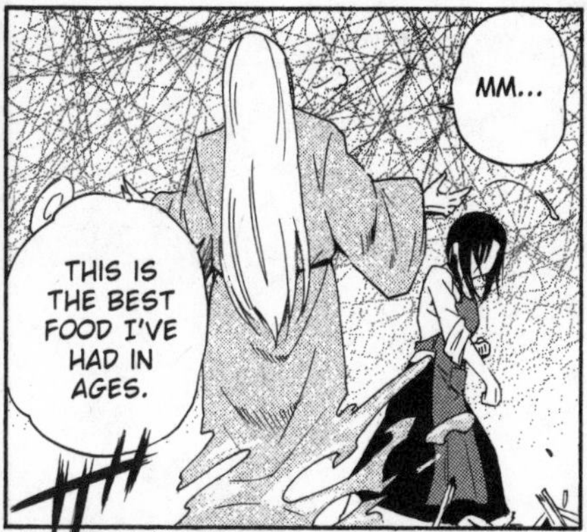
MM...
THIS IS THE BEST FOOD I'VE HAD IN AGES.

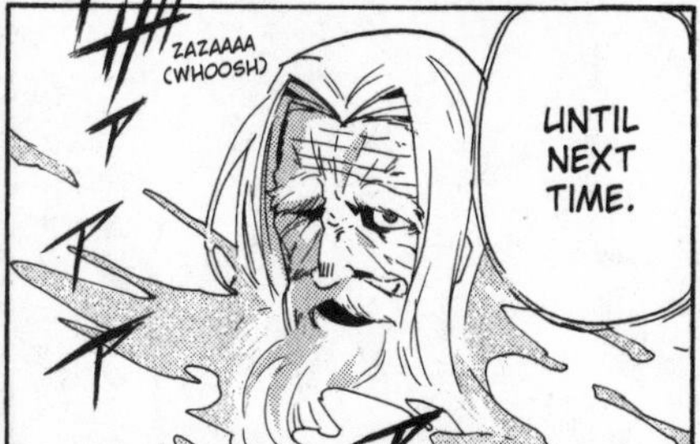
UNTIL NEXT TIME.
ZAZAAAA (WHOOSH)

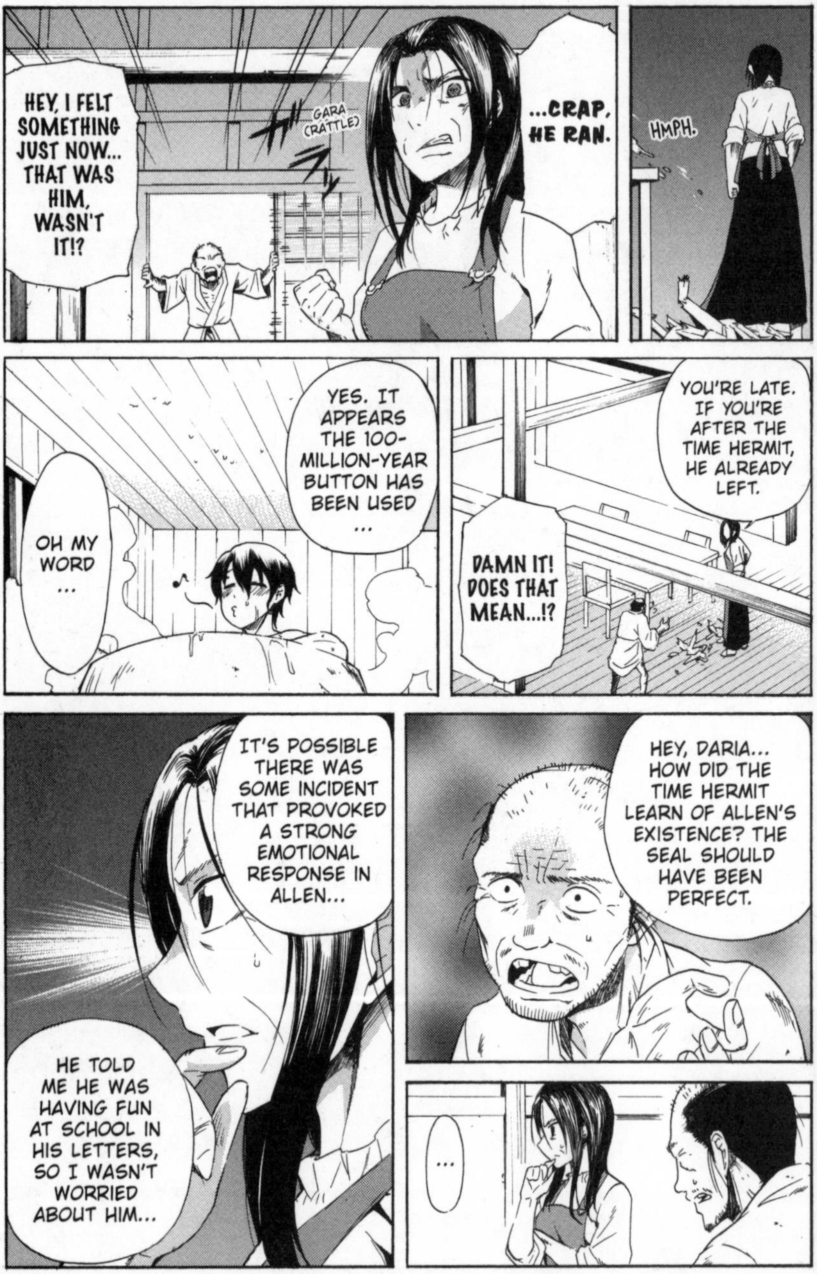
HMPH.
...CRAP, HE RAN.
GARA (RATTLE)
HEY, I FELT SOMETHING JUST NOW... THAT WAS HIM, WASN'T IT!?
YOU'RE LATE. IF YOU'RE AFTER THE TIME HERMIT, HE ALREADY LEFT.
DAMN IT! DOES THAT MEAN...!?
YES. IT APPEARS THE 100-MILLION-YEAR BUTTON HAS BEEN USED...
OH MY WORD...
HEY, DARIA... HOW DID THE TIME HERMIT LEARN OF ALLEN'S EXISTENCE? THE SEAL SHOULD HAVE BEEN PERFECT.
...
IT'S POSSIBLE THERE WAS SOME INCIDENT THAT PROVOKED A STRONG EMOTIONAL RESPONSE IN ALLEN...
HE TOLD ME HE WAS HAVING FUN AT SCHOOL IN HIS LETTERS, SO I WASN'T WORRIED ABOUT HIM...

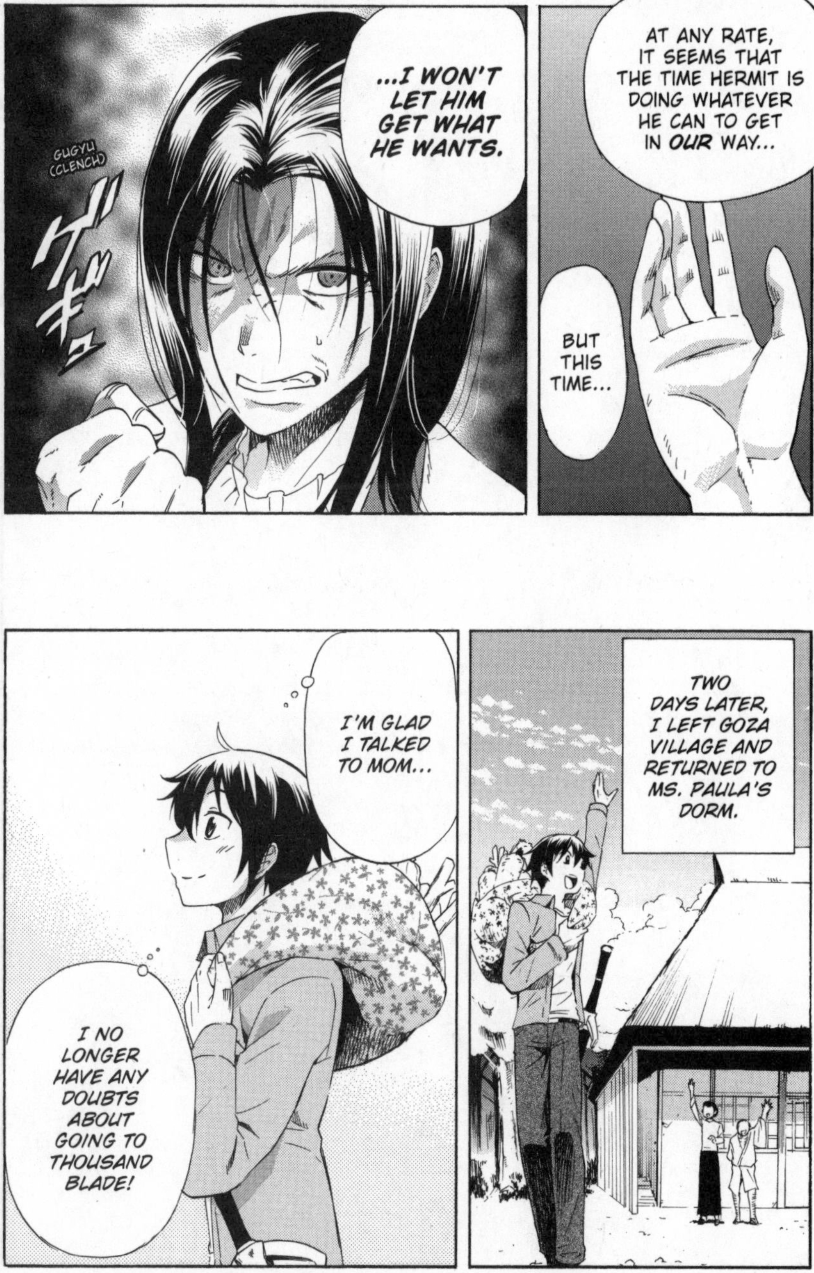
AT ANY RATE, IT SEEMS THAT THE TIME HERMIT IS DOING WHATEVER HE CAN TO GET IN OUR WAY...
BUT THIS TIME...
...I WON'T LET HIM GET WHAT HE WANTS.
GUGYU (CLENCH)
TWO DAYS LATER, I LEFT GOZA VILLAGE AND RETURNED TO MS. PAULA'S DORM.
I'M GLAD I TALKED TO MOM...
I NO LONGER HAVE ANY DOUBTS ABOUT GOING TO THOUSAND BLADE!

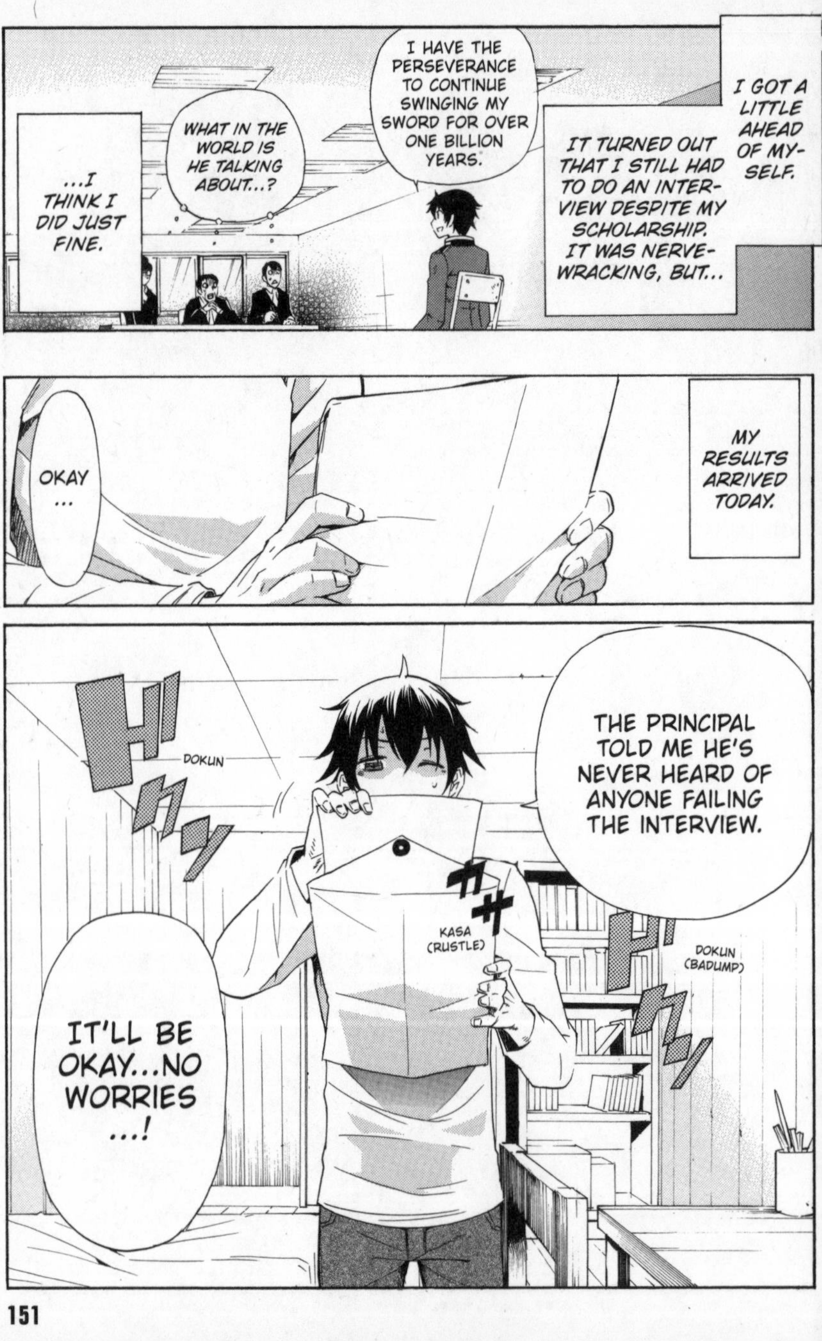
I GOT A LITTLE AHEAD OF MY-SELF.
IT TURNED OUT THAT I STILL HAD TO DO AN INTER-VIEW DESPITE MY SCHOLARSHIP. IT WAS NERVE-WRACKING, BUT...
I HAVE THE PERSEVERANCE TO CONTINUE SWINGING MY SWORD FOR OVER ONE BILLION YEARS.
WHAT IN THE WORLD IS HE TALKING ABOUT...?
...I THINK I DID JUST FINE.
MY RESULTS ARRIVED TODAY.
OKAY...
THE PRINCIPAL TOLD ME HE'S NEVER HEARD OF ANYONE FAILING THE INTERVIEW.
DOKUN (BADUMP)
KASA (RUSTLE)
DOKUN
IT'LL BE OKAY...NO WORRIES...!

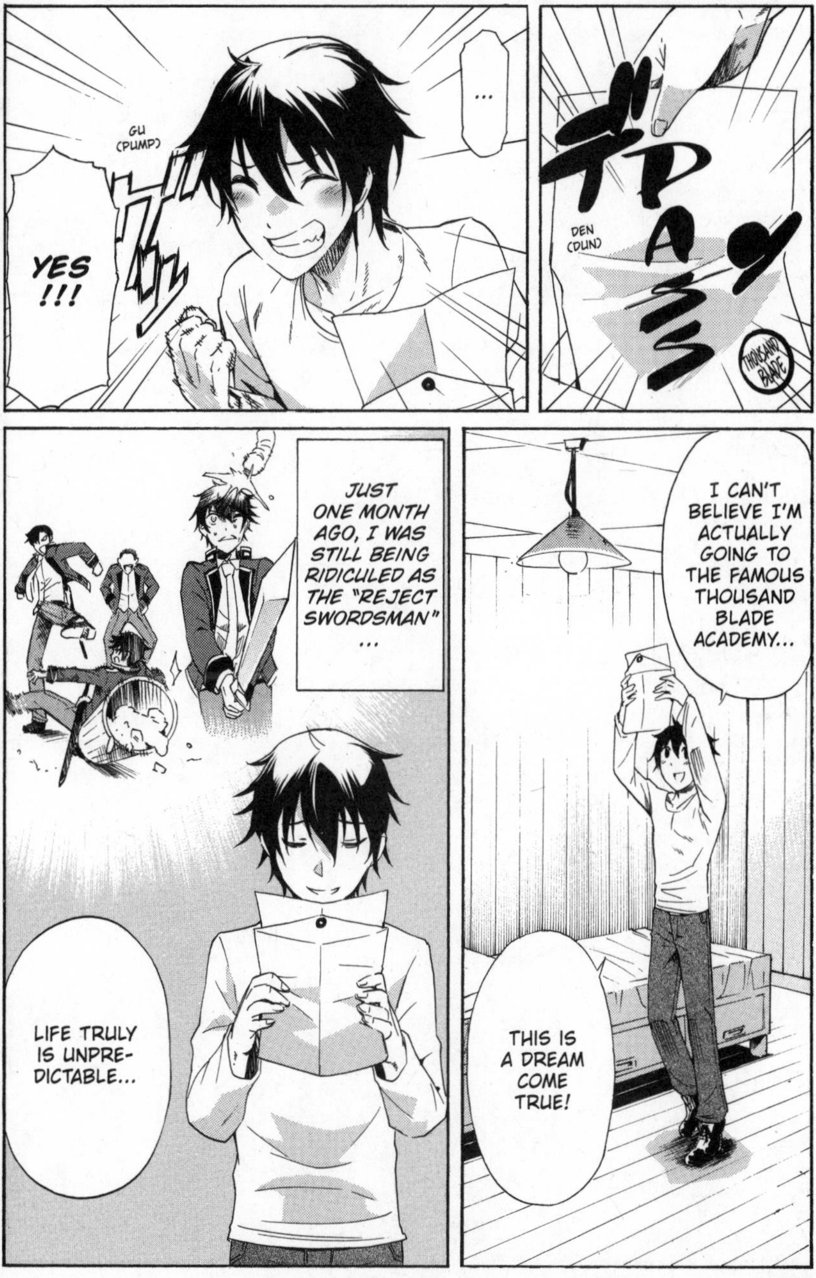
PASS
THOUSAND BLADE
DEN (DUN)
...
GU (PUMP)
YES !!!
I CAN'T BELIEVE I'M ACTUALLY GOING TO THE FAMOUS THOUSAND BLADE ACADEMY...
THIS IS A DREAM COME TRUE!
JUST ONE MONTH AGO, I WAS STILL BEING RIDICULED AS THE "REJECT SWORDSMAN"...
LIFE TRULY IS UNPRE-DICTABLE...

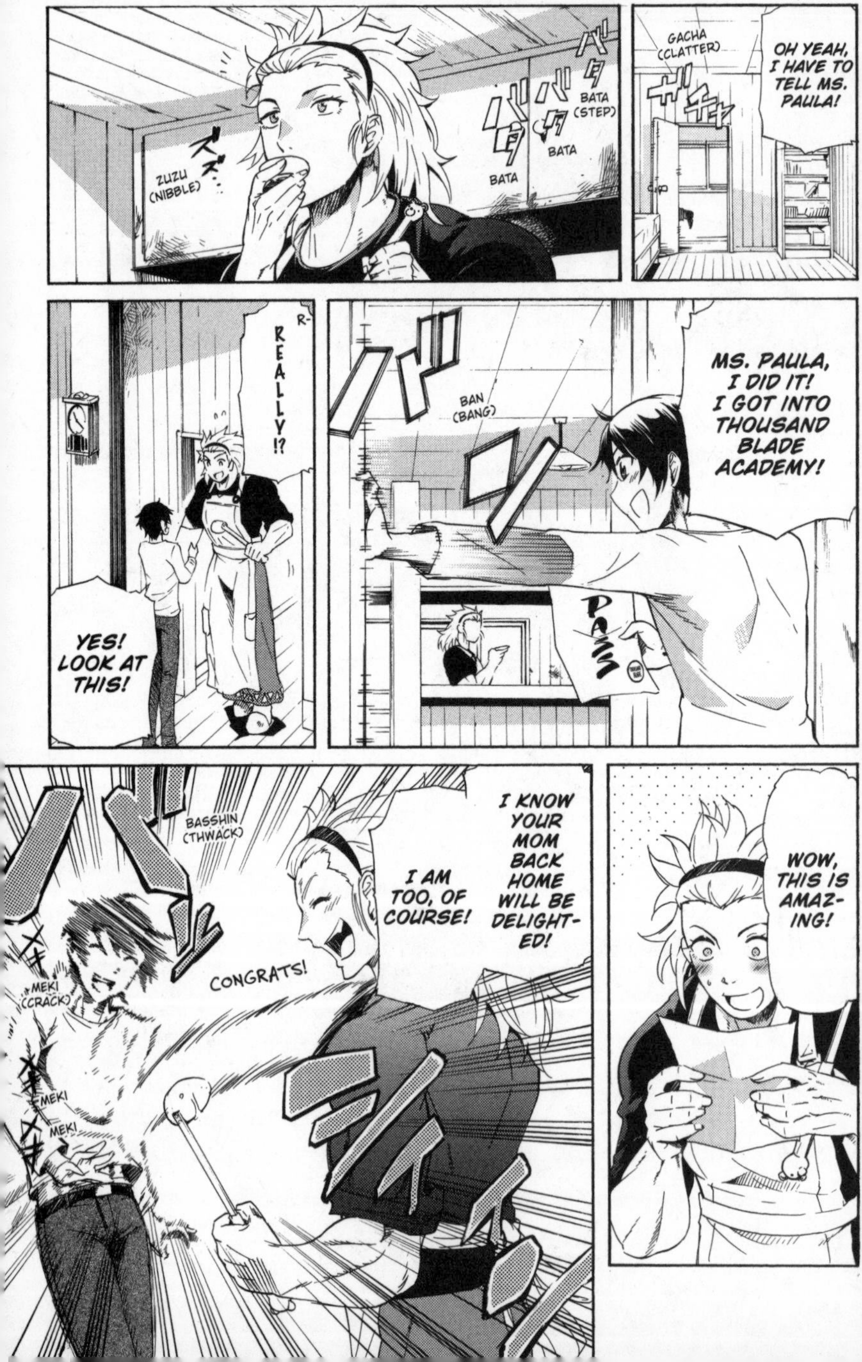
GACHA (CLATTER)
OH YEAH, I HAVE TO TELL MS. PAULA!
BATA (STEP)
BATA
BATA
ZUZU (NIBBLE)
MS. PAULA, I DID IT! I GOT INTO THOUSAND BLADE ACADEMY!
BAN (BANG)
PASS
R-REALLY!?
YES! LOOK AT THIS!
WOW, THIS IS AMAZ-ING!
I KNOW YOUR MOM BACK HOME WILL BE DELIGHT-ED!
I AM TOO, OF COURSE!
BASSHIN (THWACK)
CONGRATS!
MEKI (CRACK)
MEKI
MEKI

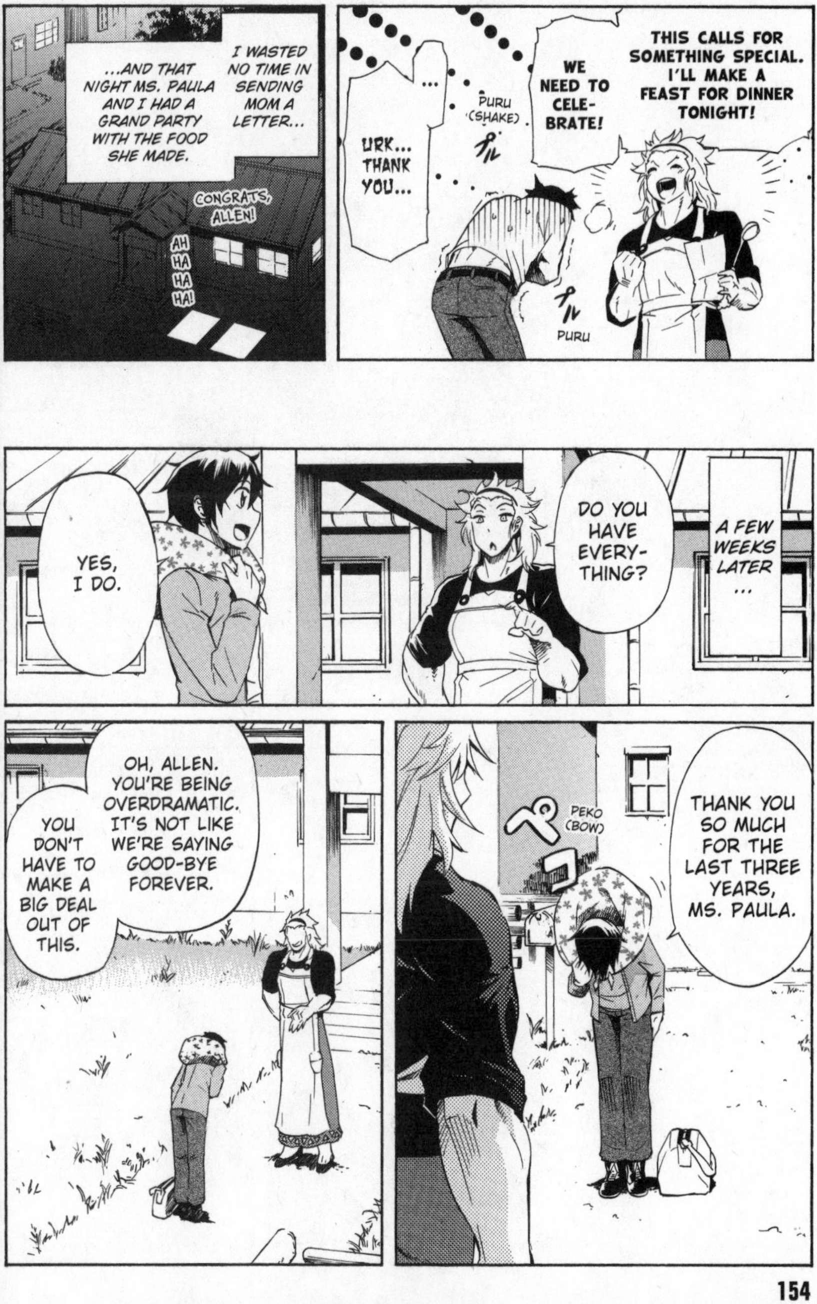
THIS CALLS FOR SOMETHING SPECIAL. I'LL MAKE A FEAST FOR DINNER TONIGHT!
WE NEED TO CELEBRATE!
...
PURU (SHAKE)
URK... THANK YOU...
PURU
I WASTED NO TIME IN SENDING MOM A LETTER...
...AND THAT NIGHT MS. PAULA AND I HAD A GRAND PARTY WITH THE FOOD SHE MADE.
CONGRATS, ALLEN!
AH HA HA HA!
A FEW WEEKS LATER...
DO YOU HAVE EVERYTHING?
YES, I DO.
THANK YOU SO MUCH FOR THE LAST THREE YEARS, MS. PAULA.
PEKO (BOW)
OH, ALLEN. YOU'RE BEING OVERDRAMATIC. IT'S NOT LIKE WE'RE SAYING GOOD-BYE FOREVER.
YOU DON'T HAVE TO MAKE A BIG DEAL OUT OF THIS.

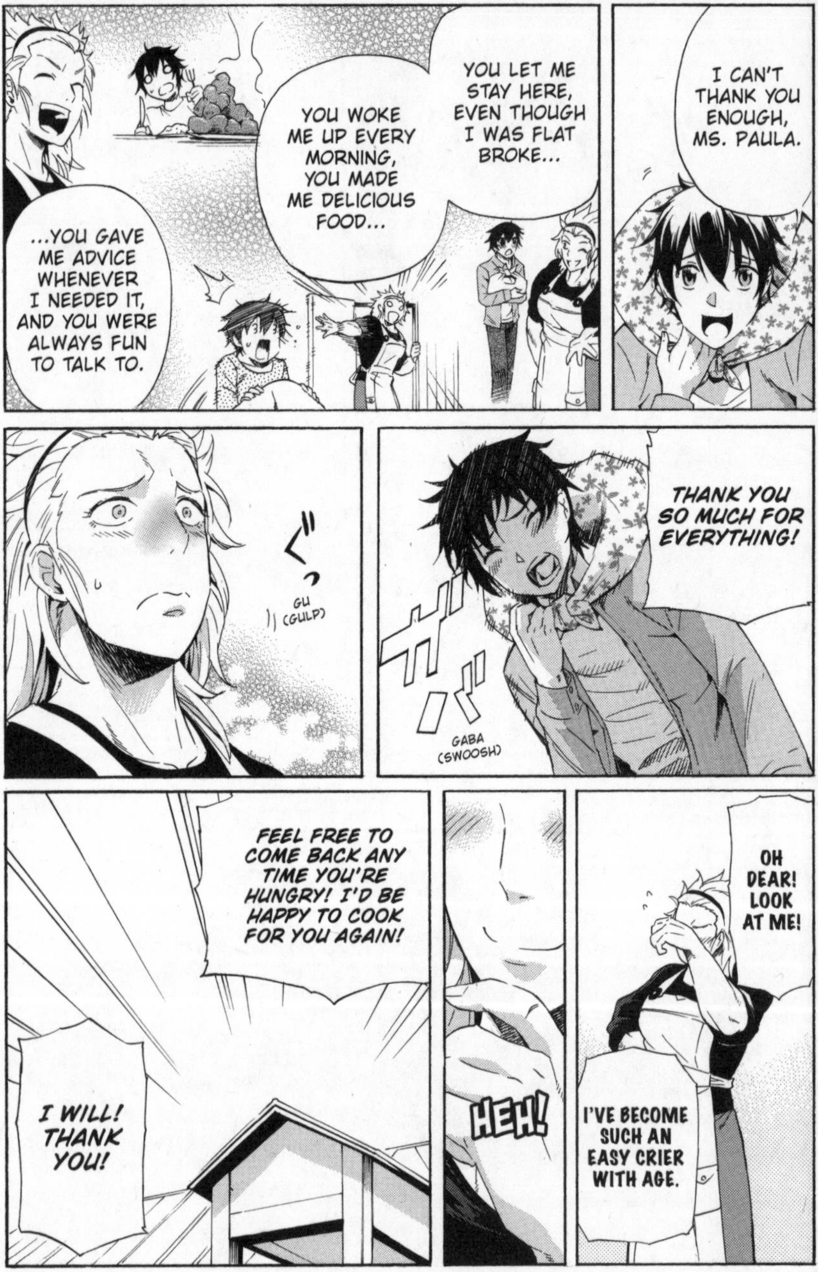
I CAN'T THANK YOU ENOUGH, MS. PAULA.
YOU LET ME STAY HERE, EVEN THOUGH I WAS FLAT BROKE...
YOU WOKE ME UP EVERY MORNING, YOU MADE ME DELICIOUS FOOD...
...YOU GAVE ME ADVICE WHENEVER I NEEDED IT, AND YOU WERE ALWAYS FUN TO TALK TO.
THANK YOU SO MUCH FOR EVERYTHING!
GABA (SWOOSH)
GU (GULP)
OH DEAR! LOOK AT ME!
I'VE BECOME SUCH AN EASY CRIER WITH AGE.
HEH!
FEEL FREE TO COME BACK ANY TIME YOU'RE HUNGRY! I'D BE HAPPY TO COOK FOR YOU AGAIN!
I WILL! THANK YOU!

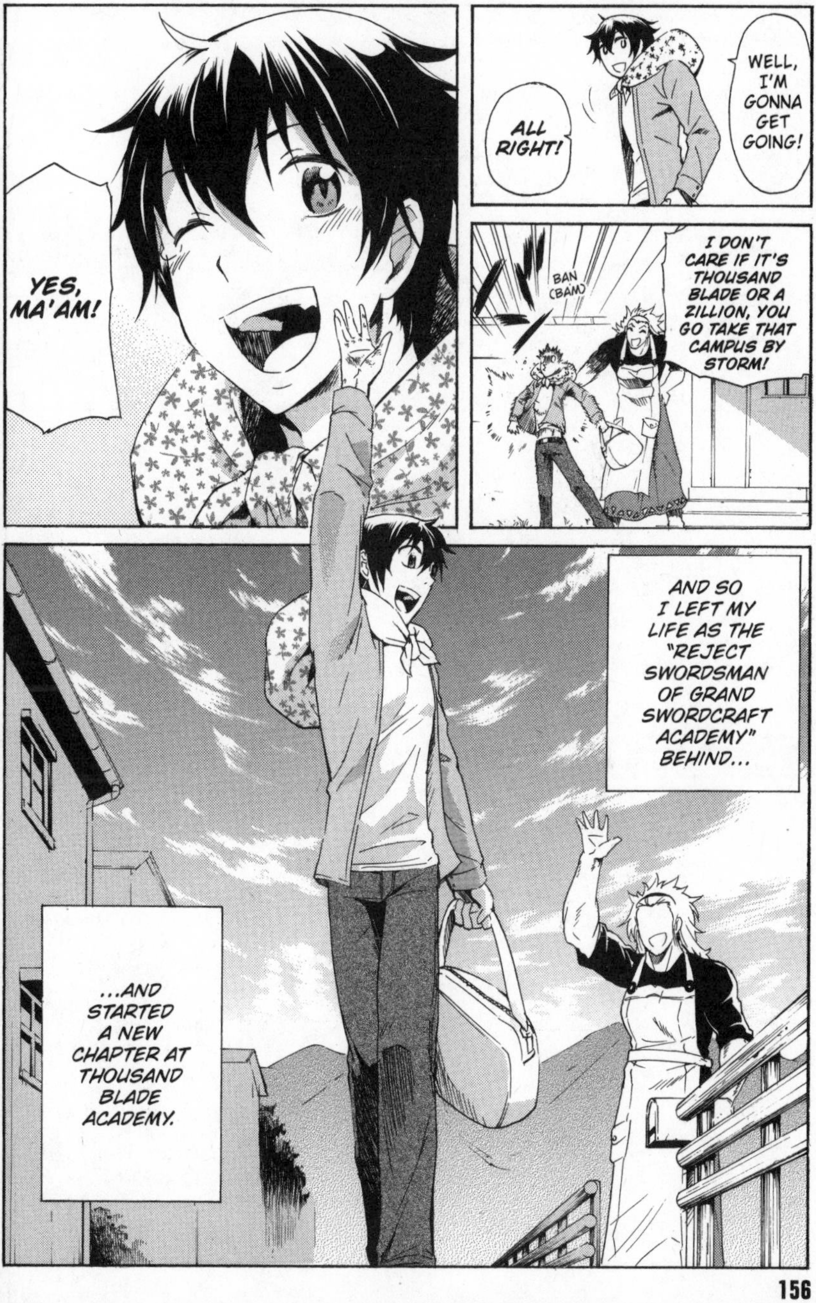
WELL, I'M GONNA GET GOING!
ALL RIGHT!
I DON'T CARE IF IT'S THOUSAND BLADE OR A ZILLION, YOU GO TAKE THAT CAMPUS BY STORM!
BAN (BAM)
YES, MA'AM!
AND SO I LEFT MY LIFE AS THE "REJECT SWORDSMAN OF GRAND SWORDCRAFT ACADEMY" BEHIND...
...AND STARTED A NEW CHAPTER AT THOUSAND BLADE ACADEMY.

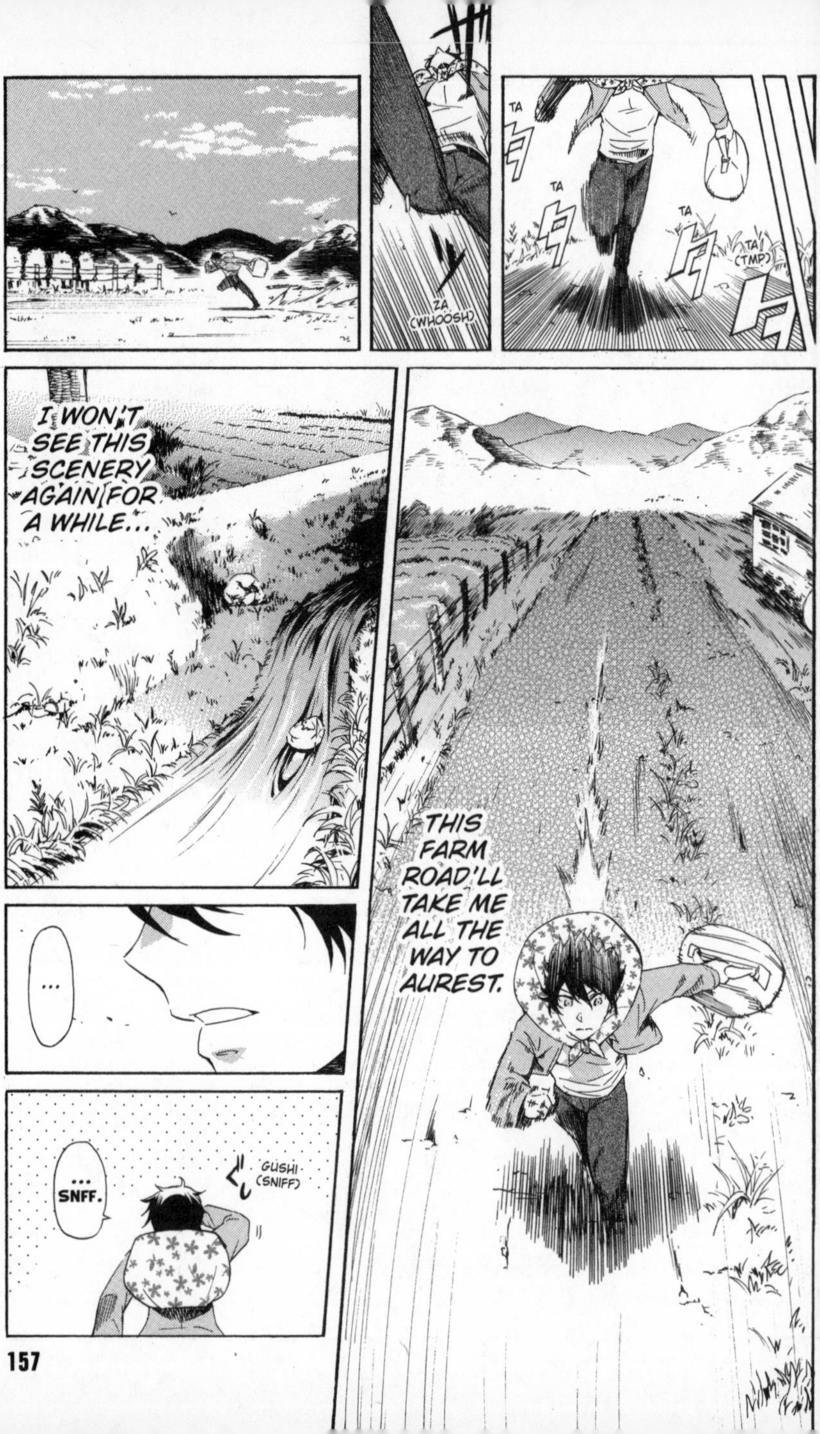
TA
TA
TA
TA (TMP)
ZA (WHOOSH)
THIS FARM ROAD'LL TAKE ME ALL THE WAY TO AUREST.
I WON'T SEE THIS SCENERY AGAIN FOR A WHILE...
...
...SNFF.
GUSHI (SNIFF)

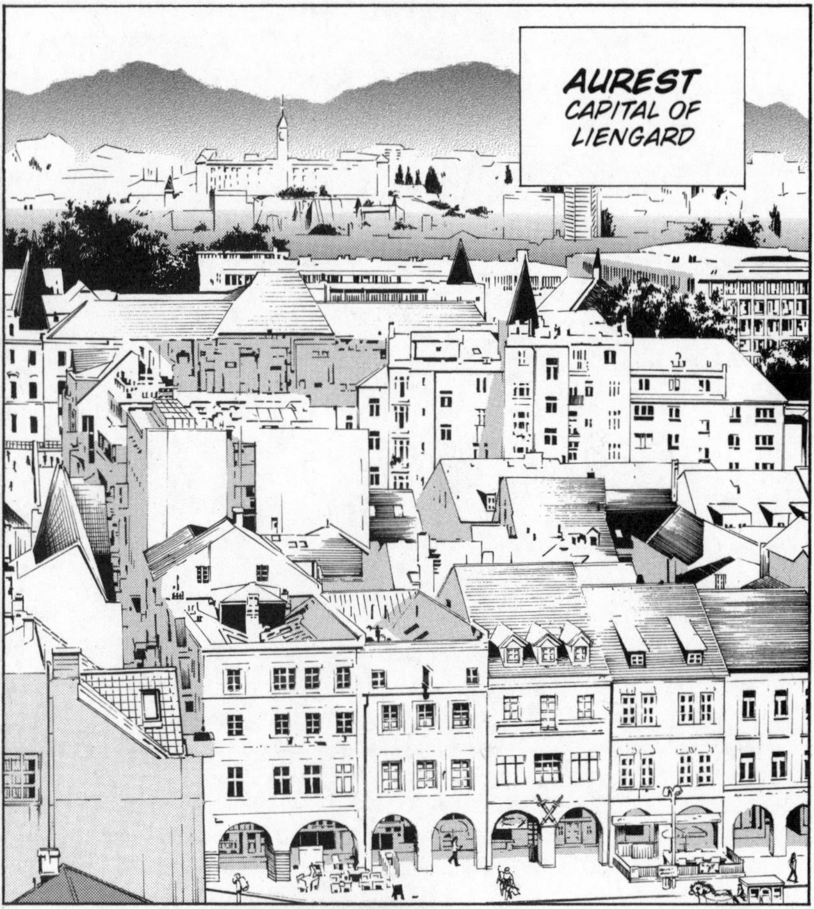
AUREST
CAPITAL OF
LIENGARD
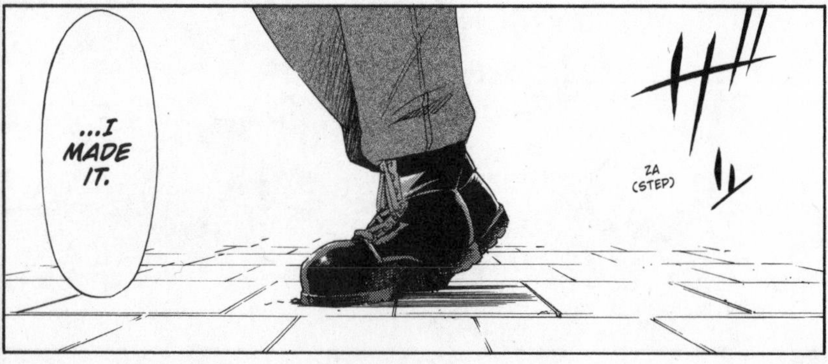
ZA
(STEP)
...I
MADE
IT.

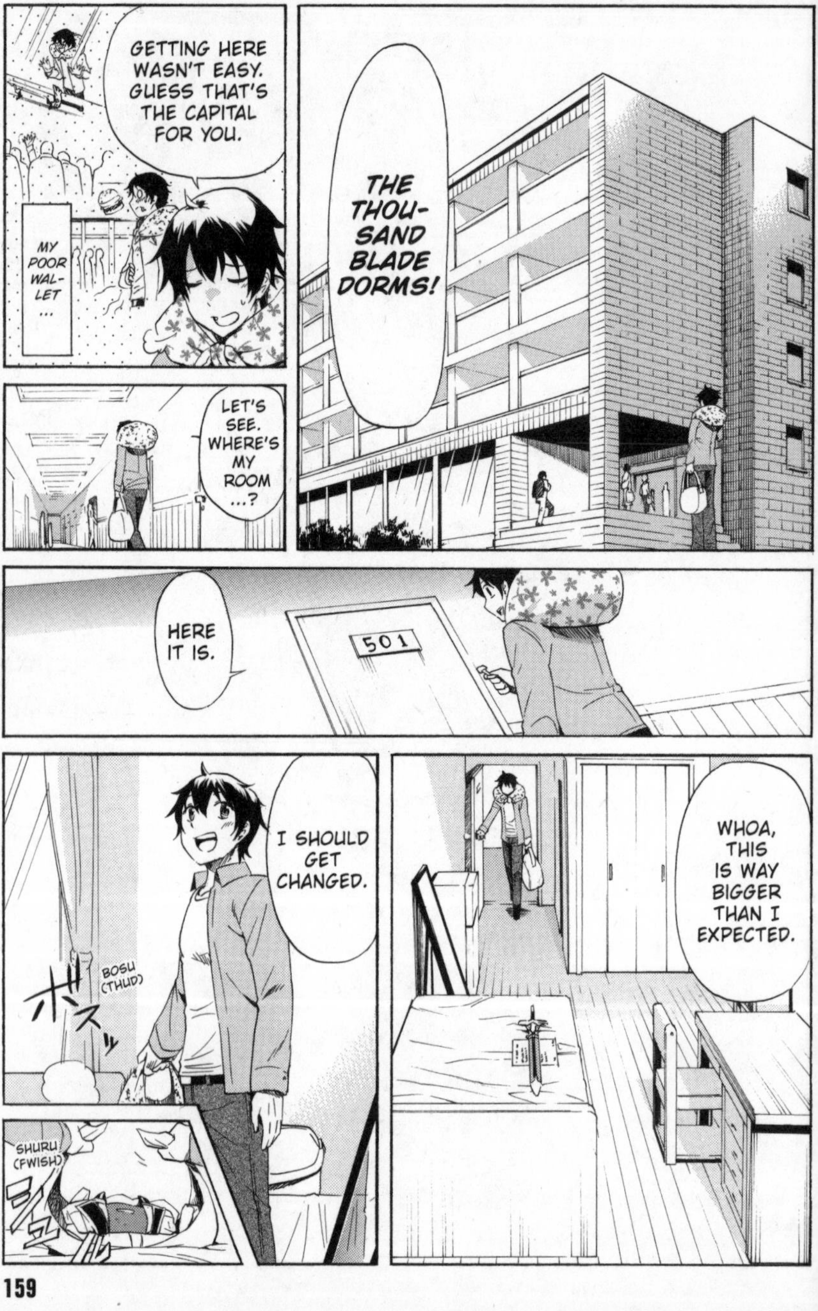
THE THOUSAND BLADE DORMS!
GETTING HERE WASN'T EASY. GUESS THAT'S THE CAPITAL FOR YOU.
MY POOR WALLET...
LET'S SEE. WHERE'S MY ROOM...?
HERE IT IS.
501
WHOA, THIS IS WAY BIGGER THAN I EXPECTED.
I SHOULD GET CHANGED.
ボスッ
BOSU (THUD)
SHURU (FWISH)

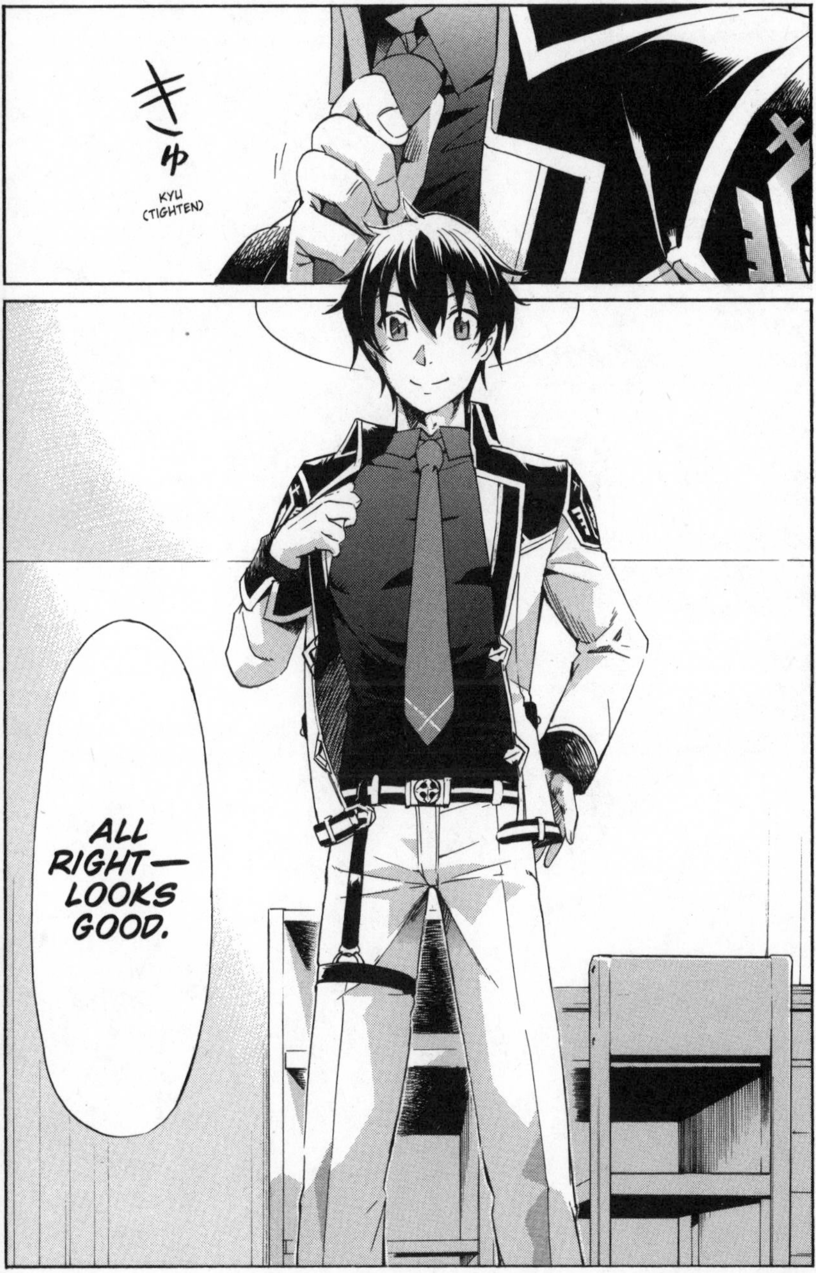
きゅ
KYU (TIGHTEN)
ALL RIGHT— LOOKS GOOD.

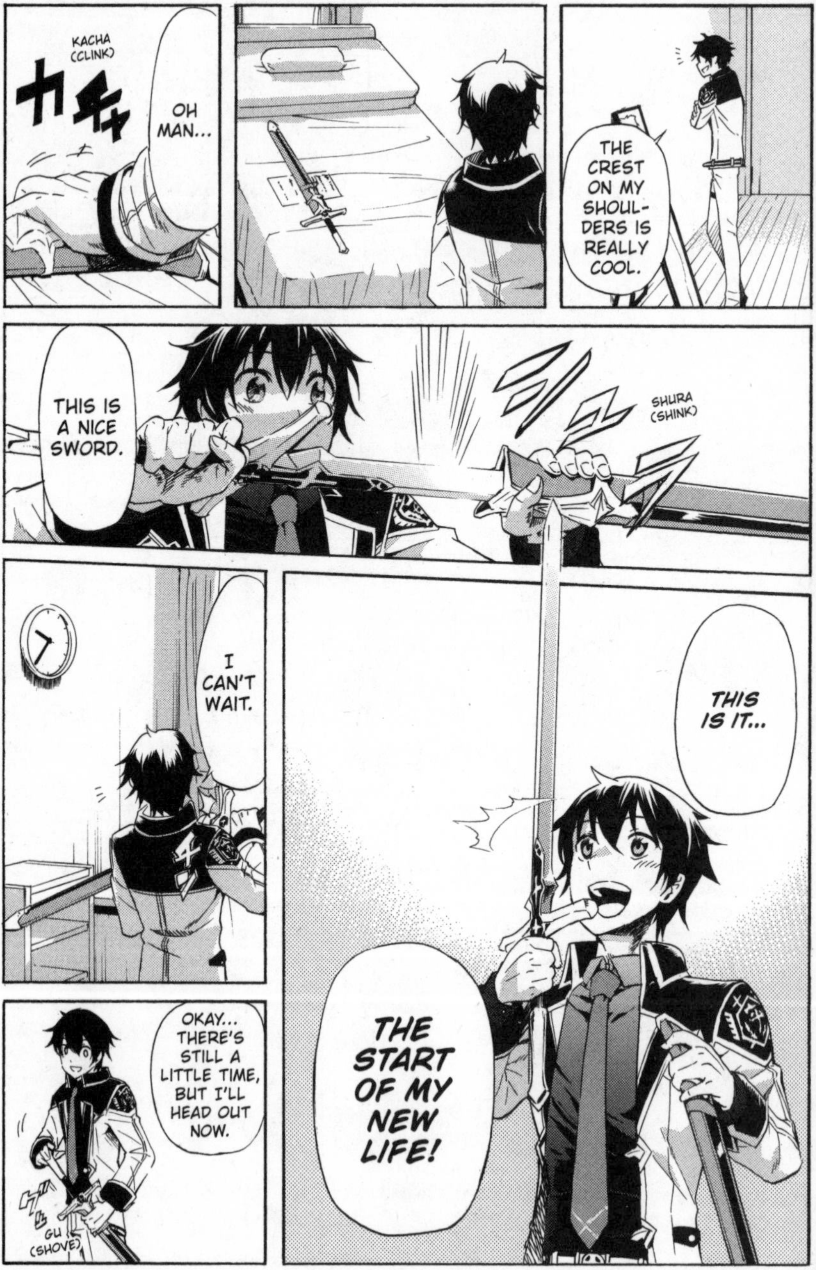
THE CREST ON MY SHOULDERS IS REALLY COOL.
OH MAN...
カチャ
KACHA (CLINK)
SHURA (SHINK)
THIS IS A NICE SWORD.
THIS IS IT...
THE START OF MY NEW LIFE!
I CAN'T WAIT.
OKAY... THERE'S STILL A LITTLE TIME, BUT I'LL HEAD OUT NOW.
GU (SHOVE)

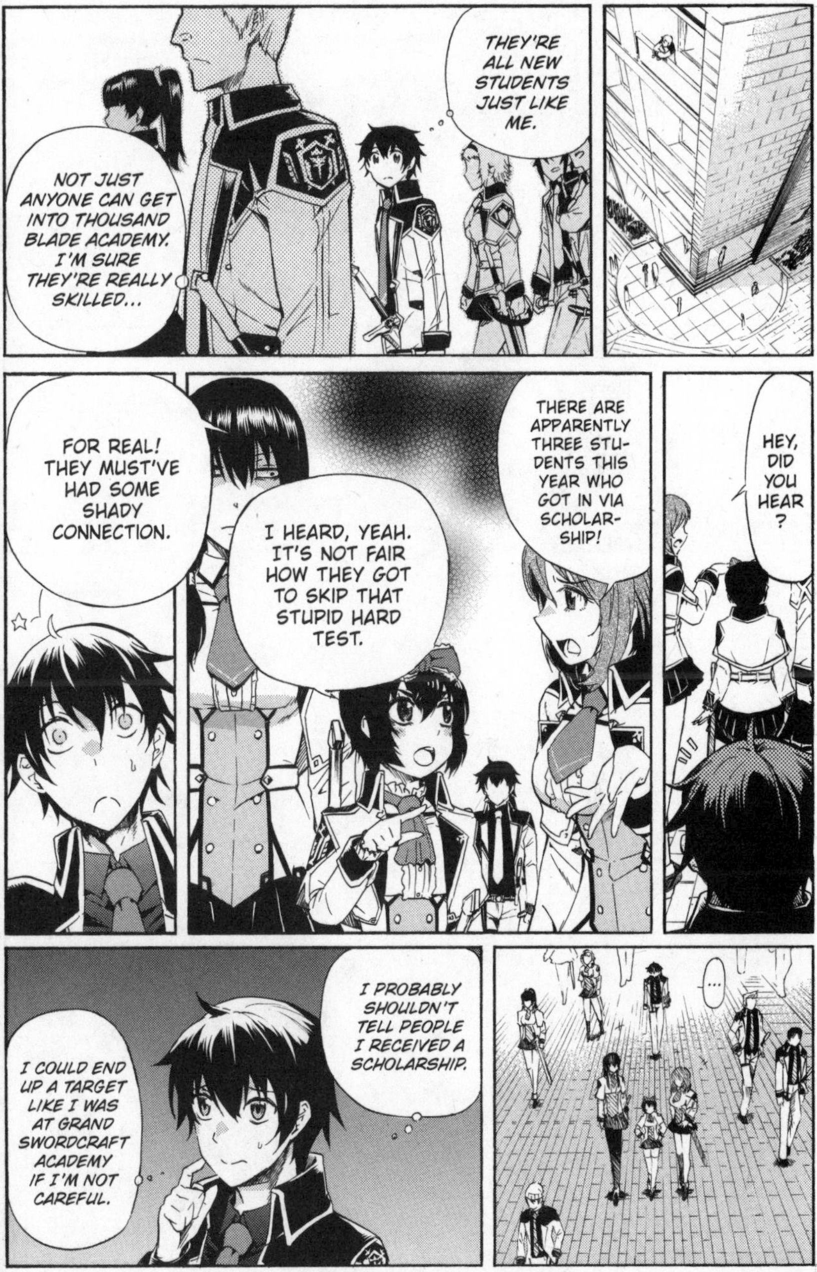
THEY'RE ALL NEW STUDENTS JUST LIKE ME.
NOT JUST ANYONE CAN GET INTO THOUSAND BLADE ACADEMY. I'M SURE THEY'RE REALLY SKILLED...
HEY, DID YOU HEAR?
THERE ARE APPARENTLY THREE STU-DENTS THIS YEAR WHO GOT IN VIA SCHOLAR-SHIP!
I HEARD, YEAH. IT'S NOT FAIR HOW THEY GOT TO SKIP THAT STUPID HARD TEST.
FOR REAL! THEY MUST'VE HAD SOME SHADY CONNECTION.
...
I PROBABLY SHOULDN'T TELL PEOPLE I RECEIVED A SCHOLARSHIP.
I COULD END UP A TARGET LIKE I WAS AT GRAND SWORDCRAFT ACADEMY IF I'M NOT CAREFUL.

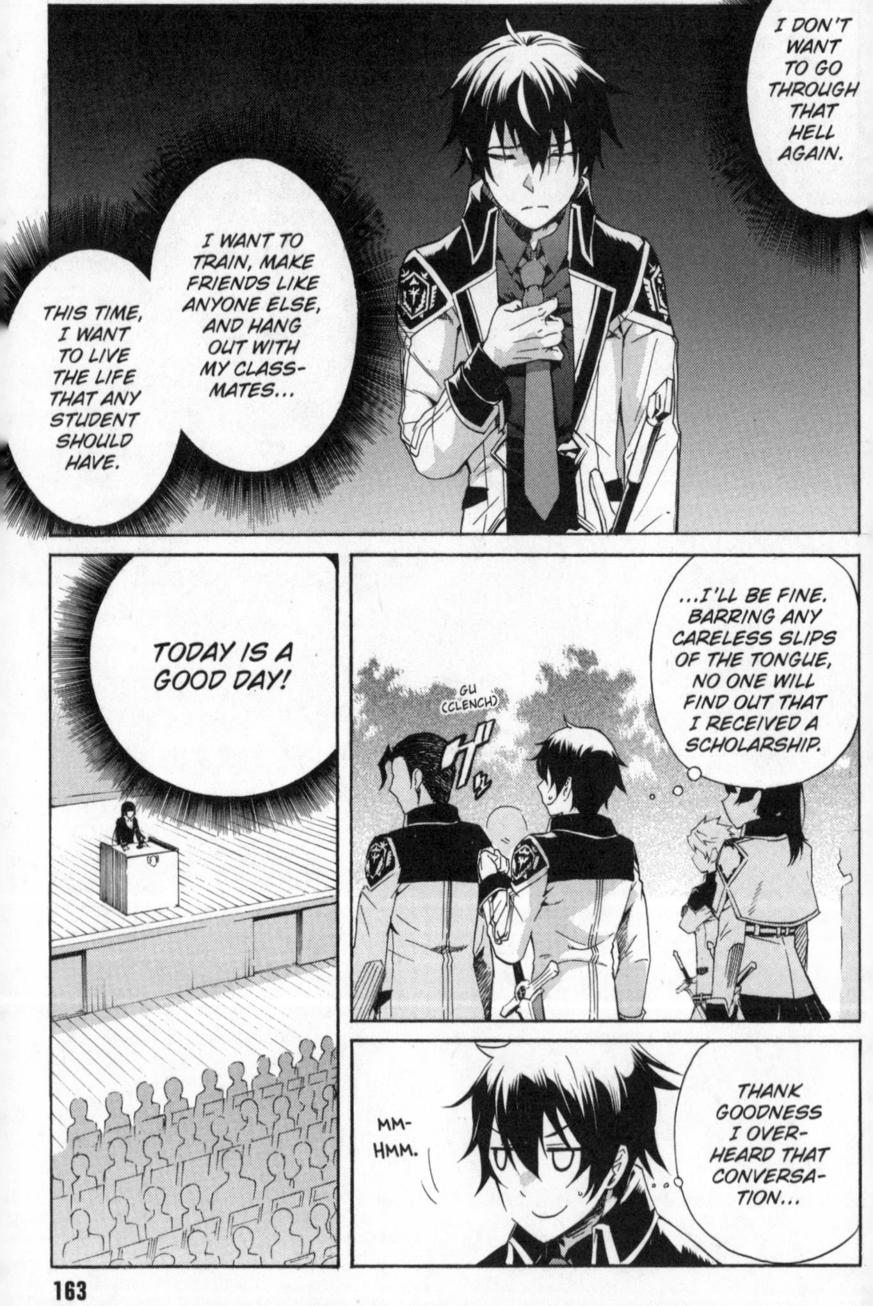
I DON'T WANT TO GO THROUGH THAT HELL AGAIN.
I WANT TO TRAIN, MAKE FRIENDS LIKE ANYONE ELSE, AND HANG OUT WITH MY CLASSMATES...
THIS TIME, I WANT TO LIVE THE LIFE THAT ANY STUDENT SHOULD HAVE.
...I'LL BE FINE. BARRING ANY CARELESS SLIPS OF THE TONGUE, NO ONE WILL FIND OUT THAT I RECEIVED A SCHOLARSHIP.
GU (CLENCH)
THANK GOODNESS I OVERHEARD THAT CONVERSATION...
MM-HMM.
TODAY IS A GOOD DAY!

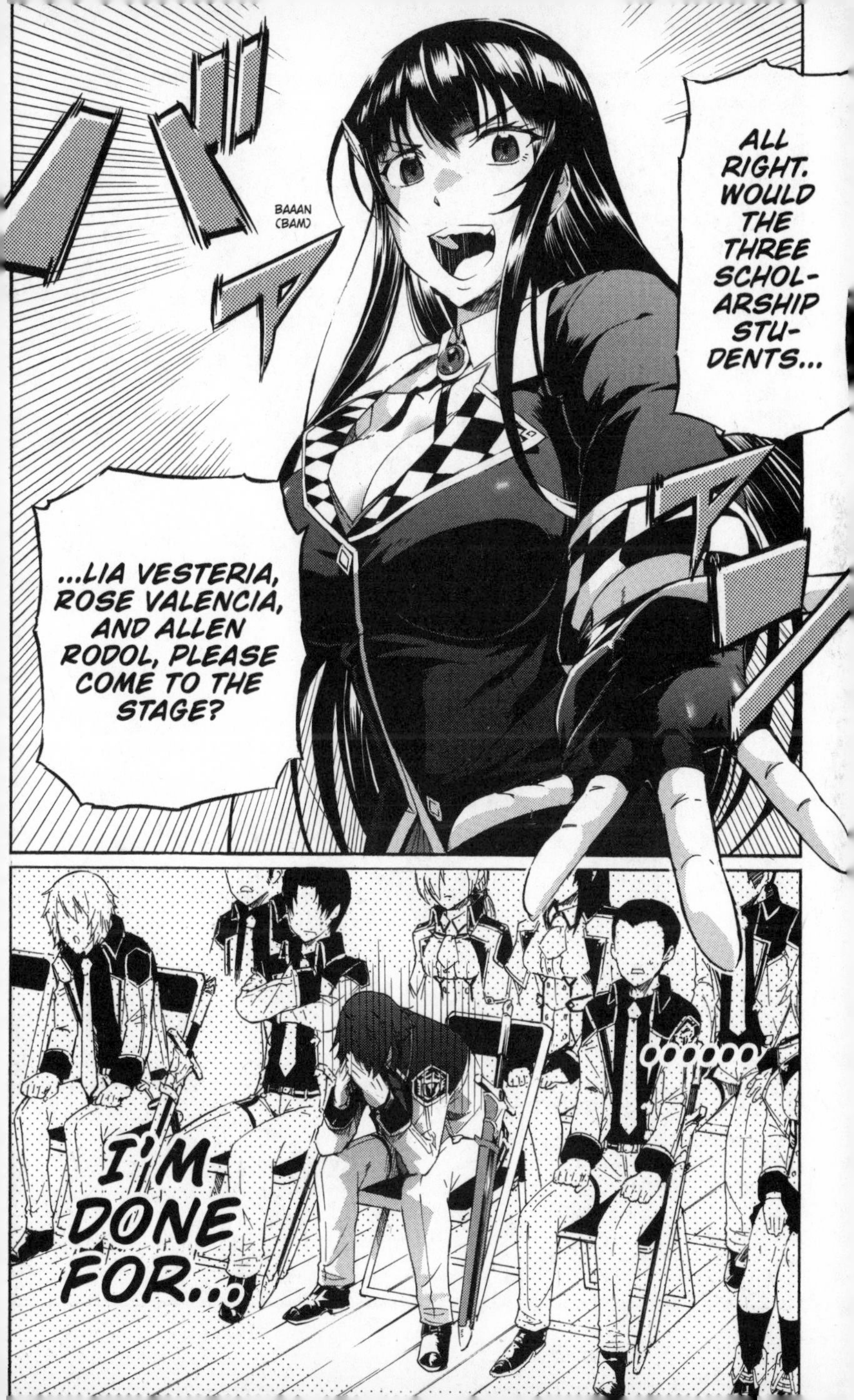
ALL RIGHT. WOULD THE THREE SCHOL-ARSHIP STU-DENTS...
BAAAN (BAM)
...LIA VESTERIA, ROSE VALENCIA, AND ALLEN RODOL, PLEASE COME TO THE STAGE?
oooooo
I'M DONE FOR...

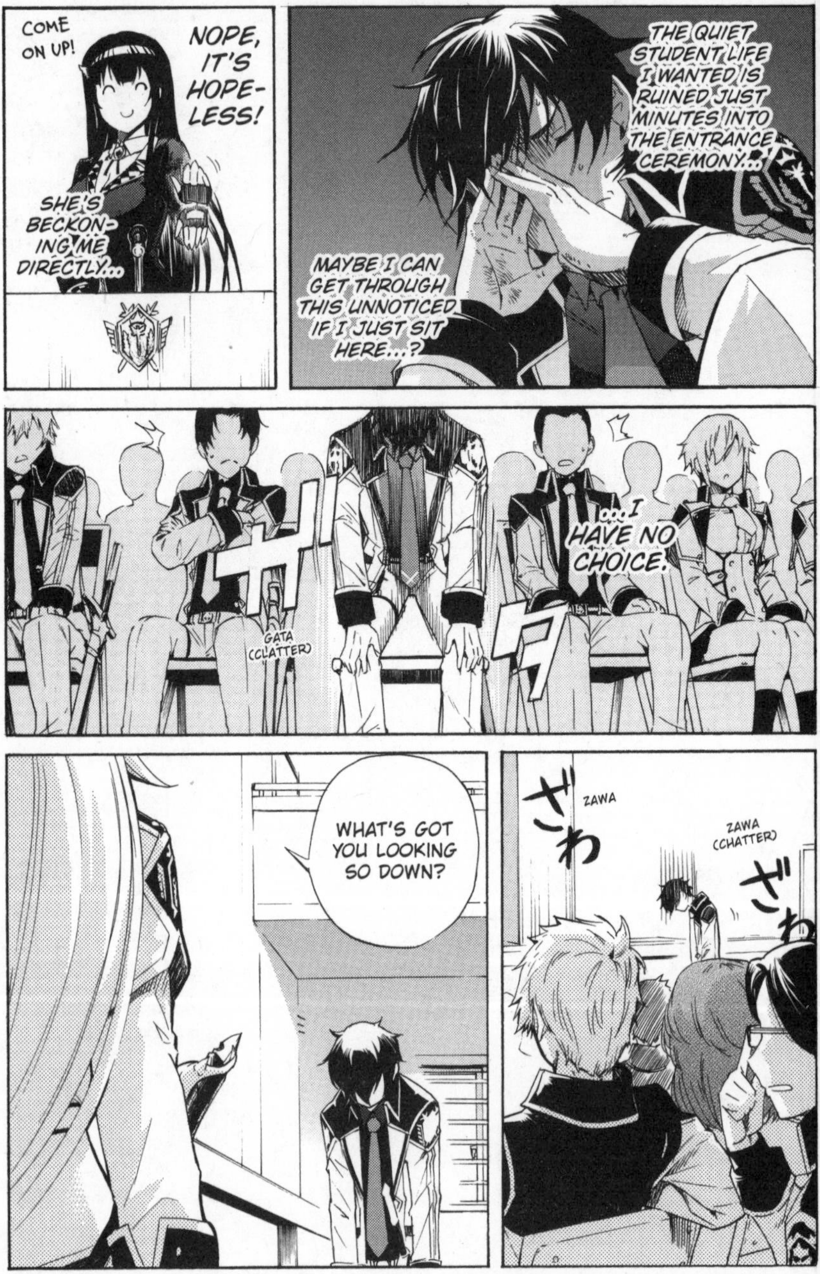

THE QUIET STUDENT LIFE I WANTED IS RUINED JUST MINUTES INTO THE ENTRANCE CEREMONY...
MAYBE I CAN GET THROUGH THIS UNNOTICED IF I JUST SIT HERE...?
COME ON UP!
NOPE, IT'S HOPELESS!
SHE'S BECKONING ME DIRECTLY...
...I HAVE NO CHOICE.
ガタ
GATA (CLATTER)
ざわ
ZAWA
ざわ
ZAWA (CHATTER)
WHAT'S GOT YOU LOOKING SO DOWN?

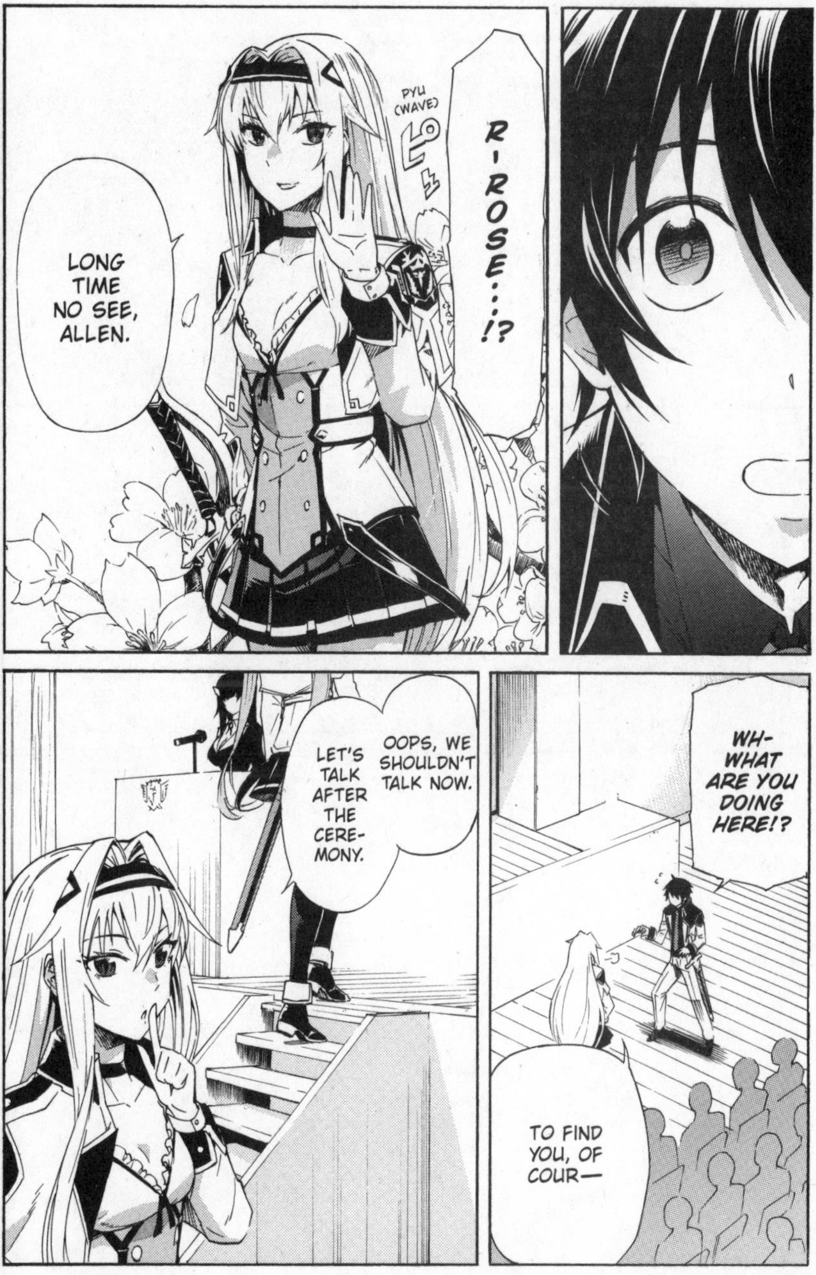
R-ROSE...!?
PYU (WAVE)
LONG TIME NO SEE, ALLEN.
WH-WHAT ARE YOU DOING HERE!?
TO FIND YOU, OF COUR—
OOPS, WE SHOULDN'T TALK NOW.
LET'S TALK AFTER THE CERE-MONY.

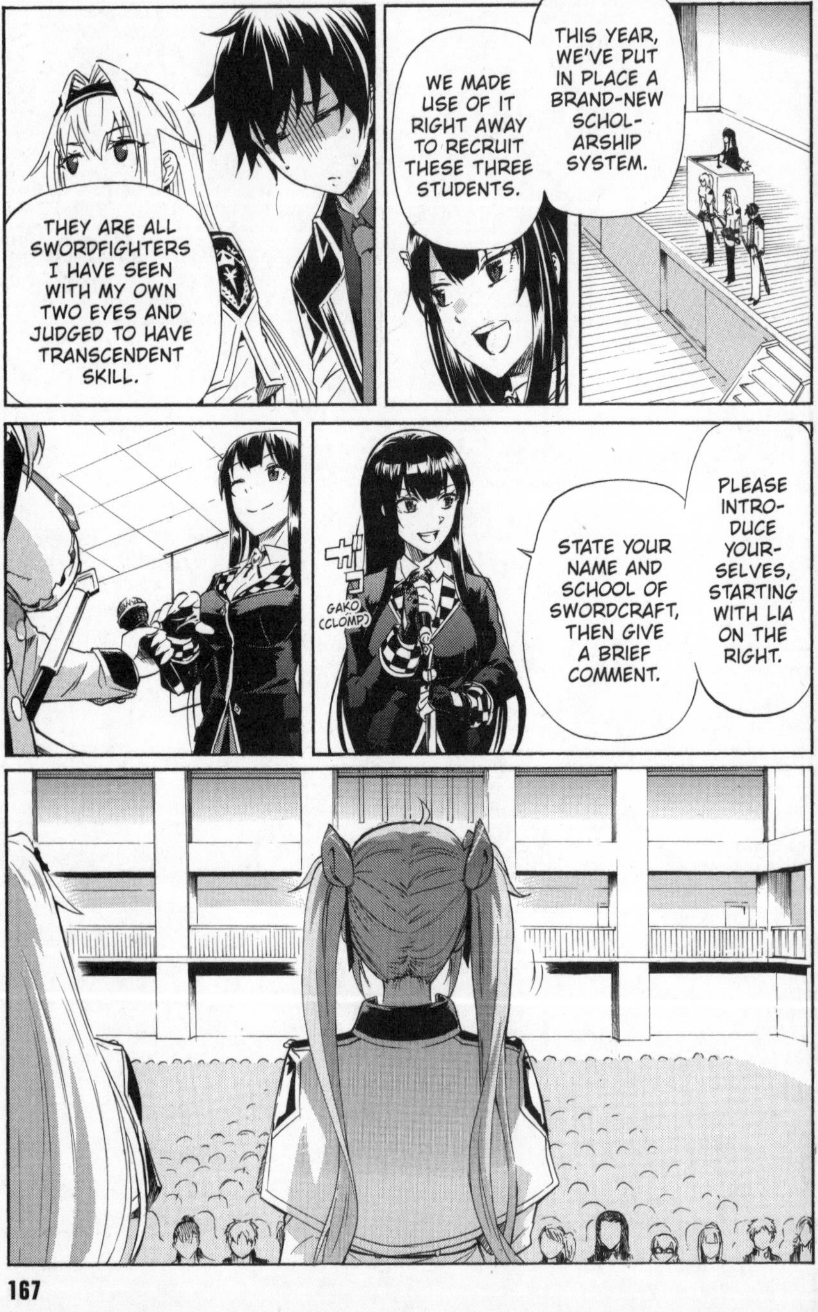
THIS YEAR, WE'VE PUT IN PLACE A BRAND-NEW SCHOLARSHIP SYSTEM.
WE MADE USE OF IT RIGHT AWAY TO RECRUIT THESE THREE STUDENTS.
THEY ARE ALL SWORDFIGHTERS I HAVE SEEN WITH MY OWN TWO EYES AND JUDGED TO HAVE TRANSCENDENT SKILL.
PLEASE INTRODUCE YOURSELVES, STARTING WITH LIA ON THE RIGHT.
STATE YOUR NAME AND SCHOOL OF SWORDCRAFT, THEN GIVE A BRIEF COMMENT.
GAKO (CLOMP)

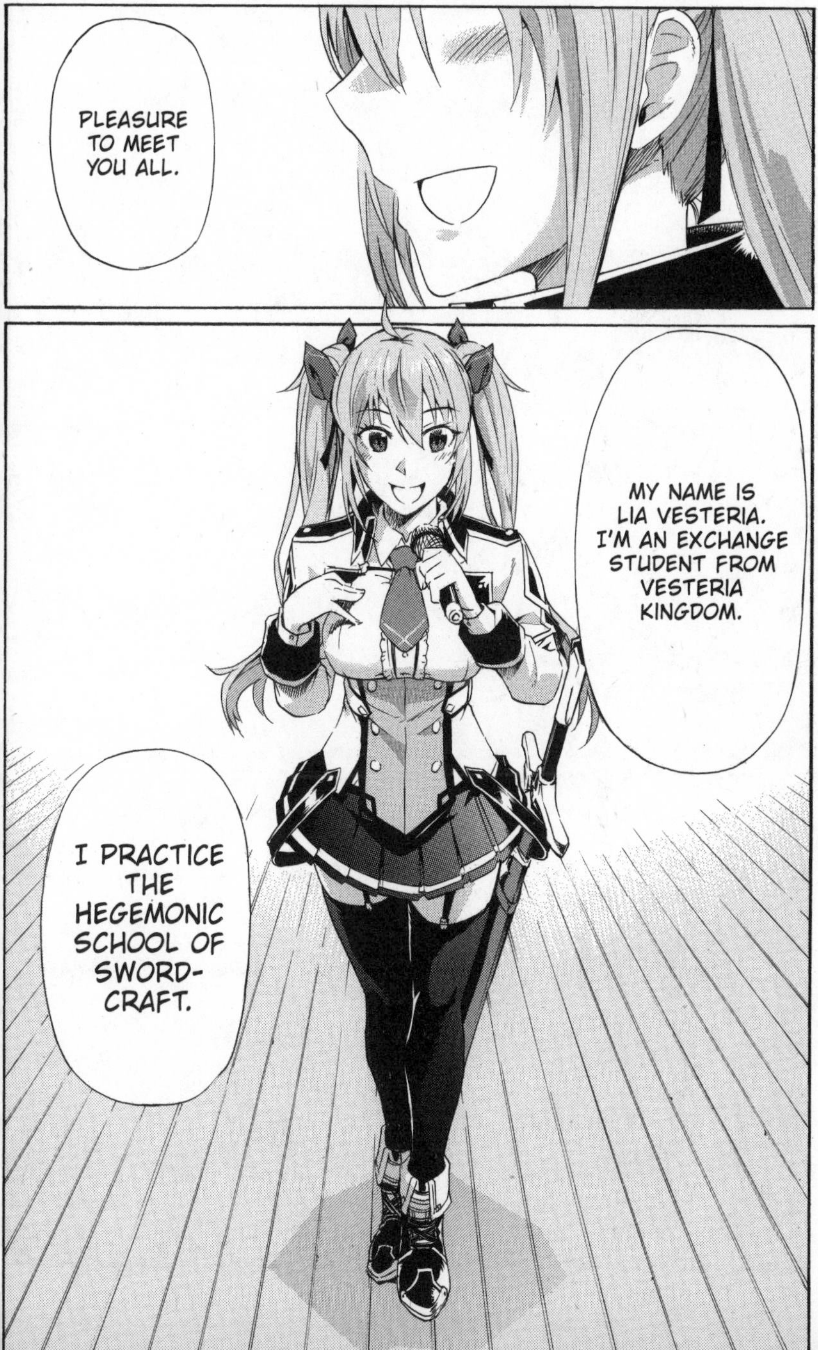
PLEASURE TO MEET YOU ALL.
MY NAME IS LIA VESTERIA. I'M AN EXCHANGE STUDENT FROM VESTERIA KINGDOM.
I PRACTICE THE HEGEMONIC SCHOOL OF SWORD-CRAFT.

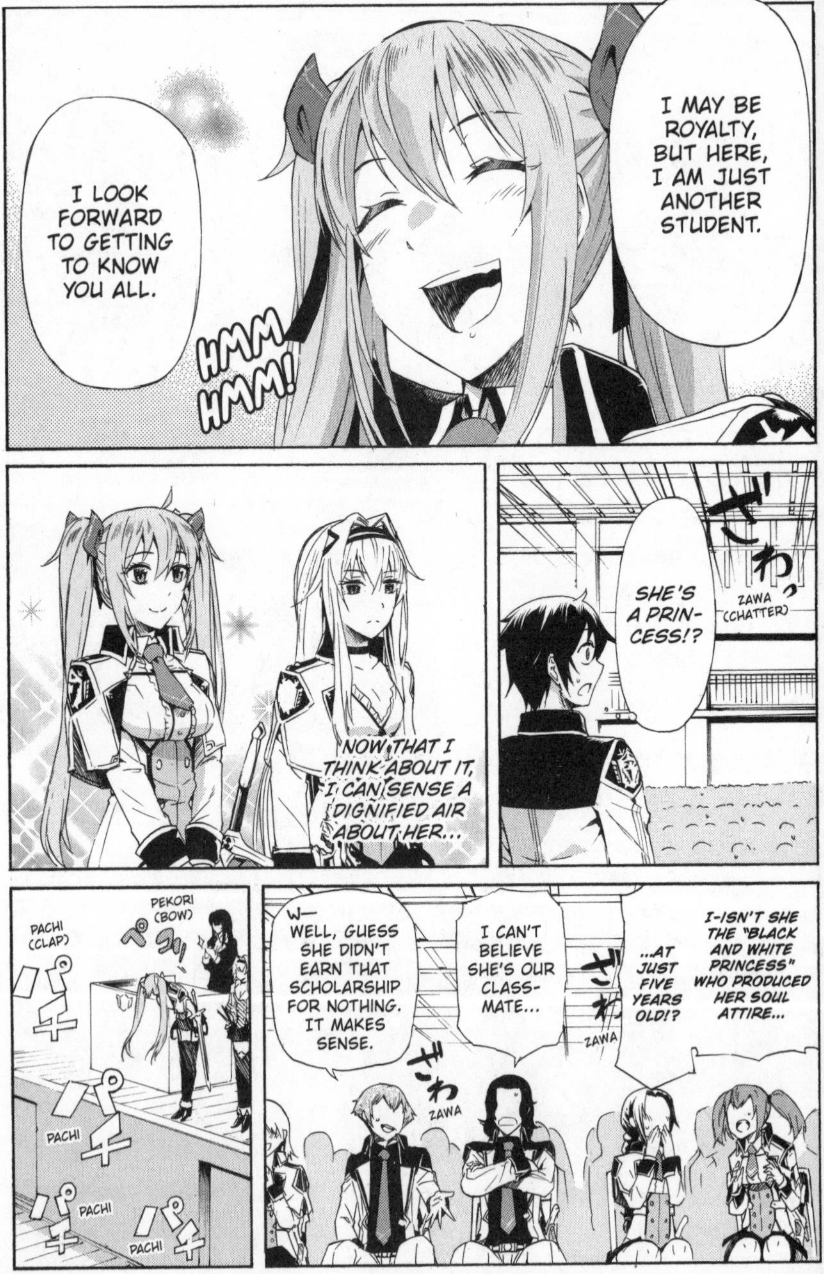
I MAY BE ROYALTY, BUT HERE, I AM JUST ANOTHER STUDENT.
I LOOK FORWARD TO GETTING TO KNOW YOU ALL.
HMM HMM!
ざわっ
ZAWA (CHATTER)
SHE'S A PRIN-CESS!?
NOW THAT I THINK ABOUT IT, I CAN SENSE A DIGNIFIED AIR ABOUT HER...
I-ISN'T SHE THE "BLACK AND WHITE PRINCESS" WHO PRODUCED HER SOUL ATTIRE...
...AT JUST FIVE YEARS OLD!?
ざわ
ZAWA
I CAN'T BELIEVE SHE'S OUR CLASS-MATE...
W— WELL, GUESS SHE DIDN'T EARN THAT SCHOLARSHIP FOR NOTHING. IT MAKES SENSE.
ざわ
ZAWA
ペコッ
PEKORI (BOW)
パチ
PACHI (CLAP)
パチ
PACHI
パチ
PACHI
パチ
PACHI

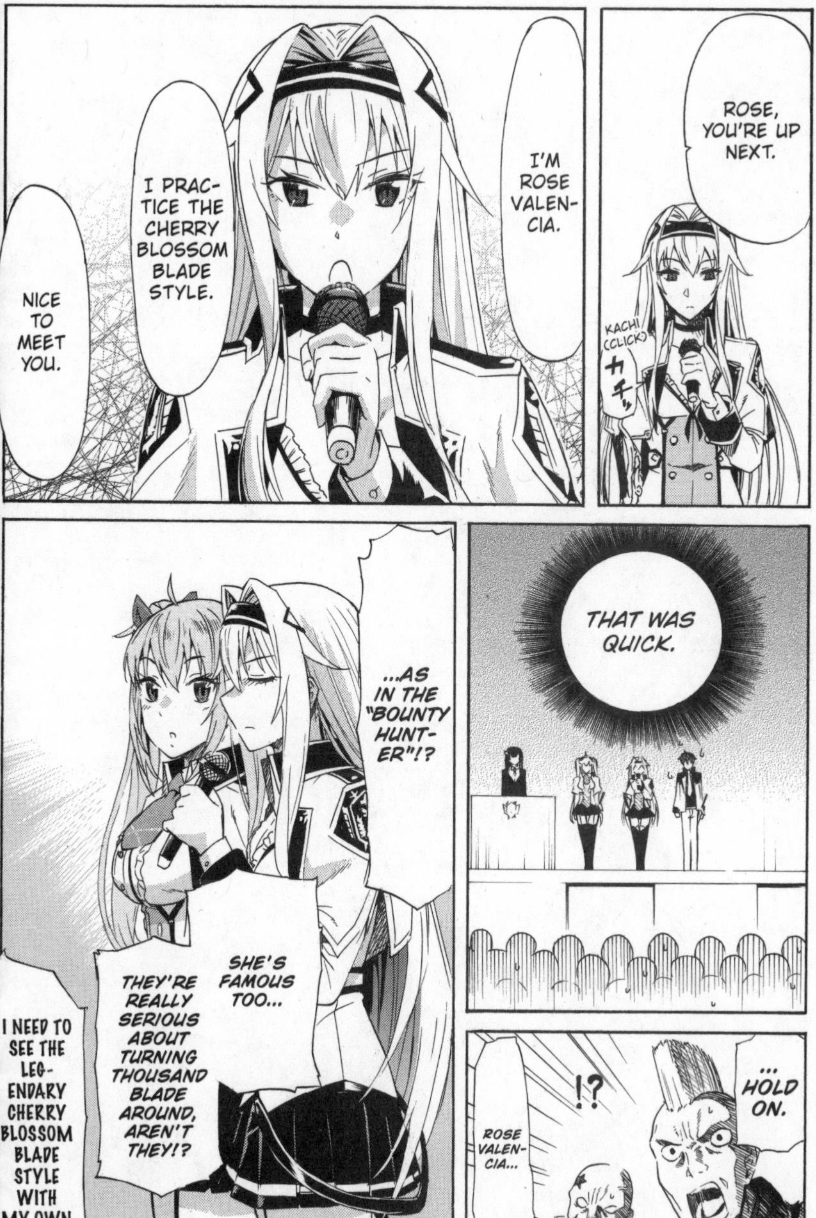
ROSE, YOU'RE UP NEXT.
KACHI (CLICK)
カチッ
I'M ROSE VALENCIA.
I PRACTICE THE CHERRY BLOSSOM BLADE STYLE.
NICE TO MEET YOU.
THAT WAS QUICK.
...HOLD ON.
!?
ROSE VALENCIA...
...AS IN THE "BOUNTY HUNTER"!?
SHE'S FAMOUS TOO...
THEY'RE REALLY SERIOUS ABOUT TURNING THOUSAND BLADE AROUND, AREN'T THEY!?
I NEED TO SEE THE LEGENDARY CHERRY BLOSSOM BLADE STYLE WITH MY OWN EYES.

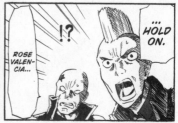

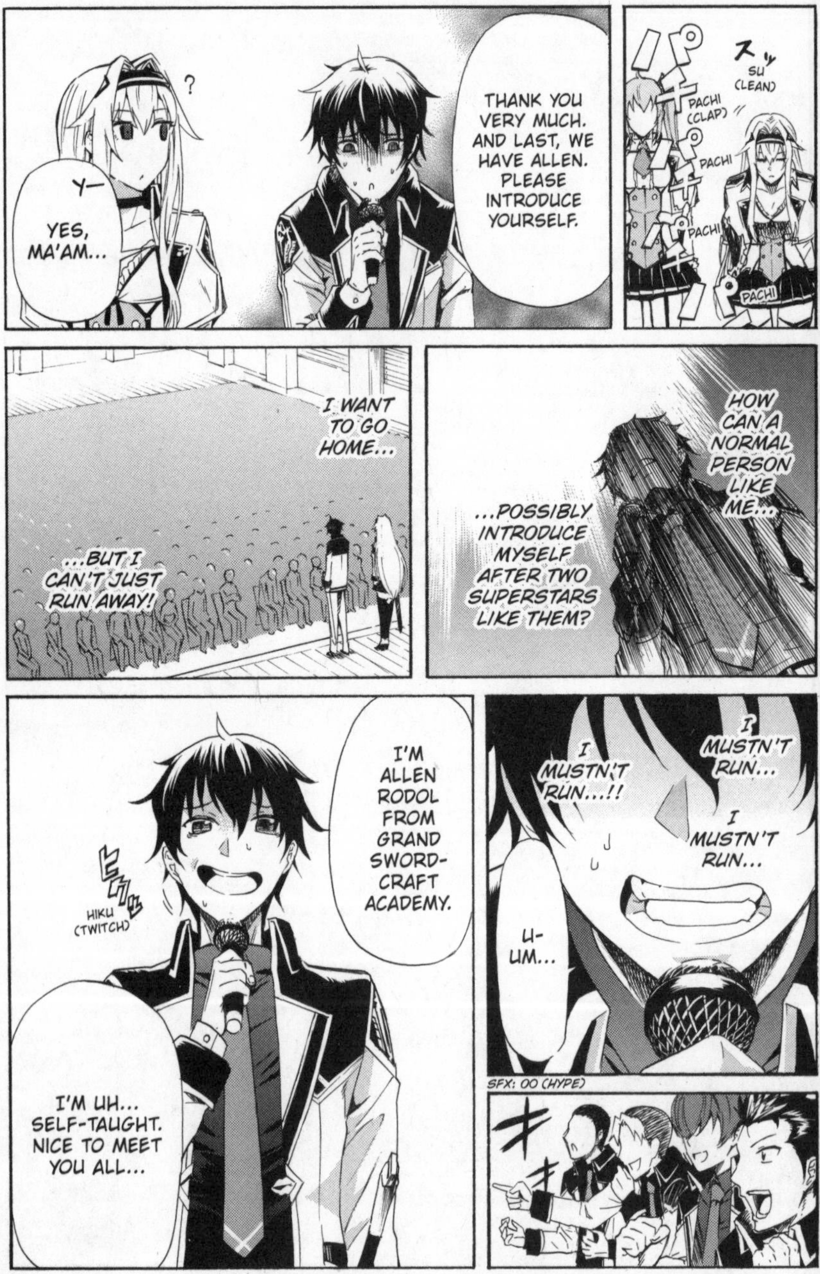
SU (LEAN)
PACHI (CLAP)
PACHI
PACHI
PACHI
THANK YOU VERY MUCH. AND LAST, WE HAVE ALLEN. PLEASE INTRODUCE YOURSELF.
YES, MA'AM...
HOW CAN A NORMAL PERSON LIKE ME...
...POSSIBLY INTRODUCE MYSELF AFTER TWO SUPERSTARS LIKE THEM?
I WANT TO GO HOME...
...BUT I CAN'T JUST RUN AWAY!
I MUSTN'T RUN...
I MUSTN'T RUN...
I MUSTN'T RUN...!!
U-UM...
SFX: OO (HYPE)
I'M ALLEN RODOL FROM GRAND SWORD-CRAFT ACADEMY.
HIKU (TWITCH)
I'M UH... SELF-TAUGHT. NICE TO MEET YOU ALL...

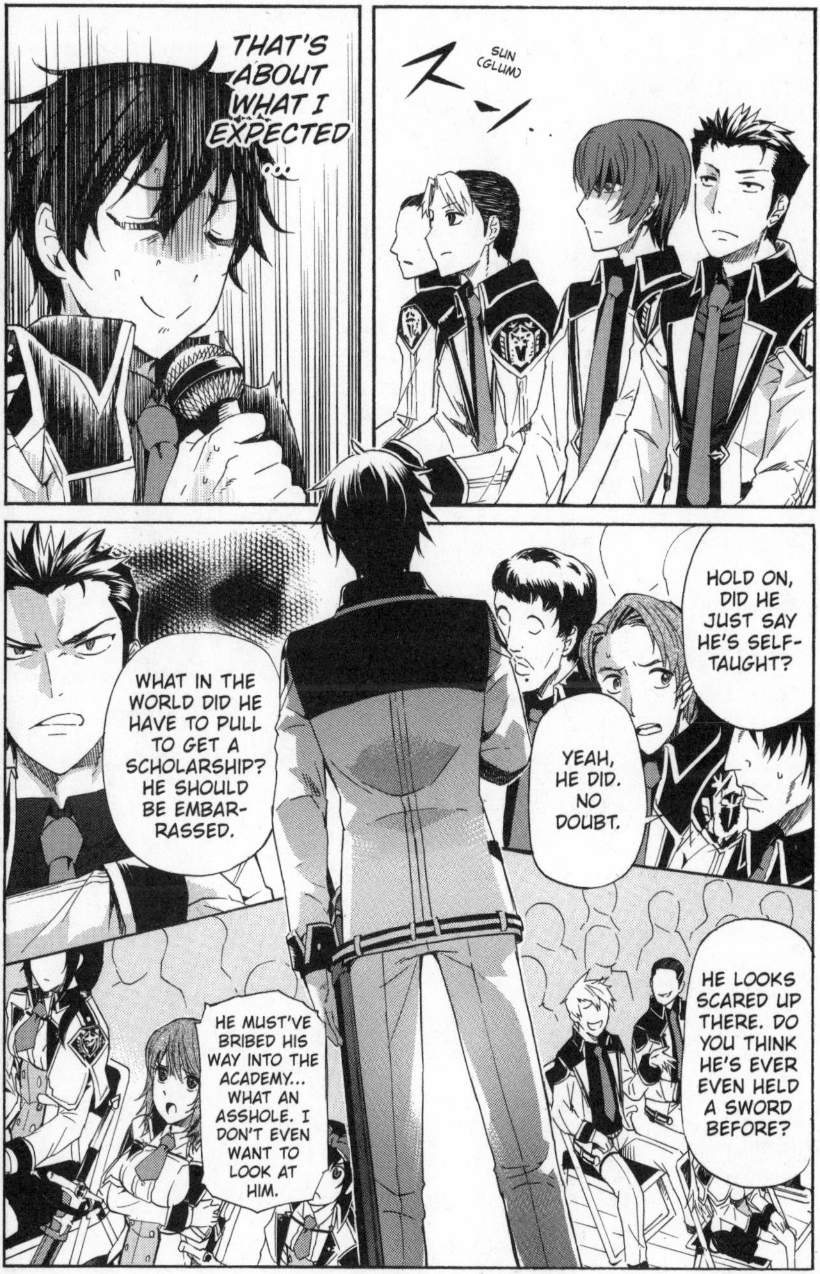
SUN (GLUM)
THAT'S ABOUT WHAT I EXPECTED...
HOLD ON, DID HE JUST SAY HE'S SELF-TAUGHT?
YEAH, HE DID. NO DOUBT.
WHAT IN THE WORLD DID HE HAVE TO PULL TO GET A SCHOLARSHIP? HE SHOULD BE EMBARRASSED.
HE LOOKS SCARED UP THERE. DO YOU THINK HE'S EVER EVEN HELD A SWORD BEFORE?
HE MUST'VE BRIBED HIS WAY INTO THE ACADEMY... WHAT AN ASSHOLE. I DON'T EVEN WANT TO LOOK AT HIM.

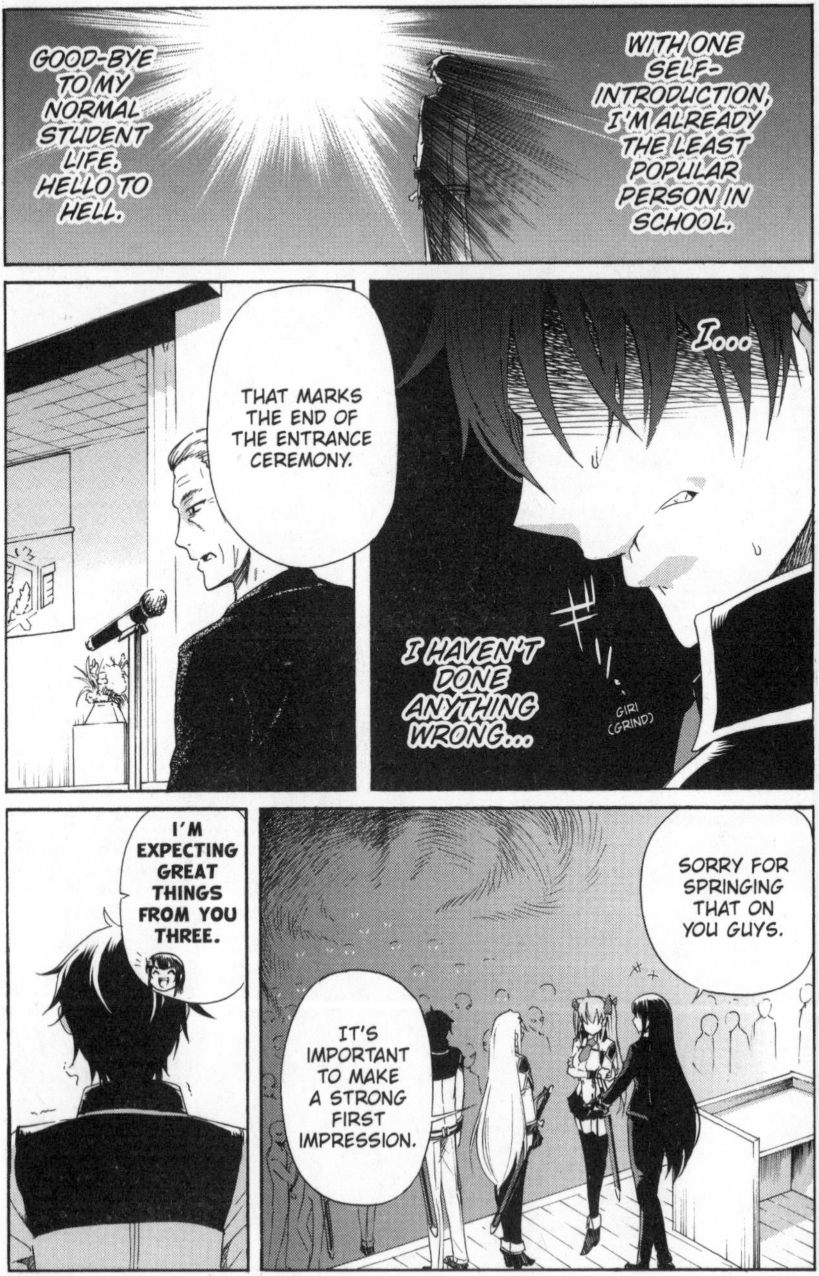
WITH ONE SELF-INTRODUCTION, I'M ALREADY THE LEAST POPULAR PERSON IN SCHOOL.
GOOD-BYE TO MY NORMAL STUDENT LIFE. HELLO TO HELL.
I...
I HAVEN'T DONE ANYTHING WRONG...
GIRI (GRIND)
THAT MARKS THE END OF THE ENTRANCE CEREMONY.
SORRY FOR SPRINGING THAT ON YOU GUYS.
IT'S IMPORTANT TO MAKE A STRONG FIRST IMPRESSION.
I'M EXPECTING GREAT THINGS FROM YOU THREE.

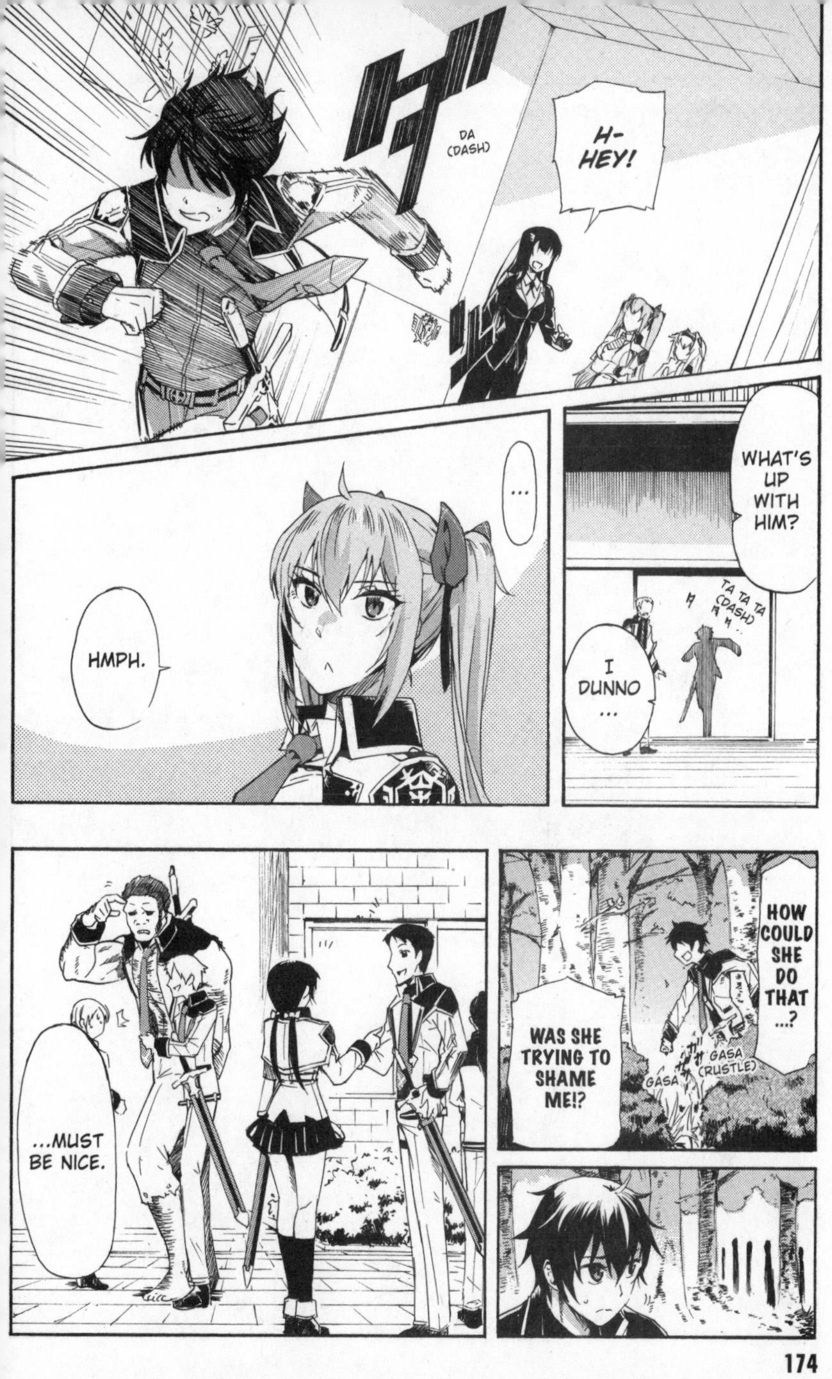
H- HEY!
DA (DASH)
WHAT'S UP WITH HIM?
TA TA TA (DASH)
I DUNNO ...
...
HMPH.
HOW COULD SHE DO THAT ...?
WAS SHE TRYING TO SHAME ME!?
GASA GASA (RUSTLE)
...MUST BE NICE.

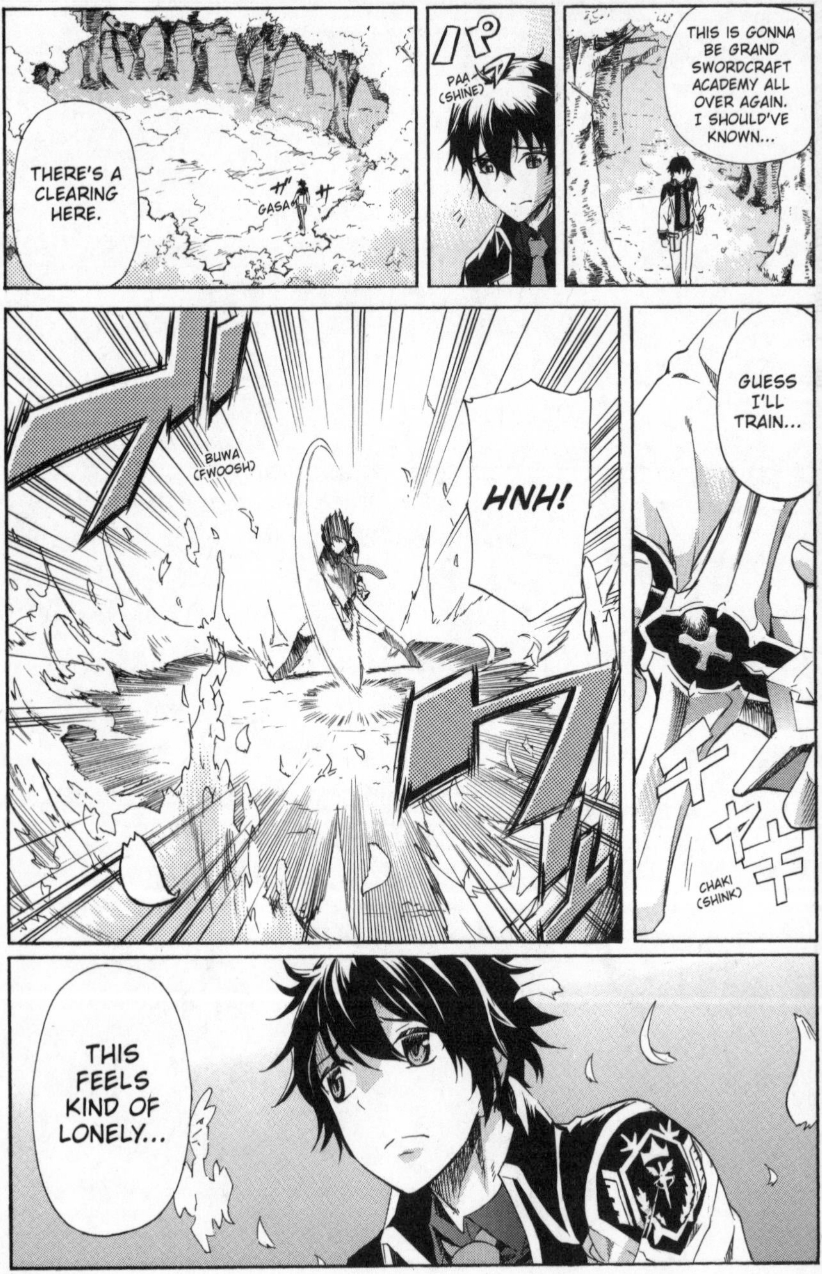
THIS IS GONNA BE GRAND SWORDCRAFT ACADEMY ALL OVER AGAIN. I SHOULD'VE KNOWN...
PAA (SHINE)
THERE'S A CLEARING HERE.
GASA
GUESS I'LL TRAIN...
CHAKI (SHINK)
BUWA (FWOOSH)
HNH!
THIS FEELS KIND OF LONELY...

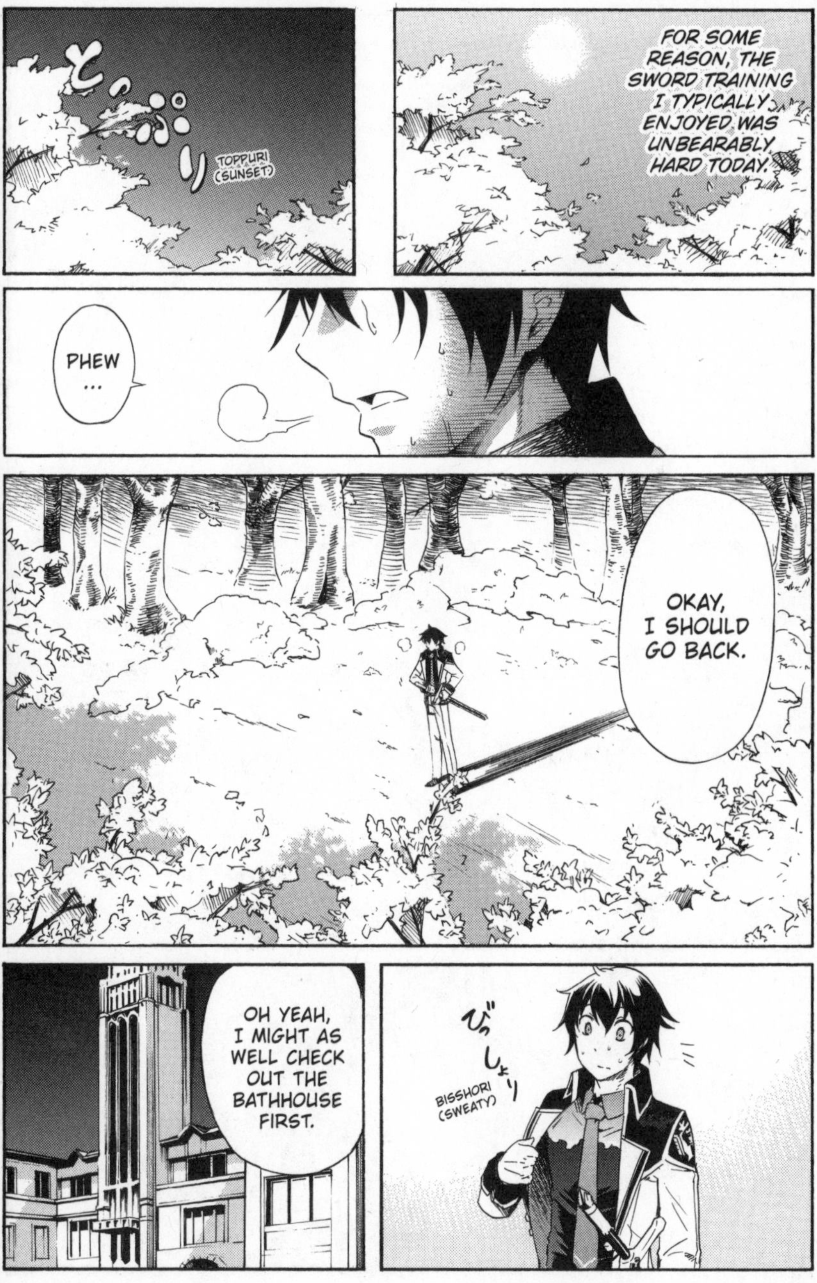
FOR SOME REASON, THE SWORD TRAINING I TYPICALLY ENJOYED WAS UNBEARABLY HARD TODAY.
とっぷり
TOPPURI (SUNSET)
PHEW ...
OKAY, I SHOULD GO BACK.
びっしょり
BISSHORI (SWEATY)
OH YEAH, I MIGHT AS WELL CHECK OUT THE BATHHOUSE FIRST.

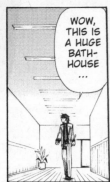

WOW, THIS IS A HUGE BATH-HOUSE...

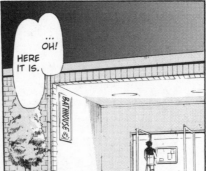

...OH! HERE IT IS.

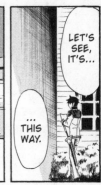

LET'S SEE, IT'S...

...THIS WAY.

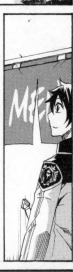

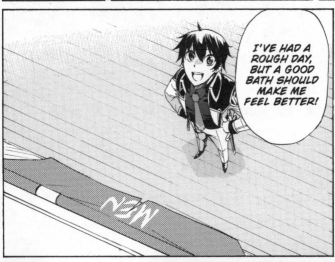

I'VE HAD A ROUGH DAY, BUT A GOOD BATH SHOULD MAKE ME FEEL BETTER!

MEN

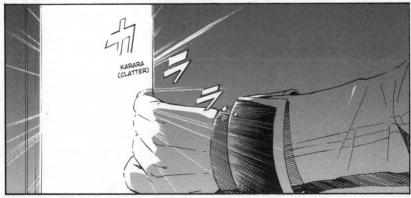

KARARA (CLATTER)

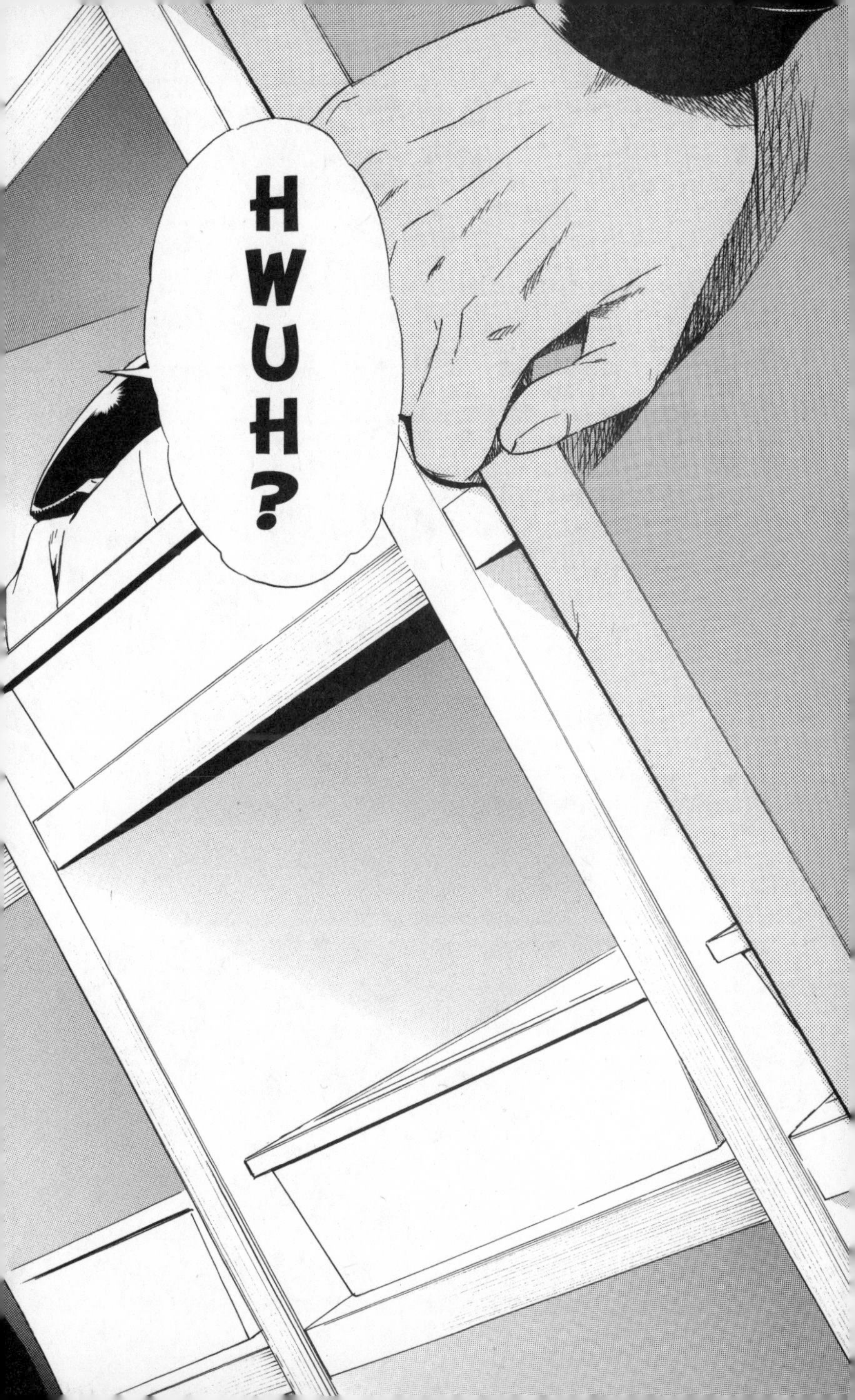
HWUH?

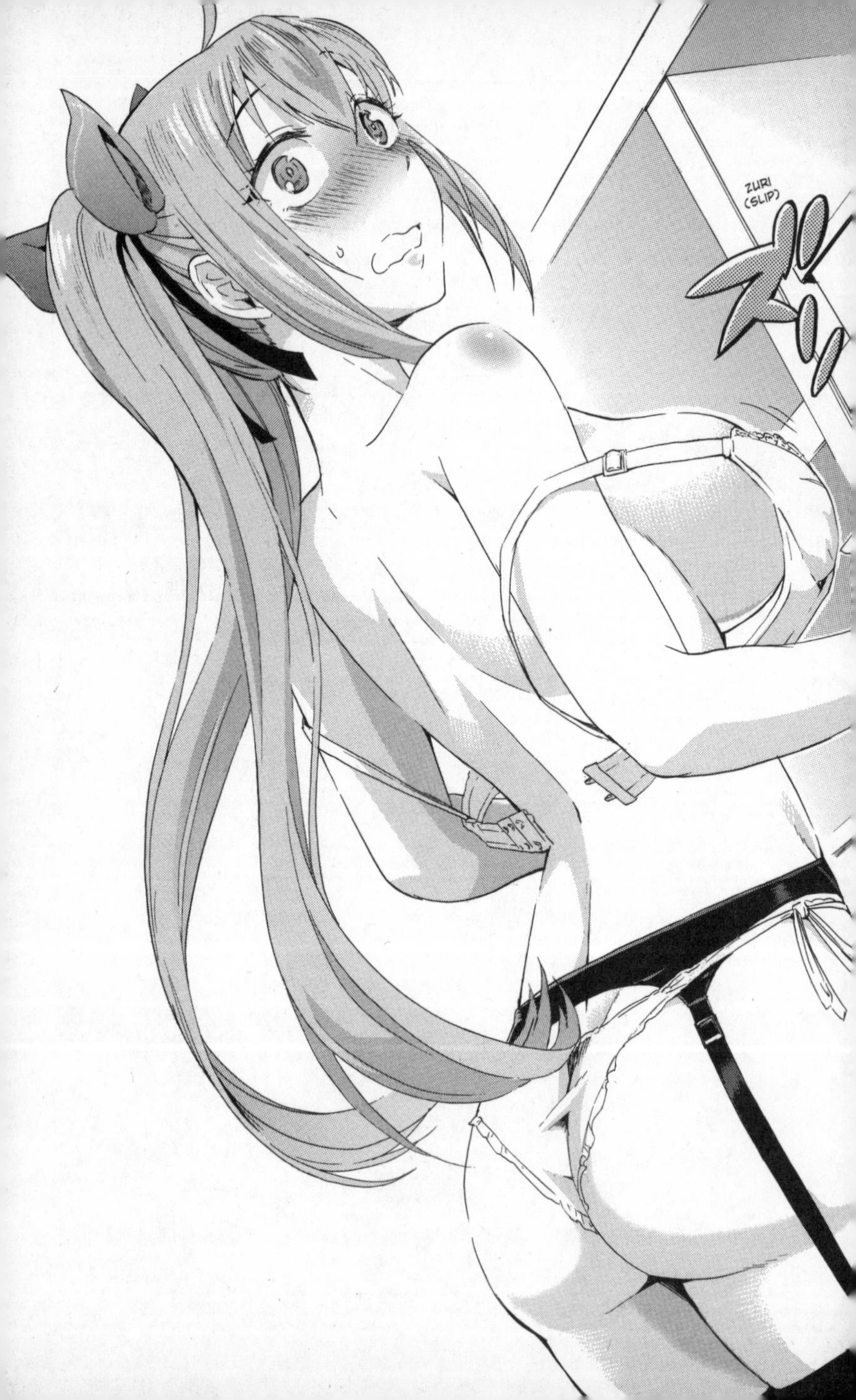
ZURI (SLIP)

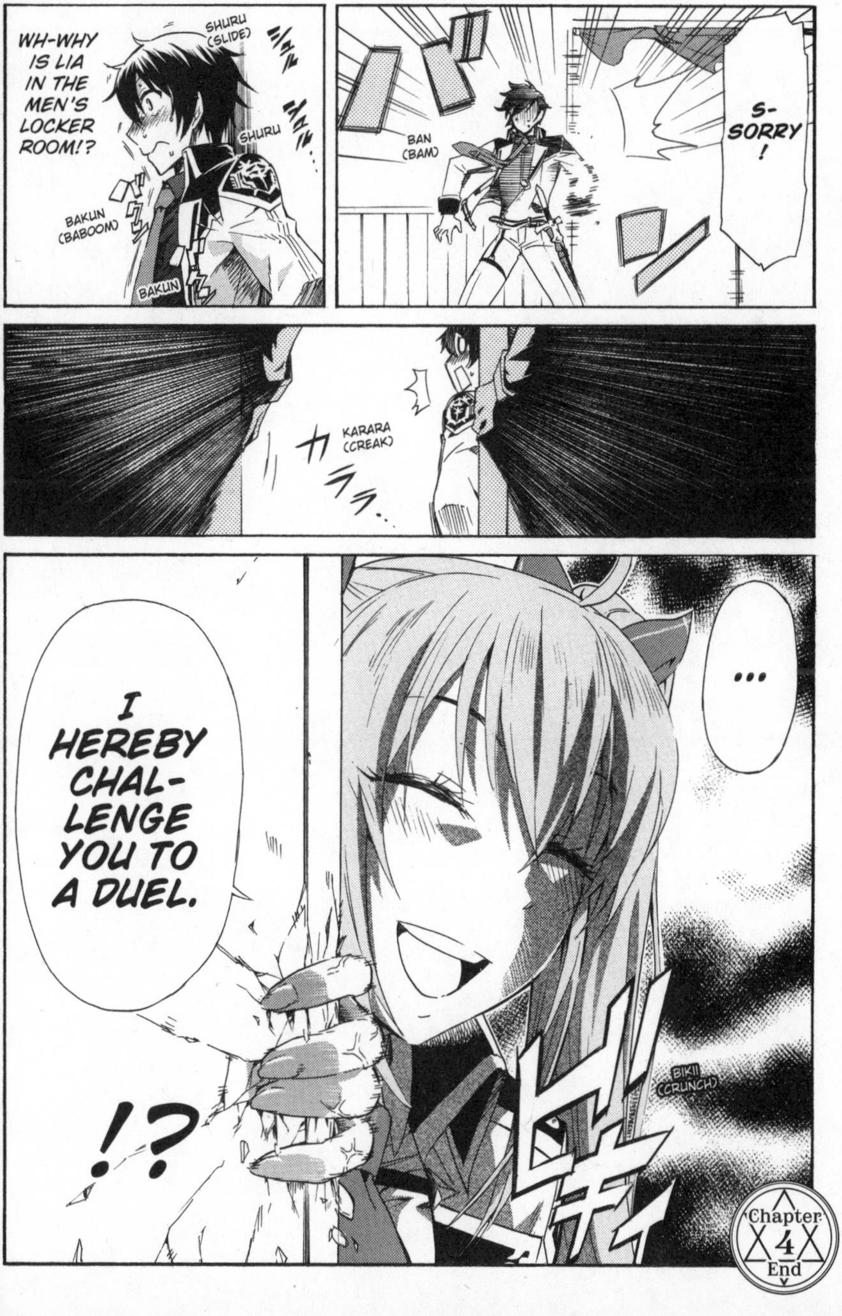
S-SORRY!
BAN (BAM)
SHURU (SLIDE)
WH-WHY IS LIA IN THE MEN'S LOCKER ROOM!?
SHURU
BAKUN (BABOOM)
BAKUN
KARARA (CREAK)
...
I HEREBY CHAL-LENGE YOU TO A DUEL.
BIKII (CRUNCH)
!?
Chapter 4 End

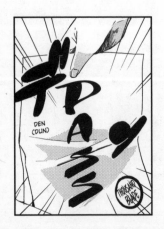

DEN
(DUN)

THOUSAND
BLADE

I KEPT PRESSING THE 100-MILLION-YEAR BUTTON AND CAME OUT ON TOP

~THE UNBEATABLE REJECT SWORDSMAN~

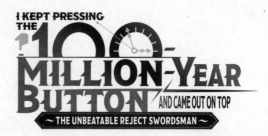

Chapter 5

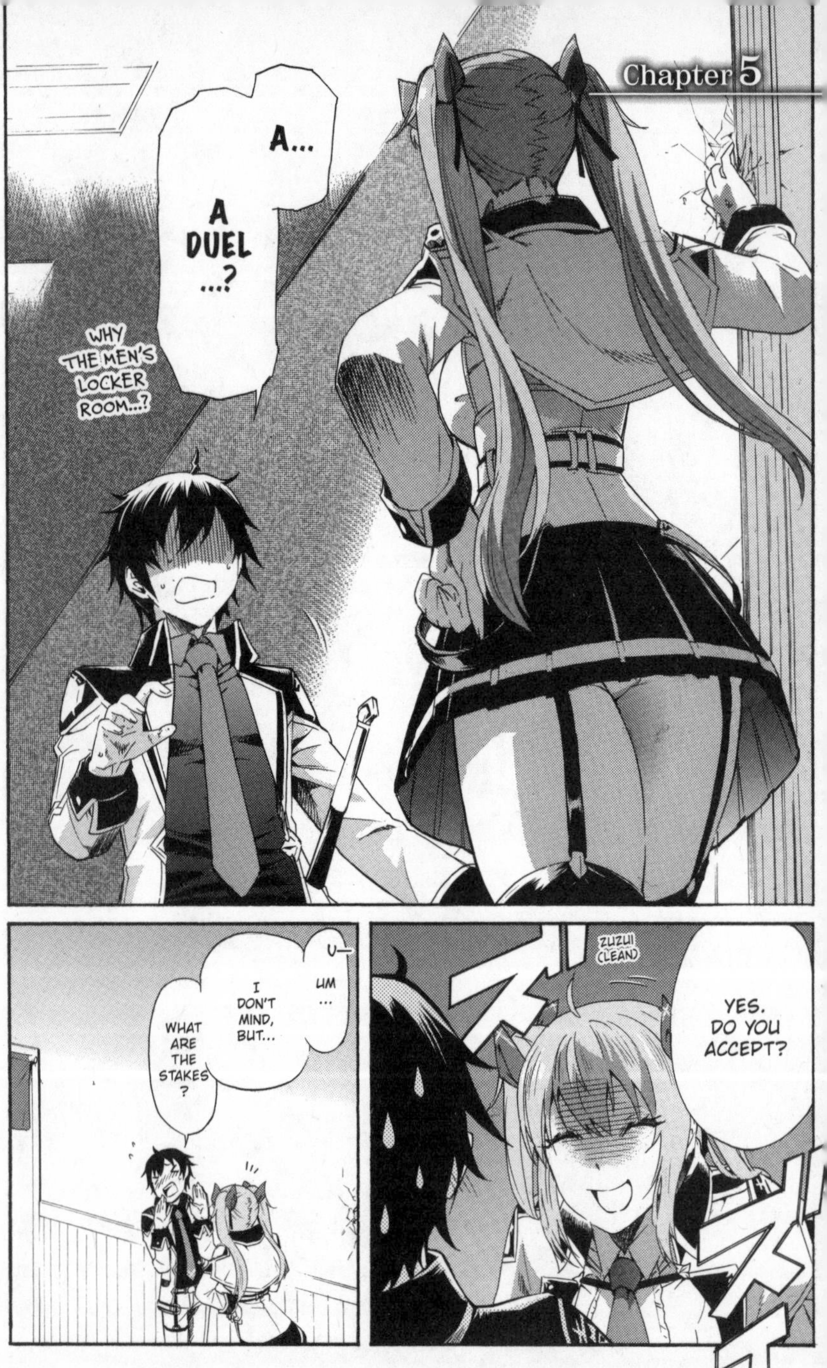
A...
A DUEL ...?
WHY THE MEN'S LOCKER ROOM...?
ZUZUI CLEAND
YES. DO YOU ACCEPT?
U— UM ...
I DON'T MIND, BUT...
WHAT ARE THE STAKES?

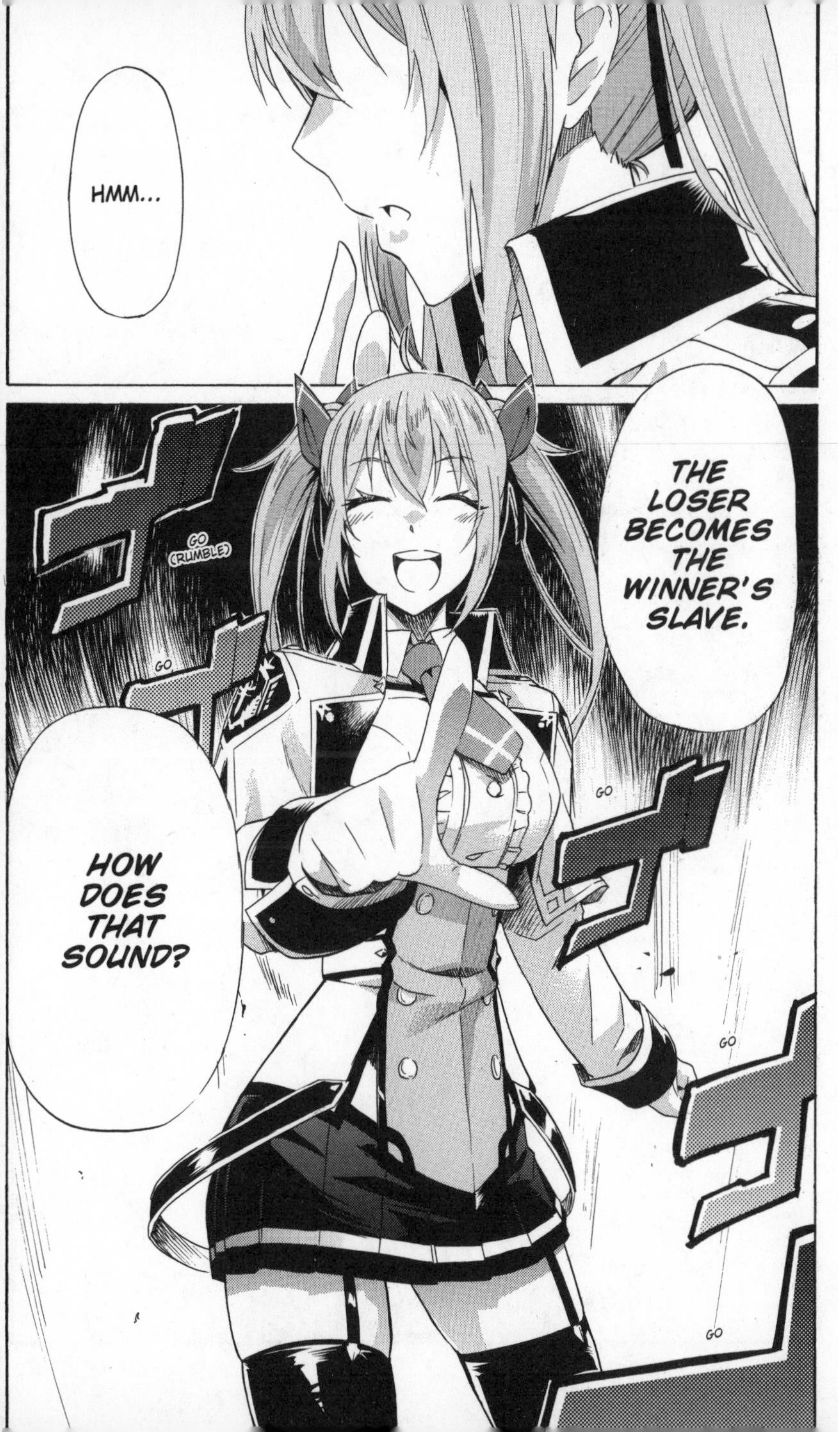
HMM...
THE LOSER BECOMES THE WINNER'S SLAVE.
GO (RUMBLE)
GO
GO
GO
GO
HOW DOES THAT SOUND?

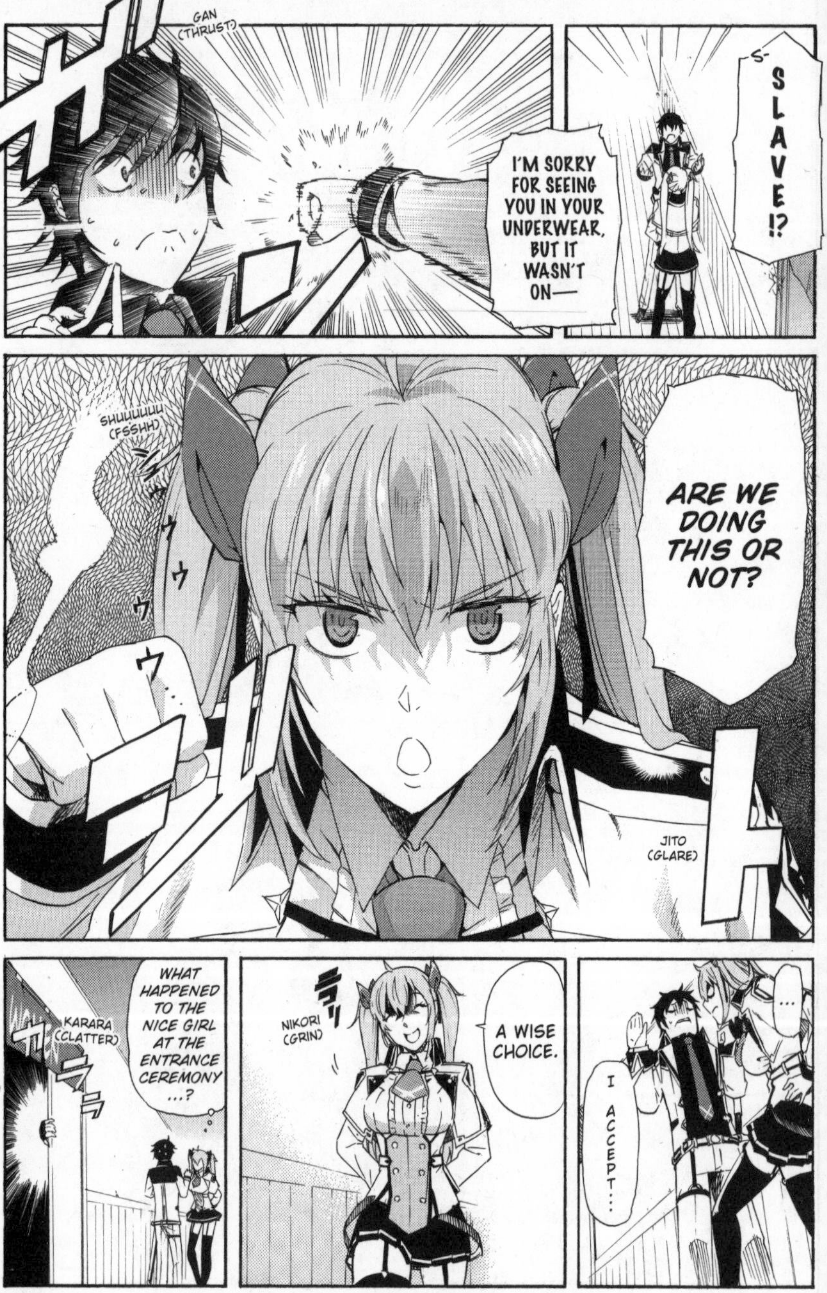
S-
SLAVE!?
I'M SORRY FOR SEEING YOU IN YOUR UNDERWEAR, BUT IT WASN'T ON—
GAN (THRUST)
ARE WE DOING THIS OR NOT?
SHUUUUUUU (FSSHH)
JITO (GLARE)
...
I ACCEPT...
A WISE CHOICE.
NIKORI (GRIN)
WHAT HAPPENED TO THE NICE GIRL AT THE ENTRANCE CEREMONY...?
KARARA (CLATTER)

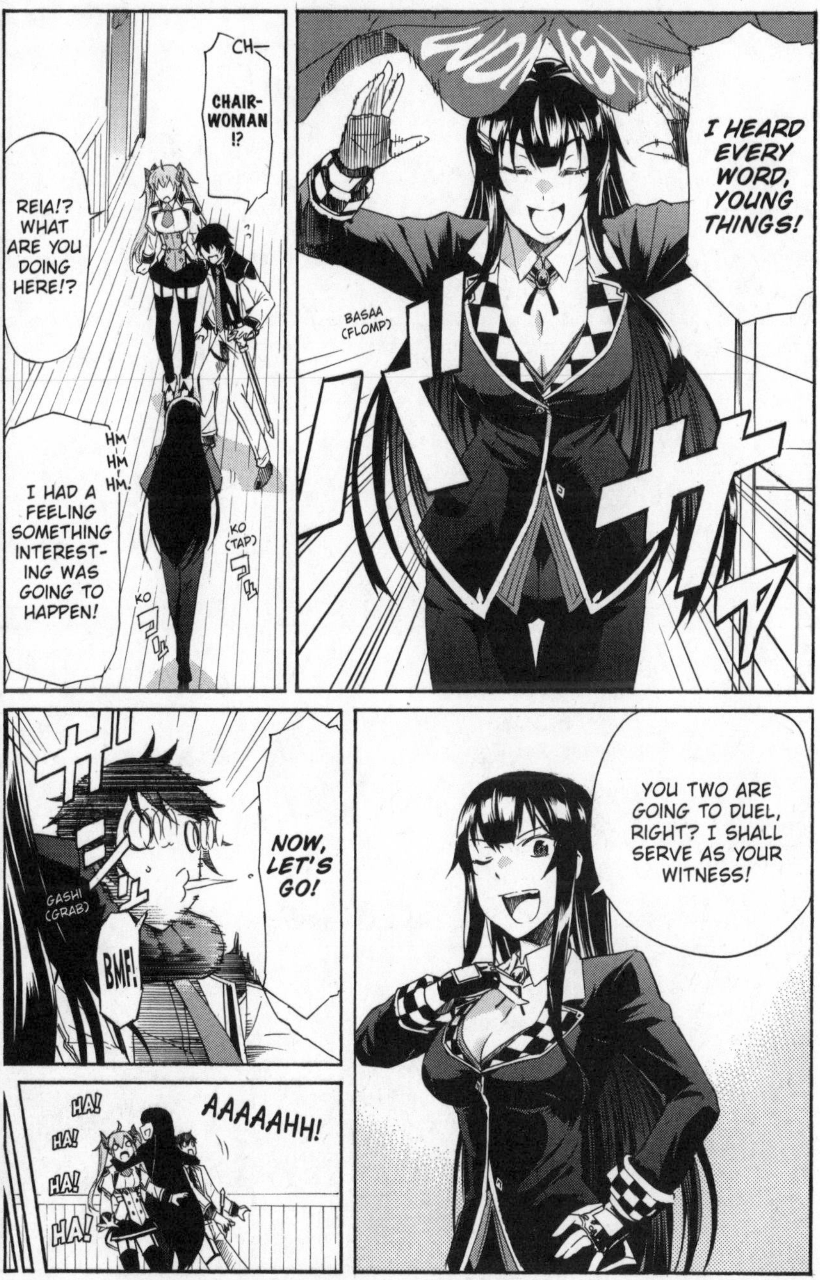
I HEARD EVERY WORD, YOUNG THINGS!
BASAA (FLOMP)
CH—
CHAIR-WOMAN!?
REIA!? WHAT ARE YOU DOING HERE!?
HM HM HM.
I HAD A FEELING SOMETHING INTEREST-ING WAS GOING TO HAPPEN!
KO (TAP)
KO
YOU TWO ARE GOING TO DUEL, RIGHT? I SHALL SERVE AS YOUR WITNESS!
NOW, LET'S GO!
GASHI (GRAB)
BMF!
AAAAAHH!
HA!
HA!
HA!
HA!

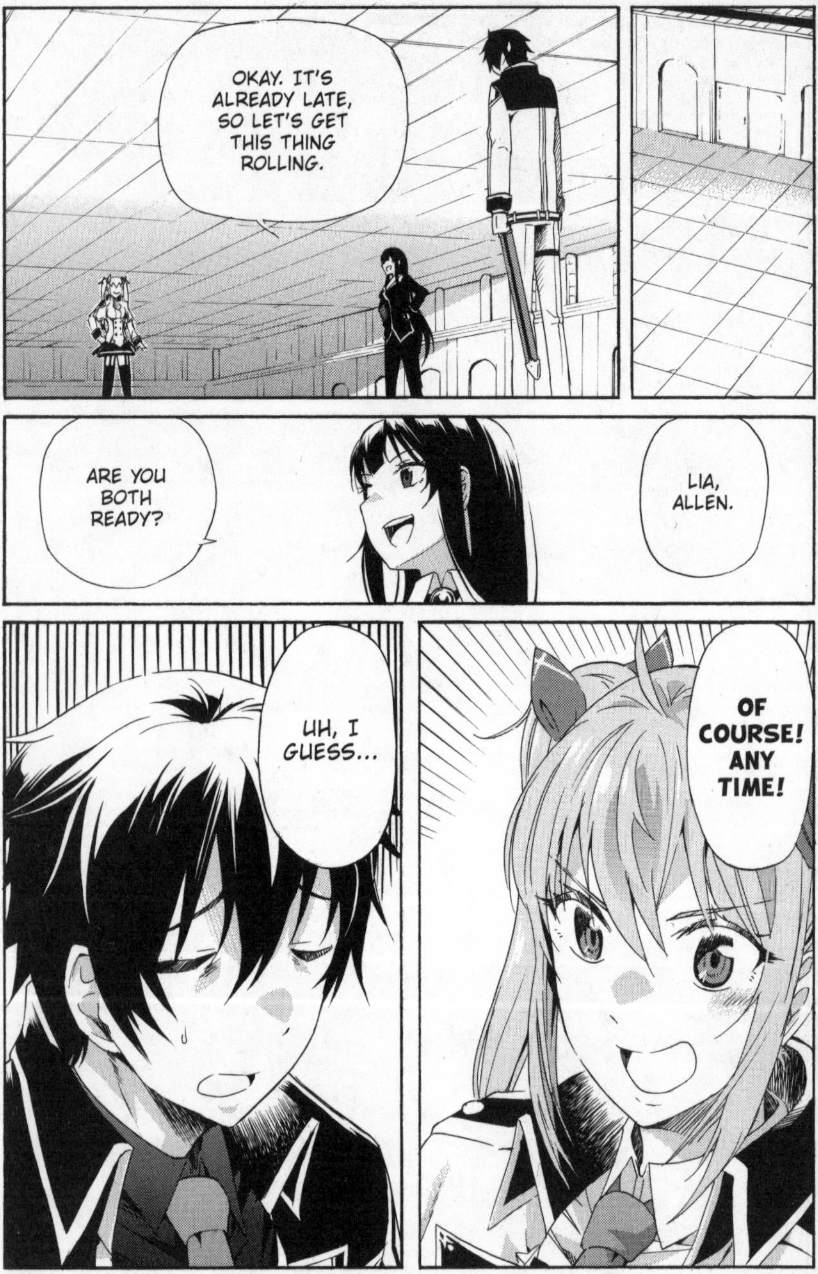
OKAY. IT'S ALREADY LATE, SO LET'S GET THIS THING ROLLING.
LIA, ALLEN.
ARE YOU BOTH READY?
OF COURSE! ANY TIME!
UH, I GUESS...

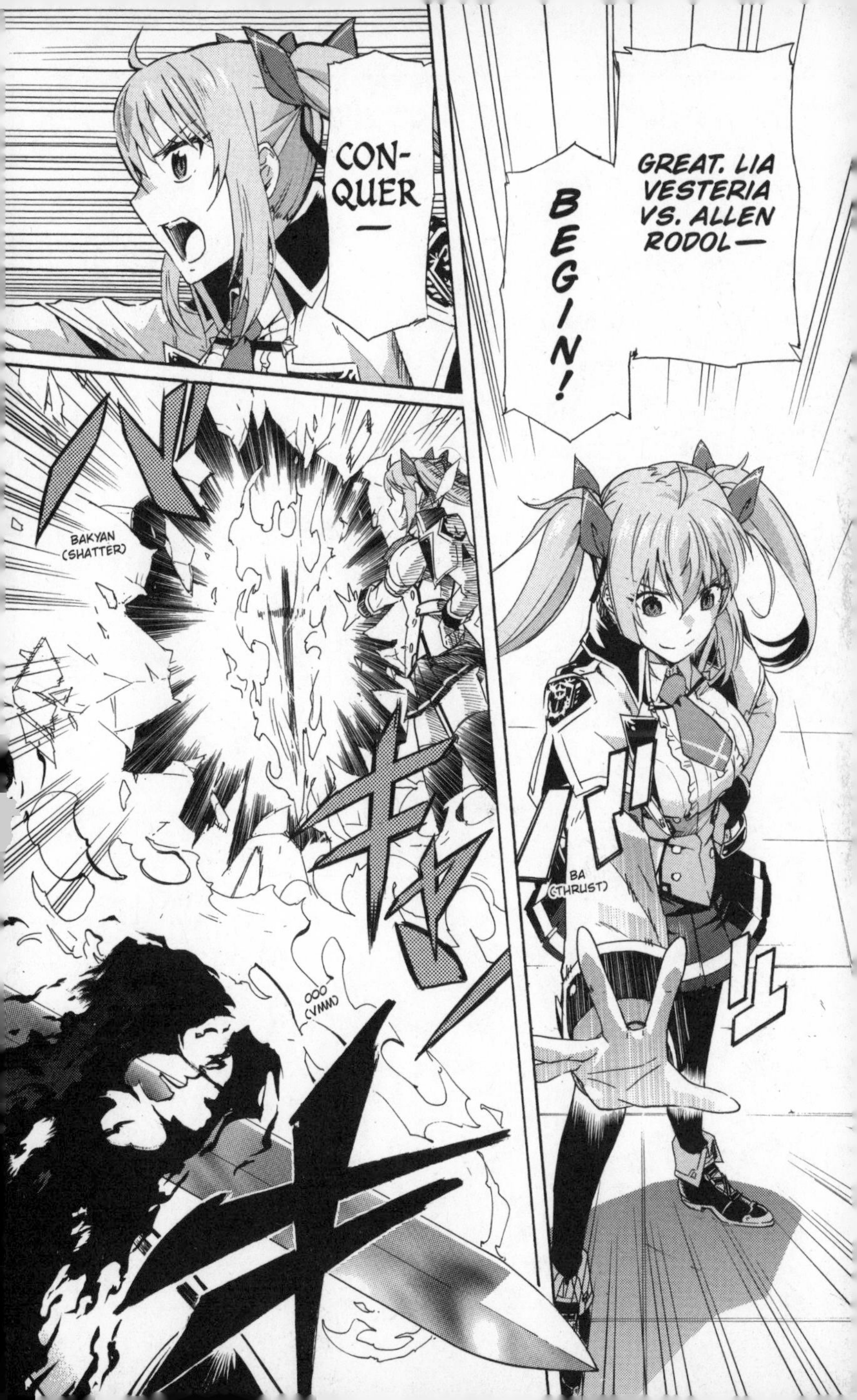
GREAT. LIA VESTERIA VS. ALLEN RODOL—
BEGIN!
BA (THRUST)
CON-QUER—
BAKYAN (SHATTER)
OOO (VMM)

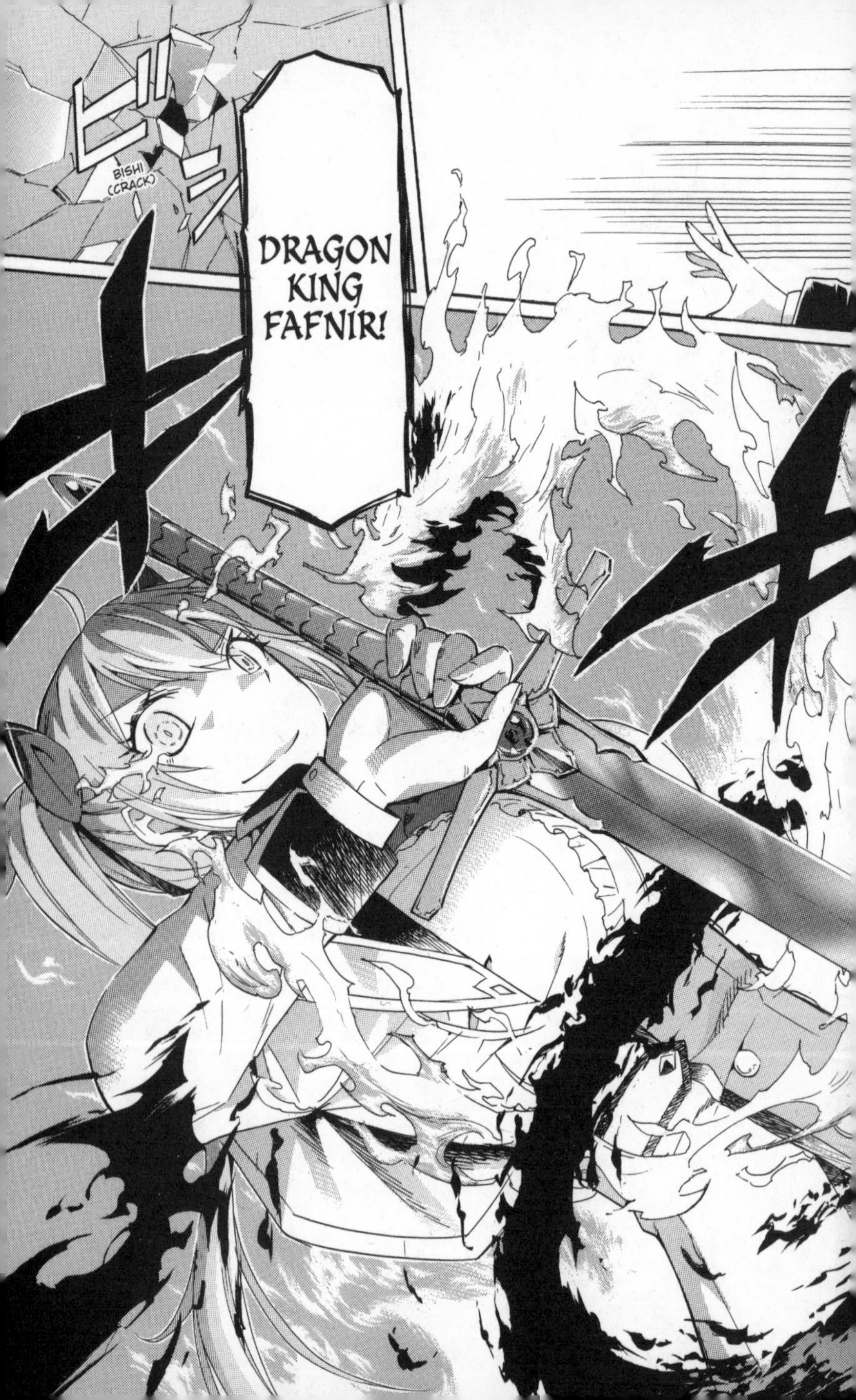
ビシ
BISHI (CRACK)
DRAGON KING FAFNIR!

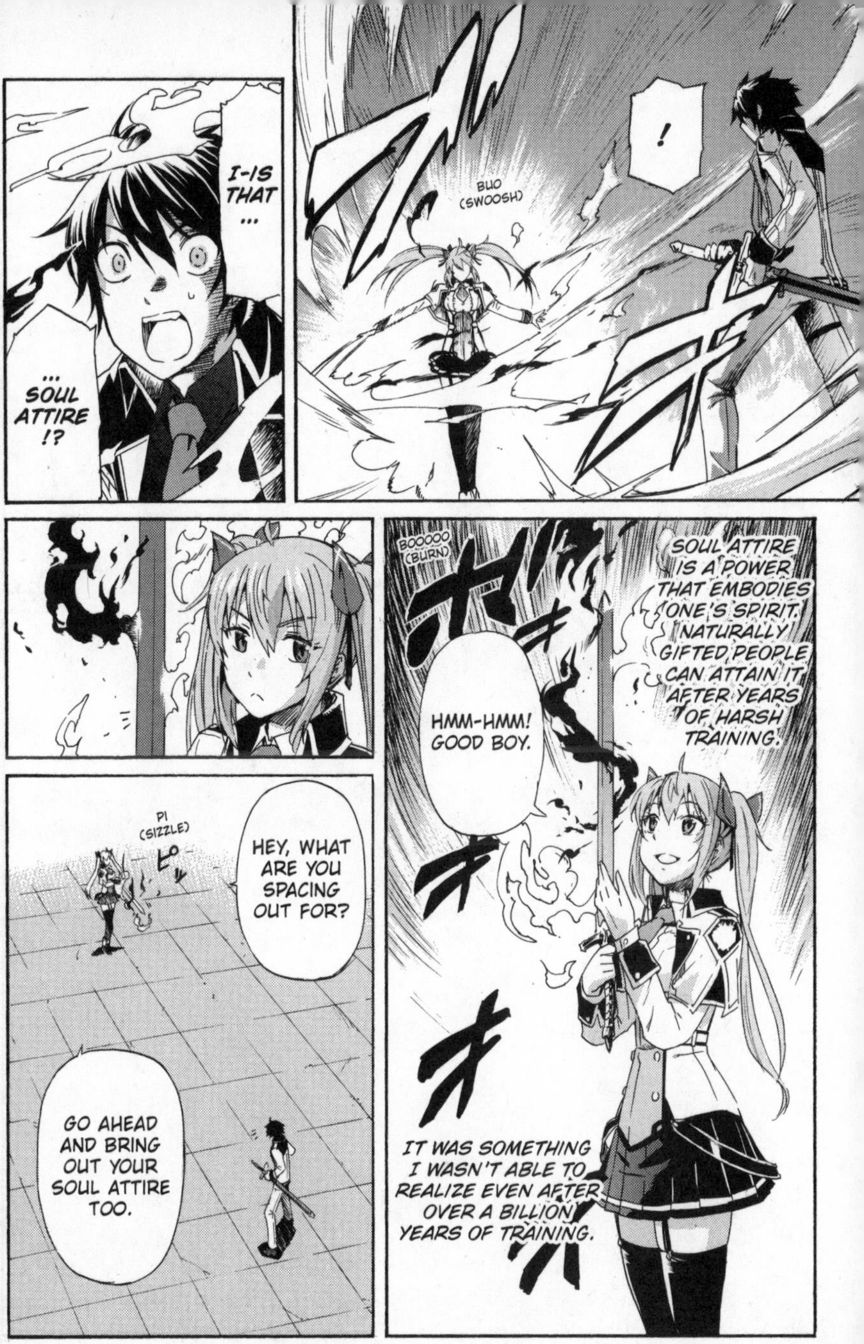
!
BUO (SWOOSH)
I-IS THAT ...
... SOUL ATTIRE !?
BOOOOO (BURN)
SOUL ATTIRE IS A POWER THAT EMBODIES ONE'S SPIRIT. NATURALLY GIFTED PEOPLE CAN ATTAIN IT AFTER YEARS OF HARSH TRAINING.
HMM-HMM! GOOD BOY.
IT WAS SOMETHING I WASN'T ABLE TO REALIZE EVEN AFTER OVER A BILLION YEARS OF TRAINING.
PI (SIZZLE)
ピッ
HEY, WHAT ARE YOU SPACING OUT FOR?
GO AHEAD AND BRING OUT YOUR SOUL ATTIRE TOO.

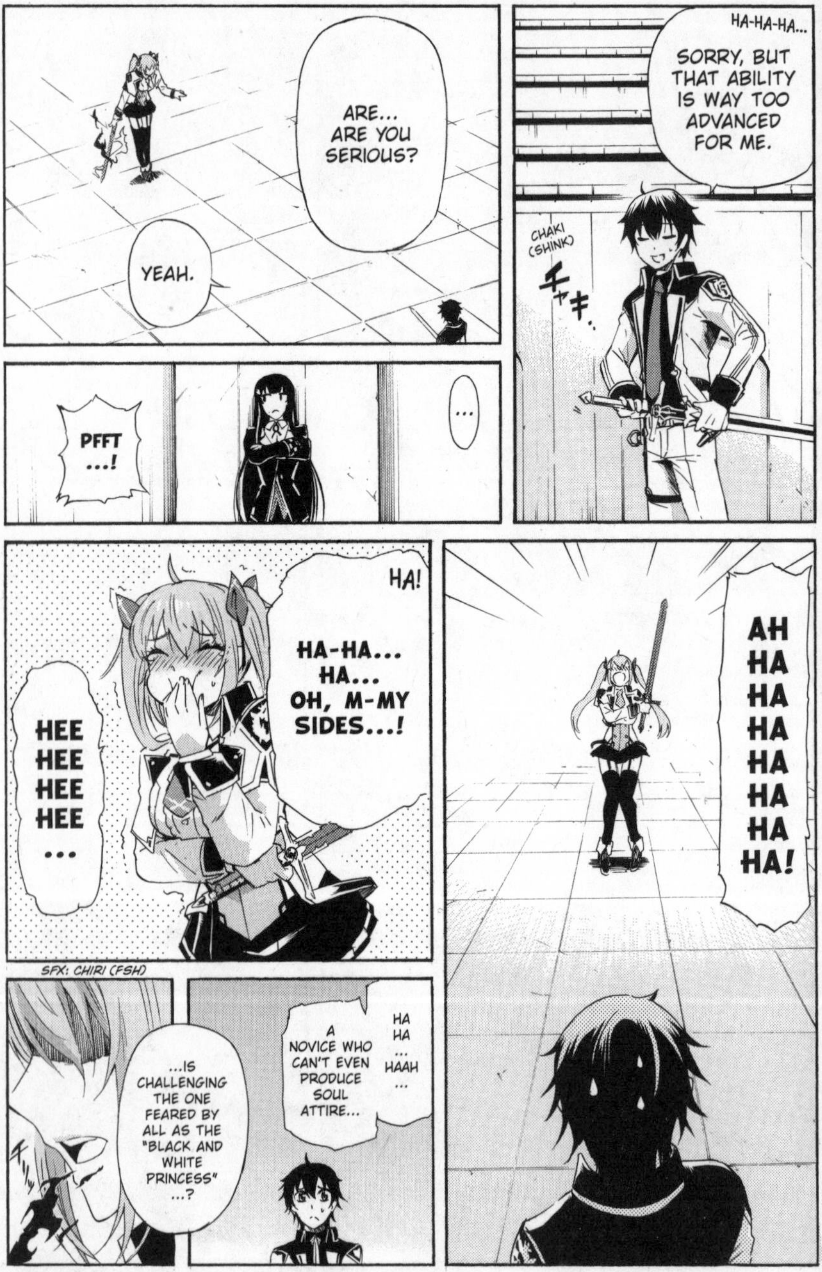
HA-HA-HA...
SORRY, BUT THAT ABILITY IS WAY TOO ADVANCED FOR ME.
CHAKI (SHINK)
ARE... ARE YOU SERIOUS?
YEAH.
...
PFFT ...!
AH HA HA HA HA HA HA HA HA!
HA!
HA-HA... HA... OH, M-MY SIDES...!
HEE HEE HEE HEE ...
SFX: CHIRI (FSH)
HA HA ... HAAH ...
A NOVICE WHO CAN'T EVEN PRODUCE SOUL ATTIRE...
...IS CHALLENGING THE ONE FEARED BY ALL AS THE "BLACK AND WHITE PRINCESS" ...?

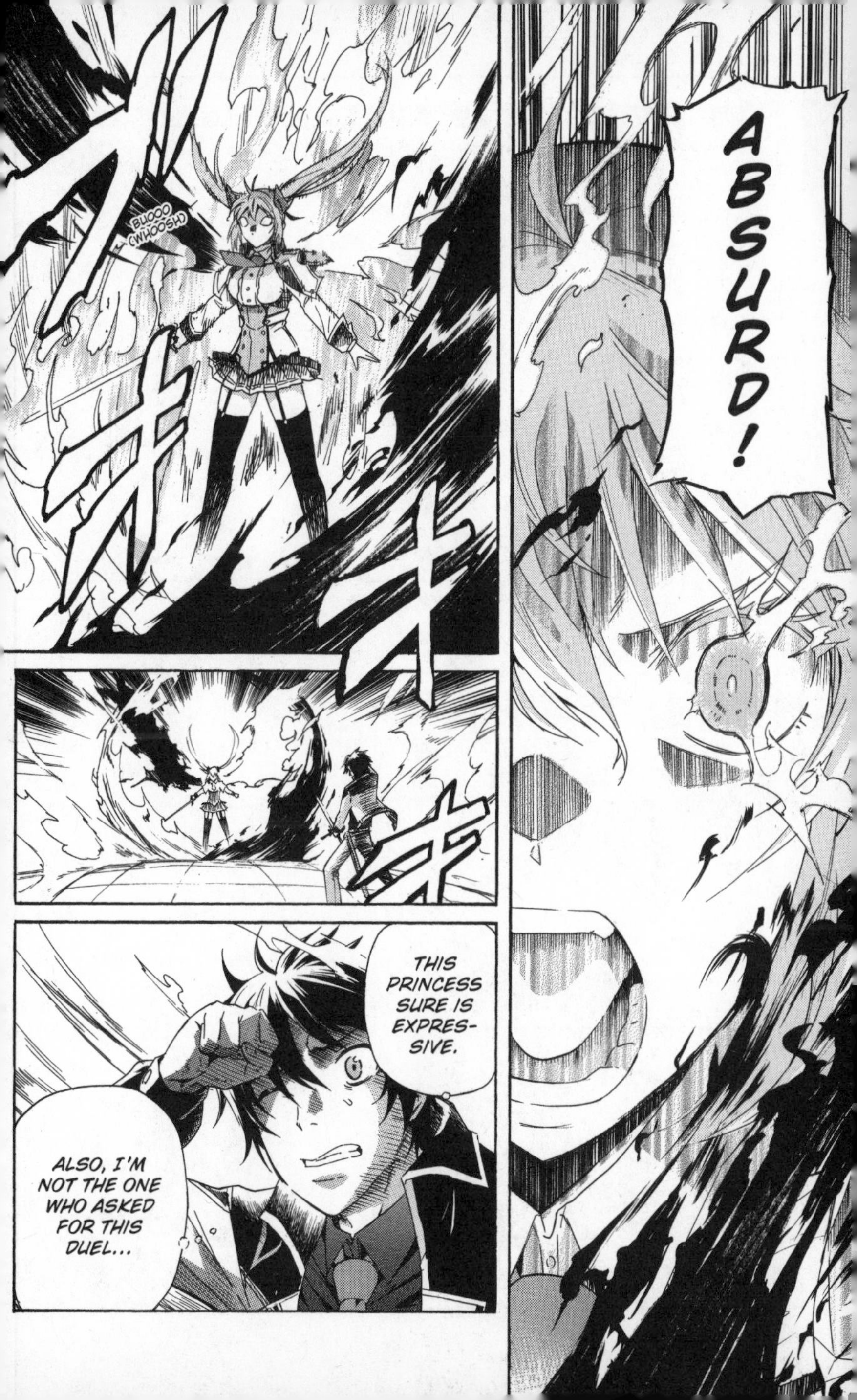

ABSURD!
BUOOO (WHOOSH)
THIS PRINCESS SURE IS EXPRES-SIVE.
ALSO, I'M NOT THE ONE WHO ASKED FOR THIS DUEL...

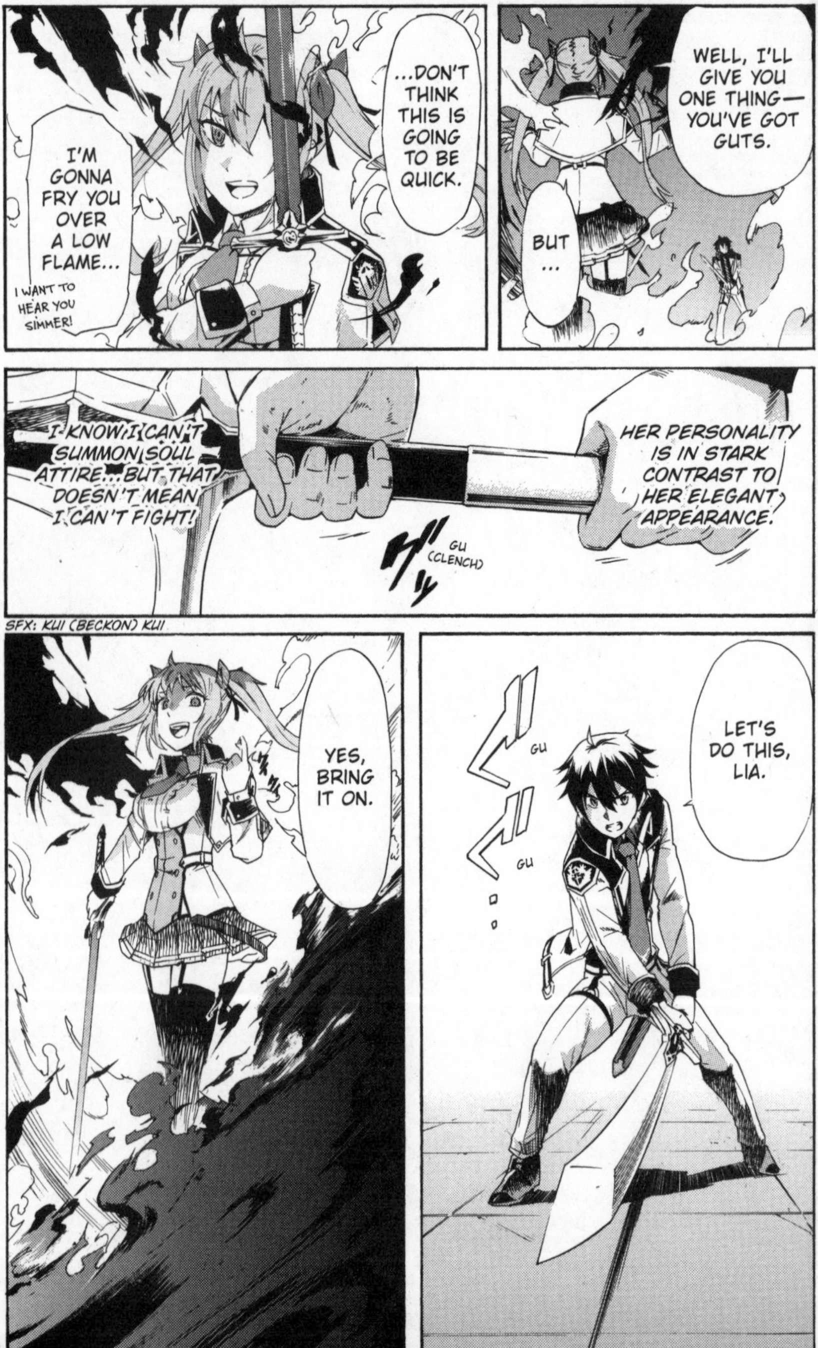
WELL, I'LL GIVE YOU ONE THING— YOU'VE GOT GUTS.
BUT ...
...DON'T THINK THIS IS GOING TO BE QUICK.
I'M GONNA FRY YOU OVER A LOW FLAME...
I WANT TO HEAR YOU SIMMER!
HER PERSONALITY IS IN STARK CONTRAST TO HER ELEGANT APPEARANCE.
GU (CLENCH)
I KNOW I CAN'T SUMMON SOUL ATTIRE... BUT THAT DOESN'T MEAN I CAN'T FIGHT!
SFX: KUI (BECKON) KUI
LET'S DO THIS, LIA.
GU
GU
YES, BRING IT ON.

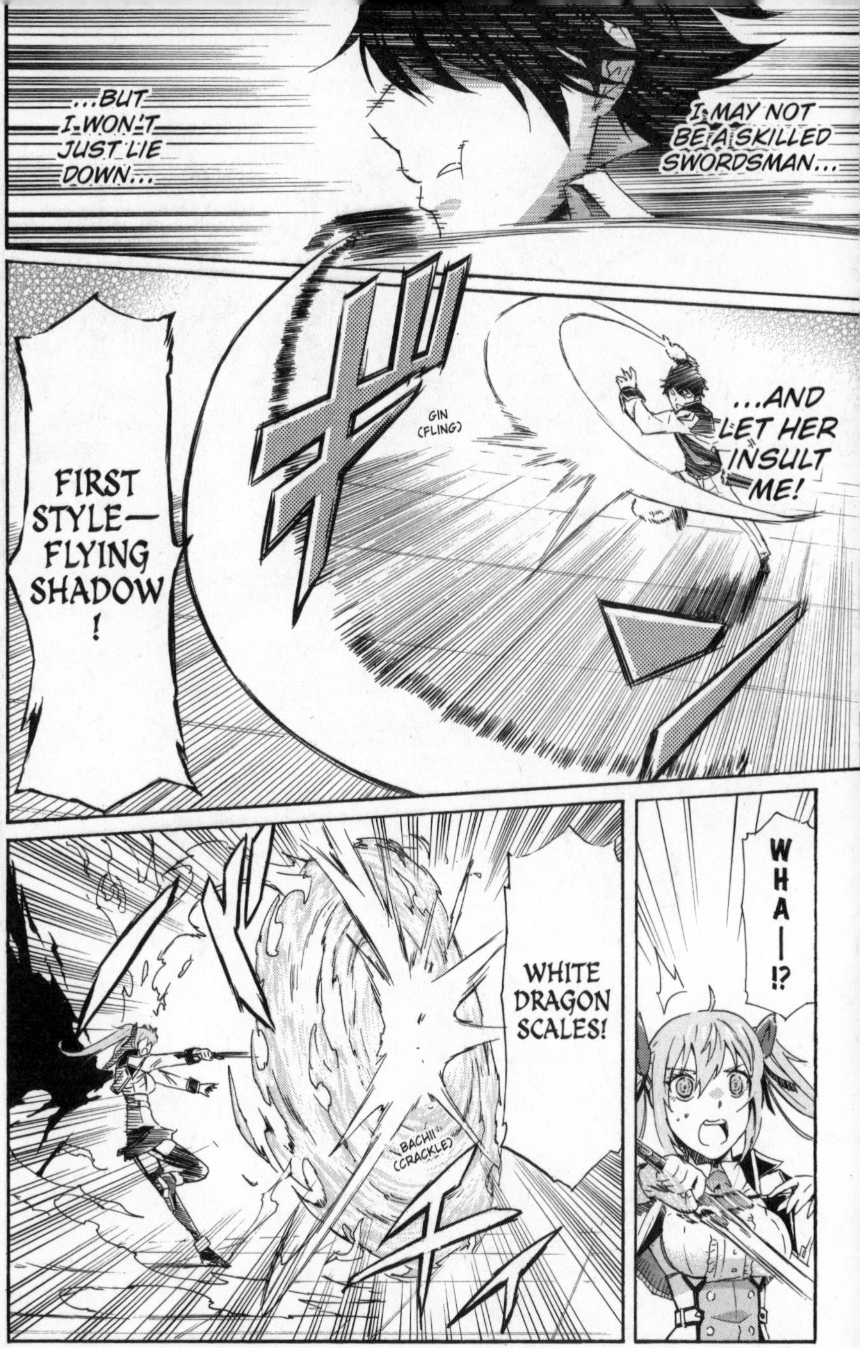
I MAY NOT BE A SKILLED SWORDSMAN...
...BUT I WON'T JUST LIE DOWN...
...AND LET HER INSULT ME!
GIN (FLING)
FIRST STYLE—FLYING SHADOW!
WHA—!?
WHITE DRAGON SCALES!
BACHII (CRACKLE)

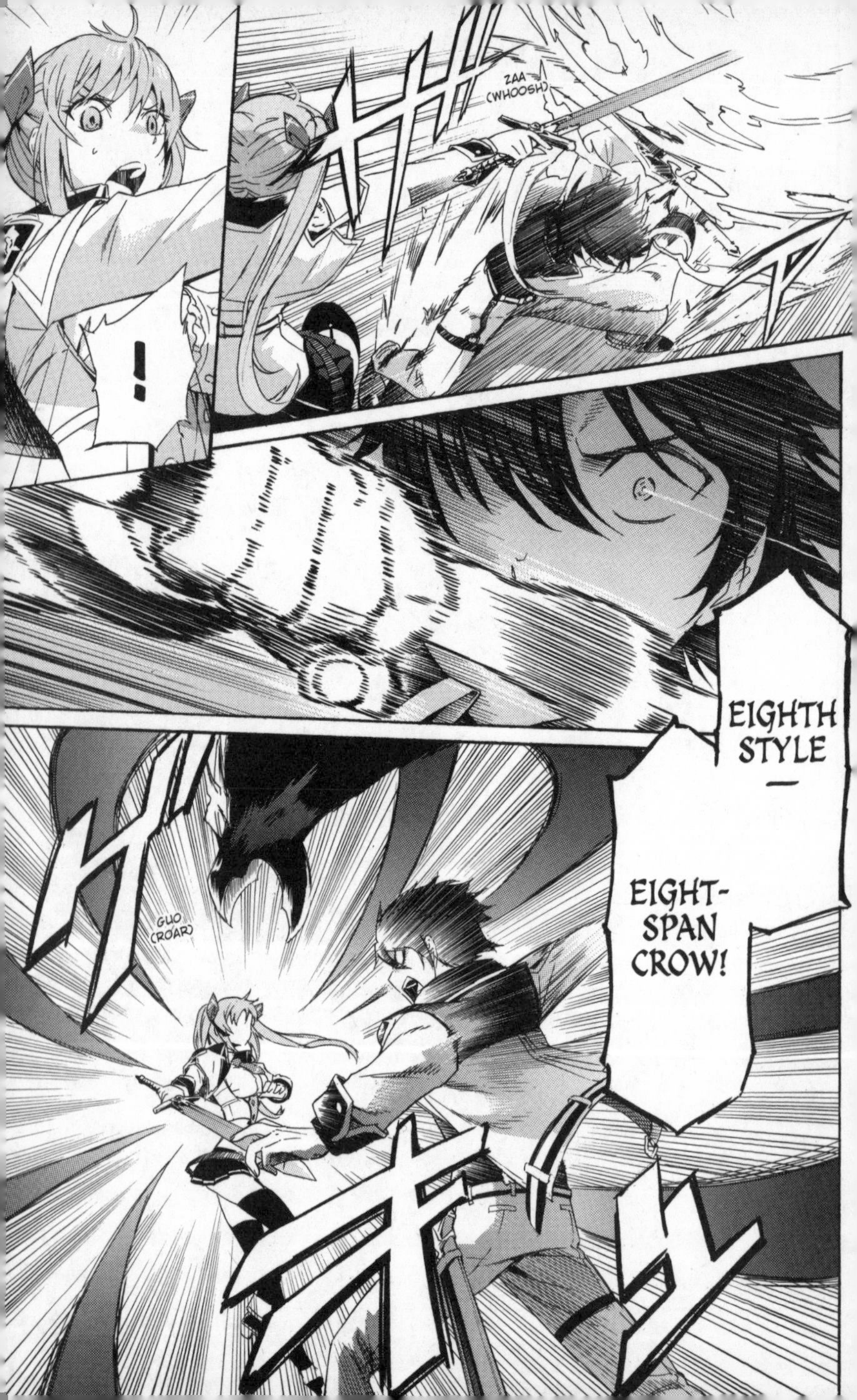
ZAA (WHOOSH)
!
EIGHTH STYLE —
EIGHT-SPAN CROW!
GUO (ROAR)

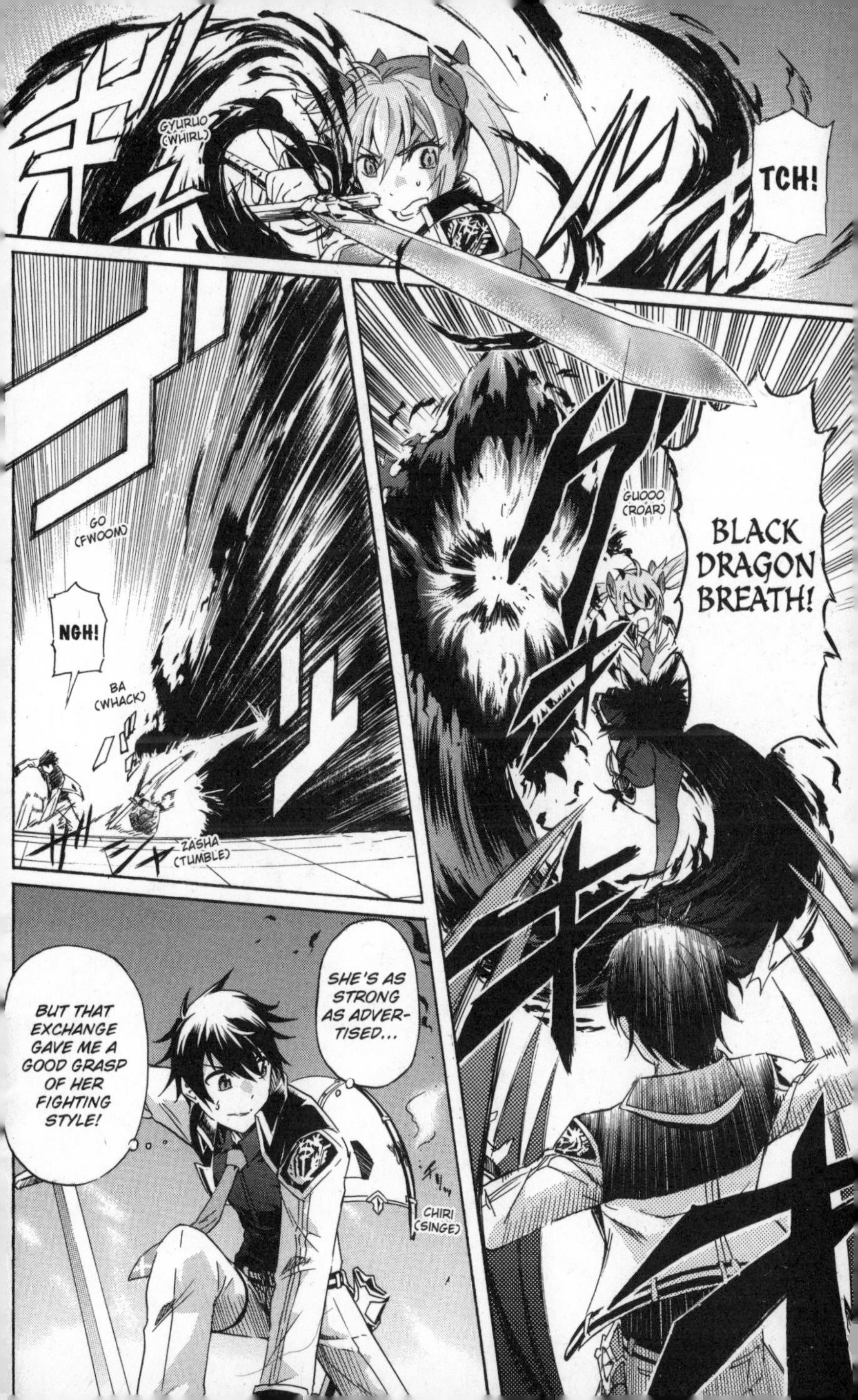
GYURUO (WHIRL)
TCH!
GUOOO (ROAR)
BLACK DRAGON BREATH!
GO (FWOOM)
NGH!
BA (WHACK)
ZASHA (TUMBLE)
SHE'S AS STRONG AS ADVER-TISED...
BUT THAT EXCHANGE GAVE ME A GOOD GRASP OF HER FIGHTING STYLE!
CHIRI (SINGE)

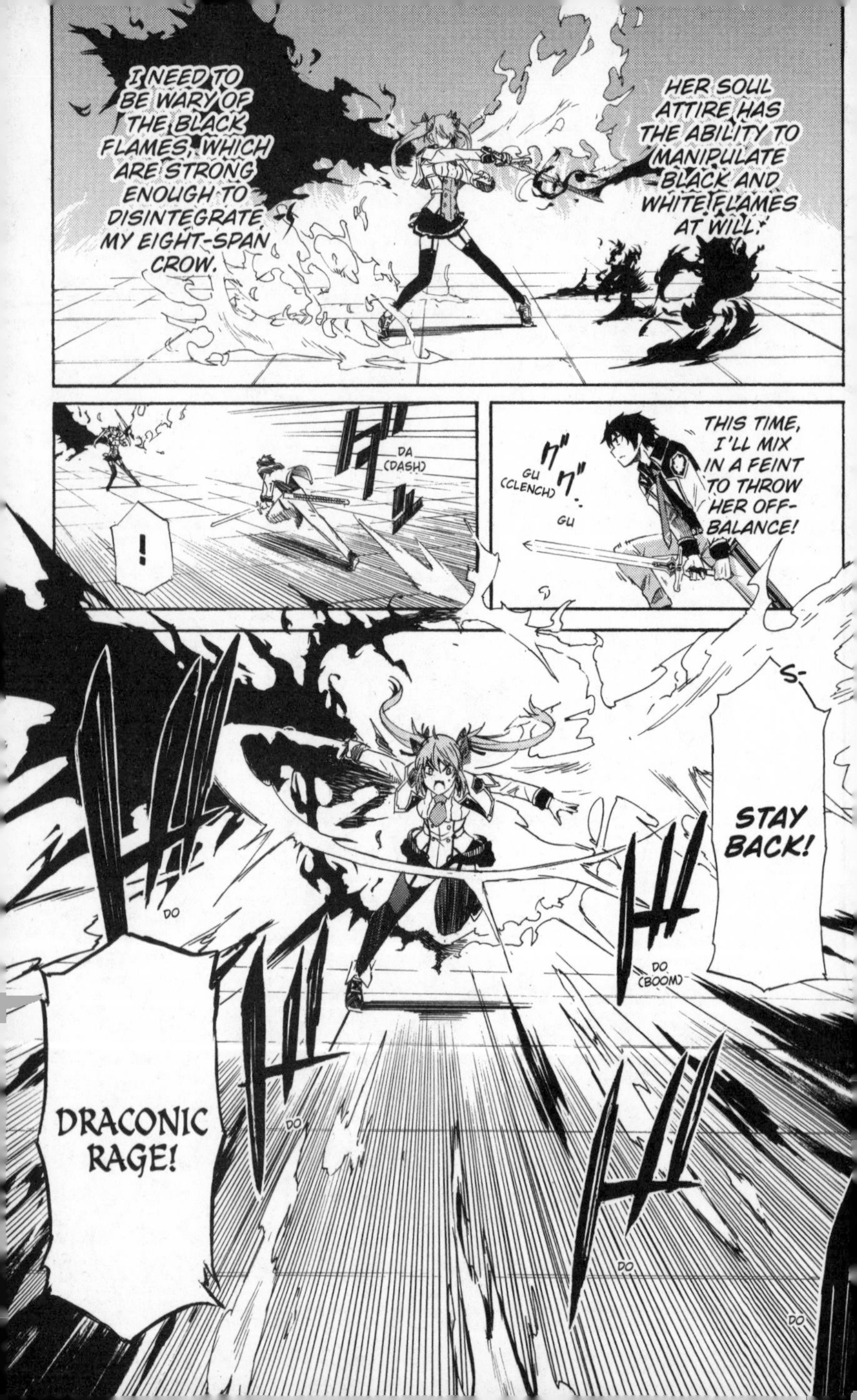
HER SOUL ATTIRE HAS THE ABILITY TO MANIPULATE BLACK AND WHITE FLAMES AT WILL.
I NEED TO BE WARY OF THE BLACK FLAMES, WHICH ARE STRONG ENOUGH TO DISINTEGRATE MY EIGHT-SPAN CROW.
THIS TIME, I'LL MIX IN A FEINT TO THROW HER OFF-BALANCE!
GU (CLENCH)
GU
DA (DASH)
!
S-
STAY BACK!
DO (BOOM)
DO
DRACONIC RAGE!
DO
DO
DO

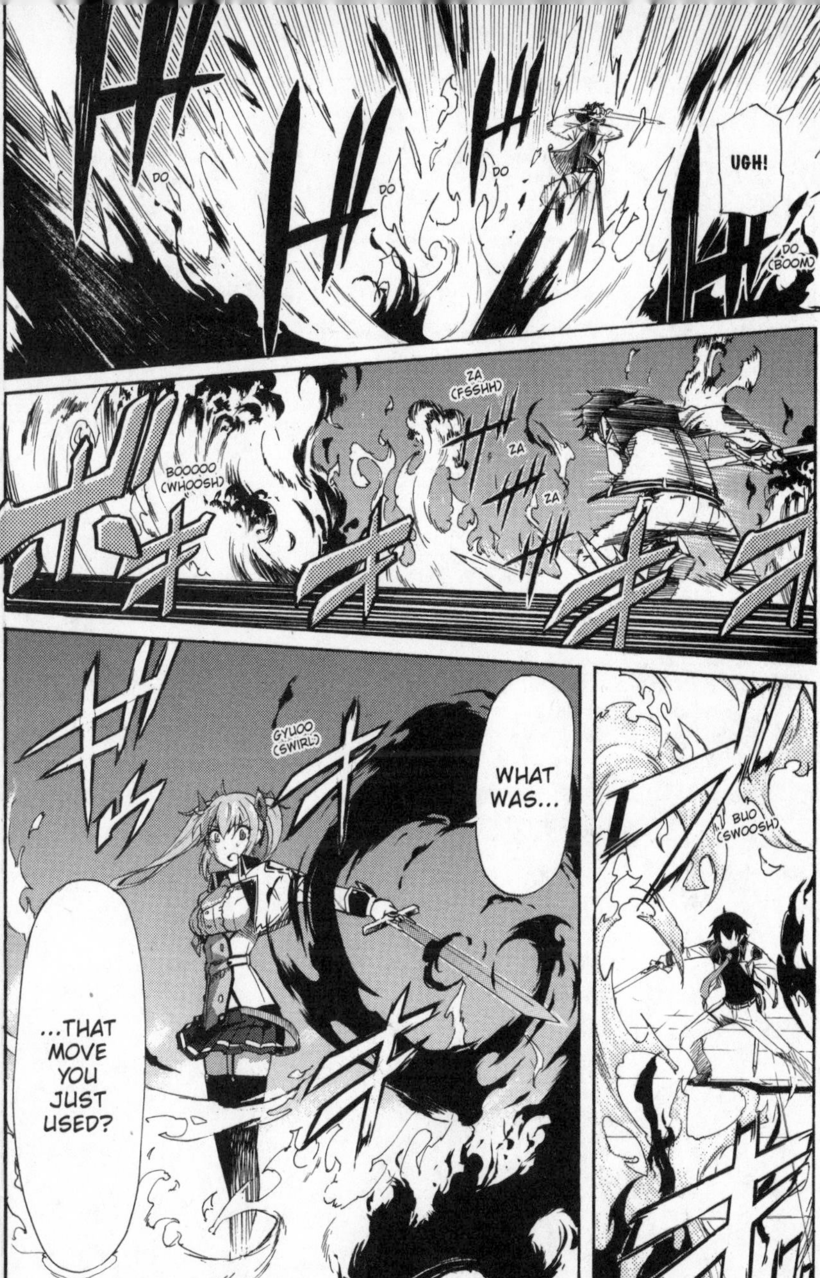
UGH!
DO (BOOM)
DO
DO
DO
ZA (FSSHH)
ZA
ZA
BOOOOO (WHOOSH)
BUO (SWOOSH)
WHAT WAS...
GYUOO (SWIRL)
...THAT MOVE YOU JUST USED?

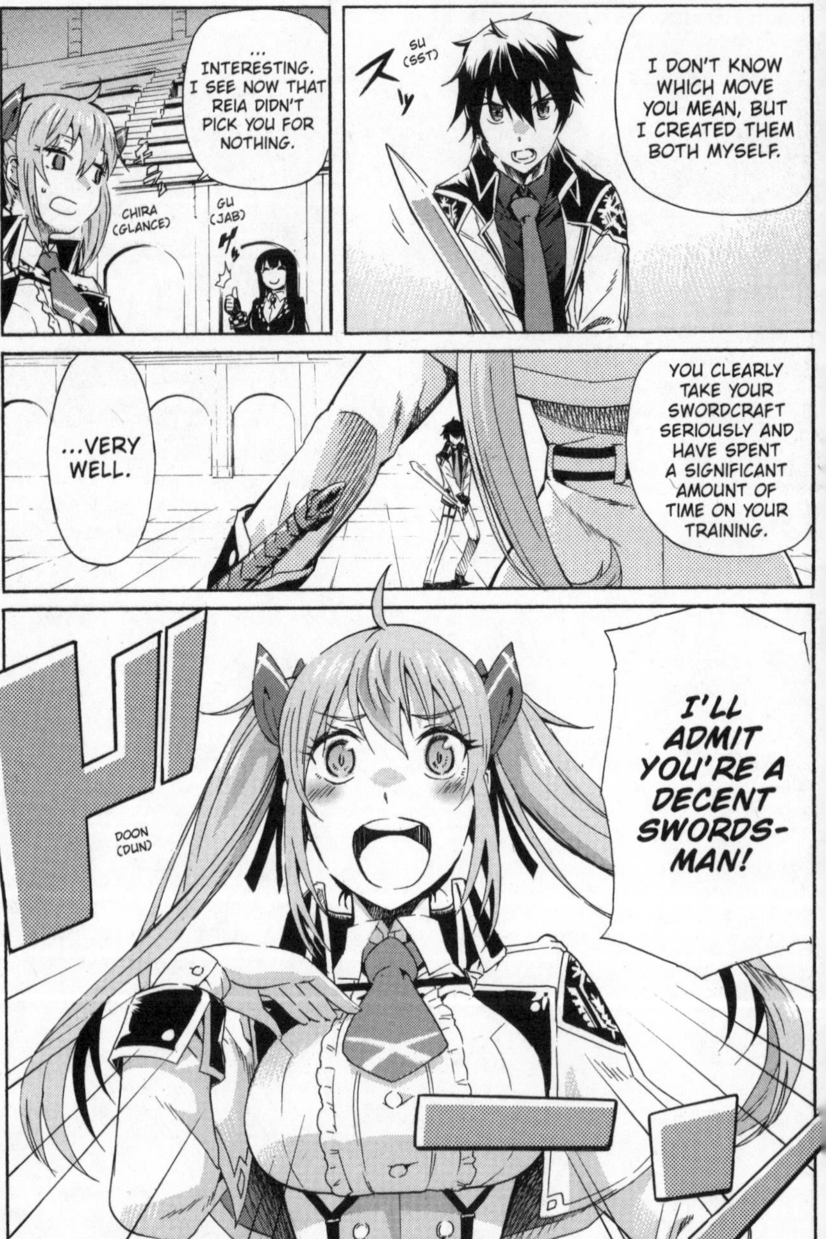
SU (SST)
I DON'T KNOW WHICH MOVE YOU MEAN, BUT I CREATED THEM BOTH MYSELF.
... INTERESTING. I SEE NOW THAT REIA DIDN'T PICK YOU FOR NOTHING.
CHIRA (GLANCE)
GU (JAB)
YOU CLEARLY TAKE YOUR SWORDCRAFT SERIOUSLY AND HAVE SPENT A SIGNIFICANT AMOUNT OF TIME ON YOUR TRAINING.
...VERY WELL.
I'LL ADMIT YOU'RE A DECENT SWORDS-MAN!
DOON (DUN)

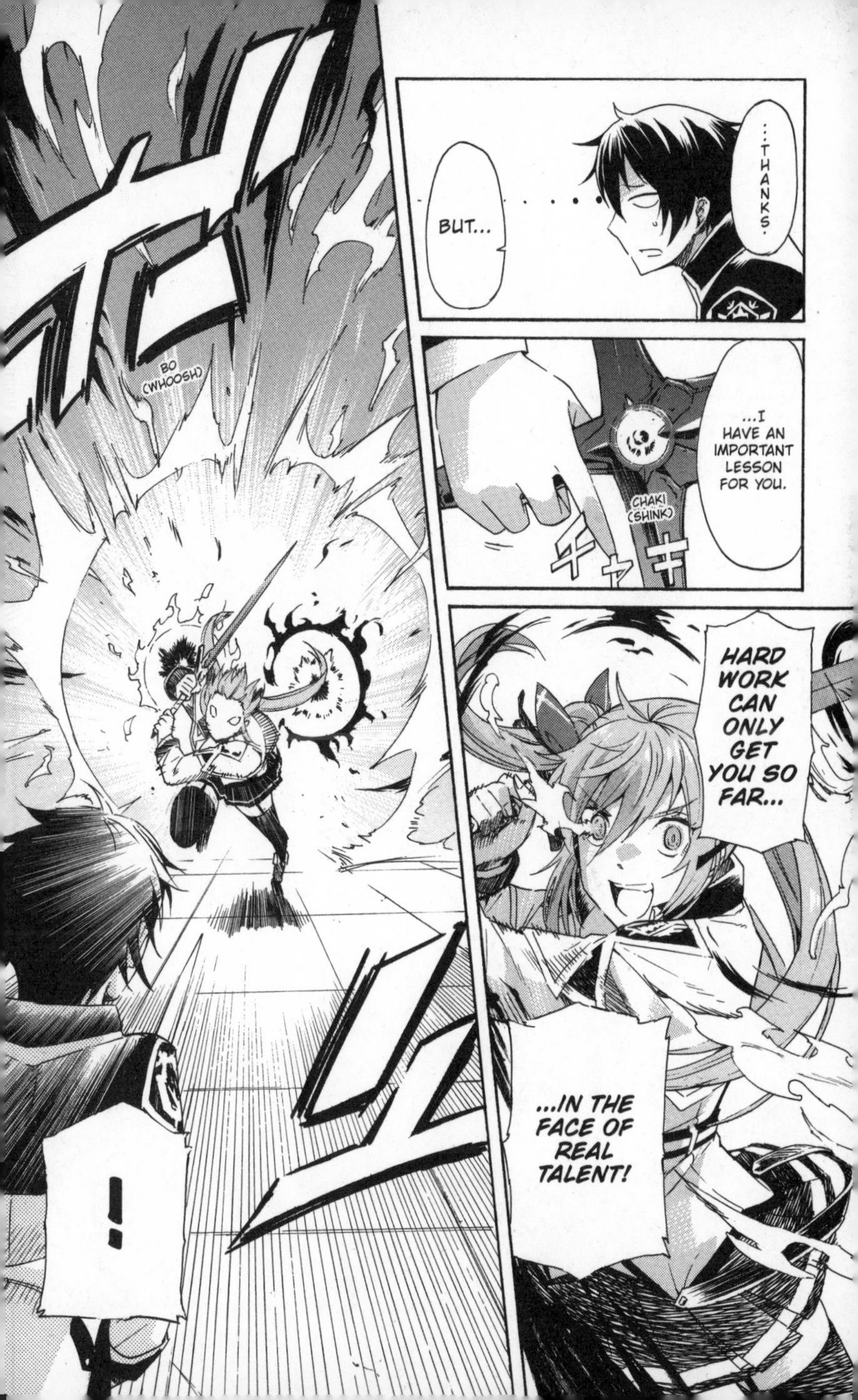
...THANKS.
BUT...
...I HAVE AN IMPORTANT LESSON FOR YOU.
CHAKI (SHINK)
HARD WORK CAN ONLY GET YOU SO FAR...
...IN THE FACE OF REAL TALENT!
BO (WHOOSH)
!

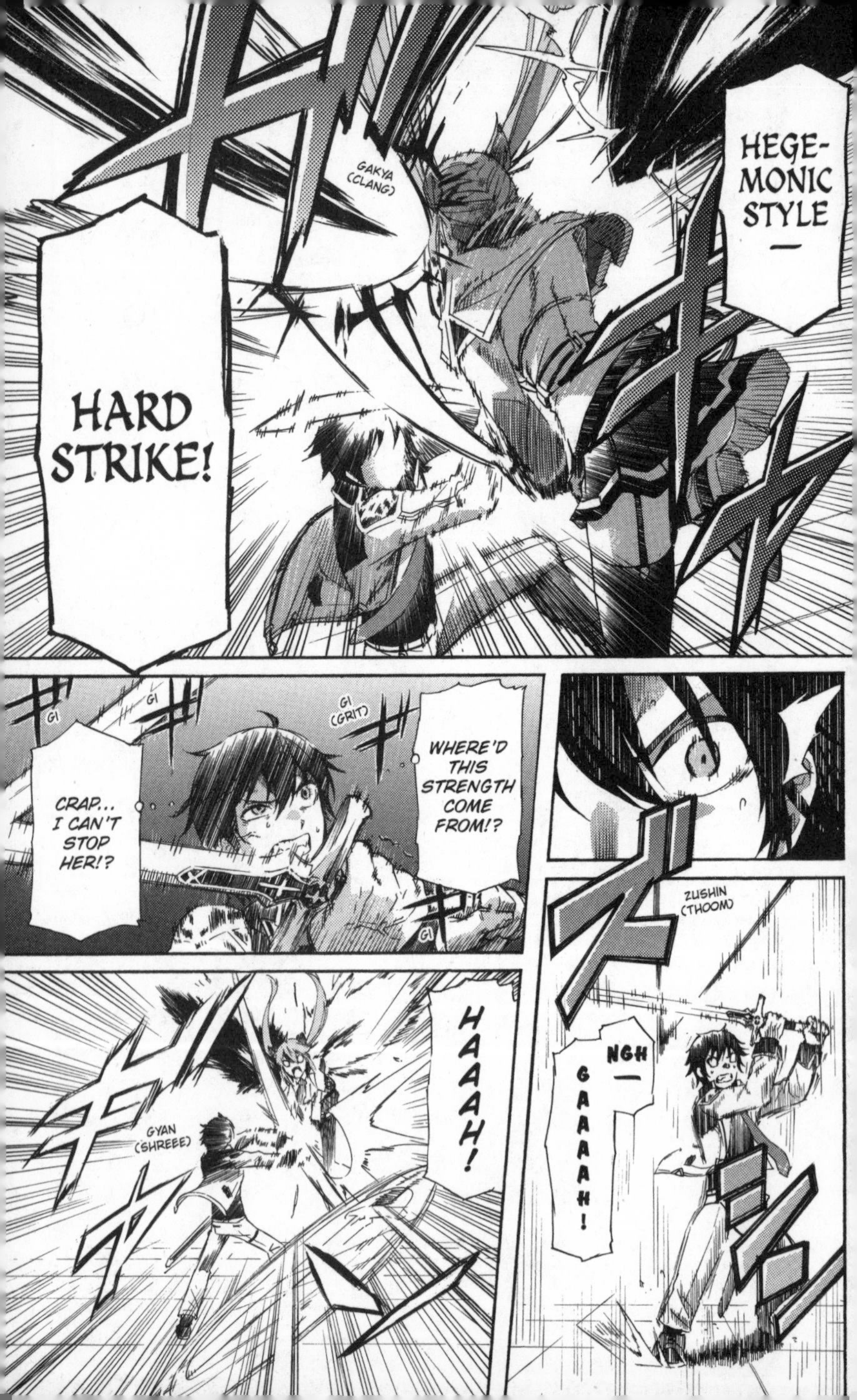
HEGE-MONIC STYLE —
GAKYA (CLANG)
HARD STRIKE!
ZUSHIN (THOOM)
NGH — GAAAAAH!
GI (GRIT)
WHERE'D THIS STRENGTH COME FROM!?
GI
GI
CRAP... I CAN'T STOP HER!?
GI
HAAAAH!
GYAN (SHREEE)

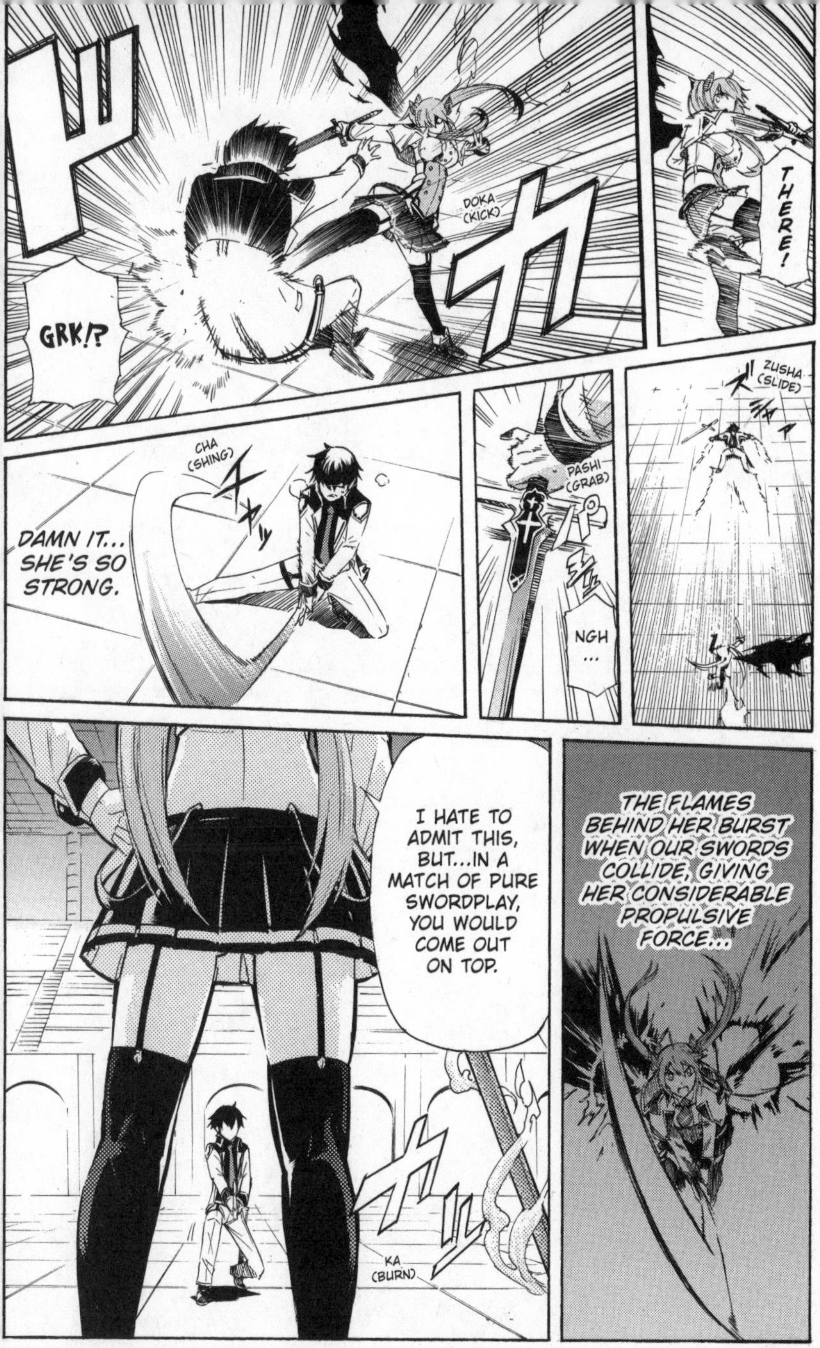
THERE!
DOKA (KICK)
GRK!?
ZUSHA (SLIDE)
PASHI (GRAB)
NGH...
CHA (SHING)
DAMN IT... SHE'S SO STRONG.
THE FLAMES BEHIND HER BURST WHEN OUR SWORDS COLLIDE, GIVING HER CONSIDERABLE PROPULSIVE FORCE...
I HATE TO ADMIT THIS, BUT...IN A MATCH OF PURE SWORDPLAY, YOU WOULD COME OUT ON TOP.
KA (BURN)

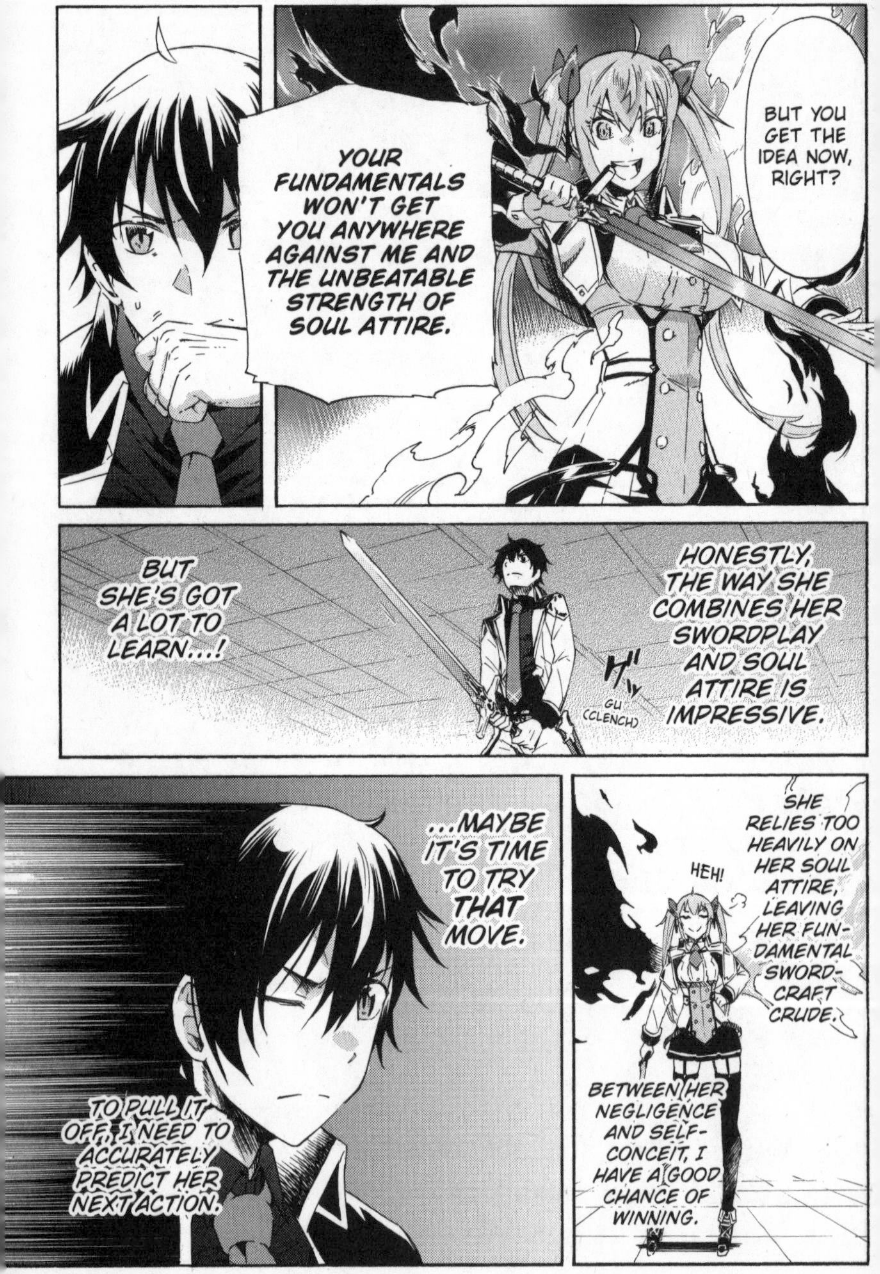

BUT YOU GET THE IDEA NOW, RIGHT?
YOUR FUNDAMENTALS WON'T GET YOU ANYWHERE AGAINST ME AND THE UNBEATABLE STRENGTH OF SOUL ATTIRE.
HONESTLY, THE WAY SHE COMBINES HER SWORDPLAY AND SOUL ATTIRE IS IMPRESSIVE.
GU (CLENCH)
BUT SHE'S GOT A LOT TO LEARN...!
SHE RELIES TOO HEAVILY ON HER SOUL ATTIRE, LEAVING HER FUN-DAMENTAL SWORD-CRAFT CRUDE.
HEH!
BETWEEN HER NEGLIGENCE AND SELF-CONCEIT, I HAVE A GOOD CHANCE OF WINNING.
...MAYBE IT'S TIME TO TRY THAT MOVE.
TO PULL IT OFF, I NEED TO ACCURATELY PREDICT HER NEXT ACTION.

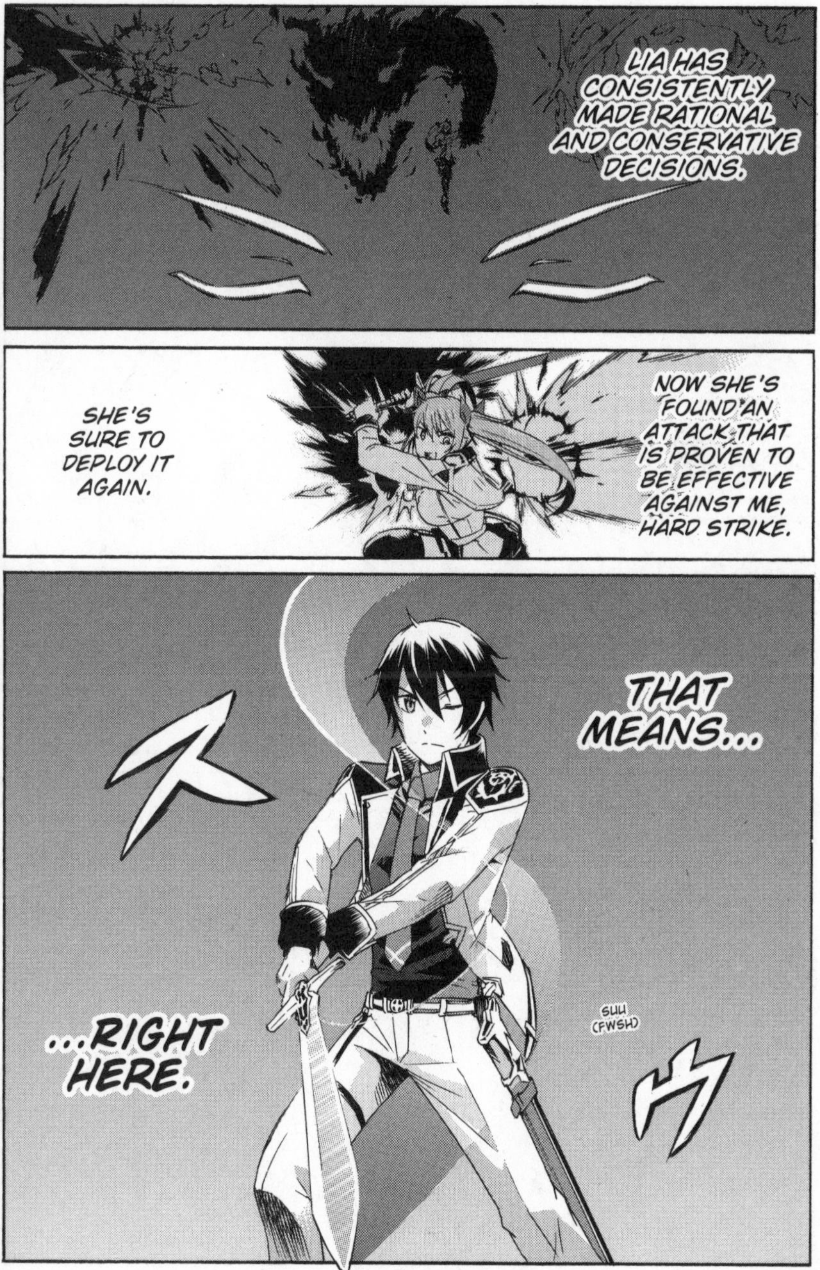
LIA HAS CONSISTENTLY MADE RATIONAL AND CONSERVATIVE DECISIONS.
NOW SHE'S FOUND AN ATTACK THAT IS PROVEN TO BE EFFECTIVE AGAINST ME, HARD STRIKE.
SHE'S SURE TO DEPLOY IT AGAIN.
THAT MEANS...
ス
SUU (FWSH)
ウ
...RIGHT HERE.

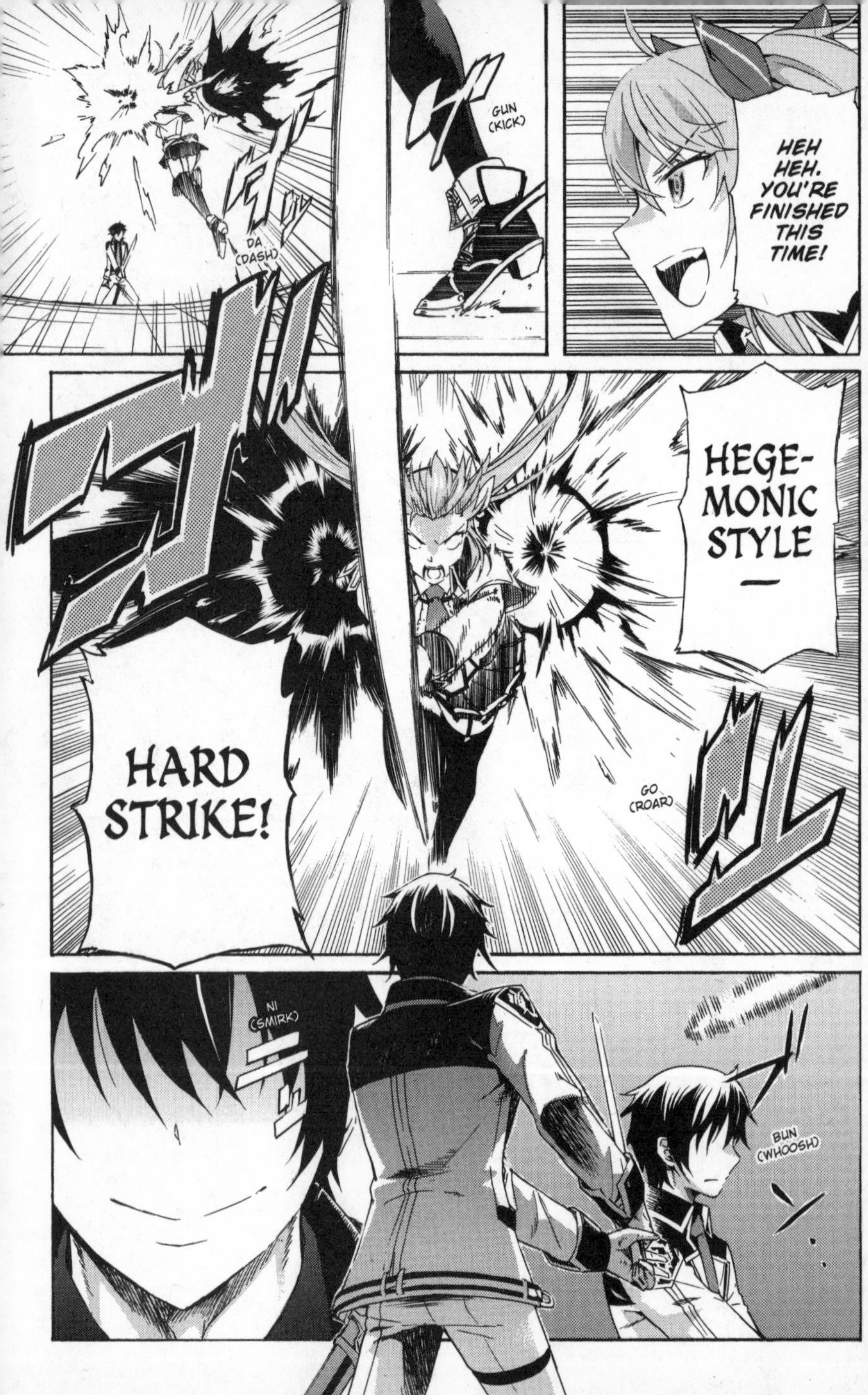
HEH HEH. YOU'RE FINISHED THIS TIME!
GUN (KICK)
DA (DASH)
HEGE-MONIC STYLE —
HARD STRIKE!
GO (ROAR)
BUN (WHOOSH)
NI (SMIRK)

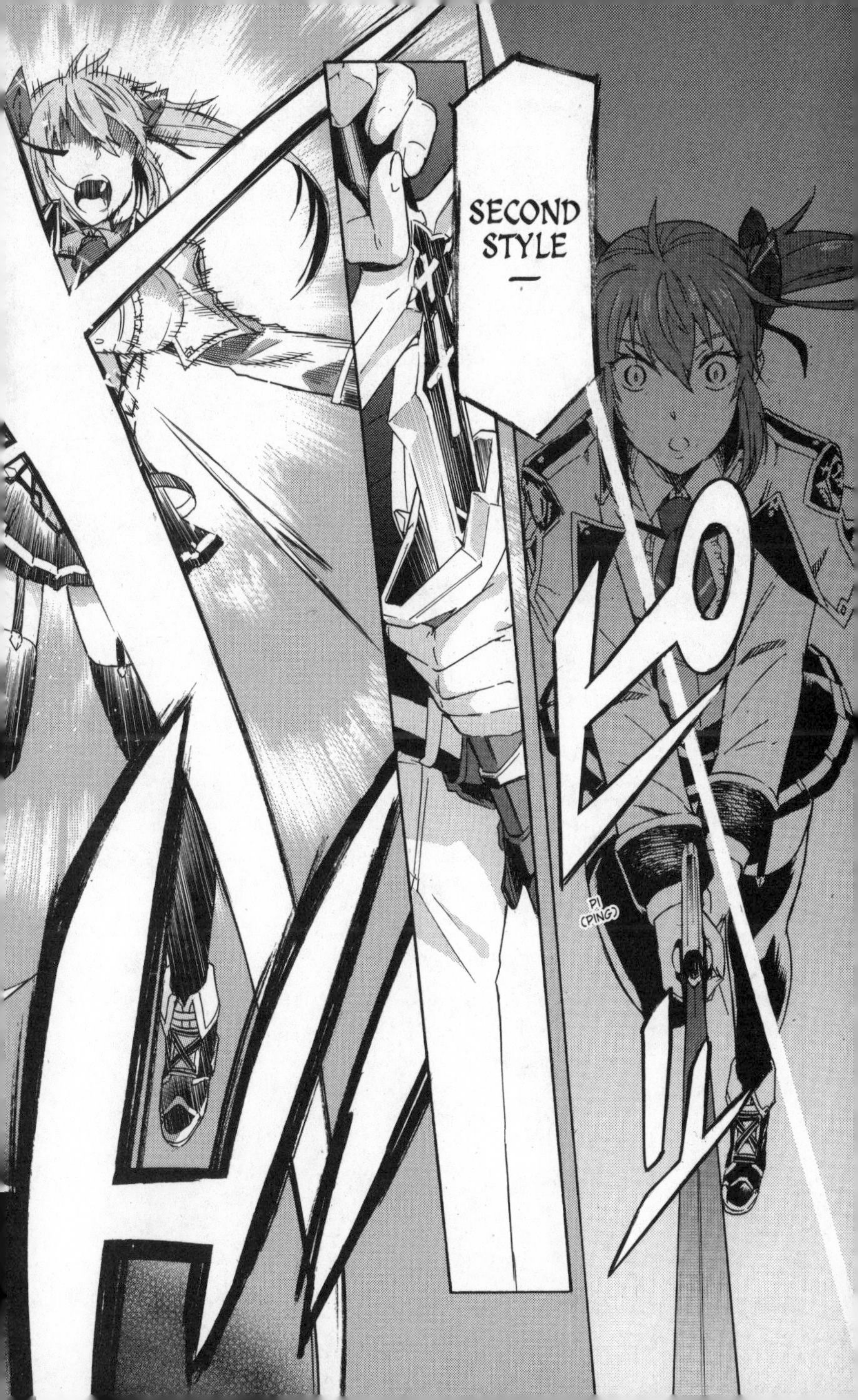
SECOND STYLE
—
PI (PING)

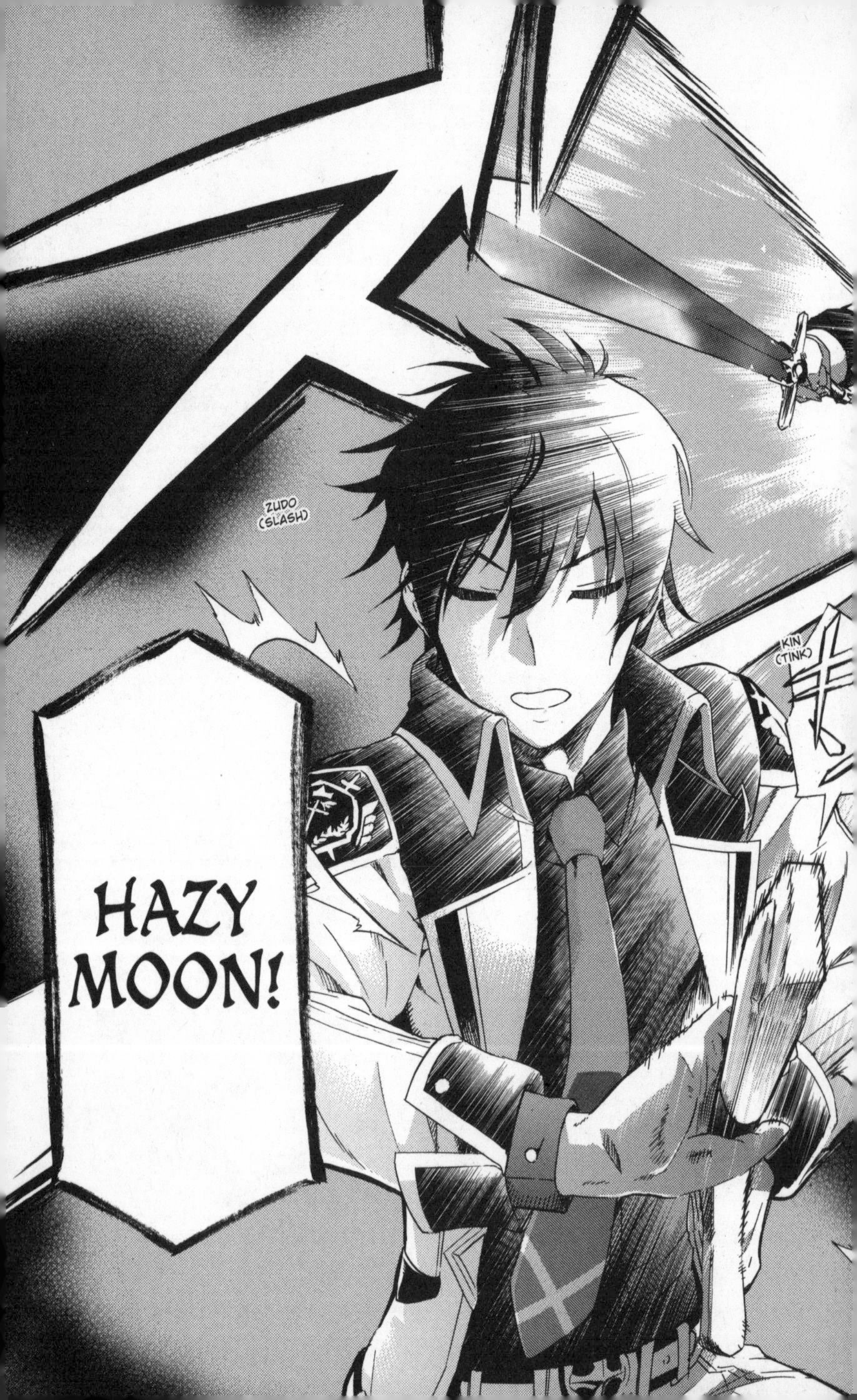
KIN
(TINK)
ZUDO
(SLASH)
HAZY MOON!

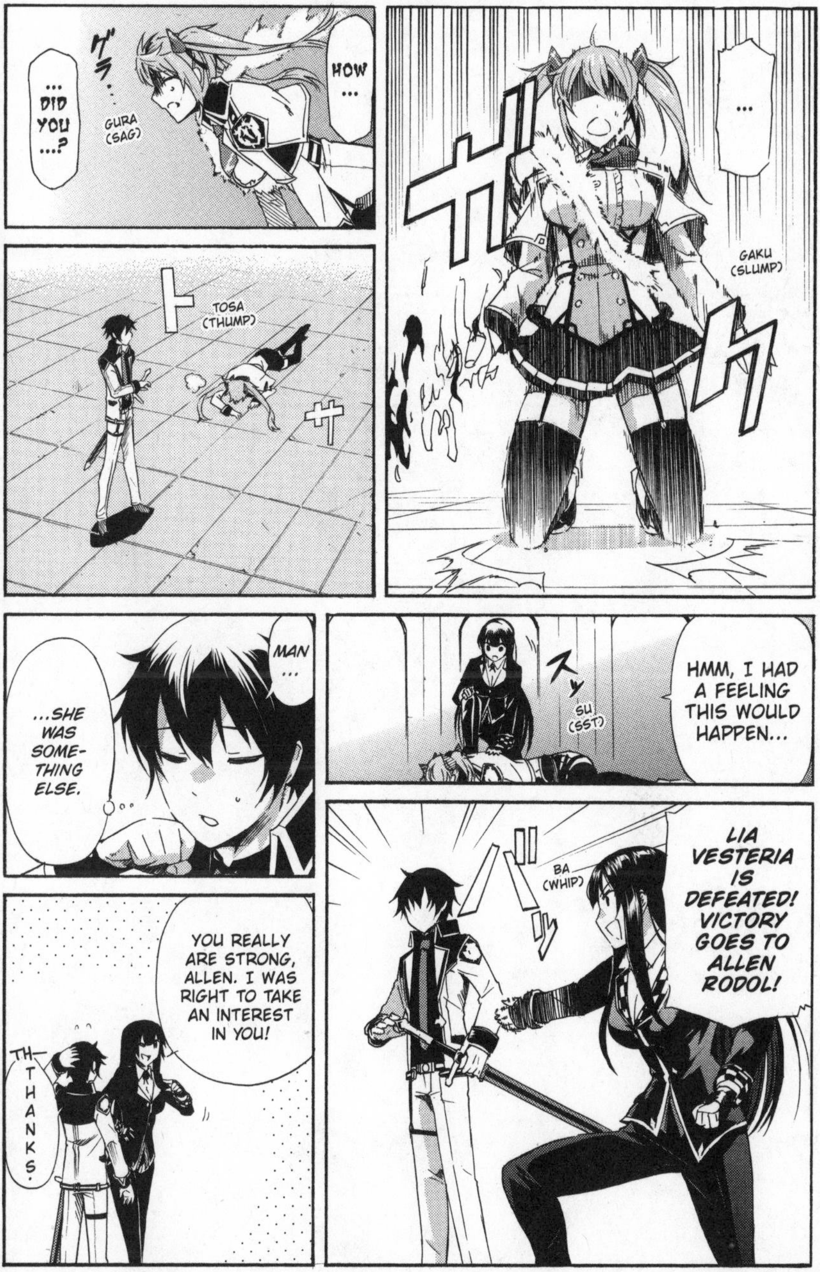
...
GAKU (SLUMP)
HOW ...
... DID YOU ...?
GURA (SAG)
TOSA (THUMP)
HMM, I HAD A FEELING THIS WOULD HAPPEN...
SU (SST)
MAN ...
...SHE WAS SOMETHING ELSE.
LIA VESTERIA IS DEFEATED! VICTORY GOES TO ALLEN RODOL!
BA (WHIP)
YOU REALLY ARE STRONG, ALLEN. I WAS RIGHT TO TAKE AN INTEREST IN YOU!
TH— THANKS.

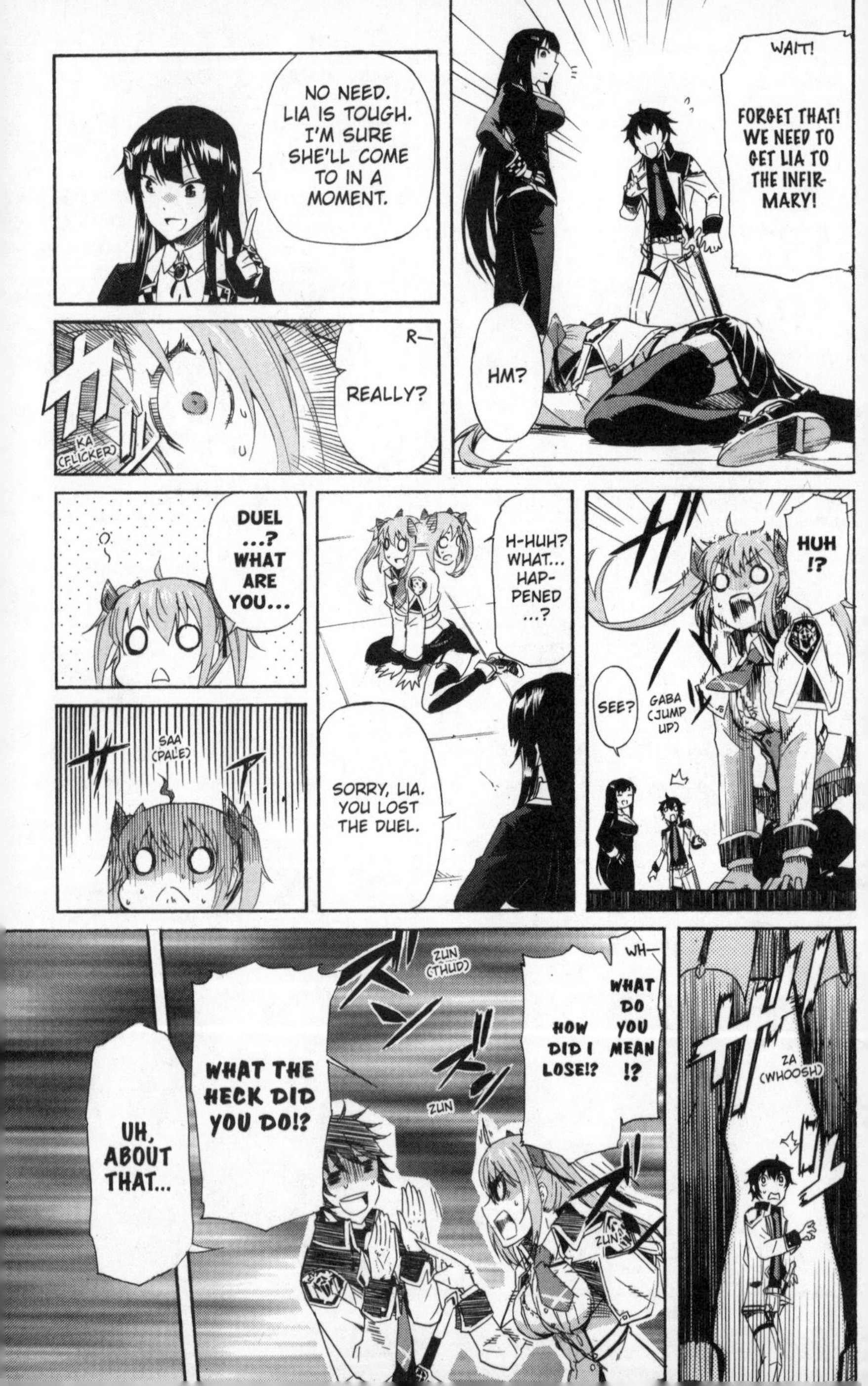
WAIT!
FORGET THAT! WE NEED TO GET LIA TO THE INFIRMARY!
HM?
NO NEED. LIA IS TOUGH. I'M SURE SHE'LL COME TO IN A MOMENT.
KA (FLICKER)
R— REALLY?
HUH !?
SEE?
GABA (JUMP UP)
H-HUH? WHAT... HAPPENED ...?
SORRY, LIA. YOU LOST THE DUEL.
DUEL ...? WHAT ARE YOU...
SAA (PALE)
ZA (WHOOSH)
WH— WHAT DO YOU MEAN !?
HOW DID I LOSE!?
ZUN (THUD)
WHAT THE HECK DID YOU DO!?
ZUN
ZUN
UH, ABOUT THAT...

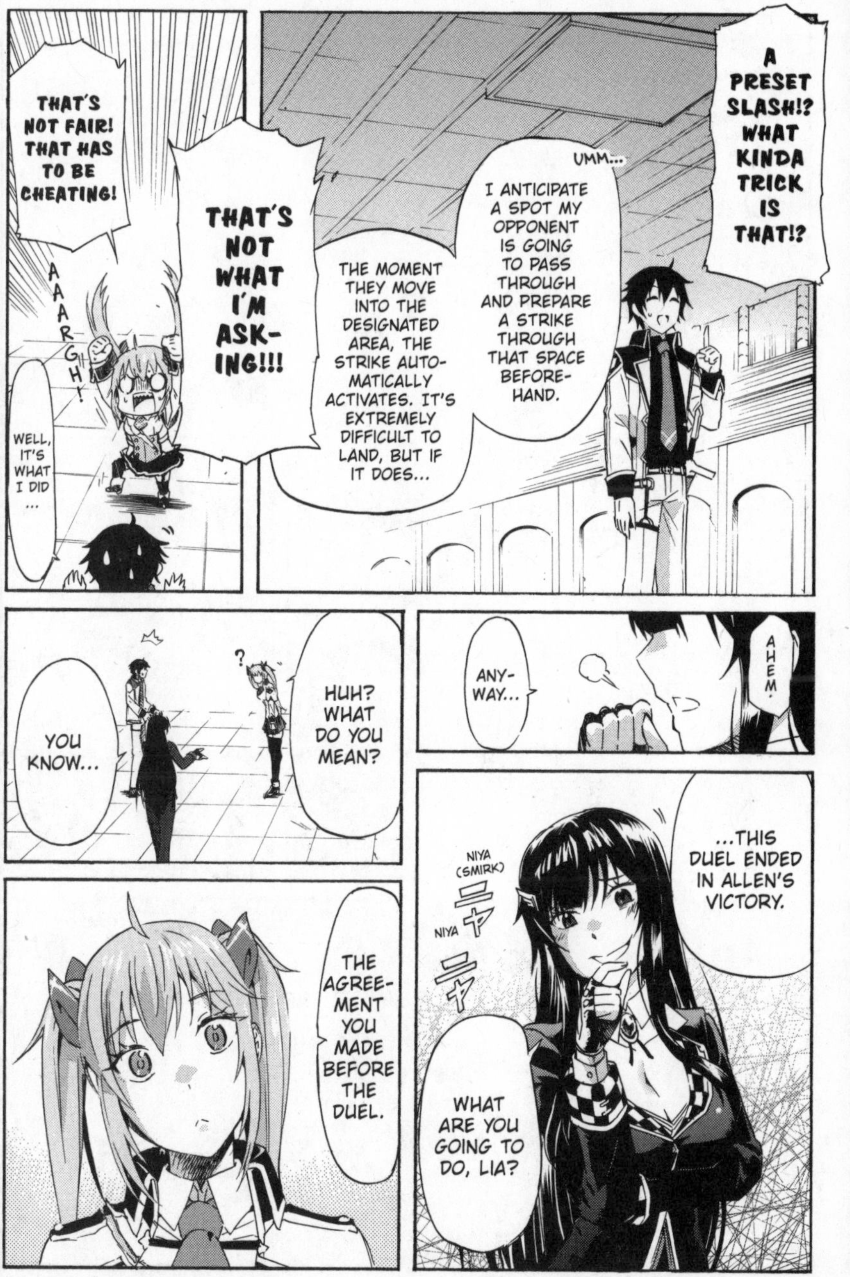
A PRESET SLASH!? WHAT KINDA TRICK IS THAT!?
UMM...
I ANTICIPATE A SPOT MY OPPONENT IS GOING TO PASS THROUGH AND PREPARE A STRIKE THROUGH THAT SPACE BEFOREHAND.
THE MOMENT THEY MOVE INTO THE DESIGNATED AREA, THE STRIKE AUTOMATICALLY ACTIVATES. IT'S EXTREMELY DIFFICULT TO LAND, BUT IF IT DOES...
THAT'S NOT WHAT I'M ASKING!!!
THAT'S NOT FAIR! THAT HAS TO BE CHEATING!
AAARGH!
WELL, IT'S WHAT I DID...
AHEM.
ANYWAY...
HUH? WHAT DO YOU MEAN?
YOU KNOW...
...THIS DUEL ENDED IN ALLEN'S VICTORY.
NIYA (SMIRK)
NIYA
WHAT ARE YOU GOING TO DO, LIA?
THE AGREEMENT YOU MADE BEFORE THE DUEL.

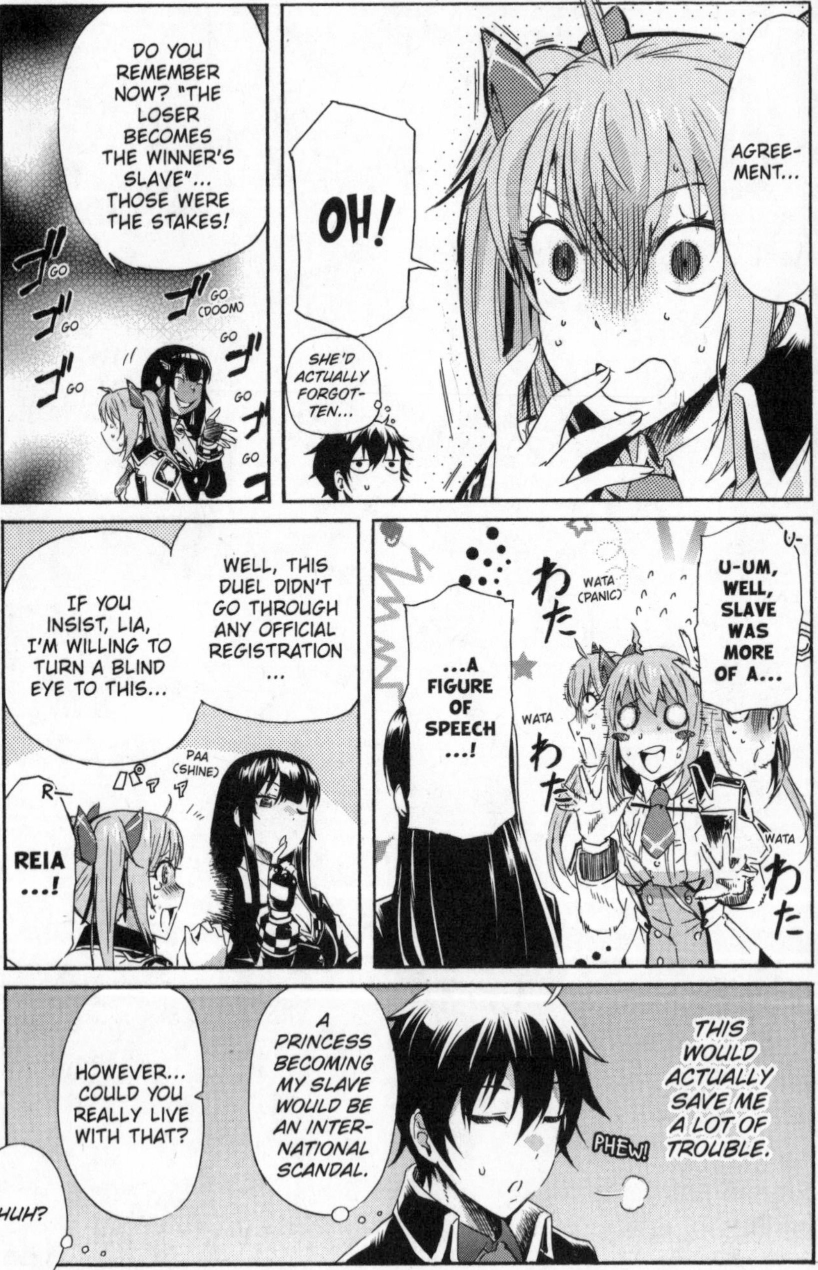
AGREE-MENT...
OH!
SHE'D ACTUALLY FORGOT-TEN...
DO YOU REMEMBER NOW? "THE LOSER BECOMES THE WINNER'S SLAVE"... THOSE WERE THE STAKES!
GO GO GO GO (DOOM)
GO GO GO GO
U-
U-UM, WELL, SLAVE WAS MORE OF A...
...A FIGURE OF SPEECH...!
WATA (PANIC)
WATA
WATA
WELL, THIS DUEL DIDN'T GO THROUGH ANY OFFICIAL REGISTRATION...
IF YOU INSIST, LIA, I'M WILLING TO TURN A BLIND EYE TO THIS...
PAA (SHINE)
R— REIA...!
THIS WOULD ACTUALLY SAVE ME A LOT OF TROUBLE.
PHEW!
A PRINCESS BECOMING MY SLAVE WOULD BE AN INTER-NATIONAL SCANDAL.
HOWEVER... COULD YOU REALLY LIVE WITH THAT?
HUH?

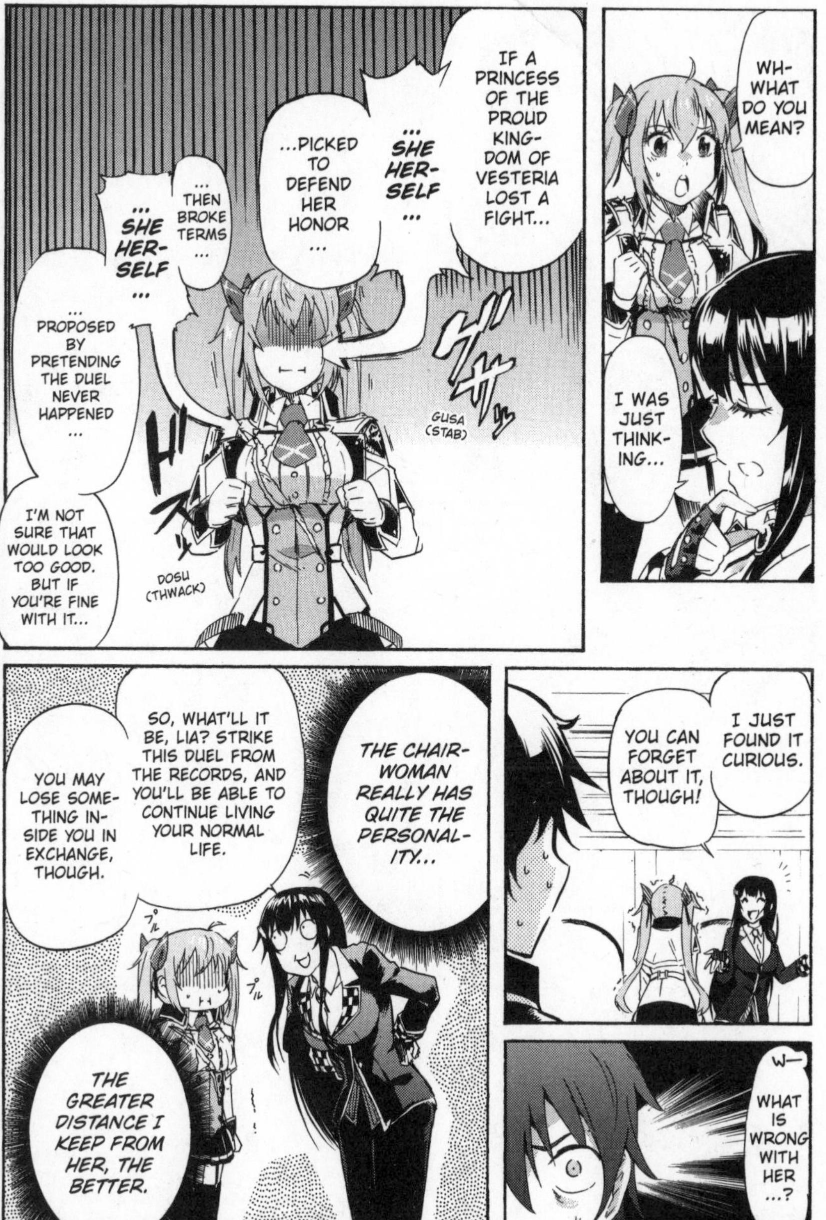
WH-WHAT DO YOU MEAN?
I WAS JUST THINKING...
IF A PRINCESS OF THE PROUD KINGDOM OF VESTERIA LOST A FIGHT...
...SHE HERSELF...
...PICKED TO DEFEND HER HONOR...
...SHE HERSELF...
...THEN BROKE TERMS...
GUSA (STAB)
...SHE HERSELF...
...PROPOSED BY PRETENDING THE DUEL NEVER HAPPENED...
I'M NOT SURE THAT WOULD LOOK TOO GOOD. BUT IF YOU'RE FINE WITH IT...
DOSU (THWACK)
I JUST FOUND IT CURIOUS.
YOU CAN FORGET ABOUT IT, THOUGH!
W— WHAT IS WRONG WITH HER...?
THE CHAIRWOMAN REALLY HAS QUITE THE PERSONALITY...
SO, WHAT'LL IT BE, LIA? STRIKE THIS DUEL FROM THE RECORDS, AND YOU'LL BE ABLE TO CONTINUE LIVING YOUR NORMAL LIFE.
YOU MAY LOSE SOMETHING INSIDE YOU IN EXCHANGE, THOUGH.
THE GREATER DISTANCE I KEEP FROM HER, THE BETTER.
SFX: PURU (SHAKE) PURU

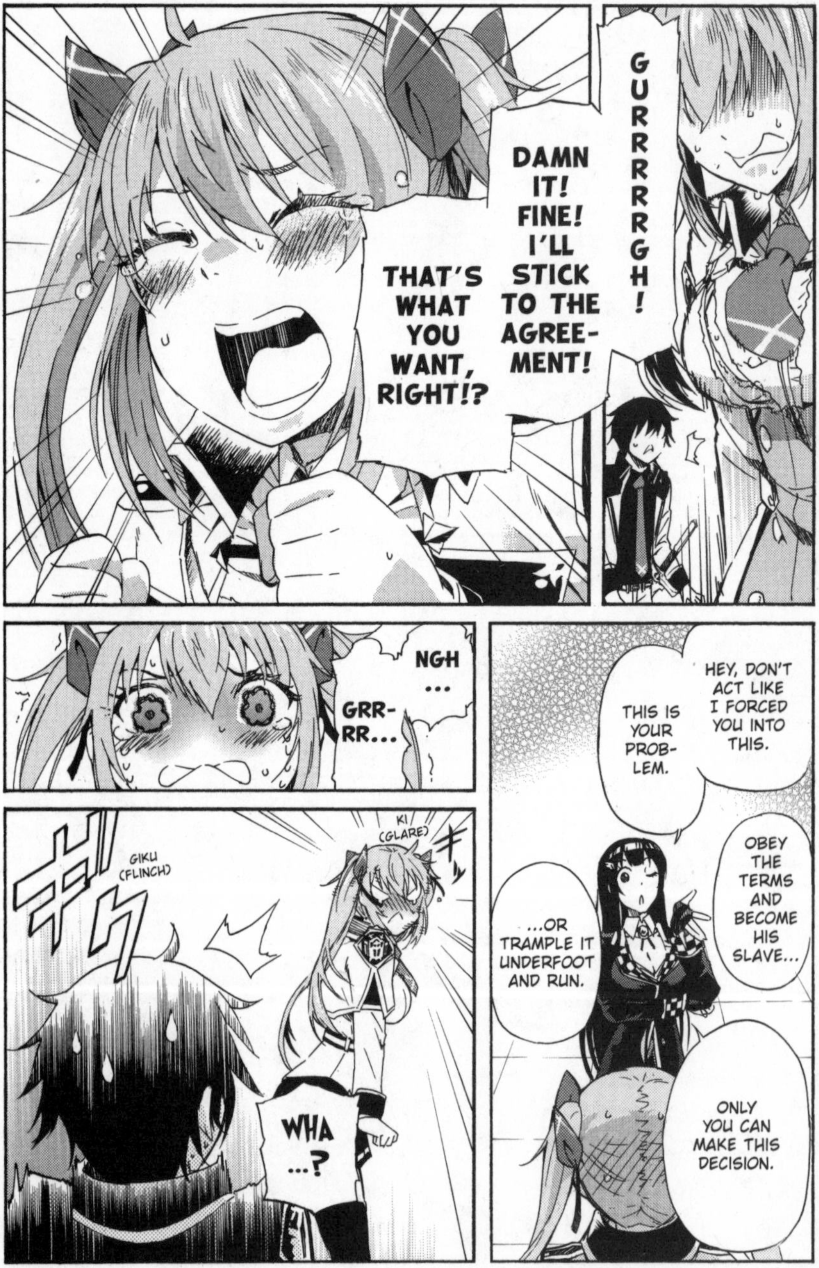
GURRRRRGH!
DAMN IT! FINE! I'LL STICK TO THE AGREEMENT!
THAT'S WHAT YOU WANT, RIGHT!?
HEY, DON'T ACT LIKE I FORCED YOU INTO THIS.
THIS IS YOUR PROBLEM.
OBEY THE TERMS AND BECOME HIS SLAVE...
...OR TRAMPLE IT UNDERFOOT AND RUN.
ONLY YOU CAN MAKE THIS DECISION.
NGH...
GRR-RR...
KI (GLARE)
GIKU (FLINCH)
WHA...?

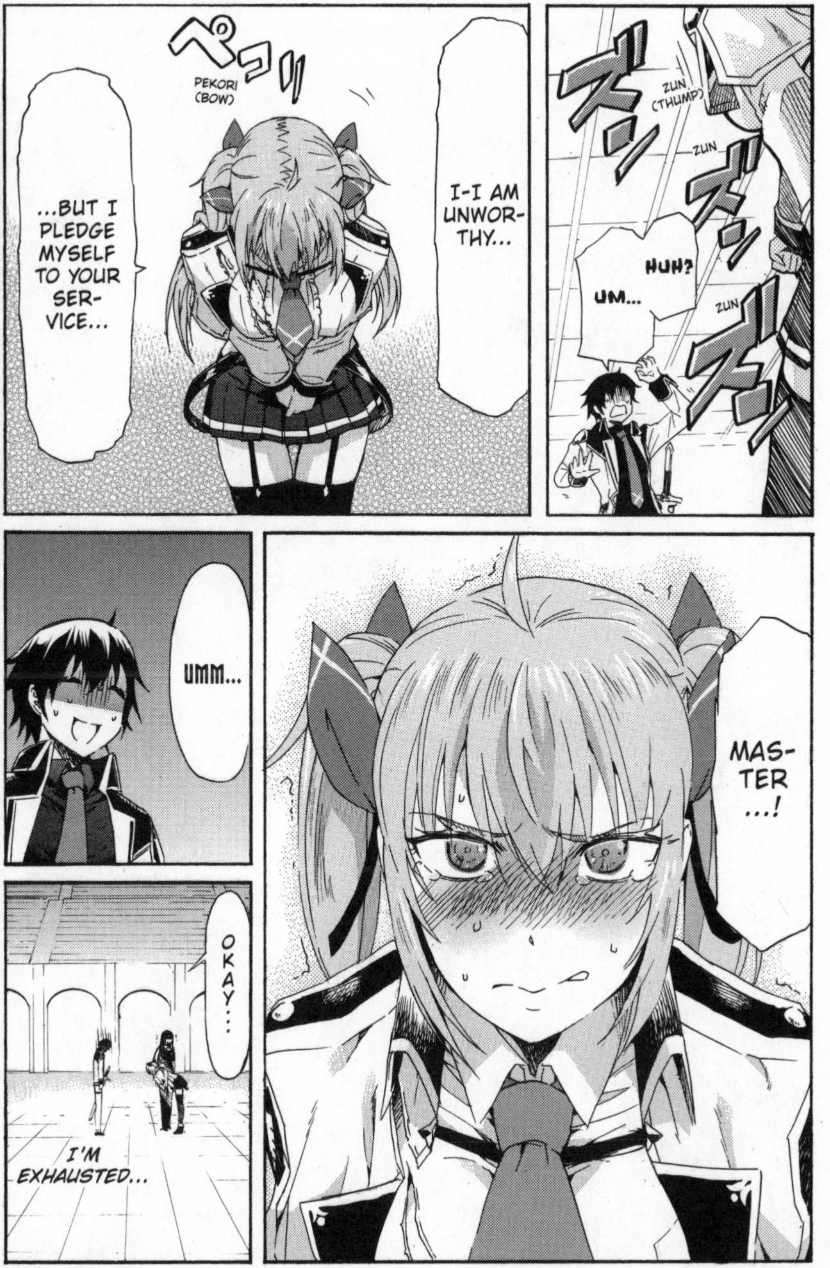
ZUN (THUMP)
ZUN
HUH? UM...
ZUN
PEKORI (BOW)
I-I AM UNWORTHY...
...BUT I PLEDGE MYSELF TO YOUR SERVICE...
MASTER...!
UMM...
OKAY...
I'M EXHAUSTED...

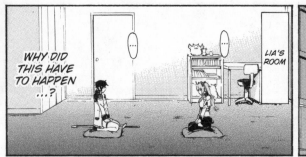

LATER
LIA'S ROOM
...
...
WHY DID THIS HAVE TO HAPPEN ...?
A SLAVE NEEDS TO DEVOTE EVERYTHING TO THEIR MASTER!
KEEP THAT IN MIND! I'M GONNA HAVE ALL OF ALLEN'S STUFF SENT HERE TOMORROW. TOODLE-OO!
HEY ...
BI (FWIP)
A PRINCESS JUST BECAME A SLAVE TO SOME NOBODY, AND NOW THEY'RE LIVING UNDER THE SAME ROOF.
IF THE VESTERIA ROYAL FAMILY FINDS OUT ABOUT THIS...
HAAH ...
CHIRA (GLANCE)
WE'RE GOING TO BE LIVING TOGETHER FROM NOW ON...

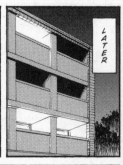

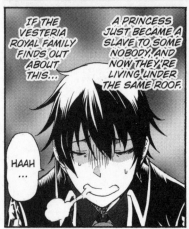

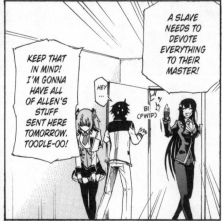

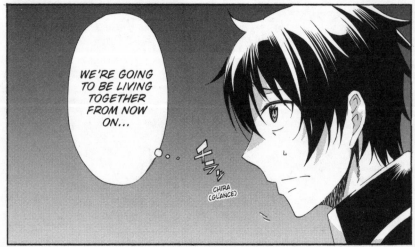

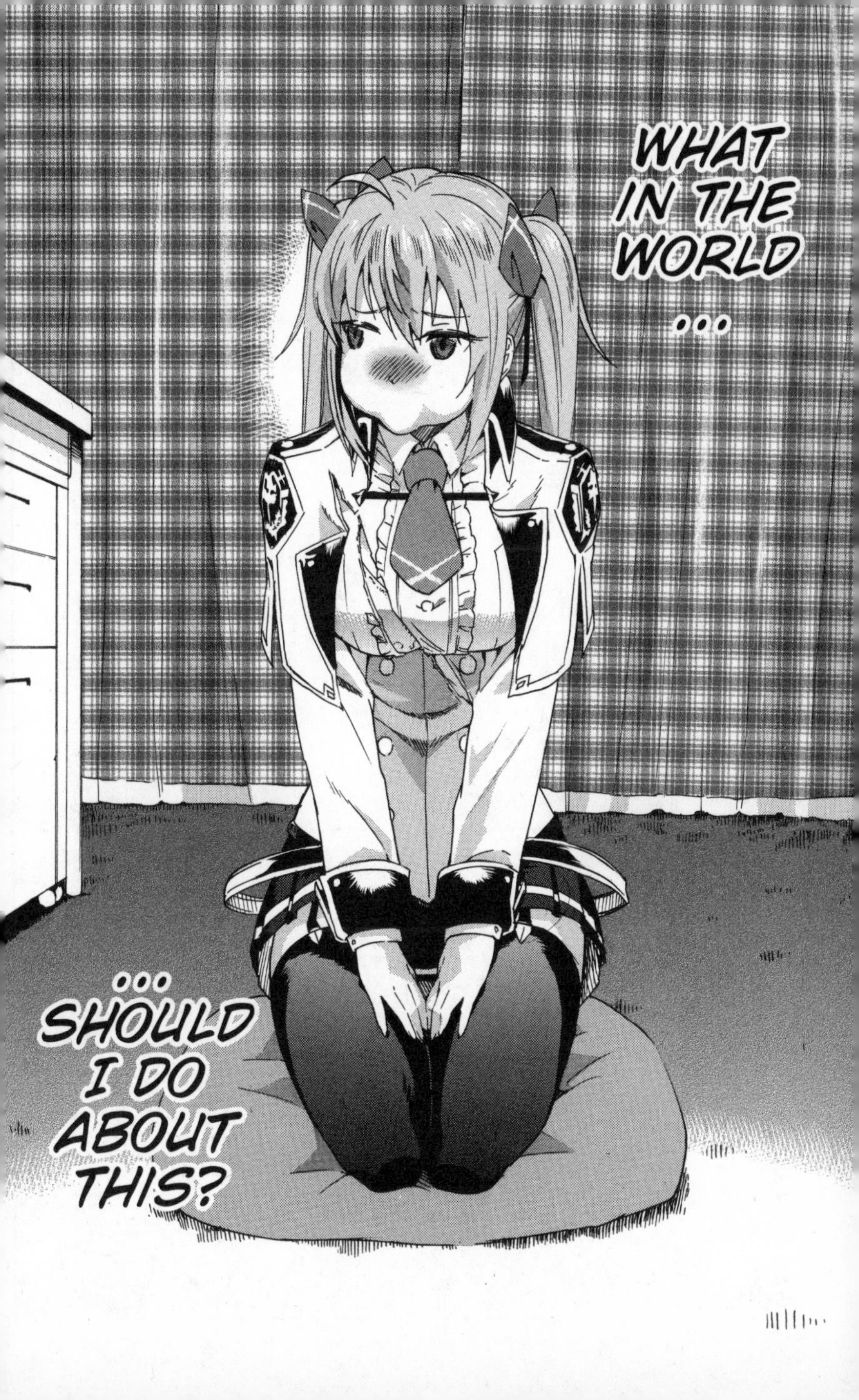
WHAT IN THE WORLD ...
...SHOULD I DO ABOUT THIS?

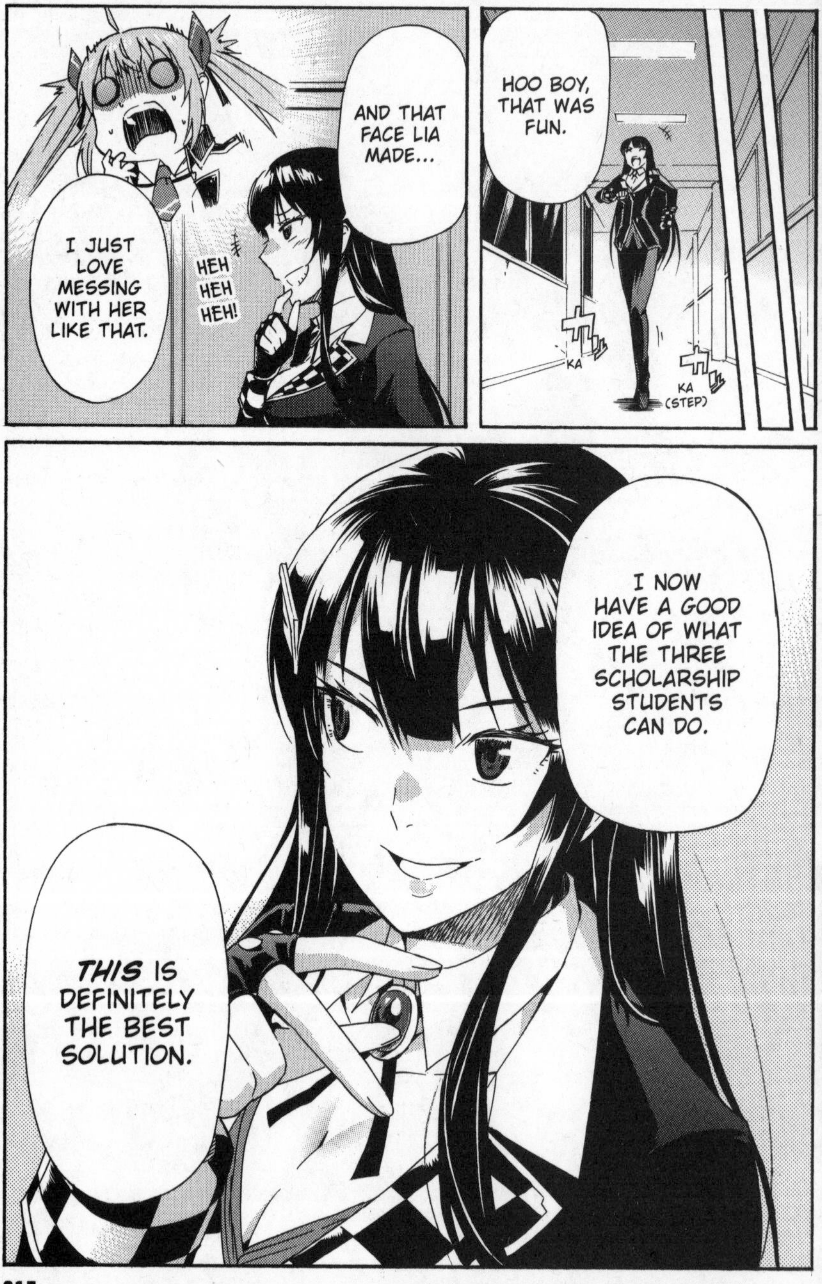

HOO BOY, THAT WAS FUN.
KA
KA (STEP)
AND THAT FACE LIA MADE...
HEH HEH HEH!
I JUST LOVE MESSING WITH HER LIKE THAT.
I NOW HAVE A GOOD IDEA OF WHAT THE THREE SCHOLARSHIP STUDENTS CAN DO.
THIS IS DEFINITELY THE BEST SOLUTION.

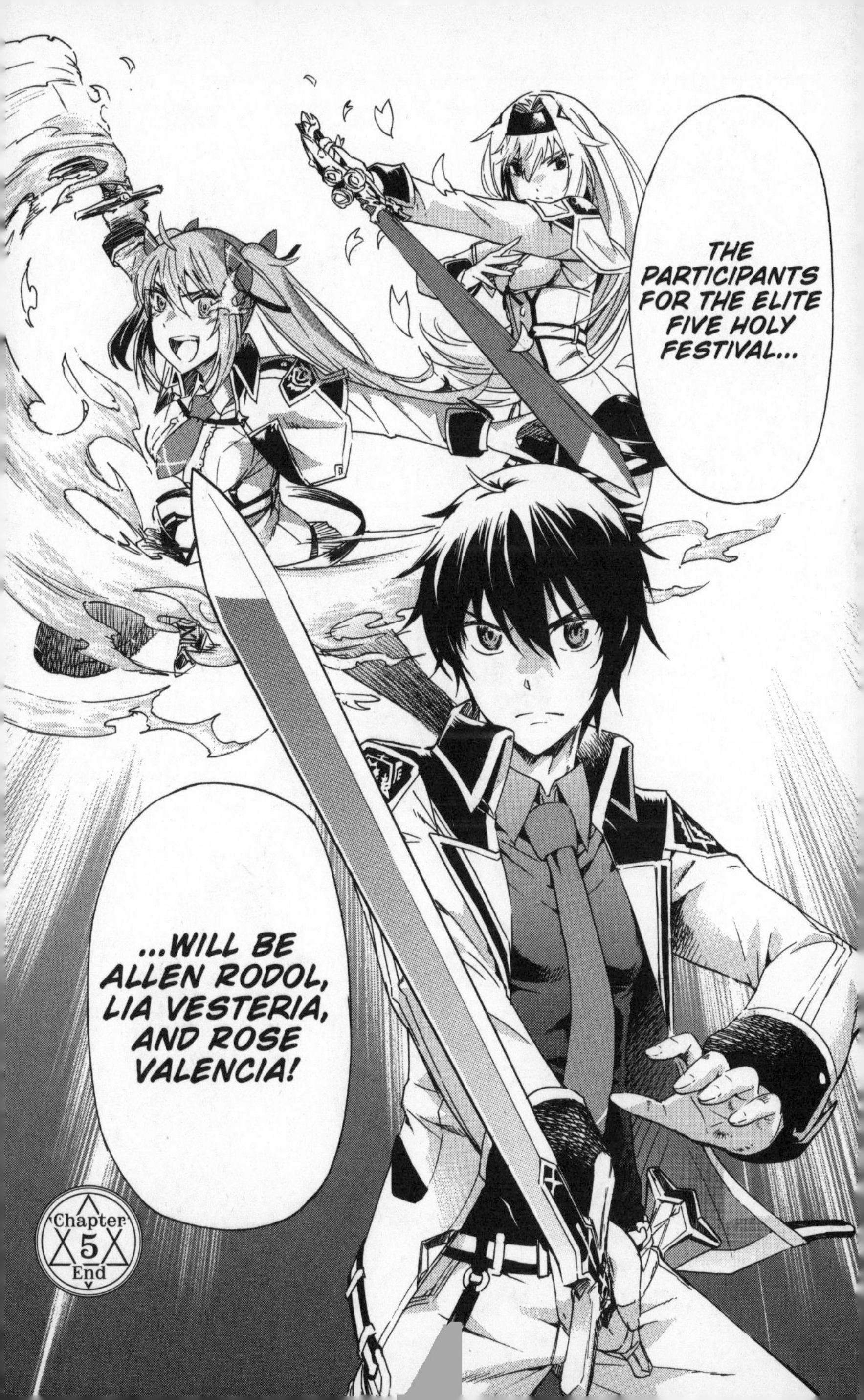
THE PARTICIPANTS FOR THE ELITE FIVE HOLY FESTIVAL...
...WILL BE ALLEN RODOL, LIA VESTERIA, AND ROSE VALENCIA!
Chapter 5 End

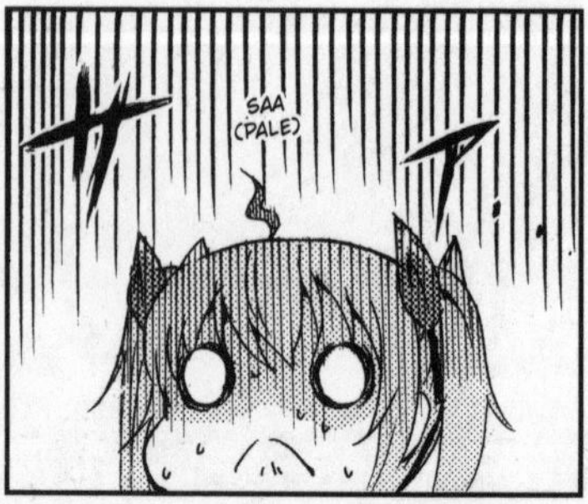
SAA
(PALE)

I KEPT PRESSING THE 100-MILLION-YEAR BUTTON AND CAME OUT ON TOP

~THE UNBEATABLE REJECT SWORDSMAN~

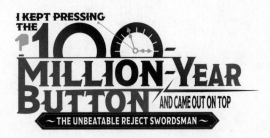

AFTERWORD

THANK YOU VERY MUCH FOR BUYING THE FIRST VOLUME OF THE *100-MILLION-YEAR BUTTON* MANGA! IT IS THANKS TO YOU ALL THAT IT WAS ABLE TO REACH THE SHELVES. I HAVE A LONG WAY TO GO, BUT I'M GOING TO WORK HARD TO CAPTURE WHAT MAKES THE ORIGINAL WORK SO COOL! HOW WILL THE RELATIONSHIPS BETWEEN THESE THREE DEVELOP? LOOK FORWARD TO VOLUME TWO!

YUTARO SHIDO

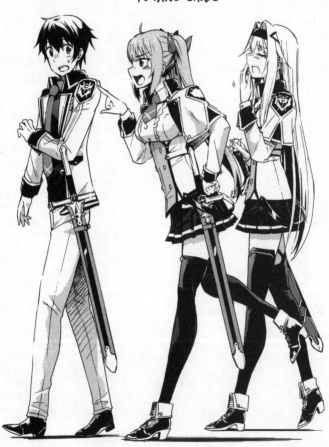

Preview

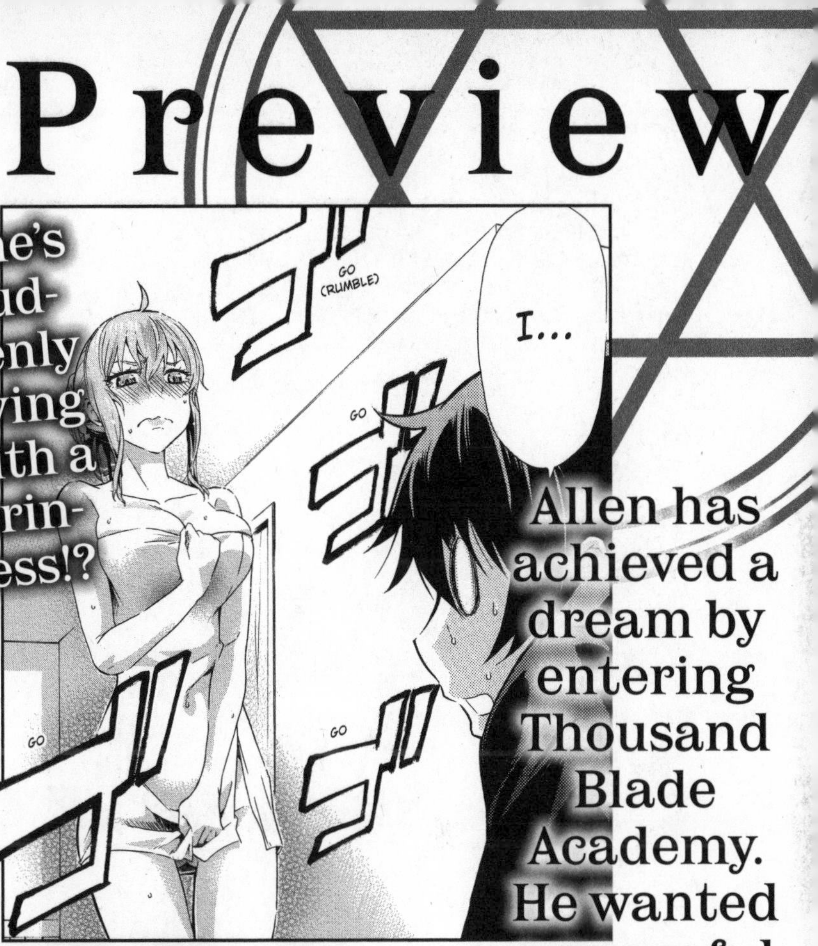

I...
GO (RUMBLE)
GO
GO
GO

Allen has achieved a dream by entering Thousand Blade Academy. He wanted a peaceful student life, but instead...

...he's suddenly living with a princess!?

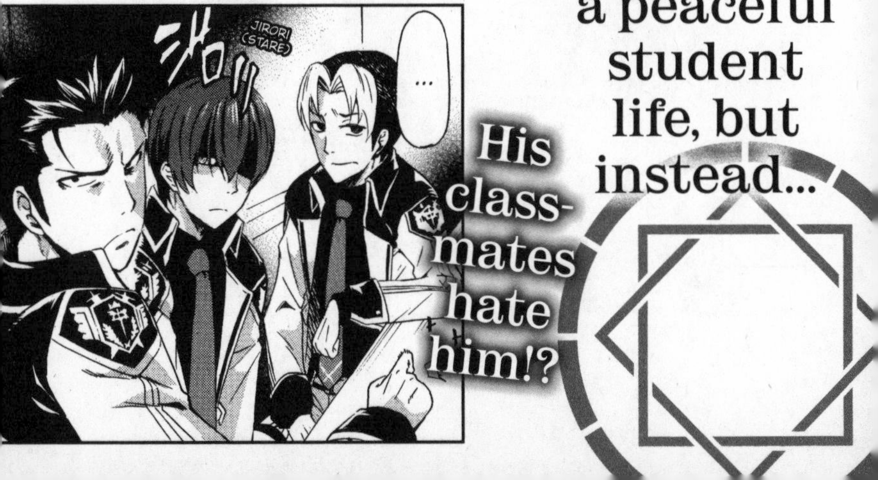

...
JIRORI (STARE)

His classmates hate him!?

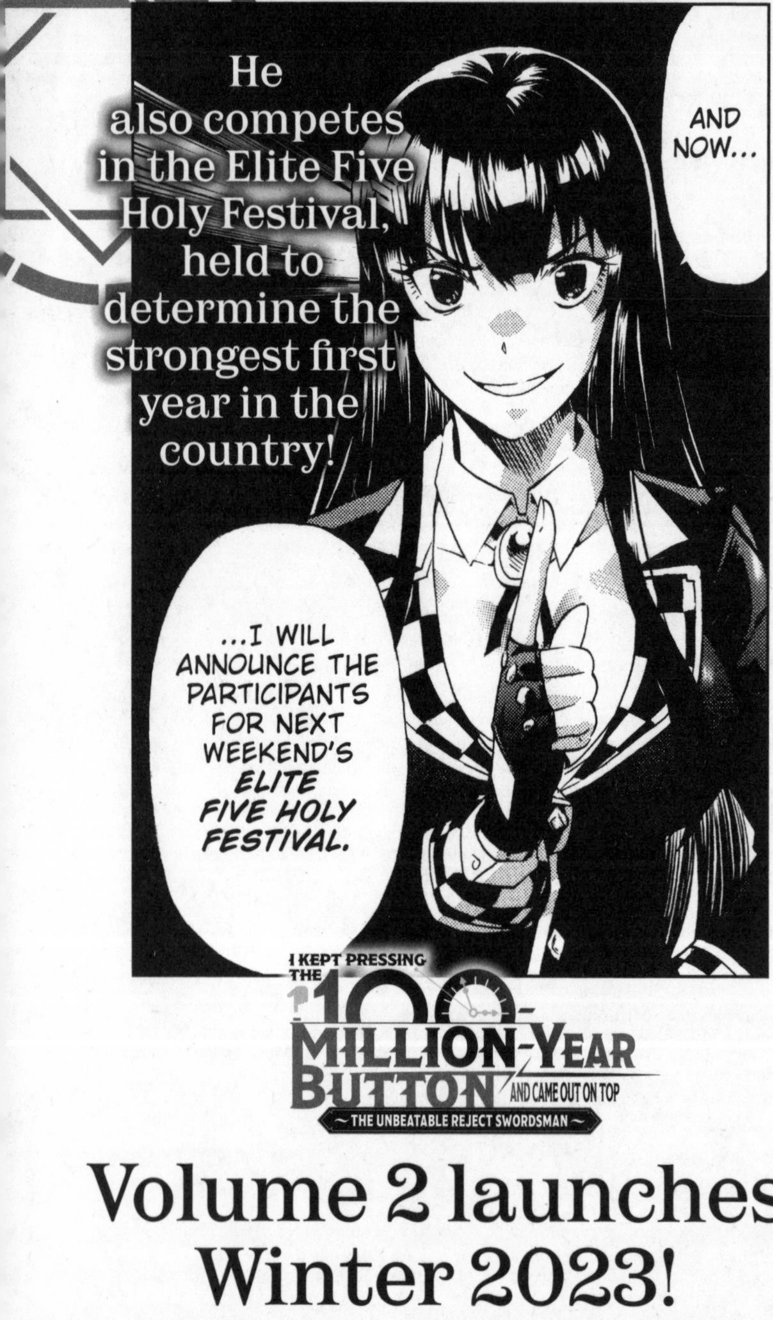
AND NOW...
He also competes in the Elite Five Holy Festival, held to determine the strongest first year in the country!
...I WILL ANNOUNCE THE PARTICIPANTS FOR NEXT WEEKEND'S *ELITE FIVE HOLY FESTIVAL.*

I KEPT PRESSING THE 100-MILLION-YEAR BUTTON AND CAME OUT ON TOP 1

~THE UNBEATABLE REJECT SWORDSMAN~

YUTARO SHIDO

Original Story
SYUICHI TSUKISHIMA

Character Design
MOKYU

Translation **LUKE HUTTON** Lettering **ARBASH MUGHAL**

ICHIOKUNEN BUTTON WO RENDA SHITA ORE WA, KIZUITARA SAIKYO NI NATTE ITA ~RAKUDAI KENSHI NO GAKUIN MUSO~ Volume 1

First published in Japan in 2020 by KADOKAWA CORPORATION, Tokyo. English translation rights arranged with KADOKAWA CORPORATION, Tokyo through TUTTLE-MORI AGENCY, INC., Tokyo.

Yen Press
150 West 30th Street, 19th Floor
New York, NY 10001

Visit us!
yenpress.com • facebook.com/yenpress • twitter.com/yenpress
yenpress.tumblr.com • instagram.com/yenpress

First Yen Press Edition: October 2022
Edited by Yen Press Editorial: Jacquelyn Li, Carl Li
Designed by Yen Press Design: Andy Swist

Yen Press is an imprint of Yen Press, LLC.
The Yen Press name and logo are trademarks of Yen Press, LLC.

The publisher is not responsible for websites (or their content) that are not owned by the publisher.

Library of Congress Control Number: 2022940150
ISBNs: 978-1-9753-5067-3 (paperback)
978-1-9753-5068-0 (ebook)

10 9 8 7 6 5 4 3 2 1

WOR

Printed in the United States of America

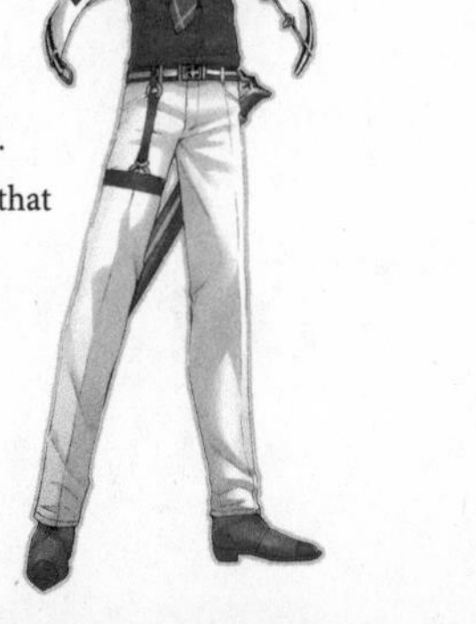

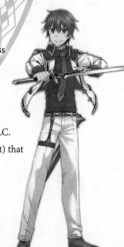

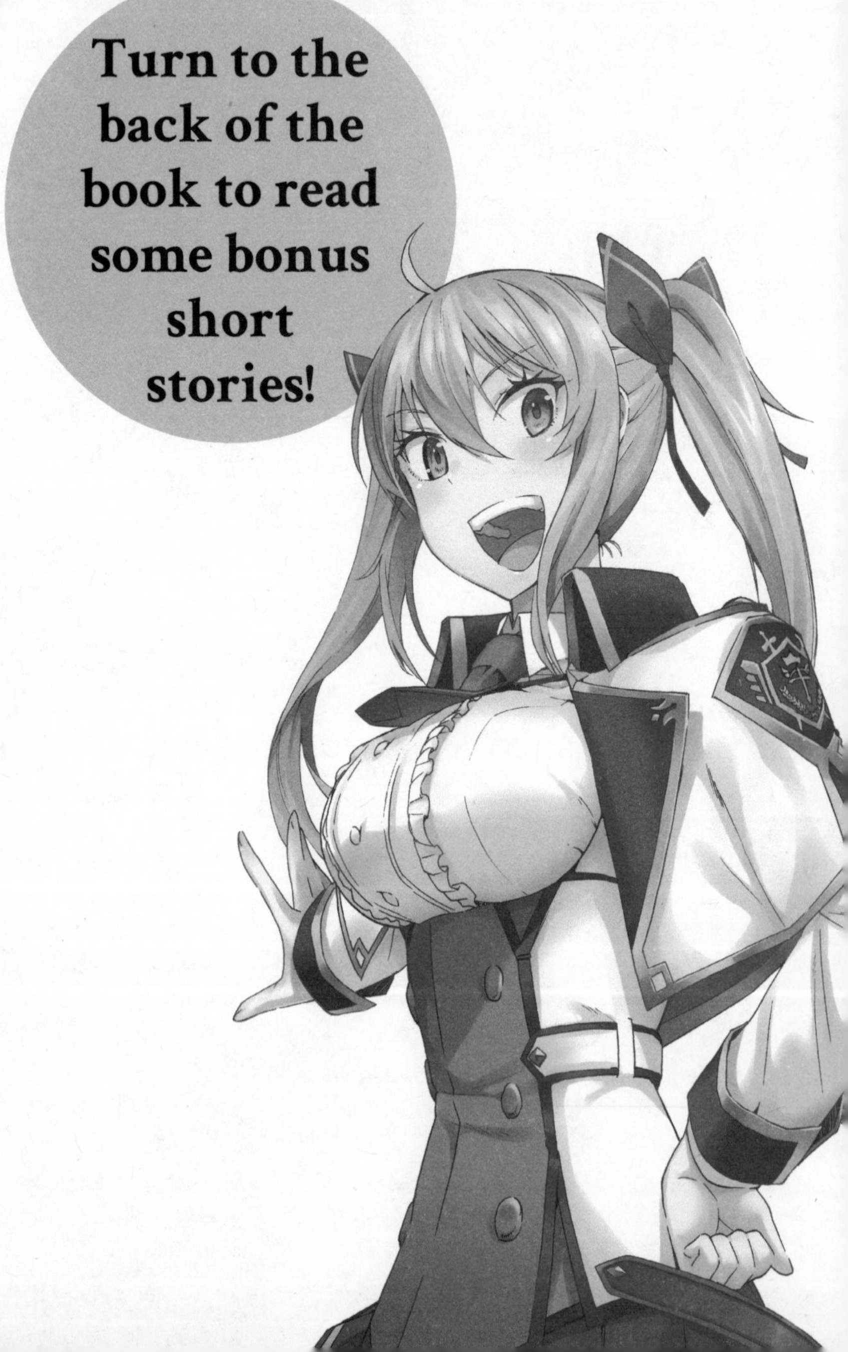
Turn to the back of the book to read some bonus short stories!